THE Ridgeway

53 large-scale maps & guides to 24 towns and villages

PLANNING – PLACES TO STAY – PLACES TO EAT

AVEBURY TO IVINGHOE BEACON

NICK HILL &
HENRY STEDMAN

TRAILBLAZER PUBLICATIONS

Contents

Contents

ABOUT THIS BOOK

This guidebook contains all the information you need. The hard work has been done for you so you can plan your trip without the usual pile of assorted books, maps and guides. When you're all packed and ready to go, there's comprehensive public transport information to get you to and from the Ridgeway and 53 detailed walking maps (1:20,000) and 21 town plans to help you find your way along it. The guide includes:

- Where to stay: from campsites to luxurious hotels
- Details of walking companies if you'd prefer an organised holiday and baggage-carrying services if you just want your luggage carried
- Suggested itineraries for all types of walkers
- Answers to all your questions: when to go, how challenging it is, what to pack and the approximate cost of the whole walking holiday.
- Walking times in both directions; route descriptions are written from west to east
- GPS waypoints (downloadable from www.trailblazer-guides.com)
- Details of cafés, pubs, teashops, takeaways and restaurants as well as shops and supermarkets for supplies
- Rail, bus and taxi information for all places along the path
- Street plans of the main towns and villages
- Historical, cultural and geographical background information.

❑ MINIMUM IMPACT FOR MAXIMUM INSIGHT

Nature's peace will flow into you as the sunshine flows into trees. The winds will blow their freshness into you and storms their energy, while cares will drop off like autumn leaves. **John Muir** (one of the world's earliest and most influential environmentalists, born in 1838)

It is no surprise that, since the time of John Muir, walkers and adventurers have been concerned about the natural environment; this book seeks to continue that tradition. By developing a deeper ecological awareness through a better understanding of nature and by supporting rural economies, local businesses, sensitive forms of transport and low-impact methods of farming and land-use we can all do our bit for a brighter future.

As we work harder and live our lives at an ever faster pace a walking holiday is a chance to escape from the daily grind and the natural pace gives us time to think and relax. This can have a positive impact not only on our own well-being but also on that of the area we pass through. There can be few activities as 'environmentally friendly' as walking.

INTRODUCTION

The Ridgeway stretches for **87 miles (139km)** across the very heart of England, a journey that encompasses no fewer than five counties, beginning in Wiltshire, at Avebury, and passing through Oxfordshire, Berkshire and Hertfordshire before finally ending its meandering way at Ivinghoe Beacon in Buckinghamshire (see back of the book for overview map). Though now one of the 15 National Trails of England and Wales, the path actually started life around 5000 years ago – a thoroughfare for prehistoric man to make his way across the country on higher (and thus drier) ground. It's no surprise, therefore, you'll often see it described on promotional literature as the oldest road in the country – and there may well be some truth to that.

The Ridgeway stretches for 87 miles (139km) across the very heart of England

Perhaps the main joy of the Ridgeway is that so much evidence of its extensive history is still visible. From the moment you arrive in magical **Avebury** – a UNESCO World Heritage Site thanks to the concentric **stone circles** that ring the village, including the largest stone circle in the whole of Western Europe – the prehistoric sites

Avebury Stone Circle (see p86) at the very start at the walk.

The Thames between Goring and Streatley where another national trail, the Thames Path, crosses the Ridgeway.

come thick and fast. Between the village and the actual start of the trail is **West Kennet Avenue**, originally lined with about 100 pairs (give or take a few) of giant sarsen stones in parallel lines; only some of which now remain. And no sooner do you set off from the start of the trail proper, at **Overton Hill**, than your gaze is diverted towards to a set of three tumuli to the right of the path – ancient barrows (burial mounds) that are almost as old as the road itself.

Indeed, before your first day on the trail is over you will have encountered the huge Iron Age forts of **Barbury Castle** and **Liddington Castle** and the wonderfully preserved **Neolithic long barrow at Wayland's Smithy** – at around 5500 years old it's as old as the trail itself! And just a little further on you come upon the most striking ancient landmark of them all, the magnificent **Uffington White Horse**: lines of trenches filled with crushed chalk that, together, form a highly stylised outline of a 100m-long white horse. So striking and enigmatic is it that it is said to have influenced not only all the other white horses that adorn many a hillside round these parts, but it has also even been described as a forerunner of much of modern-day's minimalist art!

But the Ridgeway's charms are not merely confined to remnants of its distant past, as fascinating as these may be. There are the landscapes through which it passes and the panoramas you can enjoy from it too. From the moment you take your first steps on the trail you are immediately taken up onto high ground; thereafter the views of the countryside change endlessly with the light and reach endlessly to the horizon. The first half of the trail is open to the elements but it is exhilarating. On sunny days the air is wonderful, filling you with energy and physical well-being. It is also one of the most enjoyable sections of the Ridgeway; in blissful solitude you can look down at the towns and villages far below, with only the occasional friendly dog-walker or fellow Ridgeway trekker to break the isolation every once in a while.

Then, at about the halfway point, the Ridgeway changes character. Dropping down to the **Thames** at the pretty Siamese twin villages of **Streatley** and **Goring**, the path leaves the voluptuous Wessex Downs in favour of the **Chiltern Hills**. From here on woodlands become the dominant theme, with luxuriant woodland bearding the trail's many ascents and descents. But scattered amongst the trees are several small, picturesque villages, such as **Wigginton** and **Aldbury**, as well as a number of market towns – **Princes Risborough**, **Wendover** and **Tring** – all of which lie either on the trail or within easy walking distance of it. Plus there's also the rare opportunity to walk through the Chequers Estate, the traditional country home of the prime minister!

Eventually, of course, trees finally relent and thin out and, climbing above the butterfly Mecca of Albury Nowers, you catch your first glimpse of your ultimate destination, **Ivinghoe Beacon**, up ahead in the distance. It's a fairly punishing way to end a trek, but you'll be rewarded by some spectacular, panoramic views of the countryside below; plus, of course, the warm feeling that comes with having completed one of the country's great walks.

Prehistoric sites, gorgeous rolling countryside and exquisite little villages huddled around cosy, half-timbered pubs. And, if that's not enough, it should

(Below) Looking back to Silbury Hill from West Kennet Long Barrow (see p90), Avebury.

also be pointed out that walking the Ridgeway is *not* difficult. It can be done in five days but this won't leave much time for relaxation, or for enjoying the countryside you are walking through. So allow time to explore, to dally, to soak in the sun and smell the flowers. The Ridgeway, after all, is a path to savour, not hurry through; so allow six or, even better, seven days for your hike along this most ancient of trails – you'll be mightily glad that you did.

History

The Ridgeway is very ancient. It's often described as 'the oldest road in Britain' and it's clear that parts of the route were in use 5000 years ago or more. The Ridgeway, as we know it today, is in fact the middle section of the Greater Ridgeway (see pp193-4), an ancient system of tracks that stretches from Lyme Regis on the Dorset coast up to Hunstanton on the Norfolk coast. These tracks evolved over centuries as people chose the driest and most suitable paths across the countryside, for themselves and their animals – which usually meant following the higher ground.

It's often described as the 'oldest road in Britain' ... parts were in use 5000 years ago or more

During your walk you will still be able to see and touch stone structures dating back to the prehistoric days of the Ridgeway; the burial mound known as Wayland's Smithy (see box p114) dates back to around 3590BC. Bronze Age (2500BC to 800BC) stone structures still stand, with the Avebury stone circle (see box pp86-7) and West Kennet Avenue (see box p89) being by far the most famous and accessible of these. Additionally, you can see numerous Bronze Age burial mounds dotted along the Ridgeway.

From the Iron Age (beginning about 800BC) there are several important hill forts to investigate including Barbury Castle (see p97) and Uffington Castle (see p116) plus earthworks such as Grim's ditch (see box p152) also dating from this time. During the Dark Ages the Ridgeway was used as a major transport route for invading Danish Viking armies. By the late 9th century they had conquered most of Saxon England and had turned their attention to the kingdom of Wessex. In 871 they marched west along the Ridgeway from their base by the Thames at Reading only to be defeated by King Alfred at the Battle of

Wayland's Smithy (see p114) is a Neolithic long barrow. Legend tells that the shoes for the Uffington White Horse were forged here.

Ashdown, which some think took place in the area around White Horse Hill (see box p117).

Up until the 18th century the Ridgeway still consisted of a collection of routes broadly heading in approximately the same direction across the country but then the Enclosures Acts were passed by parliament and these initiated the division of previously communal open land into privately owned fields. These fields were then hedged in to protect them from passing livestock and as a result the Ridgeway was forced to follow a single, defined route.

A lovely row of thatched cottages in Ashbury, north of Wayland's Smithy.

As coaching routes to London developed they avoided the actual course of the Ridgeway so it was left largely neglected – although several towns on the path, such as Marlborough and Wendover, were important rest stops. For several hundred years, therefore, the main users of the path were drovers transporting their sheep from the West Country, and even Wales, to the large sheep fairs at East Ilsley (see p132). The width of the Ridgeway in this area, sometimes up to 20 metres, gives an idea of just how much livestock was transported on this route. At their peak the fairs held auctions for up to 80,000 sheep a day though by the early 20th century these fairs were in decline: the last one was held in 1934. From then on the path was used mainly by farmers for access to their land.

This was especially the case during World War II when many of the hillsides around the Ridgeway saw a change in use from sheep-grazed areas to cultivated fields. This was the result of a government-initiated effort to provide sufficient food for the population as imports were threatened owing to the fighting. This not only changed the visual landscape of many areas of the Ridgeway but also damaged the indigenous wildlife as powerful chemical fertilisers were used to improve the poor soil.

The first calls for the Ridgeway to be recognised as a long-distance walking trail were made in 1947 by the National Parks Committee and in the 1950s the Ramblers' Association (now Ramblers; see box p42) joined the appeal. However, it

The Ridgeway was once used mainly by drovers taking their sheep to the sheep fairs at East Ilsley. You'll see far fewer sheep now.

wasn't until 1973 that it was officially opened as a National Trail, since when, the most common use for the path has been for recreation. Only minor alterations have been made to its course since then which enables everyone to make their way along the 87-mile (139km) trail in the footsteps of the first Ridgeway pioneers from thousands of years ago.

How difficult is the Ridgeway?

If you are reasonably fit you won't encounter any problems walking the Ridgeway. There are no sections that are technically difficult and despite having a couple of steep climbs during each day's walking, it's nothing like as demanding as many other National Trails. The most important thing to do is plan your walking based on your own abilities. If you try to walk too far in one day, not only will you lose the chance to really enjoy the countryside you are walking through but you will end up exhausted and won't feel much like walking the next day.

It's nothing like as demanding as many other National Trails

If anything, the western section of the Ridgeway, up to Streatley, could be considered more difficult than the eastern section owing to its remote and exposed conditions that become very apparent during bad weather. From Streatley onwards the Ridgeway is often in woodland, or passing through fields, and goes through, or near to, numerous towns and villages.

How long do you need?

This depends on your fitness and experience. Do not try to do too much in one day if you are new to long-distance walking. Most people find that eight days is enough to complete the walk and still have time to look around the villages and enjoy the views along the way. Alternatively, the entire path can be done in five days if you are fit enough, but you won't see much of the surrounding countryside.

Most people find that eight days is enough to complete the walk and have time to look around the villages ... but it can be done in five days

(Below) Ivinghoe Beacon – journey's end.

If you're camping don't underestimate how much a heavy pack laden with camping gear will slow you down. It is also worth bearing in mind that those who take it easy on the Ridgeway see a lot more than those who sweat out long days and tend to only ever see the path in front of them. If you are walking on your own you can dictate the pace, but when walking with someone else you need to take their abilities into account and take time to enjoy their company – this may slow you down. If you don't take time to do this, you might as well be walking separately and simply meet up at the end of the day.

On all sections, but particularly the western section, you'll also need to consider how far off the path your accommodation is and build that distance into your daily total. Although some B&Bs will collect you from the Ridgeway and drop you back the next morning, not all offer this service so you do need to check when reserving

See p34 for some suggested itineraries covering different walking speeds

a room. On p34 there are some suggested itineraries covering different walking speeds that will give you an idea of what you can expect to achieve each day.

If you only have a few days it makes sense to concentrate on the 'best' parts of the Ridgeway; there is a list of recommended day/two-day walks on p31.

When to go

SEASONS

The western half of the Ridgeway follows the high ground and is very exposed so if it rains you'll certainly know about it. Likewise, if it is sunny, you'll get very hot. To compound this there is very little in the way of shelter on the western section. The eastern section, on the whole, follows lower ground and is often in sheltered woodland. You are also far closer to human habitation on this section should the weather turn really bad. The **main walking season** is from Easter (March/April) to the end of September.

Pausing for a breather at the Boer War Monument atop Coombe Hill.

The biggest attraction of walking the Ridgeway in the **spring** is to see the wild flowers in bloom, especially the carpets of bluebells in the woods. You'll also get good walking weather at this time but there will be a risk of showers and thick fog can obscure pretty much everything in the early to mid-morning. Unsurprisingly, the Easter holiday is a busy time.

Obviously **summer** is the busiest season for walkers on the Ridgeway owing to the fact that it is the main holiday period and the weather should be good. You probably still won't see many people on the western section, but the eastern section is very popular with dog-walkers and day-trippers. If you are walking on your own it can be nice to stop and chat to other walkers every once in a while. Although summer is your best bet, the weather in England is not always good at this time. Look at the forecast before you go and be prepared.

Autumn can be one of the best times of year to walk the Ridgeway. Most walkers have finished their holidays but you can still have good, clear weather and the sections of woodland walking are especially colourful. The western section is less inviting at this time owing to its exposed conditions.

The cold and often unpredictable weather in the **winter** makes walking the Ridgeway low on most people's lists of priorities. It certainly wouldn't be much fun on some of the open western sections but there is still plenty of opportunity for some good day walks on other sections if the weather is clear.

TEMPERATURE & RAINFALL

As the English climate is temperate, walking can be enjoyed at most times of the year. However, there will be plenty of days in the winter where it will be too cold for comfortable walking but equally in the summer it can sometimes be too hot.

The air **temperature** will generally be fine, it's the rain you need to watch out for. On average it rains on about one day in three in England, though more often in the winter.

Rainfall in July can be as little as half that of January in the Ridgeway area, but that's not much consolation if you are caught in a summer downpour.

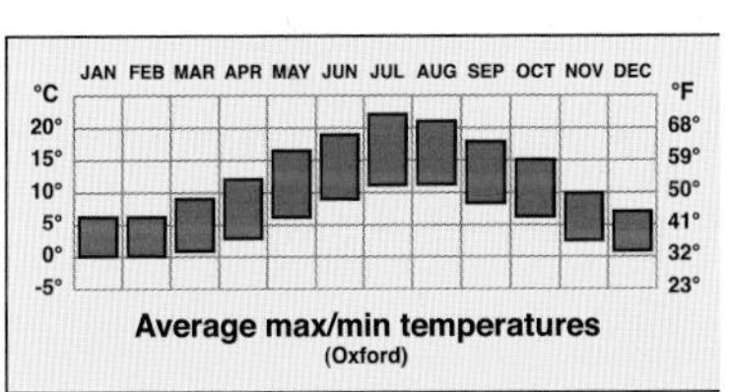

Average max/min temperatures (Oxford)

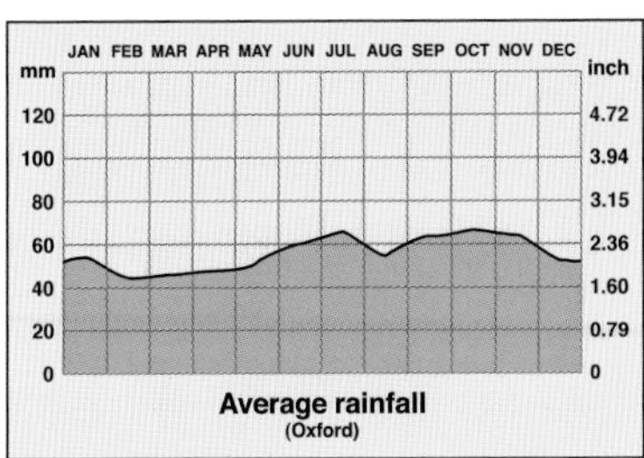

Average rainfall (Oxford)

DAYLIGHT HOURS

If walking in autumn, winter and early spring, you must take account of how far you can walk in the available light. It may not be possible to cover as many miles as you would in summer. The sunrise and sunset times in the table (opposite) are based on information for Oxford on the first of each month. This gives a rough picture for the Ridgeway. Also bear in mind that you will get a further 30-45 minutes of usable light before sunrise and after sunset depending on the weather.

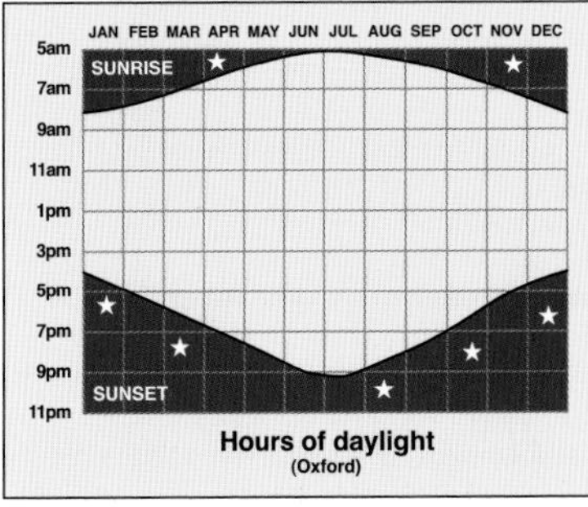

Hours of daylight (Oxford)

❑ FESTIVALS AND ANNUAL EVENTS

Year-round

● **Organised events along the Ridgeway** The National Trails Office (💻 www.nationaltrail.co.uk/ridgeway/events) promotes walks and activities along the Ridgeway **year-round**. Most weekends, especially in the summer months, there will be something going on, be it a walk along a particularly interesting section accompanied by a knowledgeable guide, a focus on specific wildlife, or a class in navigating skills.

Throughout the summer months

● **Morris dancing** During the **summer months** you can see Morris groups performing at festivals and pubs along the first half of the Ridgeway. Most performances are arranged well in advance which allows you to plan your trip to coincide with them if you so desire. See box p119 for more information about Morris dancing.

May

● **Sarsen Trail, Neolithic Marathon and Cycle Ride** (Wiltshire Wildlife Trust, 💻 www.wiltshirewildlife.org/Pages/Events) This sponsored walk in aid of the Wiltshire Wildlife Trust runs between Avebury and Old Carter Barracks, a total of 26 miles. It's held on the first Bank Holiday weekend in May. The event attracts more than 2000 walkers and you must register in advance. Alongside the walk there's also the Neolithic Marathon and Half Marathon along the same route, as well as a 50km (31+ miles) 'Neolithic Bike Route', beginning and finishing at Old Carter Barracks.

● **The Ridgeway 40** (💻 ridgeway40.org.uk) This is a 40-mile walk along the Ridgeway from Overton Hill to the YHA hostel at Streatley. You are expected to complete the walk in one day and there are checkpoints along the route. There is also a separate event for runners. The Ridgeway 40 is held annually on a weekend in May; you may want to avoid doing your walk over this weekend.

June

● The **summer solstice** (20-21st June) draws a lot of people to Avebury Stone Circle.

July

● **Marlborough Jazz** (💻 www.marlboroughjazz.com) This 3-day festival features around 60 artists and attracts more than 5000 visitors. It takes place in mid July.

● **Goring & Streatley Regatta** (💻 www.goringgapbc.org.uk) This regatta, held in mid July, is organised by Goring Gap Boat Club. The focus is on providing a family day out with a funfair and live entertainment, in addition to the boat races on the Thames.

August

● **Uffington White Horse Show** (💻 www.whitehorseshow.co.uk) This traditional country show, held on ground between Uffington and Kingston Lisle villages, is a well-organised event attracting over 10,000 visitors. Past attractions have included a fly-past by a Vulcan Bomber, stunt horses, ferret racing, morris dancing, a heavy horse show and a falconry display. It's held on the Bank Holiday weekend at the end of August.

(**Opposite**) **Top**: St Mary's Church, Uffington, known as the Cathedral in the Vale, boasts an unusual octagonal tower and a cruciform layout. **Bottom left**: Exploring West Kennet Long Barrow (see p90). **Bottom right**: With several racehorse stables in the area (see p104) you'll often see horses being exercised beside the path.

(**Overleaf**) Taking in the superb view from the Uffington White Horse (see p117). The flat-topped Dragon Hill below was where St George is said to have slain the dragon, its blood poisoning the grass and leaving a bare area of chalk on the hill. (Photo © Nick Hill).

RIDGEWAY

PLANNING YOUR WALK 1

Practical information for the walker

ROUTE FINDING

You shouldn't have any problems staying on the Ridgeway. At nearly all the junctions there are special 'Ridgeway' signposts showing the direction of the trail and these are usually also marked with the National Trail **acorn symbol**. For many stretches you barely even need these signposts as the path is clear and well-trodden. Other branching paths are also shown; note that the word 'Byway' in red warns that that section of the route may also be used by motorists. The word 'Footpath' (in yellow) indicates that the continuing section of the route is for the exclusive use of pedestrians.

In some places the standard system of chevrons and identifying colours is used. An acorn and a **yellow** chevron or yellow writing indicates that this route is a footpath, ie exclusively for pedestrians. **Blue** indicates that the trail is a bridleway and can therefore also be used by horses and cyclists. **Purple/plum** quaintly adds a pony and trap. **Red** or **white** and the word 'Byway' warns that the route can also be used by motorists.

Since other footpaths may be indicated on the waymark posts you won't go wrong if you just **follow the acorn**. All path junctions are included on the maps in this book along with relevant notes.

GPS

GPS technology is an inexpensive, well-established if non-essential, navigational aid. Within a minute of being turned on and with a clear view of the sky, **GPS receivers** will establish your position and elevation anywhere on earth to an accuracy of within a few metres.

(Opposite) Top: The view from Liddington Hill in summer, the fields yellow with oilseed rape. (Photo © Nick Hill). **Bottom**: Where the Ridgeway coincides with the Icknield Way it's often better to walk above the actual path rather than in the ditch!

Most **smartphones** also have a GPS receiver built in and mapping software available to run on it (see box p41). Don't treat a GPS as a replacement for maps, a compass and common sense. Every electronic device is susceptible to battery failure or some electronic malfunction that might leave you in the dark. GPS should be used merely as a backup to more traditional route-finding techniques and is best used in conjunction with a paper map.

Using GPS with this book – waypoints

Though a GPS system is not essential on the Ridgeway, for those who have one, GPS waypoints for the route are provided. **Waypoints** are single points like cairns. This book identifies key waypoints on the route maps. The book's waypoints correlate to the list on pp196-81 which gives the grid reference and a description. You can download the complete list as a GPS-readable .gpx file of grid references (but with no descriptions) from 💻 www.trailblazer-guides.com. It's anticipated that you won't tramp along day after day, ticking off the book's waypoints, transfixed by the screen on your GPS or smartphone; the route description and maps should be more than adequate most of the time.

It's worth repeating that 98% of people who've ever walked the Ridgeway did so without GPS so there's no need to rush out and buy one – or a new GPS-enabled smartphone for that matter. Your spending priorities ought to be on good waterproofs and above all, footwear.

ACCOMMODATION

There is plenty of accommodation along the Ridgeway and if you plan ahead you shouldn't encounter any problems finding somewhere to stay. However, most accommodation falls into the B&B category: there are some campsites but only one YHA hostel and one bunkhouse on/near the path.

On the western section, up to Streatley, there is virtually no accommodation on the Ridgeway itself and the nearest place to stay might be a mile or two off the path: for this reason, you really should book ahead otherwise you might find yourself very tired and without a bed for the night.

Camping

Wild camping (see also p54) is not strictly allowed on the Ridgeway: it's private land and although it's a public right of way this does not entitle you to stop and camp. However, if you pitch your tent on the path and move on the next morning leaving no trace of yourself, you shouldn't have any problems. In many places the path is wide enough to pitch a tent and leave room for anyone else passing by. Unless you have personally asked permission from the landowner, do not pitch your tent in fields, or woods, next to the Ridgeway.

There are some official campsites with basic facilities such as toilets and showers with prices around £5-10 per person (pp) which makes this the cheapest accommodation option. The campsites aren't usually open in winter (Oct-Mar), which is a strong hint that camping at this time of year really isn't much fun.

There simply aren't enough official campsites along the Ridgeway for you to stay at one every night of your walk so sometimes you'll have to engage in a spot of wild camping, stay in the only YHA hostel/bunkhouse, or splash out on a B&B.

YHA hostels and bunkhouses

YHA hostels and bunkhouses are cheap and allow you to travel on a budget without having to carry cumbersome camping equipment. They are also good places to meet fellow walkers and in many cases are just as comfortable as B&Bs. However, there is now only one YHA hostel actually on the Ridgeway – at Streatley – and one independent bunkhouse, at Court Hill.

Both Court Hill (see pp124-5) and Streatley (see p138) provide bedding so there is no need to carry a sleeping bag if you are expecting to be in B&Bs most other nights. Additionally both have a self-catering kitchen and provide meals.

YHA hostels are, despite their name, for anyone of any age. You can join the **Youth Hostels Association of England and Wales** (YHA; ☎ 01629 592700, freephone ☎ 0800 019 1700, 💻 www.yha.org.uk) on arrival at any hostel, or over the phone or on the internet, for £15-20 per year (the exact amount depending on your method of payment). However, if you are not a member and are planning to stay in the hostel at Streatley for only one night it is cheaper to pay the non-member rate for that night, which is an additional £3 per adult.

Bed and breakfasts

Anyone who has not stayed in a bed and breakfast (B&B) has missed out on something very British. They consist of a bed in someone's house and usually a big cooked breakfast (see p21) in the morning. For visitors from outside Britain it can provide an interesting insight into the way of life here as you often feel like a guest of the family.

What to expect The B&Bs in this guide are included primarily due to their proximity to the Ridgeway. They basically all offer the same thing but can vary greatly in terms of quality, style and price.

Many B&Bs offer en suite rooms but often this can mean a shower and toilet have been squeezed into a corner of the room. For a few pounds less you can usually get a standard room and it's rarely far to the bathroom, which may have the choice of a bath or a shower, though admittedly you might have to share with other guests. At the end of a long day's walking some people prefer to stretch out in a bath rather than squash into a shower.

A **single** room has one bed, though not all B&Bs have a single room so if you are walking alone you might have to book a twin or double room and pay a supplement (see p30). **Twin** rooms and **double** rooms are often confused but a twin room comprises two single beds while a double room has one double bed (or two twins pushed together). **Triple/quad** rooms are for three/four people: they often have one double bed and one or two single beds but sometimes these are bunk beds. Proprietors often describe rooms that sleep more than two as family rooms; in some cases the additional beds are suitable for children only.

If you think you would like an **evening meal** ask when you are booking as most B&Bs require advance warning. Alternatively, the owner may give you a lift to and from the nearest eating place if there isn't a pub or restaurant within walking distance. Some proprietors will make a **packed lunch** as long as you request it by the night before.

B&B owners may also provide a **pick-up service** from the Ridgeway and drop you off there the next morning, which can be a great help; offering to pay something towards the petrol would definitely be appreciated. Some also provide a **luggage-transfer** service for which a charge would be made; see p27.

Booking You should always book your accommodation in advance. In summer, at weekends and on public holidays there can be stiff competition for beds and in winter there's the distinct possibility that the place could be closed.

Some B&Bs have their own website and offer online/email booking but for the majority you will need to phone; it is also possible to book some places through agencies but almost always it will end up costing a bit more.

Most places ask for a deposit (about 50%) which is generally non-refundable if you cancel at short notice. Some places may charge 100% if the booking is for one night only. Always let the owner know as soon as possible if you have to cancel your booking so they can offer the bed to someone else.

Larger places take credit or debit cards. Most smaller B&Bs accept only cheques by post or payments by bank transfer for the deposit; the balance can be settled with cash or a cheque.

Guesthouses, pubs, inns and hotels

Guesthouses are usually more sophisticated than B&Bs and offer evening meals and a lounge for guests. Some **pubs** and **inns** offer accommodation; these have the added advantage of a bar downstairs so it's not far to stagger up to bed. However, the noise from tipsy punters might prove a nuisance if you want an early night.

Hotels are usually aimed more at the motoring tourist than the muddy walker and the tariff is likely to put off the budget traveller. You'll probably arrive there in the late afternoon and leave fairly early the next morning so it's hard to justify the price. However, if you want a few more luxuries in your room, or room service, it may be worth considering a hotel.

Airbnb

The rise and rise of Airbnb (💻 www.airbnb.co.uk) has seen private homes and apartments opened up to overnight travellers on an informal basis. Primarily based in cities, the concept is spreading to tourist hotspots in more rural areas, but do check thoroughly what you are getting and the precise location. Places tend to come and go far more frequently than 'normal' B&Bs but there are several possibilities for a Ridgeway walk. However, while the first couple of options listed may be in the area you're after, others may be far too far afield for walkers. At its best, this is a great way to meet local people in a relatively unstructured environment, but do be aware that these places are not registered B&Bs, so standards may vary, yet prices may not necessarily be any lower than the norm.

In pretty much all the villages and towns to the north of the Wessex Downs – Ashbury, Woolstone, Uffington etc – you can find accommodation in an Airbnb.

FOOD AND DRINK

Breakfast and lunch

Almost everywhere you stay, other than if camping, you'll be offered a full English cooked **breakfast**. A cooked breakfast includes some or all of the following: fried bacon, eggs, sausages, tomatoes, mushrooms, baked beans and fried bread – in addition to cereal and toast, washed down with a fruit juice and tea or coffee. This will certainly be enough to set you up for a day's walking – if you are thinking about calories, you'll probably want to spend the day trying to walk it off – but it may be more than you are used to or even want. If so, ask for a continental breakfast. Alternatively, if you want an early start or would prefer to skip breakfast it might be worth asking if you could have a packed lunch instead.

Many places to stay can also provide you with a packed **lunch** for an additional cost. Alternatively, packed lunches (and indeed breakfast) can be bought and made yourself. In most towns and villages you should be able to find at least one shop selling sandwiches and usually a café. If you are lucky you may be in town when there is a (farmers') market.

❑ Markets and farmers' markets along the Ridgeway

If you happen to be in town when a market, or farmers' market, is on you should definitely try to have a look at what's for sale. Generally at these types of markets whatever is being sold has been produced locally and/or by the people selling it. Farmers' markets offer an outlet for farmers to sell their produce direct to the public but also at these and general markets you will see many other small producers of high-quality niche foods.

Products that you are likely to find are seasonal fruit and vegetables; meat, poultry and game; dairy products such as local cheeses and yoghurt; eggs from hens, ducks and geese; sausages and pies; soups; farmed fish such as trout, and preserves such as chutney and jam. Many of these are likely to be organic.

Some markets are held weekly but farmers' markets may be monthly as the stallholders need time to work their way round the other markets in the area too. Below is a list of (farmers') markets in towns along the Ridgeway:

- **Marlborough** (see p73) There is a street market every Wednesday and Saturday (8.30am-3pm), High St.
- **Wantage** (see p125) Market every Wednesday and Saturday; farmers' market last Saturday of every month (8.30am-1pm), Market Place.
- **Wallingford** (see p147) Third Tuesday and fifth Saturday (when there is one) of every month (8.30am-1pm), Market Place. There is a Local Producers' Market every Saturday (10am-1pm), other than the fifth in the month, in the Regal Centre, Goldsmith's Lane (car park) and a WI country market every Friday in the Regal Centre and a street market in the town centre.
- **Princes Risborough** (see p169) Third Thursday (9am-1pm) of every month apart from January, High St.
- **Wendover** (see p176) Third Saturday of every month (9am-1pm), off the High St on the Manor Waste. Also a weekly market there on Thursdays (8am-4pm).
- **Tring** (see p182) Every other Saturday (9am-12.15pm), The Marketplace, off Brook St (🖳 www.tringfarmersmarket.co.uk).

Remember that certain stretches of the walk are devoid of anywhere to eat so look at the town and village facilities table (pp32-3) and check the information in Part 4 to make sure you don't go hungry.

❑ Real ales along the Ridgeway

Among the many pleasures of strolling on the Ridgeway is coming across country pubs and inns that you would never otherwise have visited. As you'll discover, they all have their own character and you'll end up with some very fond memories of your time spent at some of them. You'll usually have the chance to try some real ales that you might not have tried before. There are too many ales to list here and many pubs change their beers on a regular basis, but below is a selection of real ales that you are almost guaranteed to see in the course of your walk. (ABV means 'alcohol by volume' and is expressed as a percentage of how much alcohol a drink contains).

• **Ridgeway Brewery** (🖳 www.ridgewaybrewery.co.uk) Surely the most apt beers for Ridgeway walkers are those produced by Ridgeway Brewery, based in South Stoke in Oxfordshire. Their ales have only been brewed under contract by other breweries since 2003 but already have a good reputation. **Ridgeway Bitter** (ABV 4%) is their standard brew, but if you have time to linger you might like to try their stronger premium bitter, **Oxfordshire Blue** (5%). Stronger still is their **Ridgeway IPA** (5.5%) and there is also **Ivanhoe** (5.2%). These are all available in bottles and sometimes on draught, though from personal experience they can be quite elusive; if you do see any, grab the opportunity!

• **White Horse Brewery** (🖳 whitehorsebrewery.co.uk) Also very fitting for walkers of the Ridgeway, this company has been brewing since 2004. They produce three ales year-round and various seasonal beers throughout the year. You are most likely to encounter their **Bitter** (3.7%), which is perfect if you're stopping off for a few. Their excellent **Wayland Smithy** (4.4%) is tastier though has the potential to stop you in your tracks. You might also like to try a pint of their **Village Idiot** (4.1%), which is light and fruity.

• **Wadworth** (🖳 www.wadworth.co.uk) Mainly around the beginning of the Ridgeway, but even as far as Tring, you will find Wadworth ales. The best known is **6X** (4.1%); this has been brewed in Wadworth's Devizes brewery since 1921 and has a fruity, malty taste and a copper colour.

• **Arkell's** (🖳 www.arkells.com) This Swindon-based brewery produces mainly **2B** (3.2%) and **3B** (4%), which you'll see in any of the pubs they own.

• **Brakspear** (🖳 www.brakspear-beers.co.uk) You'll certainly come across Brakspear ales, especially during the middle sections. The most common is **Brakspear Bitter** which is easy enough for anyone to drink, being only 3.4%. It has an amber colour and a mild taste. It's a good beer for more prolonged rest stops and has won many national awards. Their **Oxford Gold** (4% on draught) is brewed year-round and has a light, golden colour and fruity flavour.

• **Hop Back Brewery** (🖳 www.hopback.co.uk) This brewery is in Downton, near Salisbury. Among the range of ales they produce is one that could be of particular interest to Ridgeway walkers, namely **Crop Circle**. Its ABV of 4.2% accompanied by its crisp and thirst-quenching qualities make it an ideal mid-walk drink. You might find this pint hard to find on the Ridgeway but it's available in pubs around the south-west of England.

For more information about real ales look at the website for **CAMRA** (Campaign for Real Ale) at 🖳 www.camra.org.uk.

Evening meals

There are some lovely **pubs** and **inns** on the Ridgeway but none directly on the path before Streatley. Although there are fewer freehouses than there used to be you can still sample some excellent beers (see box opposite) during or after a day's walking. Most pubs also serve food (at lunchtime and in the evenings, though not always daily) and this ranges from standard 'pub grub' to restaurant quality fare. There will usually be at least one vegetarian option. A popular lunchtime option in a pub is a 'ploughman's lunch'. This is a cold meal traditionally comprising a thick slice of cheese, bread and butter, salad, some pickles and possibly an apple, though there are many variations.

There are some quality **restaurants** in the larger towns. Additionally, most towns and some of the larger villages are riddled with cheap **takeaway** joints offering kebabs, pizzas, Chinese, Indian and fish 'n' chips; they can come in handy if you finish your walk late in the day, since they usually stay open until at least 11pm.

Buying camping supplies

If you are camping, fuel for your stove, outdoor equipment and food supplies are important considerations. Plan your journey carefully as, particularly on the western half of the Ridgeway, there aren't many opportunities to stock up without embarking on a fair trek to the nearest shop and back.

Drinking water

Depending on the weather you will need to drink as much as two to four litres of water a day. If you're feeling lethargic it may well be that you haven't drunk enough, even if you're not particularly thirsty.

Drinking directly from streams and rivers is tempting, but is not a good idea. Streams that cross the path tend to have flowed across farmland where you can be pretty sure any number of farm animals have relieved themselves. Combined with the probable presence of farm pesticides and other delights it is best to avoid drinking from these streams.

There are drinking **water taps** at some points along the Ridgeway and these are marked on the maps. Where these are thin on the ground you can usually ask a friendly shopkeeper or pub staff to fill your bottle or pouch for you – from a tap, of course. When you are filling your bottle have a good drink from it then fill it again so you leave the tap with a full bottle and don't feel like drinking half of it 100 metres down the path. When you reach a water tap, remember to check that is working before you drink your remaining water.

MONEY

As there are no banks and few post offices on the western half of the Ridgeway, you should take plenty of **cash** for this stretch. Unless you leave the Ridgeway and go to Wantage you won't find a bank/ATM till Goring and after that you'll have to wait until Princes Risborough unless you leave the path. In towns without a bank there is often now an ATM in a garage or at a newsagent but be aware that many of these charge £1.25-1.95 regardless of the amount you withdraw.

Small independent shops rarely accept payment by debit/credit card and require you to pay in cash, as will most B&Bs and campsites. Shops that do take cards, such as supermarkets, will sometimes advance cash against a card (cash-back) as long as you buy something (usually at least £5) at the same time, but these are few and far between on the Ridgeway. See also p40 and the town and village facilities table, pp32-3.

❑ Information for foreign visitors

• **Currency** The British pound (£) comes in notes of £50, £20, £10 and £5, and coins of £2 and £1. The pound is divided into 100 pence (usually referred to as 'p', pronounced 'pee') which come in 'silver' coins of 50p, 20p, 10p and 5p, and 'copper' coins of 2p and 1p.

A guide to currency **exchange rates** can be found on 🖳 www.xe.com/ucc; however, the actual rate used by post offices, banks and travel agents varies.

• **Business hours** Most **village shops** are open Monday to Friday 9am-5pm and Saturday 9am-12.30pm. Many choose longer hours and some open on Sundays as well. Occasionally you'll come across a local shop that closes at lunchtime on one day during the week, usually a Wednesday or Thursday; this is a throwback to the days when all towns and villages had an 'early closing day'. **Supermarkets** are open Monday to Saturday 8am-8pm (sometimes up to 15 hours a day) and on Sunday from about 9am to 5 or 6pm, though main branches of supermarkets can only open for six hours on a Sunday; most choose 10am-4pm or 11am-5pm.

Main **post offices** generally open Monday to Friday 9am-5pm and Saturday 9am-12.30pm; **banks** typically open at 9.30/10am Monday to Friday and close at 3.30/4pm, though in some places both post offices and banks may open only two or three days a week and/or in the morning, or limited hours, only. **ATMs (cash machines)** located outside a bank, shop, post office or petrol station are open all the time, but any that are inside will be accessible only when that place is open.

Pub hours are less predictable; although many open daily 11am-11pm, opening hours in rural areas and during quieter periods (early weekdays, or in the winter months) are often more limited: typically Monday to Saturday 11am-3pm & 5 or 6-11pm, and Sunday 11am/noon-3pm & 7-10.30/11pm. The last entry time to most **museums and galleries** is usually half an hour/an hour, before the official closing time.

• **Public (bank) holidays** Most businesses are shut on 1st January, Good Friday (March/April), Easter Monday (March/April), the first and last Monday in May, the last Monday in August, 25th December and 26th December.

• **School holidays** School holiday periods in England are generally: a one-week break late October, two weeks around Christmas/New Year, a week in mid February, two weeks around Easter, a week in late May/early June (to coincide with the bank holiday on the last Monday in May), and six weeks from late July to early September.

• **Documents/entry charges** If you are a member of a National Trust (NT) organisation in your country bring your membership card as you should be entitled to free entry to National Trust properties and sites in the UK. English Heritage (EH) also have a membership card allowing free access to their sites. Some NT and EH properties have two entry charges: one standard charge and one that is proportionately higher because it includes Gift Aid; this can only be used by UK tax payers.

• **Travel/medical insurance** The **European Health Insurance Card** (EHIC) entitles EU nationals (on production of the EHIC card) to necessary medical treatment under the UK's National Health Service while on a temporary visit here.

Using the Post Office for banking

Several banks in Britain have agreements with the Post Office allowing customers to make cash withdrawals using a debit card (with a PIN number) at branches throughout the country.

As many towns along the Ridgeway have a post office this can be a very useful service. However, check with the Post Office Helpline (☎ 0345-611 2970

However, this is not a substitute for proper medical cover on your travel insurance for unforeseen bills and for getting you home should that be necessary. Also consider cover for loss or theft of personal belongings, especially if you're camping or staying in hostels, as there will be times when you'll have to leave your luggage unattended.

• **Weights and measures** Following a European Commission directive, milk in Britain can still be sold in pints (1 pint = 568ml), as can beer in pubs, though most other **liquids** including petrol (gasoline) and diesel are now sold in litres.

Road **distances** can also continue to be given in miles (1 mile = 1.6km) rather than kilometres, and yards (1yd = 0.9m) rather than metres.

The population remains divided between those who still use inches (1 inch = 2.5cm) and feet (1ft = 0.3m) and those who are happy with centimetres and millimetres; you'll often be told that 'it's only a hundred yards or so' to somewhere, rather than a hundred metres or so.

Most **food** is sold in metric weights (g and kg) but the imperial weights of pounds (lb: 1lb = 453g) and ounces (oz: 1oz = 28g) are often displayed too. The **weather** – a frequent topic of conversation – is also an issue: while most forecasts predict temperatures in °C, many people continue to think in terms of °F (see temperature chart on p15 for conversions).

• **Time** During the winter the whole of Britain is on Greenwich Meantime (GMT). The clocks move one hour forward on the last Sunday in March, remaining on British Summer Time (BST) until the last Sunday in October.

• **Smoking** Smoking in enclosed public places is banned. The ban relates not only to pubs and restaurants, but also to B&Bs, hostels and hotels. These latter have the right to designate one or more bedrooms where the occupants can smoke, but the ban is in force in all enclosed areas open to the public – even in a private home such as a B&B. Should you be foolhardy enough to light up in a no-smoking area, which includes pretty well any indoor public place, you could be fined £50, but it's the owners of the premises who suffer most if they fail to stop you, with a potential fine of £2500.

• **Telephones** The international access code for Britain is ☎ 44, followed by the area code minus the first 0, and then the number you require. Within the UK, to call a number with the same code as the landline phone you are calling from, the code can be omitted: dial the number only. It is cheaper to ring at weekends (from midnight on Friday till midnight on Sunday), and after 7pm and before 7am on weekdays. To protect against vandalism some public phones accept debit/credit cards only; the minimum cost for a call is 60p.

Mobile (cell) phone reception is quite reliable along the Ridgeway. If you're using a mobile phone that is registered overseas, consider buying a local SIM card to keep costs down; also remember to bring a universal adaptor so you can charge your phone.

• **Emergency services** For police, ambulance, fire and mountain rescue dial ☎ 999, or the EU standard number ☎ 112.

Mon-Fri 8.15am-6pm, Sat 8.30am-2pm, 🖳 www.postoffice.co.uk) that the post offices en route are still open and with your bank to make sure it has an agreement with the post office and you can visit the post office to withdraw money from your account.

OTHER SERVICES

On the western half of the Ridgeway, services are a bit scant, but on the eastern half most villages and all the towns have at least one public **telephone**, a small **shop** and a **post office**. Apart from getting cash, post offices can be used for sending home unnecessary equipment that may be weighing you down.

In Part 4 special mention is given to other services that may be of use to the walker such as: **laundrettes**, **internet access**, **pharmacies** and **tourist information centres** – the latter can be used for finding and booking accommodation among other things.

WALKING COMPANIES & LUGGAGE TRANSFER

Several UK-based companies offer self-guided holidays on the Ridgeway but only one, at the time of writing, a fully guided walk (see opposite).

Self-guided holidays

Self-guided holidays usually include detailed advice and notes on itineraries and routes, maps, accommodation including breakfast, daily baggage transfer and transport arrangements at the start and end of your walk.

- **Absolute Escapes** (☎ 0131 240 1210, 🖳 www.absoluteescapes.com; Edinburgh) Offer three itineraries: the full route in 7 days and two shorter sections, either the Wessex Downs or the Chiltern Hills, in 4 days.
- **British & Irish Walks** (☎ 01242 254353, 🖳 www.britishandirishwalks.com; Cheltenham) Offer walks along the southern section of the way, beginning in Marlborough and ending at Ogbourne St George.
- **Celtic Trails** (☎ 01291 689774, 🖳 www.celtictrailswalkingholidays.co.uk; Chepstow) Have two itineraries covering the whole walk in 9-10 days and will also tailor-make walks.
- **Contours Walking Holidays** (☎ 01629 821900, 🖳 www.contours.co.uk; Derbyshire) Operate three itineraries covering the whole route in 6-8 days and two offering part of the route: Avebury to Goring, and Goring to Ivinghoe Beacon.
- **Explore Britain** (☎ 01740 650900, 🖳 www.explorebritain.com; Durham) Operate one itinerary on the western half from Avebury to Goring.
- **Footpath Holidays** (☎ 01985 840049, 🖳 www.footpath-holidays.com; Wiltshire) In addition to offering an 8-day self-guided Ridgeway tour they are also, unusually, offering treks along the Wessex Ridgeway, linking Lyme Regis on the Dorset coast to Avebury – the starting point for the Ridgeway, plus 'Ancient Landscapes of Wessex' which are highlights and include sections of the Ridgeway.

- **Freedom Walking Holidays** (☎ 07733 885390, 🖳 www.freedomwalkingholidays.co.uk; Goring-on-Thames) Can accommodate a variety of requirements within your holiday package.
- **Load Off Your Back Walking Holidays** (☎ 01707 331133, 🖳 www.loadoffyourback.co.uk, Welwyn Garden City) Offer a range of itineraries along the whole trail as well as for sections from 3 days' walking/4 nights to 7 days' walking/8 nights.
- **Macs Adventure** (☎ 0141 530 4390, 🖳 www.macsadventure.com; Glasgow) Operate two itineraries: 8 days/7 nights and 10 days/9 nights, available from April to end September.
- **Responsible Travel** (☎ 01273 823700, 🖳 www.responsibletravel.com, Brighton) Offer an itinerary of 10 days' walking along the entire trail.
- **The Walking Holiday Company** (☎ 01600 713008, 🖳 www.thewalkingholidaycompany.co.uk; Monmouth) Operate itineraries for the whole trail and also for sections; can tailor make as required.
- **Walk the Landscape** (☎ 07718 660070, 🖳 walkthelandscape.co.uk, Banbury) Offer two itineraries for the whole trail from 6 days/7 nights to 8 days/9 nights or can tailor make.

Guided holidays

- **Walk the Landscape** (see above) Offer walks of several days or more. Please contact to discuss.

Luggage transfer

- **The Walker's Friend** (☎ 07980 458748, 🖳 www.thewalkersfriend.co.uk) They can transfer up to six bags for about £35 per day and usually people take six days to walk the whole trail so this would cost £210. They will meet walkers at the railway station on arrival; also happy to start doing transfers even if the walker has already started the walk.
- **Move along Radio Cars** (☎ 07500 118323, 🖳 aly.murray089@hotmail.co.uk) are happy to transfer luggage on the western half of the Ridgeway up to Streatley and also will pick people and luggage up at Swindon rail or coach station. Text or email contact preferred as Aly is often driving.

Some of the B&Bs listed in this guide (see Part 4) will also take your luggage on to your next overnight stop if you are staying with them. Local taxi companies can also provide this service but may be more expensive.

DISABLED ACCESS

There are no officially recognised stretches of the Ridgeway open for wheelchair users, though that doesn't mean it isn't possible to use some stretches of the path. Particularly on the western half there are no stiles and only a handful of gates, none of which would prove problematic for a wheelchair user. On the downside though, the route on this section often consists of rutted tracks that can also be very muddy after rain. An area on this half that is accessible is around Barbury Castle (see p97). There is a car park here and although the castle itself would prove very difficult for a wheelchair user, the area around it is beautiful and provides excellent views over the surrounding countryside. The eastern half of the Ridgeway is less isolated and the route passes through several towns that could make good starting points. The path heading east from Wendover (see p177) is accessible, but not particularly exciting. Where the Ridgeway crosses a road there is often a car park and driving to one of these enables you to get into the open countryside quickly with little effort.

The project to replace stiles with wide gates has now been completed. National Trails staff work to maintain the gates in partnership with landowners. They also work with landowners and others to keep the track in good condition, but weather conditions and use by vehicles still damage some stretches of track.

MOUNTAIN-BIKING

The Ridgeway and trails leading off it are very popular with mountain-bikers. However, not all of it is open to them. The western section from Avebury to Streatley is totally open and has only a short section of road and relatively few gates compared to the eastern section. The paths along this portion are generally wide and shouldn't present a problem for mountain-bikers. From Streatley heading east most sections of the Ridgeway are closed to cyclists except for an 8-mile (13km) stretch from Britwell Hill (near Watlington) to Wainhill (near Bledlow). This, of course, doesn't deter some cyclists who do use the designated footpaths despite doing so illegally.

Conditions on the Ridgeway during the summer months are pretty good for cyclists though some sections of heavily rutted path might cause problems. Also be aware of flint on some sections of the path as it can cause punctures.

Details of cycle sales, repair and service shops in towns on or near the route are given in the route guide.

HORSE RIDERS

The same sections of the Ridgeway that are open to cyclists are also open to horse riders. In practice, most horse riders use only short sections of the path which link into many other bridleways. Deeply rutted tracks can be problematic for horses and you should also be aware of the flinty sections of path that can injure horses' hooves.

MOTOR VEHICLES

Despite many people's opposition, motor vehicles are allowed to use selected stretches of the Ridgeway. Since 2006 only five short sections have been open to cars and motorcycles. The total length of these sections is about 17 miles and all but one mile of that is west of the Thames. Of the five sections that are open, four can only be used between May and September.

Although you will rarely come across a car or 4x4 on the Ridgeway you are far more likely to be overtaken by motorcyclists, often riding in groups, which you'll hear coming from a long way off.

It's obvious that motor vehicles do serious damage to the Ridgeway tracks that they use and the effects of this damage are most keenly felt by walkers. It's not much fun walking on a deeply rutted, muddy track for several miles.

TAKING DOGS ALONG THE RIDGEWAY

[See also pp191-2] You are allowed to take your dog on all sections of the Ridgeway. Indeed, the majority of people you meet will be accompanied by at least one dog. Henry Stedman, who updated this 4th edition, took his dog Daisy (a veteran of many a long-distance trail) along the whole of the path without any problem. Indeed, **Daisy thinks that the Ridgeway is the best trail for dogs she has yet been on**. The relative lack of fields with livestock in them (only two fields with cows in encountered by Henry and Daisy, and only one with sheep – though this of course could vary from year to year) and the small number of busy roads mean that fairly obedient dogs (ie ones that aren't liable to jump fences and will come to heel on command) can be left off the leash for much of the trip. True, the (slight) possibility that motor vehicles will be on the trail is a potential hazard that you won't find on other national trails; but time your walk to a season when these are not allowed and you should have a safe walk for your dog – and a stress-free walk for you. Do be careful near the horse gallops, however, particularly those stretches where there is only a white rail between you and the gallop and dogs can get onto the gallop easily; the sheer speed of the horses and the thunder of their hooves can easily unnerve or excite your pet – and mayhem may ensue.

As the owner, you are fully responsible for your dog's behaviour. Dogs should always be kept on leads while around livestock (see box p57). Having said this, if you are harassed by cattle because of your dog, the Ramblers/NFU recommend letting the dog off the lead.

Budgeting

The amount of money you need to take with you depends on your accommodation plans and how you're going to eat. If you camp and cook your own meals your expenses can be very low, but most people prefer to have at least some of their meals cooked for them and even the hardiest camper may be tempted into the occasional B&B when the rain is falling. Also, don't forget all those little things that inevitably push up your daily bill: postcards, stamps, cream teas, ice-creams, beer, buses here, buses there and more beer; it all adds up!

CAMPING

You can survive on as little as £15 per person (pp) if you use the cheapest sites and cook all your own food from staple ingredients. Nevertheless, most people find that the best-laid plans to survive on the bare minimum soon fall flat after a couple of hard days' trekking. Always budget for unforeseen expenses and, of course, the end-of-day pint of beer which costs around £3.50. Assuming such liquid treats and the occasional takeaway or pub meal a budget of £20-25 per day is far more realistic.

HOSTELS AND BUNKHOUSES

Since there is only one bunkhouse (see pp124-5) and one YHA hostel (see p138) on/near the path using only this kind of accommodation is not feasible for this walk. Accommodation costs from £17pp per night and both places offer meals – breakfast and a packed lunch each cost about £6-7 and an evening meal about £9-12 – but also have a self-catering kitchen.

B&B-STYLE ACCOMMODATION

Rates can be as little as £25pp per night assuming two people are sharing a room but are more often £30-35pp, particularly for guesthouses and hotels, and can even be over £50pp for the most luxurious places. If wanting sole occupancy of a room there is likely to be a supplement; this is usually about £10-15 less than the full room rate, in some cases you may have to pay the full room rate.

Add on the price of lunch (though if you have had a cooked breakfast you may not want much), an evening meal, beer and other expenses and you can expect to need at least £60-80pp per day. However, rates can be substantially less if you are planning to stay in one place for three or more nights and are also usually lower during the winter months.

If you are on a budget you could always ask to go without breakfast which will probably result in a reduction.

Itineraries

This route in this guidebook has been divided into stages but these are not rigid daily stages. It's structured to make it easy for you to plan your own itinerary. If you have a week to spare you can walk the Ridgeway in one go. However, many people decide to walk it in sections over a longer period. Or you might simply want to pick out the best parts for a series of day walks.

To help you plan your walk look at the **planning map** (see opposite inside back cover) and the **table of town & village facilities**, see pp32-3, which gives a rundown on the essential information you need regarding accommodation possibilities and services. Alternatively, you could follow one of the suggested **itineraries**, see box p34, that are based on walking speed.

There is also a list of recommended linear day and two-day (weekend) walks (see box opposite) that cover the highlights of the Ridgeway.

The **public transport map** and the table of **bus services** are on pp48-51.

Once you have an idea of your approach turn to **Part 5** for detailed information on accommodation, places to eat and drink, as well as other services in each town and village on the route. Also in Part 4 you will find summaries of the route to accompany the detailed trail maps.

❑ THE BEST DAY AND TWO-DAY WALKS

The desire of most walkers is to tackle the whole Ridgeway in one go but sometimes this isn't possible. Spare time, good weather, transport and money all need to be found at the same time. For this reason many choose to walk the Ridgeway in separate sections, maybe over a series of summer weekends. Others might not be so concerned about walking every inch of the official path and might only want to walk the best bits. Simply getting out and walking any part of the Ridgeway will be rewarding, but listed below are some especially enjoyable parts. If you're feeling ambitious and the weather is on your side, you could try completing a two-day walk in one day. For details of public transport services to/from the places listed below see pp47-51.

Day walks

- **Avebury to Ogbourne St George** 9½ miles/15km (Alternative start route D, see pp91-3, & pp96-104) This path starts at Avebury Stone Circle and walks the quiet high ridge to the Iron Age fort of Barbury Castle where there are magnificent views northwards; it then goes onto Smeathe's Ridge and finally down into the pleasant village of Ogbourne St George where there is a pub to relax in.
- **Foxhill to White Horse Hill** 5 miles/8km (see pp109-18) Start outside The Burj restaurant at the Foxhill crossroads and quickly climb up onto the open high ground for stunning views, visit the ancient burial site at Wayland's Smithy and finish at White Horse Hill, the site of an Iron Age hill fort, Dragon Hill, and the original white horse.
- **White Horse Hill to East Ilsley** 15 miles/24km (see pp118-34) If you fancy a bit of time on your own, this is the most isolated section of the Ridgeway path. It keeps to the high ground with only a few road crossings and a handful of farms on the entire stretch. Make sure the weather is good as there is virtually no shelter.
- **Streatley to Wallingford** 7 miles/11.5km (see pp138-50) Begin in the Thames-side village of Streatley and walk into Goring before following the bank of the Thames northwards through the delightful villages of South and North Stoke. The path then heads into the old town of Wallingford.
- **Wendover to Ivinghoe Beacon** 10 miles/16km (see pp174-89) From the attractive town of Wendover the path takes you through the best woodland walking on the Ridgeway, coming close to the village of Wigginton should you choose to stop off for lunch. The final section takes on Ivinghoe Beacon, a long, steep climb through woodland and finally some excellent open walking with increasingly fantastic views.

Two-day (weekend) walks

- **Avebury to White Horse Hill** 22 miles/35.5km (Alternative start route D, see pp91-3, & pp96-118) This takes in many of the most interesting ancient sites along the Ridgeway. The walking is mainly along broad, grassy tracks with few steep climbs. There is no accommodation near the middle of this walk so, depending on where you stay, you'll either have a short first day and long second, or vice versa.
- **East Ilsley to Watlington** 22 miles/35.5km (see pp134-60) This walk takes in a bit of each of the Ridgeway's main attractions – first, isolated walking, then, the path along the Thames and finally, some fine woodland walking. You can stay in Wallingford to divide the journey neatly into two days.

TOWN AND

Place name (Places in brackets are a short walk off the Ridgeway)	**Distance from previous place** approx miles/km (Distances in brackets indicate how far the place is from the nearest point on the Ridgeway)	**ATM (cash machine) or bank**	**Post Office** (✔) means limited opening hours	**Tourist Information** Tourist Info Centre (TIC), Tourist Info Point (TIP)
(Marlborough)		✔	✔	TIP
(Avebury)		ATM ONLY	(✔)	
(West Overton)				
(East Kennett)				
Overton Hill	0			
(Ogbourne St George)	9/14.5 (+0.6/1)			
(Liddington)	6.5/10.5 (+0.6/1)			
Foxhill	1/1.5			
(Bishopstone)	1.2/2 (+0.6/1)			
(Ashbury)	1.5/2.5 (+0.6/1)		(✔)	
(Woolstone)	2/3 (+1.2/2)			
(Uffington)	0 (+1.7/2.5)			
(Sparsholt Firs)	2.5/4 (+0.6/1)			
(Sparsholt)	0 (+1.5/2.5)			
(Letcombe Regis)	3.9/6 (+1.5/2.5)			
(Court Hill)	0.6/1 (+0.3/0.5)			
(Wantage)	0 (+2/3)			TIP
(East Ilsley)	8.2/13 (+1/1.5)			
(Compton)	0 (+1.5/2.5)		✔	
(Aldworth)	2.7/4.5 (+1.2/2)			
Streatley	3/5			
Goring	0.3/0.5	✔	✔	TIP
South Stoke	1.5/2.5			
North Stoke	2.5/4			
(Wallingford)	1.2/2 (+1.2/2)	✔	✔	TIC
(Crowmarsh Gifford)	0 (+0.7/1.2)			
Nuffield	4/6.5			
(Watlington)	5.5/9 (+0.6/1)	ATM ONLY	✔	
(Lewknor)	2.5/4 (+0.5/0.8)			
(Kingston Blount)	1.7/2.5 (+0.6/1)			
(Chinnor)	1.5/2.5 (+0.3/0.5)	ATM ONLY	✔	
Princes Risborough	5.3/8.5 (+0.2/0.3)	✔	✔	TIC
Wendover	6.2/10	✔	✔	TIP
Wigginton	6.2/10			
(Tring)	0 (+1/1.5)	✔	✔	TIC
(Aldbury)	2/3 (0.6/1)	ATM ONLY	✔	
Ivinghoe Beacon	3.1/5			
(Ivinghoe)	3.4/5.5 (+1.2/2)		✔	

VILLAGE FACILITIES

Eating Place ✓ = one; ✓✓ = two; ✓✓✓ = 3+	Food Store	Campsite	Hostel/ Bunkhouse YHA = YHA hostel	B&B-style accommodation* ✓ = one ✓✓ = two; ✓✓✓ = 3+	Place name (places in brackets are a short walk off the Ridgeway: see opposite for distances)
✓✓✓	✓			✓✓✓	(Marlborough)
✓✓	✓			✓✓✓	(Avebury)
✓					(West Overton)
				✓	(East Kennett)
					Overton Hill
✓				✓✓✓	(Ogbourne St George)
✓				✓✓	(Liddington)
✓					Foxhill
✓				✓✓	(Bishopstone)
✓✓	✓			✓	(Ashbury)
✓				✓	(Woolstone)
✓	✓				(Uffington)
		✓		✓✓	(Sparsholt Firs)
✓				✓	(Sparsholt)
✓				✓✓	(Letcombe Regis)
✓		✓	Bunkhouse		(Court Hill)
✓✓✓	✓			✓✓✓	(Wantage)
✓✓				✓✓	(East Ilsley)
✓	✓			✓	(Compton)
✓					(Aldworth)
✓✓			YHA	✓✓✓	Streatley
✓✓✓	✓			✓✓✓	Goring
✓				✓✓	South Stoke
					North Stoke
✓✓✓	✓			✓✓✓	(Wallingford)
✓✓	✓	✓		✓	(Crowmarsh Gifford)
					Nuffield
✓✓✓	✓	✓		✓✓	(Watlington)
✓				✓	(Lewknor)
				✓	(Kingston Blount)
✓✓✓	✓			✓	(Chinnor)
✓✓✓	✓			✓✓	Princes Risborough
✓✓✓	✓			✓	Wendover
✓				✓	Wigginton
✓✓✓	✓			✓✓✓	(Tring)
✓✓	✓			✓	(Aldbury)
					Ivinghoe Beacon
✓✓✓	✓	✓		✓	(Ivinghoe)

* does not include Airbnb options

WHICH DIRECTION?

The generally accepted way to walk the Ridgeway is from west to east though it really doesn't matter. As the two halves are very different you might base your

SUGGESTED ITINERARIES

CAMPING & BUNKHOUSE/HOSTEL

	Relaxed pace		Medium pace		Fast pace	
Night	Place	Approx Distance miles/km	Place	Approx Distance miles/km	Place	Approx Distance miles/km
0	Overton Hill		Overton Hill		Overton Hill	
1	Ogbourne St G*	9.6/15.5	Ogbourne St G*	9.6/15.5	Ogbourne St G*	9.6/15.5
2	Sparsholt Firs	14.5/23	Sparsholt Firs	14.5/23	Court Hill	19/30.5
3	Court Hill	4.5/7	Court Hill	4.5/7	Streatley§	14/22.5
4	Streatley§	14/22.5	Streatley§	14/22.5	Watlington	15/24
5	Crowmarsh G	7.3/12	Crowmarsh G	7.3/12	Princes Risboro'*	11.2/18
6	Watlington	9.6/15	Watlington	9.6/15	Ivinghoe Beacon	17.5/28
7	Princes Risboro'*	11.2/18	Princes Risboro'*	11.2/18		
8	Wigginton*	12.4/20	Ivinghoe Beacon	17.5/28		
9	Ivinghoe Beacon	5.1/8				

§No campsite but hostel accommodation is available
*No campsites or hostels but alternative accommodation is available

STAYING IN B&B-STYLE ACCOMMODATION

	Relaxed pace		Medium pace		Fast pace	
Night	Place	Approx Distance miles/km	Place	Approx Distance miles/km	Place	Approx Distance miles/km
0	Overton Hill		Overton Hill		Overton Hill	
1	Ogbourne St G	9.6/15.5	Bishopstone	17.7/28.5	Bishopstone	17.7/28.5
2	Bishopstone	8.7/14	Letcombe Rgs	9.9/15.5	East Ilsley	18.7/30
3	Letcombe Rgs	9.9/15.5	Goring	14.8/23.5	Watlington	20.7/33
4	East Ilsley	8.8/14	Watlington	14.7/23.5	Wendover	17.2/26.5
5	Wallingford	11.2/18.5	Princes Risboro'	11/18	Ivinghoe Beacon	11.3/18
6	Watlington	9.5/15.5	Wigginton	12.4/20		
7	Princes Risboro'	11/18	Ivinghoe Beacon	5.1/8		
8	Wigginton	12.4/20				
9	Ivinghoe Beacon	5.1/8.5				

Note: Airbnb options are not included in the above

decision on what type of scenery and terrain you'd like to tackle first. Neither section is particularly demanding but the western section is far more isolated and really isn't much fun in bad weather. The eastern section, being in woodlands for much of the time, is far more sheltered and relaxing.

Availability of public transport heading in either direction along the Ridgeway is similar so this shouldn't have much bearing on which direction you choose to walk in.

Although the maps in Part 4 of this book follow the Ridgeway from west to east, there are timings on all the maps for walking in either direction.

SUGGESTED ITINERARIES

The itineraries in the box opposite are based on different accommodation types: one is for those who prefer to camp or stay in hostels/bunkhouses where possible; the other is for those who choose to stay in B&B-style accommodation. Each is divided into three options based on walking speeds. They are only suggestions so feel free to adapt them to your needs. **Don't forget** to add your travelling time before and after the walk.

SIDE TRIPS

There are plenty of good circular and linear walks from the Ridgeway. Information about all these routes can be obtained from local tourist information centres/points (see box p42), the National Trails website, or from the relevant county/district councils (see box p62).

- **Aldbourne Circular Route** This is a 12-mile (19.5km) route which for several miles uses the Ridgeway. It takes in Aldbourne village, several Bronze Age burial mounds, the deserted village of Snap (see p105), Liddington Castle (see p108) and Sugar Hill. The trail is waymarked and it's also marked on OS Explorer map Nos 157 and 170.
- **Ashbury Circular Walk** This 10-mile (16km) walk from the village of Ashbury (see p114) takes the walker through some beautiful countryside once the initial steep climb has been completed. The path crosses the Ridgeway and heads to Alfred's Castle, an Iron Age hillfort, before reaching Ashdown House, a 17th-century Dutch-style property owned by the National Trust. From here it returns to the Ridgeway via a different route and takes in Wayland's Smithy (see box p114), before heading back down the hill to Ashbury. The trail is waymarked and although the paths are marked on OS Explorer map No 170, they aren't labelled.
- **Lambourn Valley Way** This 20-mile (32km) route starts at Uffington White Horse and leads down into the valley to reach the village of Lambourn. It then broadly follows the River Lambourn along the valley to its end in Newbury.

This is a very peaceful walk passing through several small villages with only the crossing of the M4 to spoil the atmosphere. The route is waymarked and is also marked on OS Explorer map Nos 170 and 158.

• **East/West Ilsley Circular Route** This 6-mile (9.5km) walk is best started and finished in one of the pubs in East Ilsley. The path takes a wayward route to West Ilsley before heading up to the Ridgeway and following it for just over a mile then turning back to East Ilsley. Much of this path is on broad tracks that often run close to racehorse gallops. The route is waymarked and the paths are marked on OS Explorer map No 170.

• **Aston Rowant Discovery Trail** This is a 5.3-mile (8.5km) walk but 6.2 miles (10km) with a hotel/pub extension. The route is waymarked and is also marked on OS Explorer map No 171. See Map 34 (p161), and for full details see www.nationaltrail.co.uk/ridgeway/route/aston-rowant-discovery-trail.

• **The Chiltern Link** This 8-mile (13km) linear walk starts on Wendover High St and meanders through woods and open countryside to the town of Chesham where you can pick up the Chess Valley Walk. Several miles into the walk you reach The Lee, a tiny village with a popular pub – The Cock and Rabbit Inn (graziemille.co.uk) – that is well worth visiting. The route is waymarked and is also marked on OS Explorer map No 181.

• **Beacon View Walk** This 5-mile (8km) circular walk is usually started and finished at The Greyhound in Wigginton (see p180) and follows the course of the Ridgeway for about two miles from Hastoe Cross to the bridge over the Grand Union Canal. The route then follows the canal to Cow Roast (a village!) before heading back to Wigginton. The paths comprising the route are marked with standard signs and all paths appear on OS Explorer map No 181.

• **The Ashridge Drovers' Walk** This 6-mile (9.5km) circular walk starts and finishes at Tring Railway Station (see Map 47, p186). From there it makes for Aldbury (see p187) then up to the Bridgewater Monument where there is a visitor centre and tea shop. The route then follows the high ground to join the Ridgeway which it follows down to the railway station. The walk often follows wide, sunken lanes used in the past for droving (moving livestock). The paths comprising the route are marked with standard signs and all paths appear on OS Explorer map No 181.

• **Two Ridges Link** This 8-mile (13km) linear walk runs from Ivinghoe Beacon, the very end of the Ridgeway, to Leighton Buzzard at the start of the Greensand Ridge Walk. The walk takes you first through the villages of Ivinghoe Aston and Slapton before joining the Grand Union Canal. The trail is fully waymarked and it's also marked on OS Explorer map Nos 181 and 192.

• **Ridgeway Link Walk** This 7½-mile (12km) linear walk follows the Icknield Way from Chilterns Gateway Centre, on Dunstable Downs, to Ivinghoe Beacon (see Map 48, p189). Of course, walking the path in reverse might be more practical for Ridgeway walkers, especially if you are heading to Dunstable for transport connections. The walk passes through Whipsnade and Dagnall, both of which have a pub. Chilterns Gateway Centre is open all year and has a café, shop and toilets and there is also a car park. Although the route is well waymarked some of the paths can get rather muddy after rain. The entire route is marked as the Icknield Way on OS Explorer map No 181.

What to take

Deciding how much to take with you can be difficult. Experienced walkers know that you really should take only the bare essentials but at the same time you need to ensure you have all the equipment necessary to make the trip safe and comfortable.

KEEP YOUR LUGGAGE LIGHT

Carrying a heavy rucksack really can ruin your enjoyment of a good walk and can also slow you down, turning an easy 7-mile day into an interminable slog. Be ruthless when you pack and leave behind all those little home comforts that you tell yourself don't weigh that much really. This advice is even more pertinent to campers who have added weight to carry.

HOW TO CARRY IT

The size of your **rucksack** will depend on where you are planning to stay and how you are planning to eat. If you are camping and cooking for yourself you will probably need a minimum 70-litre rucksack which can hold the tent, sleeping bag, cooking equipment and food. Make sure your rucksack has a stiffened back and can be adjusted to fit your own back comfortably. This will make carrying the weight much easier.

When packing the rucksack make sure you have all the things you are likely to need during the day near the top or in the side pockets. This includes map, water bottle or pouch, packed lunch, waterproofs and this guidebook, of course. Make sure the hip belt and chest strap (if there is one) are fastened tightly as this helps distribute the weight with most of it being carried on your hips. Rucksacks are decorated with seemingly pointless straps, but if you adjust them correctly it can make a big difference to your personal comfort while walking.

If you plan to stay in B&B-style accommodation a 30- to 40-litre pack should be more than enough to carry everything you need.

Consider taking a small **bum bag** or **day pack** for your camera, guidebook and other essentials for when you go sightseeing or for a day walk.

A good habit to establish is to always put things in the same place in your rucksack and memorise where they are. There is nothing more annoying than having to pull everything out of your pack to find that lost banana when you're starving, or scrambling for your camera when there is a rare opportunity to photograph an owl perched on a fencepost. It's also a good idea to keep everything in **canoe bags**, **waterproof rucksack liners** or strong plastic bags. If you don't, it's bound to rain.

FOOTWEAR

Your **boots** are the single most important item of gear that can affect the enjoyment of your trek. In the summer you can use a light pair of trail shoes if you're only carrying a small pack. Make sure they have a Gore-Tex lining otherwise you could end up with wet, cold feet if there is any rain. Although the Ridgeway isn't particularly strenuous, some of the terrain can be quite rough so a good pair of walking boots is a safer bet. They must fit well and be properly broken in. It is no good discovering that your boots are slowly murdering your feet two days into a week-long trek. See p58 for more blister-avoidance advice.

The traditional wearing of a thin liner **sock** under a thicker wool sock is no longer necessary if you choose a high-quality sock specially designed for walking. A high proportion of natural fibres makes them much more comfortable. Three pairs are ample. Some walkers like to have a **second pair of shoes** to wear when they are not on the trail. Trainers, sport sandals or flip-flops are all suitable as long as they are light.

CLOTHES

Experienced walkers know the importance of wearing the right clothes. Especially up on the western part of the Ridgeway the wind, rain and sun can all be fierce and there's often no shelter if you are caught out. Modern technology in outdoor attire can seem baffling but it comes down to: a base layer to transport sweat away from your skin; a mid-layer or two to keep you warm; and an outer layer or 'shell' to protect you from the wind and rain.

Base layer

Cotton absorbs sweat, trapping it next to the skin which will chill you rapidly when you stop exercising. A thin lightweight **thermal top** made from synthetic material is better as it draws moisture away, keeping you dry. It will be cool if worn on its own in hot weather and warm when worn under other clothes in cooler conditions. A spare would be sensible. You may also like to bring a **shirt** for wearing in the evening.

Mid-layers

In the summer a woollen jumper or mid-weight polyester **fleece** will suffice. For the rest of the year you will need an extra layer to keep you warm. Both wool and fleece, unlike cotton, have the ability to stay reasonably warm when wet.

Outer layer

A **waterproof jacket** is essential year-round and will be much more comfortable (but also more expensive) if it's also 'breathable' to prevent the build up of condensation on the inside. This layer can also be worn to keep out the wind.

Leg wear

Whatever you wear on your legs it should be light, quick drying and not restricting. Many British walkers find polyester tracksuit bottoms comfortable. Polycotton or microfibre trousers are also excellent. Denim jeans should never be worn; if they get wet they become heavy, cold and bind to your legs. A pair of

shorts is nice to have on sunny days. Thermal **longjohns** or thick tights are cosy if you're camping but are probably unnecessary even in winter. **Waterproof trousers** are necessary most of the year. In summer a pair of windproof and quick-drying trousers are useful in showery weather. **Gaiters** are not really necessary but may come in useful in wet weather when the vegetation around your legs is dripping wet.

Underwear

Three changes of what you normally wear is fine. Women may find a **sports bra** more comfortable because pack straps can cause bra straps to dig into your shoulders.

Other clothes

A **warm** hat and **gloves** should always be kept in your rucksack, year-round. You never know when you might need them. In summer you should also carry a **sun hat** with you, preferably one that also covers the back of your neck. Also consider a small **towel**, especially if you are camping.

TOILETRIES

Only take the minimum: a small bar of **soap** in a plastic container (unless staying in B&B-style accommodation) which can also be used instead of shaving cream and for washing clothes; a tiny tube of **toothpaste** and a **toothbrush**; one roll of **loo paper** in a plastic bag. If you are planning to defecate outdoors you will also need a lightweight **trowel** for burying the evidence (see p53-4 for further tips). A **razor**, **deodorant**, **tampons/sanitary towels** and a high-factor **sun screen** should cover all your needs.

FIRST-AID KIT

There is a pharmacy in many towns and villages along the route so you only need a small kit to cover common problems and emergencies: pack it in a waterproof container.

A basic kit will contain **aspirin** or **paracetamol** for treating mild to moderate pain and fever; **plasters/Band Aids** for minor cuts; **Moleskin**, **Compeed**, or **Second skin** for blisters; a **bandage** for holding dressings, splints or limbs in place and for supporting a sprained ankle or a weak knee; a small selection of different-sized **sterile dressings** for wounds; **porous adhesive tape**, **antiseptic wipes**, **antiseptic cream**, **safety pins**, **tweezers** and **scissors**.

GENERAL ITEMS

Essential

The following should be in everyone's rucksack: a one-litre **water bottle** or **pouch**; a **torch** (flashlight) with spare bulb and batteries in case you end up walking after dark; **emergency food** (see p57) which your body can quickly convert into energy; a **penknife**; a **watch** with an alarm; and a suitable **bag** for packing out any rubbish you accumulate.

A **whistle** is also worth taking. It can fit in a pocket and although you are very unlikely to need it you may be grateful for it in the unlikely event of an emergency (see p57). Although the path is easy to follow, a 'Silva' type **compass** and knowing how to use it is a good idea in case you need to leave the trail when there is heavy fog.

Useful

Many would list a **camera** as essential but it can be liberating to travel without one once in a while; a **notebook** can be a more accurate way of recording your impressions. A **book** helps to pass the time on train and bus journeys. For comfort, particularly in the summer, you may wish to take a pair of **sunglasses**. Also useful are **binoculars** for observing wildlife, a **walking stick** or pole to take the shock off your knees, a **vacuum flask** for carrying hot drinks and a **mobile phone** (reception is quite reliable along the Ridgeway); if you take a mobile phone make sure you also take the charging device.

CAMPING GEAR

Campers will need a **tent** (or bivvy bag if you enjoy travelling light) which is able to withstand wet and windy weather. You should find that a 2- to 3-season **sleeping bag** is sufficient, but obviously in winter a warmer bag is a good idea. You will also need a **sleeping mat**, a **stove** and **fuel**, a **pan** with a lid that can double as a frying pan/plate (this is fine for two people), a **pan handle**, a **mug**, a **spoon** and a wire/plastic **scrubber** for washing up.

MONEY

There are no banks/ATMs on the Ridgeway between Overton Hill and Goring so unless you leave the way you will have to carry most of your money as **cash**. Between Goring and Ivinghoe Beacon most towns have at least one **ATM**. A **debit card** is the easiest way to withdraw money (see pp23-6) and debit/credit cards can be used to pay in larger shops, pubs, restaurants and hotels.

MAPS

The hand-drawn maps in this book cover the trail at a scale of just under 1:20,000: 3 1/8 inches = one mile (5cm = 1km); they provide plenty of detail and information to keep you on the right track.

If you are only walking on the Ridgeway, you shouldn't need any other maps but for side trips you will need an **Ordnance Survey** map (🖳 www.ordnancesurvey.co.uk). The entire Ridgeway route is covered on four OS Explorer/Active maps at a scale of 1:25,000. The numbers of these maps are: **157** (Marlborough & Savernake Forest), **170** (Abingdon, Wantage & Vale of White Horse), **171** (Chiltern Hills West, Henley-on-Thames & Wallingford), and **181** (Chiltern Hills North, Aylesbury, Berkhamsted & Chesham). The Explorer maps cost £8.99 each and the Active series (which are laminated) are £14.99 each; these maps are widely available in bookshops or can be ordered from the Ordnance Survey website. Members of Ramblers (see box p42) can borrow up to 10 maps for free from their library, paying only for return postage; contact them for details. Alternatively, members of the LDWA (see box p42) are entitled to a discount on maps.

A-Z Maps (🖳 www.az.co.uk) have an atlas of OS strip maps covering the entire route in their Adventure Atlas series – Ridgeway (£7.95) – at a scale of 1:25,000 (4cm = 1km).

❑ Digital mapping

There are numerous apps and software packages that provide Ordnance Survey (OS) maps for a PC, smartphone, tablet or GPS. Maps are supplied by direct download over the internet. The maps are then loaded into an application, also available by download, from where you can view them, print them and create routes on them.

Digital maps are normally purchased for an area such as a National Park, but the Ridgeway walk is available as a distinct product from some vendors. Once you own the electronic version of the map you can print any section of the map as many times as you like.

The real value of the digital maps though, is the ability to draw a route directly onto the map from your computer or smartphone. The map, or the appropriate sections of it, can then be printed with the route marked on it, so you no longer need the full versions of the OS maps. Additionally, the route can be viewed directly on your smartphone or uploaded to a GPS device, providing you with the whole route in your hand at all times while walking. If your smartphone has a GPS chip, you will be able to see your position overlaid onto the digital map on your phone.

Many websites now have free routes you can download for the more popular digital mapping products. It is important to ensure any digital mapping software on your smartphone uses pre-downloaded maps, stored on your device, and doesn't need to download them on-the-fly, as this will be impossible in the hills.

Taking OS-quality maps with you on the hills has never been so easy. Most modern smartphones have a GPS receiver built in to them and almost every device with built-in GPS functionality now has some mapping software available for it. One of the most popular manufacturers of dedicated handheld GPS devices is Garmin, who have an extensive range of map-on-screen devices; prices vary from around £100 to £600.

Smartphones and GPS devices should complement, not replace, the traditional method of navigation (a map and compass) as any electronic device is susceptible to problems and, if nothing else, battery failure. Remember, too, that battery life will be significantly reduced, compared to normal usage, when you are using the built-in GPS and running the screen for long periods.

- **Anquet** (🖳 www.anquet.com) has the Ridgeway for £14.20 using OS 1:25,000 mapping. They also have a range of Harvey maps.
- **Ordnance Survey** (🖳 www.ordnancesurvey.co.uk) will let you download and then use their UK maps (1:25,000 scale) on a mobile or tablet without a data connection for a subscription of £19.99 for a year (on their current offer).
- **Harvey** (🖳 www.harveymaps.co.uk) sell their Ridgeway map (1:40,000 scale) as a pdf download for £12.99 for use on any device.
- **Memory Map** (🖳 www.memory-map.co.uk) currently sell OS 1:25,000 Explorer mapping covering the whole of the UK for £50.

Stuart Greig (🖳 lonewalker.net)

Harvey Maps (🖳 www.harveymaps.co.uk) have a map – *Ridgeway* (£13.95) – for the entire trail but it's at a scale of 1:40,000 (2.5cm = 1km). Printed on polyethylene, it's durable, waterproof, weighs only 60g and can also be downloaded digitally for your iPhone, iPad or Android device.

RECOMMENDED READING

The Ridgeway, John Cleare, Frances Lincoln 2011; hardback; includes a history of the trail but most of the book is filled with beautiful colour photographs.

❑ SOURCES OF FURTHER INFORMATION

Trail information

The Ridgeway National Trails Office (NT; 🖳 www.nationaltrail.co.uk/ridgeway) The NT website has information concerning all aspects – history, geology, wildlife, events, future projects – of the Ridgeway and leaflets that can be downloaded. Up-to-date information is on the 'Plan your visit' page; there is also an interactive map. For any other queries you can email through the website, or call (☎ 01865 810224; Tue-Thur only). Another useful resource is **The Friends of Ridgeway** website (see p62).

Tourist information

- **Tourist Information Centres/Points (TICs/TIPs)** These are found in towns throughout Britain and provide locally specific information; TICs have staff and may be able to book accommodation whereas TIPs usually only have leaflets. There are TICs in **Wallingford** (p147), **Princes Risborough** (p169), and **Tring** (p182) and TIPs in **Marlborough** (p73), **Wantage** (p125), **Goring** (p140) and **Wendover** (p176).
- **English Tourist Board** (🖳 www.visitengland.com) The tourist board oversees all the local tourist information centres. It's a good place to find general information about the country and details about outdoor activities and local events. They can also help with arranging holidays and accommodation.
- **County/district councils** The websites for the county/district councils (see box p62) for the area covering the route can also be a useful source of tourist information.

Organisations for walkers

- **Backpackers Club** (🖳 www.backpackersclub.co.uk) A club for people who are involved or interested in lightweight camping through walking, cycling, skiing or canoeing. They produce a quarterly magazine and provide members with a comprehensive advisory and information service on all aspects of backpacking. They also organise weekend trips and publish a farm-pitch directory. Membership is £15 per year and £20 for a family.
- **The Long Distance Walkers Association** (LDWA; 🖳 www.ldwa.org.uk) An association of people with the common interest of long-distance walking. Membership includes a copy of their journal *Strider* three times per year giving details of challenge events and local group walks as well as articles on the subject. Members also receive a discount on the *UK Trailwalker's Handbook* which details 730 trails across the UK. Membership is £13 per year or £19.50 for a family.
- **Ramblers** (formerly Ramblers' Association; 🖳 www.ramblers.org.uk) Looks after the interests of walkers throughout Britain. They publish a large amount of useful information including their quarterly *Walk* magazine (£3.60 to non-members). The website also has a discussion forum. Membership costs £34.50/20.50 individual/concessionary, joint/concessionary £45.50/27.50.

Both National Trails (NT; Anthony Burton, 2013) and Cicerone (Steve Davison, 2013) publish guides to *The Ridgeway*. Also worth looking at is NT's *The Ridgeway National Trail Companion* (2014) which gives practical advice such as accommodation, where to eat and useful services.

Of course if you are a seasoned long-distance walker, or even if you are new to the game and like what you see, check out the ever-growing list of titles in the Trailblazer series (see pp205-8).

Flora and fauna field guides

RSPB Birds of Britain and Europe (Rob Hume, published by Dorling Kindersley in association with the RSPB; 3rd ed Mar 2011; £16.99, though available at various retailers for about £7) is one of many excellent bird guides though is a little bulky for carrying on the trail.

The extensive but pocket-sized *Wild Flowers* (Martin Walters; 2012), published by Collins as part of their 'Gem' series, is well worth £4.99; Collins Gem also publishes *Butterflies* (Michael Chinnery; 2012) for £5.99. The Field Studies Council (🖳 www.field-studies-council.org) publishes a series of inexpensive *Identification Guides* (fold out charts; £2.50-5) which are also practical.

There are also several **fieldguide apps** for the iPhone, including those that can aid in identifying birds by their song as well as by their appearance.

Getting to and from the Ridgeway

Both the start and finish of the Ridgeway are easily reached by public transport or car and its convenient location in the centre of southern England means that it's one of the most accessible long-distance trails in the country.

The obvious advantages of travelling to the Ridgeway by public transport are that you don't have to go back and collect your car at the end of the walk (in fact, you can't leave your car at the start point of the Ridgeway for more than a day) and you don't need to worry about the safety aspect of leaving your car unattended for a long period of time.

If you are walking the Ridgeway from one end to the other, in one go, you shouldn't need public transport at any point along the trail. If, however, you are just walking one section, or want to skip a certain stretch and move on to the next, you will. For short distances between towns you will be using the bus.

From nearly any given town or village on the Ridgeway it is fairly easy to get to a large town that has connections to the national public transport network. So, if you decide to walk only a certain section, you shouldn't have any problems getting back home, even if it does take some time and a series of buses.

On the whole, services to the majority of towns and villages are frequent on weekdays and mostly on Saturdays, but on Sundays and public holidays there is often just a limited service, or none at all. Even during the week, getting from one place to another isn't always straightforward; you often need to get a bus to a

❑ GETTING TO BRITAIN

• **By air** Most airlines serve London Heathrow (🖳 www.heathrow.com) or London Gatwick (🖳 www.gatwickairport.com). In addition a number of budget companies fly from Europe's major cities to the other London terminals at Stansted (🖳 www .stanstedairport.com) and Luton (🖳 www.london-luton.co.uk); the latter is the most convenient airport for the end of the walk (or the start if you choose to walk east to west). There are also flights to Bristol (🖳 www.bristolairport.co.uk), which is far closer to the start of the Ridgeway than London Heathrow.

For details of the airlines using these airports and the destinations served visit the relevant airport's website.

• **From Europe by train** The Eurostar (🖳 www.eurostar.com) terminal in London is St Pancras International at St Pancras station; there are connections from King's Cross St Pancras station on the London Underground to Paddington, the main station for trains to Swindon, and to Euston for services from Tring (see box opposite).

For more information about rail services from Europe contact your rail service provider or Railteam (🖳 www.railteam.eu).

• **From Europe by coach** Eurolines (🖳 www.eurolines.com) have a huge network of long-distance coach services, connecting over 600 destinations in 36 European countries as well as Morocco, to London. Check carefully, as once expenses, such as food for the journey, are taken into consideration it often does not work out much cheaper than taking a flight, particularly when compared to the prices of some of the budget airlines.

• **From Europe by car** **Ferries** operate between various ports from mainland Europe and ports on Britain's southern and eastern coasts as well as from Ireland to Britain's western coast. Look at 🖳 www.ferrysavers.com or 🖳 www.directferries .com for a full list of operating companies, routes and services. **Eurotunnel** (🖳 www .eurotunnel.com) operates a shuttle (Le shuttle) train service for vehicles via the Channel Tunnel between Calais and Folkestone taking just 35 mins.

town from where you can then catch a bus to your destination. This can mean that you might have to finish walking early to ensure you get your bus connections.

NATIONAL TRANSPORT

By rail [see box opposite]

The most convenient railway station for the start of the Ridgeway is **Swindon** (12½ miles/20km away). Swindon is on the main line from London Paddington to Bristol; it takes about an hour from London to Swindon and about half an hour from Bristol to Swindon (services are operated by Great Western Railway). From Swindon you'll need to take one of the regular local bus services (see box pp50-1) to Marlborough and change there for the Thamesdown No 42 service which stops at West Kennett, just a few hundred metres from Overton Hill.

In the middle of the Ridgeway, Great Western Railway has services to **Goring & Streatley** on the London Paddington to Oxford line.

The nearest railway station to the end of the path is **Tring** (3¾ miles/6km away). You will walk past this station on your way up to Ivinghoe Beacon. Tring is on London Midland's London Euston to Northampton line; Euston to Tring takes about 40 minutes.

Chiltern Railways operate services to **Princes Risborough** and **Wendover** (both on the Ridgeway). There are also services to Little Kimble and Saunderton, both of which are fairly close to the Ridgeway.

All timetable and fare information can be found at **National Rail Enquiries** (☎ 08457 484950, 💻 www.nationalrail.co.uk). You can also purchase tickets over the phone through the relevant train operating company, or online at 💻 www.thetrainline.com and 💻 www.qjump.co.uk. It is often possible now to buy a train ticket that includes bus travel at your destination. For further information visit the Plusbus website (💻 www.plusbus.info).

If you think you may want to book a taxi when you arrive visit 💻 www.traintaxi.co.uk for details of taxi companies operating at railway stations throughout England.

❑ RAIL SERVICES

Great Western Railway (💻 www.gwr.com)

• London Paddington to **Swindon** via Reading and Didcot Parkway, Mon-Sat 3-4/hr, Sun 1-2/hr
Note: services from Swansea, Cardiff Central, Bristol Parkway/Temple Meads, and Cheltenham Spa to London Paddington generally stop at Swindon)

• London Paddington to Oxford (stopping service) via Twyford, Reading, Pangbourne, **Goring & Streatley**, Cholsey & Didcot Parkway, Mon-Sat 2/hr, Sun 1/hr

• Twyford to Henley-on-Thames, Mon-Sat 1-2/hr, Sun 1/hr

• London Paddington to Exeter St David's/Plymouth via Reading, Newbury & Pewsey, Mon-Sat 13/day (7-8/day call at Newbury & Pewsey), Sun 10/day (4-5/day call at Newbury & Pewsey)

• Reading to Bedwyn via Newbury & Hungerford, Mon-Sat 1/hr, Sun one every two hours

Chiltern Railways (💻 www.chilternrailways.co.uk)

• London Marylebone to **Princes Risborough** via High Wycombe, daily 2/hr

• London Marylebone to Aylesbury via High Wycombe, Saunderton, **Princes Risborough**, Monks Risborough & Little Kimble, daily 1/hr

• London Marylebone to Aylesbury via **Wendover**, Mon-Sat 2/hr, Sun 1-2/hr

London Midland (💻 www.londonmidland.com)

• London Euston to Milton Keynes via Watford Junction, Hemel Hempstead, Berkhamsted, **Tring**, Mon-Sat 1-2/hr, Sun 1/hr

• London Euston to Cheddington via Watford Junction, Hemel Hempstead, Berkhamsted & **Tring**, Mon-Sat 2-3/hr, Sun 1/hr

By coach [see box below]

National Express is the principal coach (long-distance bus) operator in Britain. Coach travel is generally cheaper but takes longer than travel by train.

Marlborough, which is just 4 miles (6.5km) from Overton Hill and the start of the Ridgeway, is conveniently located on National Express's NX402 route. From Marlborough it's a local bus ride (services are frequent and quick) to the West Kennett bus stop, just a few hundred metres from Overton Hill.

Alternatively, some National Express services stop in Swindon from where you can take a local bus to Marlborough (see box pp50-1).

The nearest place to Ivinghoe Beacon at which National Express coaches stop is Hemel Hempstead (10 miles/16km) from where you can get a local bus to Tring (see box pp50-1). **Green Line** also operates services to Hemel Hempstead from London Victoria.

Most of the **Oxford Tube** bus services between London and Oxford call at Lewknor, a good starting point for a walk to Princes Risborough or Wendover. If you are planning to walk from Wantage ask for a connector ticket from London rather than a single/return ticket as there will then be no additional charge for the journey from Oxford to Wantage on Stagecoach's X30 (see box below). The

❑ COACH SERVICES

National Express (☎ 0871 781 8181, lines open 8am-10pm daily, 🖳 www.nationalexpress.com)
Note: all London services start at London Victoria Coach Station

402 London to **Marlborough** via Heathrow Airport & Newbury, Hungerford, 1/day
401 London to **Swindon** via Heathrow Airport, 7/day (2/day continue to/start from Bristol)
302 Bristol to Northampton via Bath, Corsham, Chippenham, **Swindon** & Oxford, 1/day
707 Gatwick Airport to Northampton via Heathrow Airport, **Hemel Hempstead**, Luton Airport & Milton Keynes, 5/day
737 Stansted Airport to Oxford via Hatfield, Luton Airport, **Hemel Hempstead**, High Wycombe & Stokenchurch, 8/day
787 Heathrow Airport to Cambridge via **Hemel Hempstead**, Luton Airport, Hitchin, Letchworth, Baldock, Royston & Harston, 10/day

Oxford Bus (🖳 airline.oxfordbus.co.uk)
theairline Oxford to Heathrow Airport via **Lewknor**, daily 2/hr
theairline Oxford to Gatwick Airport via **Lewknor**, daily 1/hr

Oxford Tube (operated by Stagecoach; customer services ☎ 01865 772250, 🖳 www.oxfordtube.com)
London to Oxford via **Lewknor**, daily (24hrs/day) 1-5/hr

Green Line (☎ 0344 801 7261, 🖳 www.greenline.co.uk)
758 London to **Hemel Hempstead**, Mon-Fri 15/day, Sat & Sun 11/day

Oxford Tube operates on a first-come-first-served basis and tickets can be bought online or on the bus but only with cash for the latter.

By car

The Ridgeway is very easily accessed by car. From junction 15 of the M4 motorway it's a short drive down the A345 to Marlborough, then onto the A4 to the start at Overton Hill. You can't, however, leave your car for more than a day in the small car parking area at Overton Hill so you should find somewhere to leave it in Marlborough or maybe Avebury, though even this could be tricky.

The Ivinghoe Beacon end of the Ridgeway is best reached from junction 11 (Dunstable) of the M40 or via Aylesbury along the A41. There is a National Trust car park for Ivinghoe Beacon about half a mile (1km) south of the B489 on the minor road to Ringshall.

However, overall it's probably easier and cheaper and certainly better for the environment to use public transport.

LOCAL TRANSPORT

There are few useful train services along the Ridgeway so you will have to rely on the bus services. These, although extensive, aren't always frequent, especially at weekends, and many are being reduced due to council cutbacks.

Buses on the western half of the Ridgeway connect more of the places you might need whereas trying to get from one place to another on the eastern section can involve travelling first to a larger town, then changing buses and continuing from there. Obviously this can be quite time consuming and if you don't want to end up paying out for a taxi this is certainly one aspect of your trip that you will need to plan. Also, services to smaller towns and villages tend to finish by mid afternoon.

The public transport map on pp48-9 gives an overview of the most useful bus, coach and train routes. The bus services table on pp50-1 gives route operators, their contact details and service numbers as well as the days and approximate frequency of services in both directions. The details given are for summer services, though some of those listed operate year-round. It is essential to check the latest details before travelling: you can pick up bus timetables for free at any of the tourist information centres along the route.

If the contact details on pp50-1 prove unsatisfactory, you can contact **traveline** (☎ 0871 200 2233, 💻 www.traveline.info) which has public transport information for the whole of the UK. Alternatively contact the public transport department of the relevant county council (see box p62).

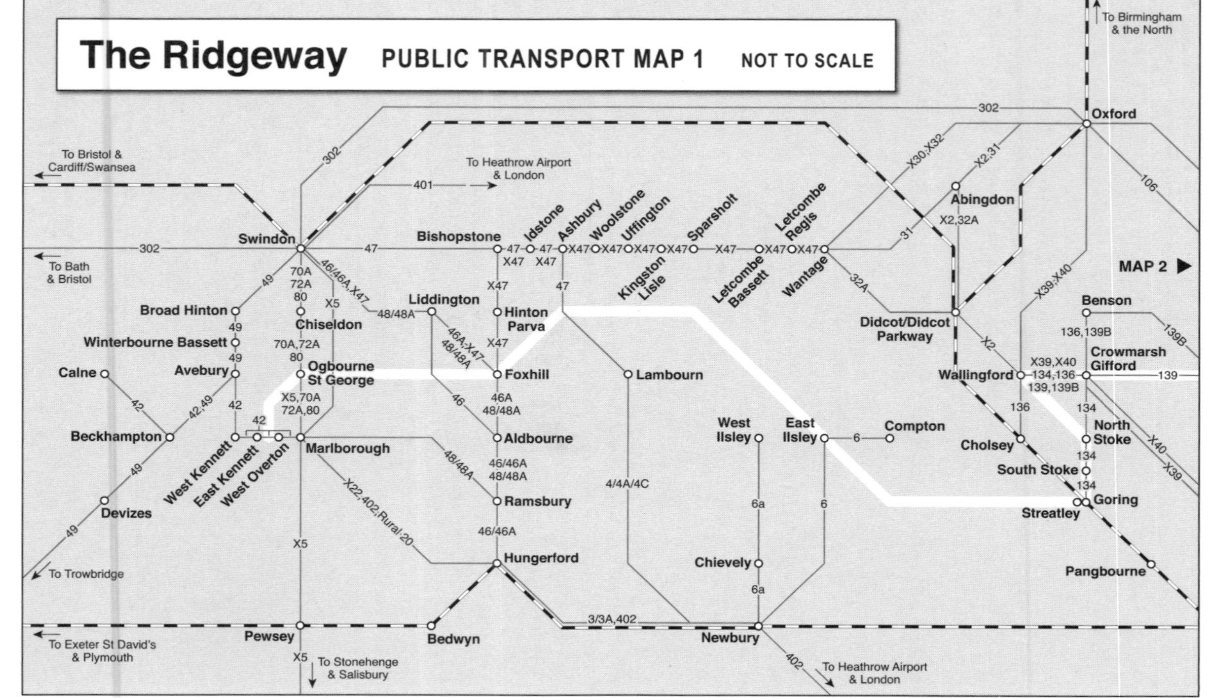
The Ridgeway
PUBLIC TRANSPORT MAP 1
NOT TO SCALE
MAP 2
To Birmingham & the North
To Bristol & Cardiff/Swansea
To Bath & Bristol
To Heathrow Airport & London
To Trowbridge
To Exeter St David's & Plymouth
To Stonehenge & Salisbury
To Heathrow Airport & London
Oxford
Swindon
Bishopstone
Idstone
Ashbury
Woolstone
Uffington
Sparsholt
Letcombe Regis
Kingston Lisle
Letcombe Bassett
Wantage
Abingdon
Didcot/Didcot Parkway
Benson
Crowmarsh Gifford
Wallingford
North Stoke
South Stoke
Cholsey
Goring
Streatley
Pangbourne
Compton
East Ilsley
West Ilsley
Chievely
Newbury
Lambourn
Broad Hinton
Winterbourne Bassett
Avebury
Calne
Beckhampton
Devizes
West Kennett
East Kennett
West Overton
Chiseldon
Ogbourne St George
Marlborough
Liddington
Hinton Parva
Foxhill
Aldbourne
Ramsbury
Hungerford
Bedwyn
Pewsey
302
106
401
47
X47
X5
70A
72A
80
70A,72A
X5,70A
72A,80
46/46A,X47
48/48A
46A,X47
46
46A
46/46A
X22,402,Rural 20
49
42
42,49
4/4A/4C
3/3A,402
402
6
6a
32A
31
X2,31
X30,X32
X2,32A
X2
X39,X40
136,139B
139B
X39,X40
134,136
139,139B
139
136
134
X40
X39

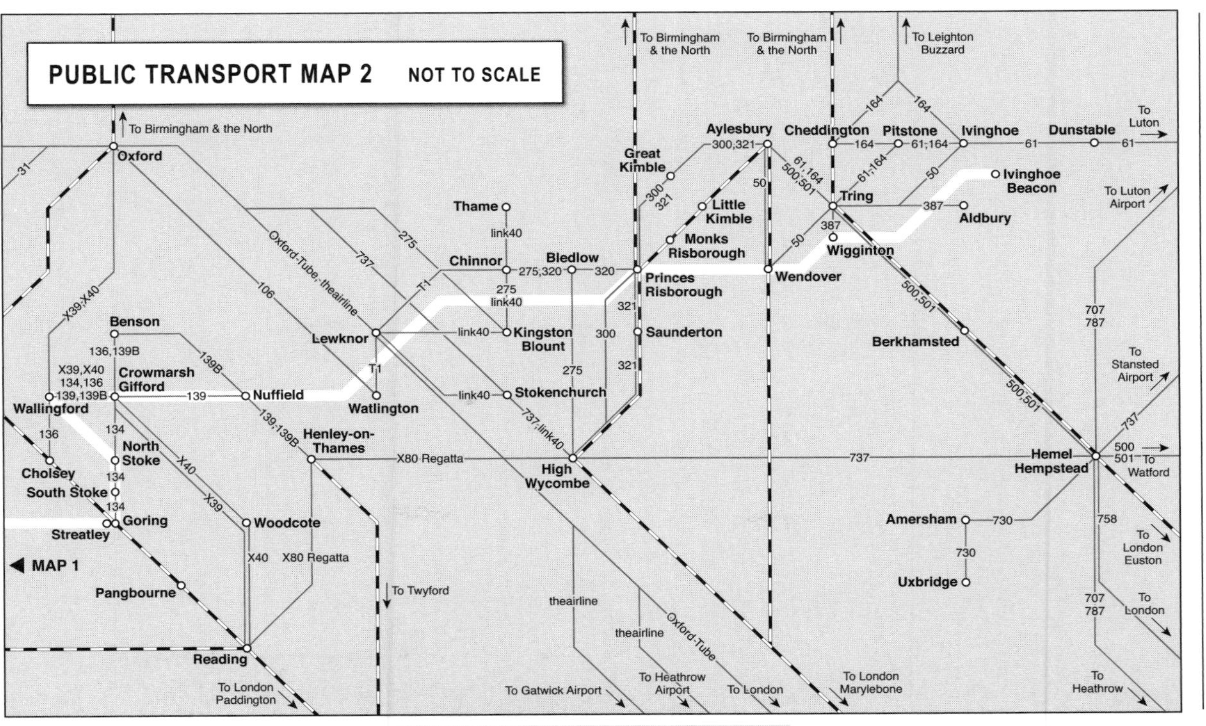
PUBLIC TRANSPORT MAP 2
NOT TO SCALE
To Birmingham & the North
Oxford
Benson
Crowmarsh Gifford
Wallingford
North Stoke
South Stoke
Cholsey
Goring
Streatley
Pangbourne
Reading
To London Paddington
MAP 1
Woodcote
Nuffield
Henley-on-Thames
To Twyford
Watlington
Lewknor
Thame
Chinnor
Kingston Blount
Stokenchurch
Bledlow
High Wycombe
To Gatwick Airport
To Heathrow Airport
To London
To London Marylebone
Great Kimble
Princes Risborough
Saunderton
Monks Risborough
Little Kimble
Aylesbury
Wendover
Cheddington
Tring
Wigginton
Pitstone
Ivinghoe
Ivinghoe Beacon
Aldbury
Dunstable
Berkhamsted
Hemel Hempstead
Amersham
Uxbridge
To Leighton Buzzard
To Luton
To Luton Airport
To Stansted Airport
To Watford
To London Euston
To Heathrow
Oxford-Tube; theairline
theairline
Oxford-Tube
X80 Regatta
737; link40

❑ LOCAL BUS SERVICES

Note: The services listed below were correct at the time of publication but may change so check before you travel. Towns/villages on/very near to the Ridgeway and also the Marlborough to Avebury walk are highlighted.

• **Arriva The Shires** (🖳 www.arrivabus.co.uk)
50 Aylesbury to RAF Halton via Stoke Mandeville & **Wendover**, Mon-Sat 2/hr (see Redline for Sun service)
61 Aylesbury to Dunstable via **Tring**, Pitstone & **Ivinghoe**, Mon-Sat 9/day
300 Aylesbury to High Wycombe via Stoke Mandeville, Great Kimble, **Princes Risborough**, Mon-Fri 5/hr, Sat 3/hr, Sun 1/hr
500 Aylesbury to Watford via **Tring**, Berkhamsted & Hemel Hempstead, Mon-Fri 3/hr, Sat 2/hr

• **Carousel** (☎ 01494 450151, 🖳 www.carouselbuses.co.uk)
link40 High Wycombe to Thame via Stokenchurch, **Lewknor** (M40 bus link), **Kingston Blount** & **Chinnor**, Mon-Sat 11-12/day
730 Uxbridge to Hemel Hempstead via Amersham, Mon-Fri 13/day, Sat 11/day
X80 Regatta High Wycombe to Reading via Henley-on-Thames, Mon-Fri 14/day, Sat 11/day

• **Connect** (West Berkshire Council Transport Services; ☎ 01635 503248, 🖳 westberks.gov.uk/transport)
47 Swindon to Lambourn via **Bishopstone**, **Idstone** & **Ashbury**, Mon-Sat 5/day

• **Go Ride CIC** (🖳 www.goridebus.co.uk)
134 **Wallingford** to **Goring** via **Crowmarsh Gifford**, **North Stoke** & **South Stoke**, Mon-Sat 5-7/day

• **Kennections** (Reading Buses ☎ 0118 959 4000, 🖳 www.reading-buses.co.uk)
3/3A Newbury to Hungerford, Mon-Sat 5/day
4/4A/4C Newbury to Lambourn, Mon-Sat 7/day
6 Newbury to **East Ilsley** & **Compton**, Mon-Sat 3/day
6a Newbury to **West Ilsley** via Chievely, Mon-Sat 3/day

• **Redline Buses** (☎ 01296 426786, 🖳 www.redlinebuses.com)
50 Ivinghoe to Aylesbury via **Tring**, **Wendover** & Stoke Mandeville, Sun & Bank Hols other than Xmas 2-3/day
164 Aylesbury to Leighton Buzzard via **Tring**, Marsworth, Pitstone, Cheddington, Mon-Sat 3/day, via **Ivinghoe** 1/day
320 **Chinnor** to **Princes Risborough** via Bledlow, Mon-Fri 6/day early morning and 1/day late afternoon (connects at Princes Risborough with trains to/from London); from **Princes Risborough** to **Chinnor** Mon-Fri 2/day early morning and 7/day late afternoon
321 High Wycombe to Aylesbury via Saunderton, **Princes Risborough**, Great Kimble, Mon-Fri 4/day

• **Red Rose Travel** (☎ 01296 747926, 🖳 www.redrosetravel.com)
275 High Wycombe to Oxford via Bledlow Ridge, **Chinnor**, **Kingston Blount** & Wheatley, Mon-Fri 3/day
387 **Tring** to **Aldbury**, Mon-Sat 4-6/day, Sat 6/day, **Tring** to **Wigginton**, Mon-Sat 4-5/day
501 Aylesbury to Watford via **Tring**, Berkhamsted & Hemel Hempstead, Sun 1/hr

• **Salisbury Reds** (☎ 01202 338420, 💻 www.salisburyreds.co.uk)
X5 Swindon to Salisbury via **Marlborough** & Pewsey, Mon-Sat 1/hr

• **Stagecoach** (💻 www.stagecoachbus.com)
80 Swindon to **Marlborough** via Chiseldon & **Ogbourne St George**, Mon-Sat 6/day
70A/72A Swindon to **Marlborough** via **Ogbourne St George**, Mon-Sat 3/day evening only (also operated by Thamesdown)
49 Swindon to Trowbridge (The Trans Wilts Express) via Broad Hinton, Winterbourne Bassett, **Avebury**, Beckhampton & Devizes, Mon-Sat 1/hr,
Swindon to Devizes via Broad Hinton, Winterbourne Bassett, **Avebury**, Beckhampton, Sun 6/day
31 Oxford to **Wantage** via Abingdon, daily 1/hr
X30 Oxford to **Wantage**, Mon-Sat 2/hr, Sun 1/hr

• **Thamesdown Transport** (☎ 01793 428428, 💻 www.thamesdown-transport.co.uk)
Rural 20 Hungerford to Marlborough, Mon-Fri 5/day
42 Calne to **Marlborough** via Compton Bassett, Cherhill, Beckhampton, **Avebury**, **West Kennett**, **East Kennett**, **West Overton**, Mon-Fri 7/day, Sat 6/day (note: stops are request only)
46/46A Swindon to Hungerford via **Liddington**, **Foxhill**, Aldbourne & Ramsbury, Mon-Sat 3/day but the 46 (1/day) doesn't stop at Foxhill
X47 **Wantage** to Swindon via **Letcombe Regis**, Letcombe Bassett, **Sparsholt**, Kingston Lisle, **Uffington**, **Woolstone**, **Ashbury**, **Idstone**, **Bishopstone**, Hinton Parva, **Foxhill** & **Liddington**, Sat 3/day
48/48A Swindon to **Marlborough** via **Liddington**, **Foxhill**, Aldbourne & Ramsbury, Mon-Sat 5-6/day
70A Swindon to **Marlborough** via Chiseldon & **Ogbourne St George**, Mon-Sat 2/day (also operated by Stagecoach)
72A Swindon to **Marlborough** via Wroughton, Chiseldon & **Ogbourne St George**, Mon-Sat 1/day
X22 Hungerford to **Marlborough**, Mon-Fri 2/day, Sat 1/day

• **Thames Travel/Go Ahead** (☎ 01865 785400, 💻 www.thames-travel.co.uk)
32A Abingdon to **Wantage** via Didcot Parkway, Mon-Fri 1/hr, Sat 12/day
136 Cholsey to Benson via **Wallingford**, **Crowmarsh Gifford** & Benson, Mon-Fri 1-2/hr, Sun Cholsey to **Wallingford** 4/day
139 Henley-on-Thames to **Wallingford** via **Nuffield** & **Crowmarsh Gifford**, Mon-Sat approx 1/hr
139B Henley-on-Thames to **Wallingford** via Benson, **Nuffield** & **Crowmarsh Gifford**, Sun 5/day
T1 **Watlington** to **Lewknor** & **Chinnor**, Mon-Sat 10/day, Sat 8/day (additional services start in Oxford/Cowley)
X2 Oxford to **Wallingford** via Abingdon & Didcot, Mon-Sat 2/hr, Sun 1/hr
X32 Oxford to **Wantage**, Mon-Fri 1/hr, Sat 11/day
X39 Reading to Oxford via **Wallingford** & **Crowmarsh Gifford**, Mon-Sat approx 1/hr
X40 Reading to Oxford via Woodcote, **Wallingford** & **Crowmarsh Gifford**, daily approx1/hr

2

MINIMUM IMPACT & OUTDOOR SAFETY

Minimum impact walking

ECONOMIC IMPACT

Support local businesses

Rural businesses and communities in Britain have been hit hard in recent years by a seemingly endless series of crises. In light of the economic pressures that many businesses are under there is something you can do to help: buy local.

Look and ask for local produce to buy and eat. Not only does this cut down on the amount of pollution and congestion that the transportation of food creates (the so-called 'food miles'), but also ensures that you are supporting local farmers and producers; the very people who have moulded the countryside you have come to see and who are in the best position to protect it. If you can find local food which is also organic so much the better.

It's a fact of life that money spent at local level – perhaps in a market, or at the greengrocer, or in an independent pub – has a far greater impact for good on that community than the equivalent spent in a branch of a national chain store or restaurant. While no-one would advocate that walkers should boycott the larger supermarkets, which after all do provide local employment, it's worth remembering that businesses in rural communities rely heavily on visitors for their very existence. For these shops and post offices to stay in business they must be used.

ENVIRONMENTAL IMPACT

A walking holiday in itself is an environmentally friendly approach to tourism. The following are some ideas on how you can go a few steps further in helping to minimise your impact on the natural environment while walking the Ridgeway.

Use public transport whenever possible

By using local bus services you will help to keep them operating. Although bus routes along the Ridgeway aren't always convenient for walkers, if fewer people use them they are more likely to disappear altogether. Public transport is always preferable to using private cars as it benefits everyone: visitors, locals and the environment.

Never leave litter

Leaving litter shows a total disrespect for the natural world and others coming after you. As well as being unsightly, litter kills wildlife, pollutes the environment and can be dangerous to farm animals. If you've carried everything at the start of the day you can probably carry whatever remains until you reach a rubbish bin. Put all your rubbish in a biodegradable bag so you can dispose of it in a bin in the next village. It would be very helpful if you could pick up litter left by other people too.

Is it OK if it's biodegradable? Not really. Apple cores, banana skins, orange peel and the like are unsightly, encourage flies, ants and wasps and ruin a picnic spot for others. Using the excuse that they are natural and biodegradable just doesn't cut any ice. When was the last time you saw a banana tree in England?

The lasting impact of litter A piece of orange peel left on the ground takes six months to decompose, silver foil takes 18 months, a plastic bag 10 years, clothes 15 years and an aluminium can 85 years.

Erosion

Stay on the main trail The effect of your footsteps may seem minuscule but when they are multiplied by several thousand walkers each year they become rather more significant. Avoid taking shortcuts, widening the trail or taking more than one path; your boots will be followed by many others.

Consider walking out of season Maximum disturbance by walkers coincides with the time of year when nature wants to do most of its growth and repair. In high-use areas, like that along much of the eastern section of the Ridgeway, the trail never recovers. Walking at less busy times eases this pressure while also generating year-round income for the local economy. Not only that, but it may make the walk a more relaxing experience with fewer people on the path and less competition for accommodation.

Respect all wildlife

Care for all wildlife you come across along the Ridgeway: it has as much right to be there as you. Tempting as it may be to pick wild flowers, leave them so the next people who pass can enjoy them too. Don't break branches off or damage trees in any way.

If you come across wildlife, keep your distance and don't watch for too long. Your presence can cause considerable stress, particularly if the adults are with young, or in winter when the weather is harsh and food is scarce. Young animals are rarely abandoned. If you come across young birds keep away so that their mother can return.

The code of the outdoor loo

'Going' in the outdoors is a lost art worth re-learning, for your sake and everyone else's. As more and more people discover the joys of the outdoors this is becoming an important issue.

In some parts of the world where visitor pressure is higher than in Britain walkers and climbers are required to pack out their excrement. This may become necessary here. Human excrement is not only offensive to our senses but, more importantly, can infect water sources.

Where to go Wherever possible use a toilet. Public toilets are marked on the trail maps in this guide and you will also find facilities in pubs, cafés and campsites along the Ridgeway.

If you do have to go outdoors choose a site at least 30 metres away from running water and also away from any site of historic or archaeological interest. Carry a small trowel and dig a hole about 15cm (6") deep in which to bury your excrement. It decomposes quicker when in contact with the top layer of soil or leaf mould. Use a stick to stir loose soil into your deposit as well as this speeds up decomposition even more. Do not squash it under rocks as this slows down the composting process. If you have to use rocks to cover it make sure they are not in contact with your faeces.

Toilet paper and tampons Toilet paper takes a long time to decompose whether buried or not. It is easily dug up by animals and may then blow into water sources or onto the path. The best method for dealing with it is to pack it out. Put the used paper inside a paper bag which you then place inside a biodegradable bag (or two). Then simply empty the contents of the paper bag at the next toilet you come across and throw the bag away. You should also pack out tampons and sanitary towels in a similar way: they take years to decompose and may be dug up and scattered about by animals.

Wild camping

Unfortunately, wild camping is not allowed along the Ridgeway, but it is generally tolerated if you leave no trace of yourself on the ground when you leave the next morning. Wild camping is an altogether more fulfilling experience than camping on a designated site. Living in the outdoors without any facilities provides a valuable lesson in simple, sustainable living where the results of all your actions, from going to the loo to washing your plates, can be seen.

If you do insist on wild camping on land off the Ridgeway path always ask the landowner for permission. Follow these suggestions for minimising your impact and encourage others to do likewise.

- **Be discreet** Camp alone or in small groups, spend only one night in each place and pitch your tent late and move off early.
- **Never light a fire** The deep burn caused by camp fires, no matter how small, damages the turf which can take years to recover. Cook on a camp stove instead.
- **Don't use soap or detergent** There is no need to use soap: even biodegradable soaps and detergents pollute streams. You won't be away from a shower for more than a day or so. Wash up without detergent: use a plastic or metal scourer, or failing that, a handful of fine pebbles or even some bracken or grass.
- **Leave no trace** Learn the skill of moving on without leaving any sign of having been there: no moved boulders, ripped up vegetation or dug drainage ditches.

Make a final check of your campsite before departing: pick up any litter that you or anyone else has left, so leaving the place in a better state than you found it.

ACCESS

Britain is a crowded cluster of islands with few places where you can wander as you please. Most of the land is a patchwork of fields and agricultural land and the area around the Ridgeway is no different. However, there are countless public rights of way, in addition to the official Ridgeway path, that criss-cross the land; so, what happens if you feel a little more adventurous and want to explore the downs, woodland and hills that can be found around the Ridgeway?

Rights of way

As a designated **National Trail** the Ridgeway is a **public right of way**. A public right of way is either a footpath, a bridleway or a byway: the Ridgeway is made up of all three of these.

Rights of way are theoretically established because the owner has dedicated them to public use. However, very few rights of way are formally dedicated in this way. If members of the public have been using a path without interference for 20 years or more the law assumes the owner has intended to dedicate it as a right of way. If a path has been unused for 20 years it does not cease to exist; the guiding principle is 'once a highway, always a highway'.

On a public right of way you have the right to 'pass and repass along the way' which includes stopping to rest or admire the view, or to consume refreshments. You can also take with you a 'natural accompaniment' which includes a dog but obviously could also be a horse on bridleways and byways. All 'natural accompaniments' must be kept under close control (see box p50 and p191).

Farmers and land managers must ensure that paths are not blocked by crops or other vegetation, or otherwise obstructed, that the route is identifiable and the surface is restored soon after cultivation. If crops are growing over the path you have every right to walk or ride through them, following the line of the right of way as closely as possible. If you find a path blocked or impassable you should report it to the appropriate **highway authority**. Highway authorities are responsible for maintaining public rights of way. Along the Ridgeway the highway authorities are **Wiltshire County Council**, **Swindon Borough Council**, **Oxfordshire County Council**, **West Berkshire Council**, **Buckinghamshire County Council** and **Hertfordshire County Council** (see box p62). The councils are also the surveying authorities with responsibility for maintaining the official definitive maps of the public rights of way.

Right to roam

The Countryside & Rights of Way Act 2000 (CRoW), or 'Right to Roam' as dubbed by walkers, gives the public access to areas of countryside, deemed to be uncultivated open country, in England and Wales – this essentially means moorland, heathland, downland and upland areas. Some land is covered by

❏ THE COUNTRYSIDE CODE

The Countryside Code, originally described in the 1950s as the Country Code, was revised and relaunched in 2004, in part because of the changes brought about by the CRoW Act (see p55); it was updated again in 2012 and also in 2014. The Code seems like common sense but sadly some people still appear to have no understanding of how to treat the countryside they walk in. An adapted version of the 2014 Code – launched under the logo 'Respect. Protect. Enjoy.' – is given below:

Respect other people

- **Consider the local community and other people enjoying the outdoors** Be sensitive to the needs and wishes of those who live and work there. If, for example, farm animals are being moved or gathered keep out of the way and follow the farmer's directions. Being courteous and friendly to those you meet will ensure a healthy future for all based on partnership and co-operation.
- **Leave gates and property as you find them and follow paths unless wider access is available** A farmer normally closes gates to keep farm animals in, but may sometimes leave them open so the animals can reach food and water. Leave gates as you find them or follow instructions on signs. When in a group, make sure the last person knows how to leave the gates.

Follow paths unless wider access is available, such as on open country or registered common land (known as 'open access land'). Leave machinery and farm animals alone – if you think an animal is in distress try to alert the farmer instead.

Use gates, stiles or gaps in field boundaries if you can – climbing over walls, hedges and fences can damage them and increase the risk of farm animals escaping. The Ridgeway path is well supplied with stiles where it crosses field boundaries. On some of the side trips you may find the paths less accommodating. If you have to climb over a gate because you can't open it always do so at the hinged end. Also be careful not to disturb ruins and historic sites. Stick to the official Ridgeway path across arable/pasture land. Minimise erosion by not cutting corners or widening the path.

Protect the natural environment

- **Leave no trace of your visit and take your litter home** Take special care not to damage, destroy or remove features such as rocks, plants and trees. Take your litter with you (see p53); litter and leftover food doesn't just spoil the beauty of the countryside, it can be dangerous to wildlife and farm animals.

Fires can be as devastating to wildlife and habitats as they are to people and property – so be careful with naked flames and cigarettes at any time of the year.

- **Keep dogs under effective control** This means that you should keep your dog on a lead or keep it in sight at all times, be aware of what it's doing and be confident it will return to you promptly on command. Across farmland dogs should always be kept on a short lead. During lambing time they should not be taken with you at all (see box opposite). Always clean up after your dog and get rid of the mess responsibly – 'bag it and bin it'. (See also p29 and pp191-2).

Enjoy the outdoors

- **Plan ahead and be prepared** You're responsible for your own safety: be prepared for natural hazards, changes in weather and other events. Wild animals, farm animals and horses can behave unpredictably if you get too close, especially if they're with their young – so give them plenty of space.
- **Follow advice and local signs** In some areas temporary diversions are in place; take notice of these and other local trail advice. Walking on the Ridgeway is pretty much hazard-free but ensure you follow the simple guidelines outlined opposite.

❑ Lambing
A great deal of the Ridgeway passes through private farmland some of which is pasture for sheep. Lambing takes place from mid March to mid May and dogs should not be taken along the path at this time. Even a dog secured on a lead is liable to disturb a pregnant ewe. If you should see a lamb or ewe that appears to be in distress contact the nearest farmer.

restrictions (ie high-impact activities such as driving a vehicle, cycling, horse-riding are not permitted) and some land is excluded (such as gardens, parks and cultivated land). Full details are given on the Natural England website (see box p62).

With more freedom in the countryside comes a need for more responsibility from the walker. Remember that wild open country is still the workplace of farmers and home to all sorts of wildlife. Have respect for both and avoid disturbing domestic and wild animals.

Outdoor safety

AVOIDANCE OF HAZARDS

With good planning and preparation most hazards can be avoided. This information is just as important for those out on a day walk as for those walking the entire Ridgeway.

Ensure you have **suitable clothes** (see pp38-9) to keep you warm and dry whatever the conditions, and a spare change of inner clothes. A compass, whistle, torch and first-aid kit should be carried and are discussed further on pp39-40. The **emergency signal** is six blasts on a whistle or six flashes with a torch.

Remember to take your **mobile phone** (and ensure it is fully charged); you can get a decent signal on nearly all the Ridgeway and not only will you be able to contact someone in an emergency, but the signal from your phone can be traced to pinpoint your location.

Take plenty of **food** with you for the day and at least one litre of **water** although more would be better, especially on the long western stretches. It is a good idea to fill up your bottle whenever you pass a water tap as they aren't very common. You will eat far more walking than you do normally so make sure you have enough for the day, as well as some high-energy snacks (chocolate, dried fruit, biscuits) in the bottom of your pack for an emergency.

Stay alert and **know exactly where you are** throughout the day. The easiest way to do this is to regularly check your position on the map. If visibility suddenly decreases with mist and cloud, or there is an accident, you will be able to make a sensible decision about what action to take based on your location.

If you choose to walk alone you must appreciate and be prepared for the increased risk. It's a good idea to leave word with someone about where you are going and remember to contact them when you have arrived safely.

WEATHER FORECASTS

The western section of the Ridgeway is particularly exposed. The difference in conditions between the villages below the Ridgeway and the path itself can be quite dramatic. You often only notice just how cold and windy it is when you stop for a few minutes.

You can get a localised 5-day forecast from 💻 www.bbc.co.uk/weather; just type in the name of the place for which you want information. Alternatively check newspaper, TV, radio or one of the telephone forecasts before you set off. Plan the day accordingly and always anticipate that the weather may change.

HEALTH

Blisters

It is important to break in new boots before embarking on a long walk. Make sure the boots are comfortable and try to avoid getting them wet on the inside. Air your feet at lunchtime, keep them clean and change your socks regularly. If you feel any hot spots stop immediately and apply a few strips of zinc oxide tape and leave them on until the area is pain free or the tape starts to come off.

If you have left it too late and a blister has developed you should surround it with 'moleskin' or any other blister kit to protect it from abrasion. Popping it can lead to infection. If the skin is broken keep the area clean with antiseptic and cover with a non-adhesive dressing material held in place with tape.

Hypothermia

Also known as exposure, this occurs when the body can't generate enough heat to maintain its normal temperature, usually as a result of being wet, cold, unprotected from the wind, tired and hungry. It is usually more of a problem in upland areas. However, even on the Ridgeway in bad weather the body can be exposed to strong winds and driving rain making the risk a real one. The western stretches of the path are particularly exposed and there are few villages making it difficult to get help should it be needed.

Hypothermia is easily avoided by wearing suitable clothing, carrying and consuming enough food and drink, being aware of the weather conditions and checking the morale of your companions. Early signs to watch

❑ Dealing with an accident

- Use basic first aid to treat the injury to the best of your ability.
- Work out exactly where you are. If possible leave someone with the casualty while others go to get help. If there are only two people, you have a dilemma.
- If you decide to get help leave all spare clothing and food with the casualty.
- Telephone ☎ 999 and ask for the ambulance service.

for are feeling cold and tired with involuntary shivering. If this occurs, find some shelter as soon as possible and warm the person up with a hot drink and some chocolate or other high-energy food. If possible give them another warm layer of clothing and allow them to rest until feeling better.

If the patient's condition deteriorates, strange behaviour, slurring of speech and poor co-ordination will become apparent and they can quickly progress into unconsciousness, followed by coma and death. You should get the patient out of wind and rain quickly, improvising a shelter if necessary. Rapid restoration of bodily warmth is essential and is best achieved by bare-skin contact: someone should get into the same sleeping bag as the patient, both having stripped to their underwear, putting any spare clothing under or over them to build up heat. Send urgently for help.

Hyperthermia

Hyperthermia is the general name given to a variety of heat-related ailments. Not something you would normally associate with England, heatstroke and heat exhaustion are serious problems nonetheless. Symptoms of **heat exhaustion** include thirst, fatigue, giddiness, a rapid pulse, raised body temperature, low urine output and, if not treated, delirium and finally a coma. The best cure is to drink plenty of water.

Heatstroke is another matter altogether, and even more serious. A high body temperature and an absence of sweating are early indications, followed by symptoms similar to hypothermia (see opposite) such as a lack of coordination, convulsions and coma. Death will follow if treatment is not instantly given. Sponge the victim down, wrap them in wet towels, fan them, and get help immediately.

Sunburn

It can easily happen even on overcast days and especially if you have a fair complexion. The only surefire way to avoid it is to stay wrapped up, but that's not really an option. What you must do, therefore, is to smother yourself in sunscreen (with a minimum factor of 15) and apply it regularly throughout the day. Don't forget your lips, nose, ears, the back of your neck if wearing a T-shirt, and even under your chin to protect against rays reflected up off the ground.

3 THE ENVIRONMENT & NATURE

At first glance, the Ridgeway path doesn't seem to be very distinctive. It doesn't have wide beaches or impressive mountains like many other long-distance trails in the UK. But when you look closer you see a wide variety of terrains and habitats from one end of the path to the other: grasslands, chalk downs, beech woodlands and a section along the banks of the River Thames. These varied environments are home to an equally diverse collection of animals, birds and plants. This book is not designed to be a comprehensive guide to all the wildlife you may encounter, but serves as an introduction to the flora and fauna the walker is likely to find along the Ridgeway.

Making that special effort to look out for wildlife and appreciating what you are seeing will enhance your enjoyment of the walk. To take it a step further is to understand a little more about the species you may encounter, appreciating how they interact with each other and learning a little about the conservation issues that are so pertinent today.

Conservation of the Ridgeway

NATURAL ENGLAND

The official responsibilities of Natural England are to 'enhance biodiversity and our landscapes and wildlife in rural, urban, coastal and marine areas; promote access, recreation and public well-being, and contribute to the way natural resources are managed, so they can be enjoyed now and for future generations'. Essentially this organisation gives advice and information, designates **Sites of Special Scientific Interest** (SSSIs), **National Parks**, **Areas of Outstanding Natural Beauty** (AONBs), manages **National Nature Reserves** (NNRs) and enforces existing regulations. Natural England also manages England's National Trails: they provide most of the funding and resources for path maintenance and promote the conservation of wildlife, geology and wild places in England.

Although no part of the Ridgeway is inside a National Park, the route does lie within two pieces of land designated **Areas of Outstanding Natural Beauty** which are administered by the relevant local authorities. The western part of the path is in the 1730 sq km

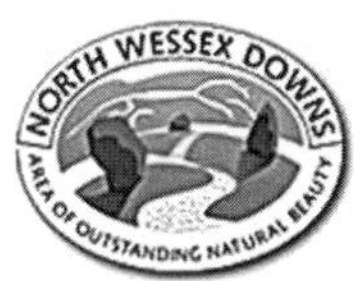

North Wessex Downs AONB that was created in 1972. It lies within the County Council boundaries of Wiltshire, Hampshire and Oxfordshire. The eastern part of the trail is included in the 833 sq km **Chilterns AONB** that was created in 1965 and lies within the County Council boundaries of Bedfordshire, Buckinghamshire, Hertfordshire and Oxfordshire.

There are over 220 **NNR**s in England and the course of the Ridgeway includes Fyfield Down NNR (see p81), just a couple of miles from the beginning of the route and Aston Rowant NNR (see Map 35, p162) near Watlington. These two areas are also **SSSI**s along with over 4100 others in England. Other SSSIs along the Ridgeway include White Horse Hill SSSI and Chinnor Chalk Pit SSSI. **Special Areas of Conservation** (SACs) are designated by the European Union's Habitats Directive and provide an extra tier of protection to the areas that they cover. Along the Ridgeway, Aston Rowant NNR and SSSI is also a SAC along with the Chilterns' beechwoods and Hackpen Hill (see 97). More information on NNRs, SSSIs and SACs can be found on the Natural England website (see box p62).

There is no doubt that these designations play a vital role in safeguarding the land they cover for future generations. However, the very fact that we rely on these labels for protecting limited areas begs the question: what are we doing to the vast majority of land that remains relatively unprotected? Surely we should be aiming to protect the natural environment outside protected areas just as much as within them.

Ridgeway Partnership

The Ridgeway Partnership took over the management, development and promotion of the Ridgeway in April 2015; before that Natural England oversaw a National Trails Management Group that administered both the Ridgeway and the Thames Path national trails. The main groups in The Ridgeway Partnership are Oxfordshire Country Council, other local authorities (see box p62), Natural England, North Wessex Downs AONB, Chilterns Conservation Board and other stakeholders, such as The Friends of the Ridgeway. The Partnership has set up a Strategic Links Project to identify the main routes used by walkers, cyclists and horse riders from the Ridgeway to local amenities; to do this they need the help of volunteers but also landowners and the Highway authorities, and of course feedback from anyone using the Ridgeway (see box p194). Once linking

❑ National Trails

The Ridgeway is one of 15 National Trails in England and Wales. These are Britain's flagship long-distance paths which grew out of the post-war desire to protect the country's special places, a movement which also gave birth to National Parks and AONBs (see opposite). The first National Trail was the Pennine Way in 1965. Since then over 2500 miles (4000km) of walking routes have been designated.

❑ **Statutory bodies**

• **Department for Environment, Food and Rural Affairs** (🖳 www.gov.uk/defra) Government ministry responsible for sustainable development in the countryside.

• **Natural England** (🖳 www.gov.uk/government/organisations/natural-england) See p60.

• **Historic England** (🖳 historicengland.org.uk) Created in April 2015 as a result of dividing the work done by English Heritage (see below). Historic England is the government department responsible for looking after and promoting England's historic environment and is in charge of the listing system, giving grants and dealing with planning matters.

• **Forestry Commission** (🖳 www.forestry.gov.uk) Government department for establishing and managing forests, including Hale Wood (see p178), for a variety of uses.

• **County/Borough Councils: Wiltshire** (🖳 www.wiltshire.gov.uk); **Oxfordshire** (🖳 www.oxfordshire.gov.uk); **Buckinghamshire** (🖳 www.buckscc.gov.uk); **Hertfordshire** (🖳 www.hertfordshire.gov.uk); **Swindon** (🖳 www.swindon.gov.uk); **West Berkshire Council** (🖳 www.westberks.gov.uk).

routes have been identified any necessary improvement work will be carried out; general maintenance is done by the Ridgeway National Trails team.

CAMPAIGNING AND CONSERVATION ORGANISATIONS

The **Friends of the Ridgeway** (🖳 www.ridgewayfriends.org.uk) group focuses specifically on the trail and is particularly vocal on the subject of motorised vehicles using and damaging the tracks. They also have a volunteer scheme for people who wish to get actively involved in preserving the Ridgeway.

The **National Trust** (🖳 www.nationaltrust.org.uk) is a charity with over three million members which aims to protect, through ownership, threatened coastline, countryside, historic houses, castles, gardens and archaeological remains. The Trust manages land and sites along the Ridgeway including the sites in the Avebury area (see pp84-93), the Uffington White Horse area (pp116-17) and the nearby Wayland's Smithy neolithic long barrow (p114). However, all these sites are actually owned by English Heritage.

Often seeming to overlap the work of the National Trust, **English Heritage** (🖳 www.english-heritage.org.uk) actually looks after, champions and advises the government on historic buildings and places, whereas the National Trust focuses more on country houses. However, in April 2015 English Heritage was divided into a new charitable trust that retains the name English Heritage and a non-departmental public body, Historic England (see box above). Most of the sites around Avebury (see pp84-93) are English Heritage properties though a number are actually managed by the National Trust.

The Wildlife Trusts (🖳 www.wildlifetrusts.org) is the umbrella organisation for the 47 wildlife trusts in the UK. Regional branches relevant to the Ridgeway are: **Wiltshire Wildlife Trust** (🖳 www.wiltshirewildlife.org); **Berks, Bucks & Oxon Wildlife Trust** (BBOWT; 🖳 www.bbowt.org.uk);

Hertfordshire & Middlesex Wildlife Trust (H&MWT; 🖳 www.hertswildlifetrust.org.uk). Reserves include a 70-acre site (Oakley Hill, managed by BBOWT, Map 36), on Chinnor Hill, which has a mixture of open grassland and woodland comprising oak, ash and beech. Aldbury Nowers Nature Reserve (managed by H&MWT), see box p188, has butterflies and wildflowers. Another reserve, Dancersend & Crong Meadow, is between Wendover and Hastoe.

The **Woodland Trust** (🖳 www.woodlandtrust.org.uk) aims to conserve, restore and re-establish native woodlands throughout the UK: it cares for over a thousand woods around the UK. The Ridgeway passes through one of their woods, Tring Park (pp178-9), towards the end of the trail.

Butterfly Conservation (🖳 butterfly-conservation.org) was formed in 1968. They now have 32 branches throughout the British Isles and operate over 34 nature reserves and also sites where butterflies are likely to be found. The branches relevant to the Ridgeway are Wiltshire (🖳 www.wiltshire-butterflies.org.uk) and the Upper Thames (🖳 upperthames-butterflies.org.uk).

The **Royal Society for the Protection of Birds** (RSPB; 🖳 www.rspb.org.uk) is the largest voluntary conservation body in Europe focusing on providing a healthy environment for birds, with 200 reserves in the UK. Although the RSPB doesn't have any reserves directly on the Ridgeway they run projects on some areas of it. In particular they are involved in a scheme to encourage stone curlew to breed in the Wessex area. Their stated aim of having 350 breeding pairs nationwide was surpassed well before the stated deadline of 2015.

Flora and fauna

FLOWERS

You'll be walking amongst many different species of wild flowers on the Ridgeway, though unless you keep an eye out it can be easy to miss some of them. Despite the trail being constantly exposed to wind and direct sunlight there will still be a wide selection of common flowers at any time between March and November though the biggest selection appears during the summer months. You'll also have the chance to see some of the more uncommon flowers native to chalk grassland. The best time for spotting these is during the summer months in the areas around Barbury Castle, Uffington Castle, the Pitstone Hills and Ivinghoe Beacon.

There will be plenty of **scentless mayweed** (*Tripleurospermum inodorum*), **common mouse-ear** (*Cerastium glomeratum*) and **common vetch** (*Vicia sativa*) at any time between April and November along most stretches of the Ridgeway. Another common flower is the **red campion** (*Silene dioica*), but this is found mainly in wooded areas and hedgerows. Despite its name, you'll recognise it by the profusion of shocking pink flowers it produces. A common flower with an even more misleading name is the **black medick** (*Medicago lupulina*) that grows mainly on grassland and has yellow flowers. **Herb Robert** (*Geranium robertianum*) also flowers throughout the spring, summer and early autumn. It has attractive pink and white flowers and is found in shady, often rocky areas.

In the spring, flowers such as **greater stitchwort** (*stellaria holostea*) and **dovesfoot cranesbill** (*Geranium molle*) are common in the hedgerows while the distinctive **cowslip** (*Primula veris*) with its clusters of yellow, funnel-shaped flowers is widespread in more open areas. The **common dog** and **heath dog violets** (*Viola riviniana, V. canina*) can be found in shady, open woodlands during the spring while another violet-coloured flower, the **common field speedwell** (*Veronica persica*), prefers cultivated land.

During the late spring and summer months, the variety of flowers along the Ridgeway is at its best. An aptly named example is the **traveller's joy** or **old man's beard** (*Clematis vitalba*) that climbs over hedgerows and displays dense clumps of white, feathery flowers with a strong scent. Another climber you are likely to see is the large-leafed, white-flowered **white bryony** (*Bryonia dioica*). Summer is also when you can see the striking flowers of the **common mallow** (*Malva sylvestris*) that can grow to 150cm high. The yellow, star-shaped flowers of the medicinal **St John's wort** (*Hypericum perforatum*) can be spotted in wooded areas and is so named as it flowers around St John's Day, 24th June.

Upright hedge parsley (*Torilis japonica*) is common along the hedgerows and on the edges of woodland whereas the similar-looking **wild parsnip** (*Pastinaca sativa*) grows mainly on grassland. **Wild carrot** (*Daucus carota*) can sometimes be seen in open grassy areas, distinguished by its large dome-shaped clusters of white flowers. Large **oxeye daisies** (*Leucanthemum vulgare*) are difficult to miss and you may also see **silverweed** (*Potentilla anserina*) along the trail showing grey/silver sharply toothed leaves and yellow flowers.

Flowers that grow only on chalk grassland areas of the Ridgeway include **devil's-bit scabious** (*Scabiosa pratensis*) that can flower as late as October, **squinancywort** (*Asperula cynanchica*) that has slender stems bearing pale-pink and white flowers and **viper's bugloss** (*Echium vulgare*) with its tall thick stem and purple funnel-shaped flowers. This type of chalky ground also plays host to various orchids including the **common spotted** (*Dactylorhiza fuchsii*) that has pale leaves spotted with crimson and the **fragrant** (*Gymnadenia conopsea)* and **pyramidal** (*Anacamptis pyramidalis*), both with reddish petals but with the pyramidal variety being darker.

TREES

You'll see few trees along the western half of the Ridgeway. Most of those you do see have been planted by man over the centuries to serve a specific purpose, eg coppices, windbreaks and plantations. Though many of these are no longer maintained you can still see evidence of them if you look. The eastern half of the Ridgeway is often wooded, usually with beech.

Coppices are areas of woodland, usually oak, hazel or elm, managed by man through the periodic cutting of the trees right back to the ground; multiple

Early Purple Orchid
Orchis mascula

Spotted Orchid
Dactylorhiza fuchsii

Pyramidal Orchid
Anacamptis pyramidalis

Common Vetch
Vicia sativa

Herb-Robert
Geranium robertianum

Red Campion
Silene dioica

Lousewort
Pedicularis sylvatica

Meadow Cranesbill
Geranium pratense

Common Dog Violet
Viola riviniana

Common Knapweed
Centaurea nigra

Violet
Viola riviniana

Old Man's Beard
Clematis vitalba

Common Ragwort
Senecio jacobaea

Yarrow
Achillea millefolium

Hogweed
Heracleum sphondylium

Gorse
Ulex europaeus

Meadow Buttercup
Ranunculis acris

Marsh Marigold (Kingcup)
Caltha palustris

Bird's-foot trefoil
Lotus corniculatus

St John's Wort
Hypericum perforatum

Tormentil
Potentilla erecta

Primrose
Primula vulgaris

Cowslip
Primula veris

Honeysuckle
Lonicera periclymemum

Viper's Bugloss
Echium vulgare

Foxglove
Digitalis purpurea

Rosebay Willowherb
Epilobium angustifolium

Rowan (tree)
Sorbus aucuparia

Dog Rose
Rosa canina

Forget-me-not
Myosotis arvensis

Scarlet Pimpernel
Anagallis arvensis

Self-heal
Prunella vulgaris

Germander Speedwell
Veronica chamaedrys

Ramsons (Wild Garlic)
Allium ursinum

Bluebell
Hyacinthoides non-scripta

Ox-eye Daisy
Leucanthemum vulgare

Peacock
Inachis io
Small Tortoiseshell
Aglais urticae
Common Blue
Polyommatus icarus
Small Garden/Cabbage White
Pieris rapae
Chalkhill Blue
Lysandra coridon
Painted Lady
Cynthia cadui
Large Garden/ Cabbage White
Pieris brassicae
Red Admiral *Vanessa atalanta*
Small Copper
Lycaena phlaeas
Small Heath
Coenonympha pamphilus
White Admiral
Limenitis camilla
Meadow Brown
Maniola jurtina

fast-growing shoots then appear from the cut trees and are harvested. Many coppices were fenced to keep animals out and often the fence sat on a raised earth ridge that you can still see around many disused coppiced areas. Coppices were an important supply of wood until the mid-1800s after which demand declined. However, most coppices were still maintained and today some are being fully used once more to supply wood for charcoal, greenwood furniture and craft items.

Windbreaks, such as hedges, serve multiple purposes. They give livestock a place to shelter from the wind and also provide shade. They also prevent soil erosion and provide a habitat for varied wildlife such as birds, insects, rabbits and pheasants. With the correct maintenance a hedge can last indefinitely and they are an extremely effective way of containing animals. Despite fences providing none of these benefits, they have often been a more popular choice with farmers who want to maximise their field size or change the layout of their fields. To a small extent, hedges are starting to make a comeback as their full benefits are realised and you'll see some recently planted hedges along parts of the Ridgeway.

Plantations were most common between 1600 and 1900; popular species included oak, beech, elm and ash. It was intended that when the trees were mature they would be used for ship-building, furniture-making and other tasks. Many plantations did provide wood for these purposes, like the beech plantations on the eastern section of the Ridgeway, but others, especially the oak plantations, which took years to mature, were never used owing to the availability of cheap coal and imported timber being sourced from around the British Empire. These unused plantations form some of what are now considered traditional woodland.

During World War I there was a timber shortage that led to large conifer plantations being started. However, these weren't ready for cutting during World War II and this meant that large tracts of private woodland had to be felled. After World War I the increased need for food led to the felling of plantations and removal of hedges to increase the size of available farmland.

Today the creation of new plantations has virtually stopped. Many of the conifer plantations, started between the wars, have matured and been felled though there are still many which are managed for their timber. In a country where so many of the ancient forests have long since disappeared, plantations are now as near as some of us can get to the real thing.

BUTTERFLIES

The chalk downlands along the Ridgeway provide a habitat in which many species of butterfly can flourish. Indeed, near the end of the trail, just before Ivinghoe Beacon, is **Aldbury Nowers** (see box p188), a nature reserve and the home of over 30 species of butterfly. Given that the UK can boast only 59 species in total, that's a remarkable figure! Among their number are such rarities as **Essex skippers**, **marbled whites**, **green hairstreaks**, **brown argus** and the moth-like **grizzled and dingy skippers**.

The most common species seen during the summer along the Ridgeway is the **meadow brown** (*Maniola jurtina*), overall a dusty brown colour, but with orange patches on its forewings, inside which are black eye-spots. This is one of the most common butterflies in Europe, as well as on the Ridgeway.

Also likely to be flitting around at this time is the **small heath** (*Coenonympha pamphilus*), recognisable by its dull-orange wings edged with grey; it has black eye-spots on the underside of its forewings.

You'll probably see some **large white** (*Pieris brassicae*) and **small white** (*Pieris rapae*) butterflies too. These are both essentially white with dark-grey wing tips. On the large white, both male and female have two black eye-spots on the underside of the forewings, but only the female has them on the upper side. On the small white, both sexes have two black eye-spots on the underside of their forewings, but on the upperside, the female has two small spots and the male only a single spot.

There are several different kinds of blue butterfly that you may see on the chalklands. The most likely is the **common blue** (*Polyommatus icarus*). The male is violet-blue with a fine black edging to its wings; the female is actually brown though has a row of red spots along her wings which are edged with black.

Less common is the **chalkhill blue** (*Lysandra coridon*); the male is altogether duller than the common blue but has more extensive black and white edging around the wings. The female is dark brown and has the same wing edging.

There are usually some **small copper** (*Lycaena phlaeas*) butterflies around that are distinctive despite their size. The forewings are bright orange with heavy black spots and black fringing whereas the hindwings are predominantly black with a thick band of bright orange edging at the bottom.

Two common day-flying moths are the **five-spot burnet** (*Zygaena trifolii*) and **six-spot burnet** (*Zygaena filipendulae*). Each has very dark wings, patterned with five or six orange/red spots.

MAMMALS

You could walk the length of the Ridgeway and come to the conclusion that there isn't much wildlife on the route. Obviously walking in a group and making unnecessary noise will dramatically reduce your chances of seeing anything, but if you take some time to look carefully and become aware of your surroundings you are likely to see much more than just the back end of a rabbit diving into the undergrowth. You can be fairly certain that the wildlife you are looking for will have seen you well before you see it and will often be making its escape by the time you do. You'll have to be either very patient or very quick if you want to get photographs.

As a brief 'checklist', depending on the time of year, you can expect to see the following animals along the Ridgeway: deer, foxes, rabbits, hares, stoats, weasels, grey squirrels and perhaps even a badger.

The biggest wild animal you will see along the Ridgeway is the deer. There are two different species in this region: the **fallow deer** (*Dama dama*) and the **roe deer** (*Capreolus capreolus*). They have basically the same lifestyle, usually living in woodland but sometimes on open land with plenty of hedges and copses for cover. Both species are most likely to be seen in the early morning and early evening when they are feeding. The easiest way to tell them apart, if you are close enough, is by their size. The adult roe deer grows to about 60cm high at the shoulder while the fallow deer can be up to 90cm at the shoulder. Male fallow deer have large, flat antlers unlike the roe deer whose antlers are spiky. The rutting season for fallow deer is July and August; this is when the males fight each other both for females and territory. You are most likely to see deer in the open during these months. At other times of year you might be able to spot one or two of them together against a hedge on the edge of a field or at the perimeter of a clearing in the woods.

The much-maligned **fox** (*Vulpes vulpes*) inhabits woods and farmland. Despite relentless persecution it is a born survivor, even having adapted to life in cities where they are quite tolerant of human presence. They aren't exclusively nocturnal and in areas where they feel less threatened they are quite likely to be active during the day. Although they can be seen year-round, sightings of foxes are usually brief and at a distance, perhaps as one crosses a field.

Among other denizens of woods and farmland are a number of common but shy mammals. One of the most difficult to see is the **badger** (*Meles meles*), a sociable animal with a distinctive black-and-white-striped muzzle. Badgers live in family groups of around ten in large underground setts, coming out to root for worms on the pastureland after sunset, though they will eat practically anything. Some setts can be in use for well over a hundred years if left undisturbed by humans. They do sometimes emerge during daylight hours and the best time for spotting them is between May and September. Unfortunately, the most common sight of badgers is as a bloody mess on the road; they are one of the most frequent animal road casualties.

The animal you are most likely to see on the Ridgeway is the **rabbit** (*Oryctolagus cuniculus*). In fact, at numerous places, especially on the trail near the aptly named Warren Farm just before Streatley, you'll find it hard to miss them. You can see them at all times of year when they come out during the day and at night to find food such as grass and farm crops. Despite the fact that they won't hang around after they have detected your presence, you can still get a good look at them.

Like rabbits, **hares** (*Lepus capensis*) also feed on grass and farm crops and although they live above ground and like open countryside they are far harder to spot. They generally keep well hidden during the day, except for the months of March and April when you might see them dashing around fields or getting involved in 'boxing matches' with other hares. This isn't, as you might presume, an exclusively male preserve as mixed boxing has also been witnessed. If you are hoping to get a photo of a hare be aware that they can run at speeds up to 40mph/65kph!

The carnivorous **stoat** (*Mustela erminea*) and its smaller cousin the **weasel** (*Mustela nivalis*) are common along the Ridgeway and can be seen year-round but just as with the hares you'll have to be quick if you want to see more than the tail-end of one. They can be difficult to tell apart, especially if you only get a glimpse, but the weasel is noticeably smaller than the stoat. Weasels eat mice, shrews and birds' eggs but owing to their size stoats can tackle larger prey such as adult rabbits and farm birds. This has led to their persecution by farmers who lose poultry to them. Weasels and stoats are by nature very inquisitive so just because they dart for cover as you approach doesn't mean they might not poke their head out for another look just after you have passed.

The **grey squirrel** (*Sciurus carolinensis*) was introduced to Britain from North America in the late 19th century and its outstanding success in colonising the country is very much to the detriment of other native species including songbirds and, most famously, the red squirrel. Grey squirrels inhabit woodlands, parks and gardens and are a common sight from January to June during their breeding season. You might also see them during the autumn on the woodland floor, burying nuts to keep themselves supplied throughout the winter.

At dusk during the summer months **bats** can be seen hunting for moths and flying insects along hedgerows, over rivers and around street lamps. As the weather gets colder they will hibernate though can sometimes still be seen on warmer evenings. Bats have had a bad press thanks to Dracula and countless other horror stories but anyone who has seen one up close knows them to be harmless and delightful little creatures. As for their blood-sucking fame, the matchbox-sized species in Britain would not even be able to break your skin with their teeth let alone suck your blood. Their reputation is improving all the time thanks to the work of the many bat conservation groups around the country and all fourteen species found in Britain are protected by law. The most numerous species is the **common pipistrelle bat** (*Pipistrellus pipistrellus*).

Some other small but fairly common species which can be found in the grassland and hedgerows on the Ridgeway include the **hedgehog** (*Erinaceus europaeus*) and a variety of **voles**, **mice** and **shrews**.

BIRDS

The two halves of the Ridgeway provide distinctly different environments for birds. On the whole the western half, up to Streatley, is exposed with few trees while the eastern half is mostly wooded. Both sections provide ample opportunity for bird spotting with the western section providing the most variety. Early mornings and early evenings are generally the best times for spotting birds.

SKYLARK
L: 185MM/7.25"

The western half

One of the most common birds on the open downs is the **skylark** (*Alauda arvensis*). Its dull brown plumage with a darker stripe doesn't make it the most distinctive of birds but when in flight you can recognise it by the white edges of the outer tail feathers. It nests on the ground in a hollow and makes little attempt to conceal its eggs.

The **corn bunting** (*Emberiza calandra*) can often be heard singing its sharp jangly song along the path. It doesn't look dissimilar to the skylark though it has no white edging on its tail feathers and its beak is shorter and more rounded. You are also likely to see some **yellowhammers** (*Emberiza citrinella*) among the hedgerows and bushes along the path. Although the young birds only have a yellow head, as they grow older the entire body takes on a yellow base colour. Their song is a single repetitive note with a higher note to finish.

YELLOWHAMMER
L: 160MM/6.25"

Another common sight on this section is the **meadow pipit** (*Anthus pratensis*). Its light brown plumage, blending into buff on its underside, is marked with darker brown bars all over. You can often see it hopping quickly along the ground where it nests but it conceals its home well with thick brambles.

LAPWING/PEEWIT
L: 320MM/12.5"

The **lapwing** (*Vanellus vanellus*) with its long legs, short bill and distinctive long headcrest feeds on arable farmland. Sadly, this attractive bird is declining in numbers. The name comes from its lilting flight, frequently changing direction with its large rounded wings. It's also identified by a white belly, black and white head, black throat patch and distinctive dark green wings.

There are also several larger birds that you might see on the Ridgeway. The **buzzard** (*Buteo buteo*) is the most common and can often be seen hovering in the sky, looking for prey such as mice, rabbits and snakes. It has a deep brown plumage with a rounded black and brown banded tail. The **kestrel** (*Falco tinnunculus*) can also be seen hovering above the ground, hunting for prey. Both the male and female are of a reddish brown colour, though the male has a blueish head. Their wings are broad and flat and widely spread when hovering.

You might also be lucky enough to see an owl, even in the daytime. The **barn owl** (*Tyto alba*) is normally nocturnal, but when it has young, or if it is desperate for food, it will hunt during the day. The back of the owl is a sandy brown colour with grey spots while the front is white with brown spots. The white face is heart-shaped, set with deep, dark eyes. The legs are covered with dense, short white feathers. If you can see one of these birds perched where you can get a good look at it you really have been fortunate.

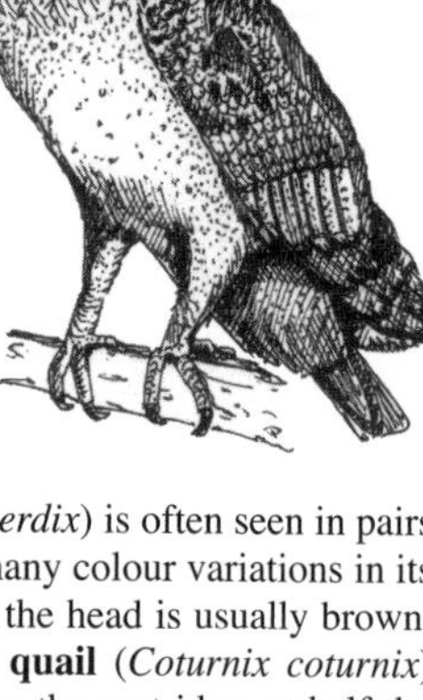

BARN OWL
L: 340MM/13.5"

Pheasants (*Phasianus colchicus*) are common around hedgerows and bushes; they can often be spotted in open fields when feeding. The male can be seen strutting around, showing off his long brown and black striped tail and colourful neck and head. The females are buff and brown all over with a shorter tail than the males. You can usually get a good look at these birds as they aren't particularly shy which might go some way to explaining why they are also the most popular game bird in England.

Other game birds you may see in the fields along the western part of the Ridgeway include the partridge and the quail. The **partridge** (*Perdix perdix*) is often seen in pairs during the spring and summer. Although there are many colour variations in its plumage, it is often light grey with brown bars and the head is usually brown. This bird feeds mainly on insects and seeds. The **quail** (*Coturnix coturnix*) feeds on similar fare, though it is much smaller than the partridge, at half the size. It is only found in England during the late spring and summer and resembles a partridge but its colouring is reddish-tan with dashes of cream and black. It's not easily spotted as it often hides in grass when disturbed.

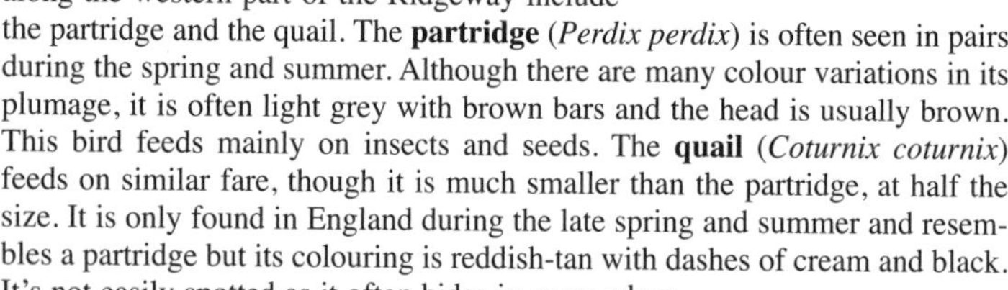

CURLEW
L: 600MM/24"

If you are very lucky, you might see a **stone curlew**, but realistically, the chances are very low. This long-legged summer visitor nests on the ground and its colouring of light brown with dark brown and cream streaks camouflages it well in such an environment. Its large yellow eyes are ideal for spotting any far-off danger from which it is more inclined to hide rather than take flight.

The eastern half

Common birds seen in the woodlands of the eastern section of the Ridgeway include the **nuthatch** (*Sitta europaea*) which can often be seen clinging to tree trunks looking for insects. It's a distinctive small bird with a blue back, white throat and chestnut-coloured underside. The nuthatch nest will often be in a hole in a tree trunk. If the hole is too big, the nuthatch will partially block it with mud, thus making it quite easy to spot.

Various species of tit also live in the woodlands with the **great tit** (*Parus major*) being the largest and one of the most common. It has a black and white head, green back, blue and white wings and a yellow underside. Other tits seen in the woodlands include the **long-tailed tit** (*Aegithalos caudatus*) which is black and white with a long black tail with white edging and the **coal tit** (*Parus ater*), another black and white specimen found in more open areas of woodland.

RED KITE
L: 650MM/25"

The numbers of **red kites** in the Chilterns are increasing owing to reintroduction programmes run by Natural England and the RSPB and there is a good chance that you will see one or more. Their large size – adults have a wingspan of around 1.8m – make them easy to spot and their long forked red tail makes them easy to identify. They have reddish brown bodies with darker wings which also have large patches of white, visible when they are in flight.

SWIFT
L: 200MM/8"

Blackbirds (*Turdus merula*) appear all along the Ridgeway and are unmistakable as the males are jet-black with orange beaks. The females are the same size but have brown bodies, graduating to black at the tail, and brown beaks.

If you, by chance, spot a **jay** (*Garrulus glandarius*) before it spots you and flies off, you are doing well. They are members of the crow family but are notoriously shy. Their plumage is a brownish-red overall with the top of the head white with black dashes. The tail is black with dark blue flashes.

SWALLOW
L: 190MM/7½"

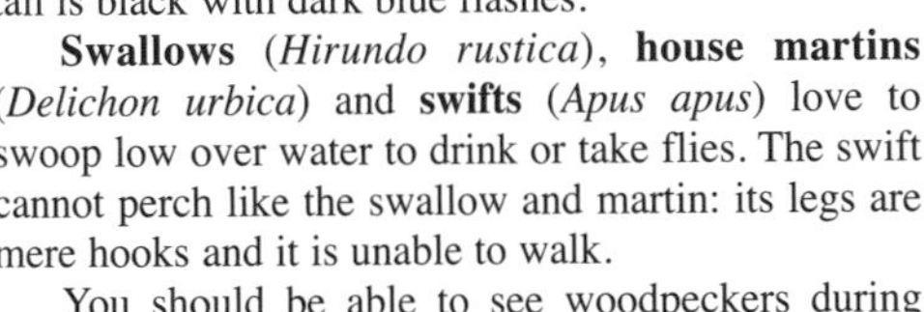

Swallows (*Hirundo rustica*), **house martins** (*Delichon urbica*) and **swifts** (*Apus apus*) love to swoop low over water to drink or take flies. The swift cannot perch like the swallow and martin: its legs are mere hooks and it is unable to walk.

HOUSE MARTIN
L: 140MM/5½"

You should be able to see woodpeckers during your walk and will certainly hear them hammering

GREEN WOODPECKER
L: 330MM/13"

away at tree trunks. The most common is the **great-spotted woodpecker** (*Dendrocopos major*) which has mainly black and white plumage enhanced by red patches on the back of its head and on its lower underside. Where the woods are on the edge of open country, you can find **green woodpeckers** (*Picus viridis*). The lifestyle of this bird is similar to that of the great-spotted woodpecker. Its striking green body, white underside and red head with black dashes make this a very attractive bird. The woodpecker bores into trees, not only to find insects and their larvae but also to hollow them out to make a nest.

GREAT SPOTTED WOODPECKER
L: 230MM/9"

MARLBOROUGH TO AVEBURY

Marlborough

Marlborough is the nearest town to the start of the Ridgeway. It has all the shops and services you might need before setting off and boasts a large array of pubs, cafés and restaurants for you to enjoy. Convenient bus links to the start of the Ridgeway, and its proximity to Avebury, also make this a useful place to base yourself before you start.

Although there is evidence of human activity in the area dating back to around 3700BC, the first mention of the town is in the Domesday Book of 1087. A royal charter was granted by King John in 1204 that allowed the town to hold markets on Wednesdays and Saturdays, a practice that remains to this day. In 1653 a devastating fire destroyed around 250 houses in Marlborough and it was decreed that from then on no house in the town could have a thatched roof. The long-term prosperity of the town was assured by its position on the old coach road between London and Bristol; the town still has an air of affluence, perhaps owing in part to the presence of the exclusive Marlborough College, founded in 1843.

SERVICES

The town's shops and services are concentrated along the High St and include a **post office** (Mon-Fri 9am-5.30pm, Sat 9am-12.30pm) in the **One Stop** convenience store (daily 6am-10pm) and various branches of **banks**, all with **ATMs**. There is also a **chemist** (Boots; Mon-Sat 8.45am-5.30pm, Wed from 9am, Sun 10am-4pm) and a **supermarket** (Waitrose; Mon-Thur 7.30am-8pm, Fri 7.30am-9pm, Sat 7.30am-8pm, Sun 10am-4pm) on the High St.

On Wednesdays and Saturdays there is a **market** on the High St (see box p21). The **tourist information point** (☎ 01672 512487, 🖳 www.marlboroughwiltshire.co.uk; Mon-Fri 10am-5.30pm), in the Town Council Building at 5 High St, has a variety of leaflets about the area.

White Horse Bookshop (☎ 01672 704001, 🖳 www.whitehorsebooks.co.uk; Mon-Sat 9am-5.30pm, Sun 11am-4pm) has a good selection of books about the local area. For outdoor equipment and supplies try **Landmark** (☎ 01672 515000, 🖳 www.landmarkstores

.com; Mon & Wed-Fri 9.30am-5.30pm, Tue & Sun 10am-5.30pm, Sat 9.30am-6pm). They have a good range of outdoor clothing and accessories in case you have forgotten something.

Bertie Maffoon's (☎ 01672 519119, 💻 www.bertiemaffoons.com; Mon-Fri 9am-5.30pm, Sat 9am-5pm), at 1 Glympton Court, Blenheim Rd, Marlborough Business Park, remains the town's premier **bicycle shop**. To get to it from the town centre follow the Salisbury Road (A346) out of town until you reach the roundabout at the top of the hill. Turn off this roundabout into the trading estate. Bertie Maffoon's is across the road from the BP petrol station.

TRANSPORT

[See public transport map and table, pp47-51] There are regular **bus** services to both Swindon and Ogbourne St George: Stagecoach's No 80, Thamesdown's No 48/48A and also their No 70A/72A services which are shared with Stagecoach; Salisbury Red's No X5 calls here en route between Swindon and Salisbury. Thamesdown's Rural 20 and X22 services operate to Hungerford and their No 42 to Calne.

National Express's 402 **coach** services (see box p46) calls here.

Taxi firms include Arrow (☎ 01672 515567, email bookings preferred: 💻 bookings@arrowph.com) and Marlborough Taxis (☎ 01672 512786), though the bus services are good so you shouldn't need them.

WHERE TO STAY

On the High St the rather grand-looking ***Castle & Ball Hotel*** (☎ 01672 515201, 💻 www.oldenglishinns.co.uk; 1S/27D/4T/2Tr/3Qd, all en suite; WI-FI; 🐕 £10 per stay) dates back to the 15th century; B&B costs vary according to season/demand etc but range between £40pp and £75pp (sgl/sgl occ and three/four sharing from £80). ***The Merlin*** (☎ 01672 512151, 💻 merlinrooms@gmail.com; 2S/1T/5D/1Qd, all en suite, 🛁; WI-FI; 🐕) is in the large, cream-coloured Georgian building and shares an entrance with the Pizza Express restaurant (see Where to eat). Rates start from £37.50pp based on two sharing (sgl £60, three/four sharing £90); note that breakfast is not available here.

Several pubs in town also offer accommodation. ***The Bear*** (☎ 01672 512134, 💻 www.thebearmarlborough.co.uk; 5D en suite, 1Tr/1Qd share shower room; WI-FI) charges from £30-37.50pp (sgl occ full room rate, three/four sharing £80-85/100. At the time of research breakfast was not provided but they were considering serving it.

Around the corner from The Bear is ***The Lamb Inn*** (☎ 01672 512668, 💻 www.thelambinnmarlborough.com; 5D/1T/1Qd, all en suite; WI-FI; 🐕) that has light, airy rooms for £35-45pp (sgl occ £60, three/four sharing £115/130).

Symbols used in text (see also p95) 🐕 Dogs allowed subject to prior arrangement
🛁 Bathtub in at least one room; Ⓛ packed lunch available if requested in advance.

At the other end of the High St is ***The Marlborough*** (☎ 01672 515011, 🖳 themarlboroughgroup.co.uk; 4D/1Tr, all en suite; WI-FI; 🐕 £14.75 per stay); the building dates from the 15th century, but it offers rather stylish rooms for £32.50-60pp (sgl occ full room rate). Breakfast is an additional £9.95pp.

Finally, one place that *doesn't* charge the full room rate for singletons is ***Green Dragon*** (☎ 01672 514847, 🖳 www.greendragonmarlborough.co.uk; 3D/1T/1Qd, all en suite, ●; WI-FI; 🐕; £40-45pp (sgl occ from £55, three/four sharing from £130).

WHERE TO EAT AND DRINK

An unusual option during the day is ***100 Chai St*** (☎ 07784 336344, 🖳 www.100chaistreet.com; Tue-Sat 11.30am-9.30pm, Sun 11.30am-3pm), on the High St, which describes itself as an authentic 'Indian Home Food and Tea Room'. To give you an idea of the kind of food you can expect, try their 'Full Englishtaani' breakfast (£9.99), including eggs, masala baked beans, *aloo tiki* (fried potatoes), minced lamb seekh kebab and bacon rashers.

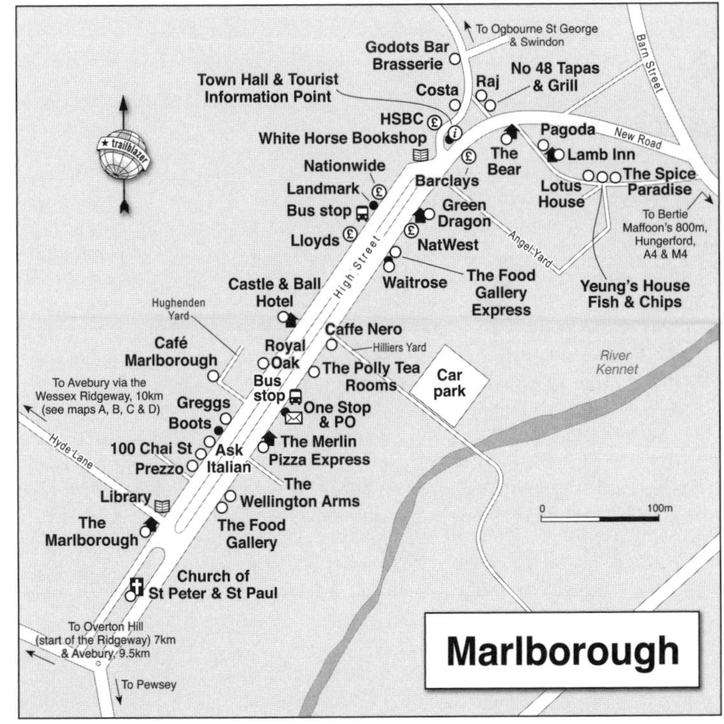

For more normal fare, ***The Food Gallery*** (☎ 01672 514069, 💻 www.thefoodgallery.co.uk; Mon-Sat 8.30am-5pm, Sun 9.30am-4pm) lies across the High St. They take great pride in the quality of their coffee and produce some excellent eat-in or takeaway sandwiches (£3-4.50). They have a smaller takeaway store, ***The Food Gallery Express*** (Mon-Fri 7.30am-3pm, Sat 8am-3pm), to the north just past Waitrose. There's also a branch of the national sandwich/snack chain ***Greggs*** (Mon-Fri 7.30am-5.30pm, Sat to 5pm).

There are more **coffee shops** in Marlborough than you can shake a cinnamon stick at, including branches of ***Caffe Nero*** (Mon-Fri 7am-6pm, Sat 7.30am-6.30pm, Sun 8am-6pm) – about the only place on the High St, other than the pubs, that allows **dogs**. Where there's a Nero there's always a ***Costa*** (Mon-Sat 7.30am-6pm, Sun 9am-5pm) too. Away from the chains, in Hughenden Yard you'll find ***Cafe Marlborough*** (☎ 01672 515200, 💻 cafemarlborough.co.uk; Tue-Sat 9am-4pm).

The Polly Tea Rooms (☎ 01672 512146, 💻 www.thepollytearooms.co.uk; Mon-Sat 8am-6pm, Sun 9am-5.30pm), which has been here since 1932, is a good place for breakfast. Apart from cooked breakfasts (from £5.50 for avocado and poached eggs up to £8.95 for a full English) they also have plenty of home-made lunches, such as their omelette made with cheese, Wiltshire ham, mushrooms, or fine herbs (£9.25). However, they are probably best known for their cream teas (£6.25).

Most of the **pubs** on the High St serve food both at lunchtime and in the evening and are licensed to serve drinks all day. You could head to ***The Wellington Arms*** (☎ 01672 512954; food daily noon-2.30pm, Tue-Sat 6-9pm) where the hearty lunchtime options include beer-battered cod (£10.95) and lasagne (£8.95), or ***The Marlborough*** (see Where to stay; food daily noon-2.30pm, Mon-Sat 6.30-9pm, Sun 6.30-8.30pm) where the food on the ever-changing menu is several notches above your average pub grub, with dishes such as pan-fried seabass with spiced lentils, *cavolo nero* (black kale) and *peperonata* (pepper stew) for £16.95.

The ***Royal Oak*** (☎ 01672 512064, 💻 www.royaloak-marlborough.co.uk; food daily 10am-9pm) has Greene King ales to go with a mixed grill (comprising a 5oz rump steak, gammon steak, chicken breast, sausage, fried egg, seasoned chips, half grilled tomato, peas and onion rings for £11.49).

Castle & Ball Hotel (see p74; food daily 11am-10pm) offers several menus including a 'value' menu with such delights as ham, egg & chips for just £4.99. Continuing on the pub crawl you might like to visit ***The Bear*** (see p74; food daily Mon-Sat noon-7.30pm, Sun 11am-4pm) for Arkell's beers and a decent Sunday lunch (from £9.95), or ***Green Dragon*** (food Mon-Fri daily 11am-9pm) to try some locally brewed 6X from the Wadworth brewery; they also serve breakfast from 8am. ***The Lamb Inn*** (see p74; food daily noon-2.30pm, Mon-Thur 6.30-9pm) also serves food; their homemade fish pie is a snip at £12.

On Kingbury St, ***No 48 Tapas & Grill*** (☎ 01672 515848; Mon 6-10pm, Tue-Thur noon-2pm & 6-10pm, Fri & Sat noon-2.30pm & 6-10.30pm) is a fun and lively place most nights, and the dishes reasonably priced (£1.20-4.95 for vegetable tapas, £3.95-5.95 for fish and £4.95-6.95 for meat tapas). Next door is the ever popular Indian restaurant, ***Raj*** (☎ 01672 515661, 💻 www.rajindiancuisine.co.uk; Mon-Sat noon-2pm, Sun noon-3pm, Mon-Sat 5.30pm-midnight, Sun 5.30-11.30pm) and is always busy. They have the usual extensive menu with most main dishes costing £5.50-11.95. On Sunday they have a buffet.

If you just want a takeaway you could head to one of three places next to each other on The Parade: ***Spice Paradise*** (☎ 01672 519959, 💻 spiceparadise-marlborough.co.uk; Wed-Mon 5-11pm); ***Yeung's House Fish & Chips*** (☎ 01672 515654; Mon-Thur noon-2pm & 5-10pm, Fri & Sat noon-2pm & 5-10.30pm); and ***Lotus House*** (☎ 01672 512715; daily 5.30-11.30pm) which cooks Chinese food for takeaway only. Alternatively, a minute or so back up the hill is ***Pagoda*** (☎ 01672 512886, 💻 www.pagodapeking.co.uk; Mon-Sat 5.30-11pm); it's a pretty standard Peking Chinese restaurant with a lengthy menu and reasonable prices (£5.60 for king prawn foo young); takeaway is available here too.

There is also a scattering of eateries serving Italian food. ***Pizza Express*** (☎ 01672 519229, 💻 www.pizzaexpress.com/marlborough; Mon-Wed 11.30am-10pm, Thur-Sat to 11pm, Sun noon-10pm), at The Merlin (see p74), has a sunny courtyard and the usual selection of pizza and pasta. On the other side of the High St, ***Ask Italian*** (☎ 01672 515797, 💻 www.askitalian.co.uk/restaurant/marlborough; Sun-Thur 8am-10pm, Fri & Sat to 11pm) has a more interesting selection and the menu changes regularly. It's always busy and has an easy-going atmosphere. Just down the way is a branch of another Italian chain, ***Prezzo*** (☎ 01672 511181, 💻 www.prezzorestaurants.co.uk; Mon-Sat noon-11pm, Sun to 10.30pm).

For something a little more stylish there's ***Godots Bar Brasserie*** (☎ 01672 514776, 💻 www.godotsrestaurant.co.uk; Tue-Sat noon-2.30pm & 7-10pm, Fri from 6pm; last orders 9.30pm), a short walk from the High St. Reservations (recommended for the evening) by phone only. Mains are simple but tasty – such as a fish burger of salmon, cod, parsley, french fries & dill mayonnaise (£11.50) – as well as sharing boards for £10-20. They have a delightful courtyard garden.

MARLBOROUGH TO AVEBURY WALK [MAP A p78, MAP B p79, MAP C p80, MAP D p82]

[See pp94-5 for notes on using the route guide and maps] If you're spending time around the beginning of the Ridgeway, the chances are you'll need to get to Avebury from Marlborough, or vice versa, at some point. You could always take one of the regular buses but walking is far more interesting.

The route in fact follows the course of the Wessex Ridgeway (see pp193-4) and is an easy 6 miles/9.5km across the Marlborough Downs with the only mildly strenuous section occurring as you approach Avebury towards the end of your trek; and the only potentially difficult section when it comes to route-finding occurs near the very beginning as you leave the town. Although most of this route is very exposed to the elements, the conditions underfoot are generally excellent, consisting mainly of hard gravel tracks. From Marlborough, where the High St joins Hyde Lane, to The Red Lion at Avebury (or vice versa) it'll take 2-3 hours.

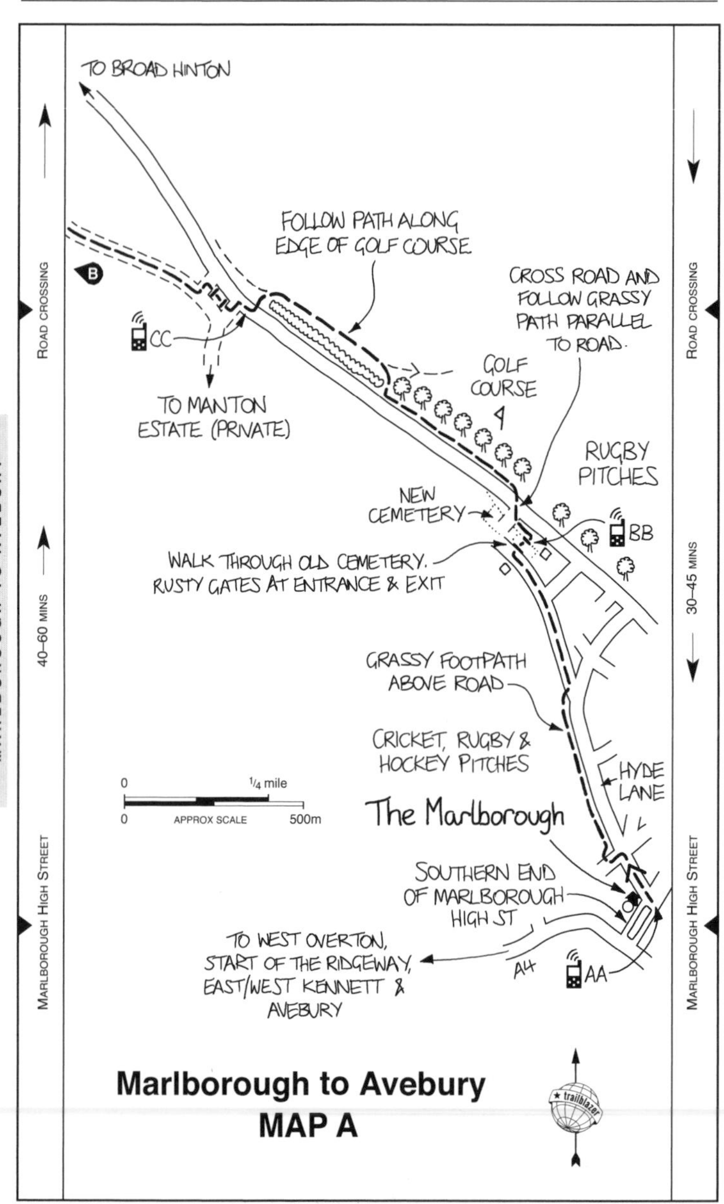
TO BROAD HINTON
FOLLOW PATH ALONG EDGE OF GOLF COURSE
CROSS ROAD AND FOLLOW GRASSY PATH PARALLEL TO ROAD.
B
CC
TO MANTON ESTATE (PRIVATE)
GOLF COURSE
RUGBY PITCHES
NEW CEMETERY
BB
WALK THROUGH OLD CEMETERY. RUSTY GATES AT ENTRANCE & EXIT
GRASSY FOOTPATH ABOVE ROAD
CRICKET, RUGBY & HOCKEY PITCHES
HYDE LANE
0
1/4 mile
0
APPROX SCALE
500m
The Marlborough
SOUTHERN END OF MARLBOROUGH HIGH ST
TO WEST OVERTON, START OF THE RIDGEWAY, EAST/WEST KENNETT & AVEBURY
A4
AA
ROAD CROSSING
40–60 MINS
MARLBOROUGH HIGH STREET
ROAD CROSSING
30–45 MINS
MARLBOROUGH HIGH STREET
MARLBOROUGH TO AVEBURY
trailblazer
Marlborough to Avebury
MAP A

The starting point in Marlborough is **Hyde Lane** which runs up the side of The Marlborough (hotel). As the road bends right you follow a track leading to two **cemeteries**, the first and oldest of which you pass through to reach a lane beyond which, on the other side, are some rugby pitches. The path takes you alongside this lane as it borders a golf course, before you cross back to its southern side and forsake it altogether by the driveway for **Manton House** where a well-established stable and stud has been operating since the 19th century.

The path is clear from here as you join a well-made gravel track. **Gallops** parallel the track for long stretches; indeed, you'll notice plenty of evidence of the racehorse business (see box p104); if you're lucky you could see some thoroughbreds being exercised. When walking on the edge of the grassy gallops instead of on the gravel track you'll notice just how soft and springy the ground is; this is one of the main reasons that this area is so favourable for training racehorses. At one point on this stretch, if you look across the fields to your right, you may just be able to make out the top of a series of **standing stones** arranged in a circle. Distant the view may be, and the stones themselves rather unimpressive when compared to the giants of Avebury, this glimpse nevertheless provides you with a brief but tantalising taste of the delights that await both at the end of this walk and on the Ridgeway itself.

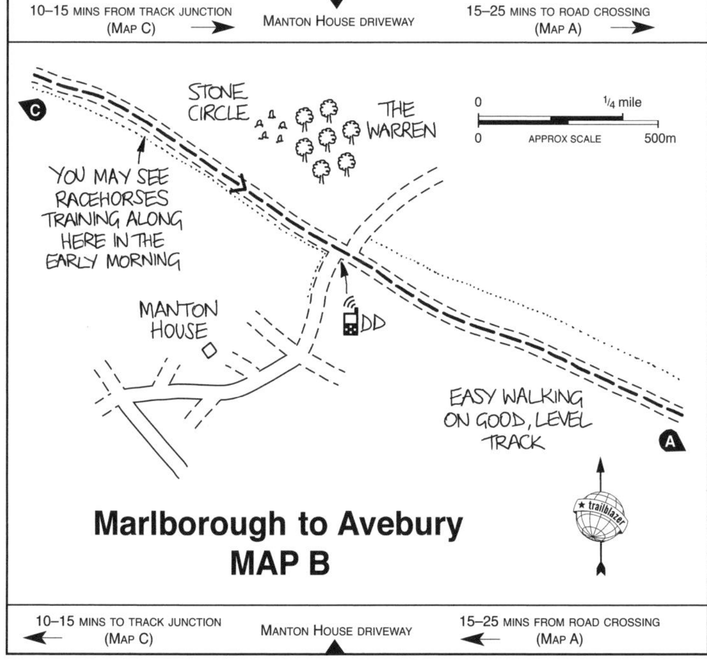

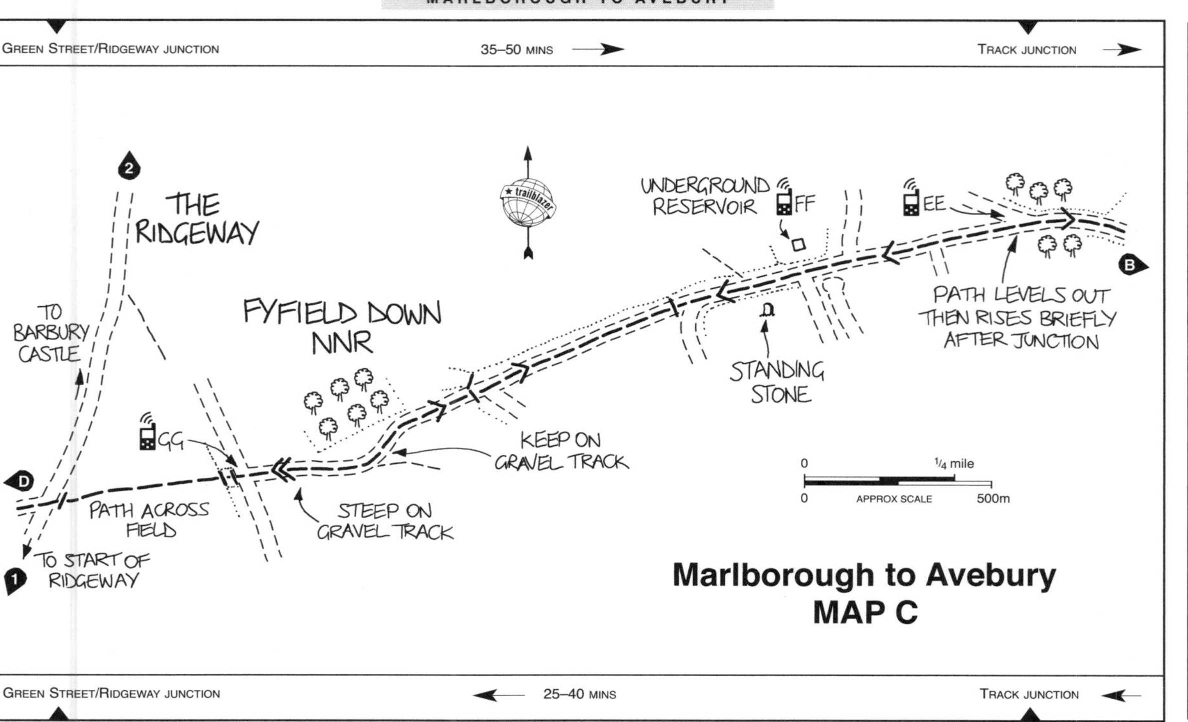
GREEN STREET/RIDGEWAY JUNCTION
35–50 MINS
TRACK JUNCTION
2
THE RIDGEWAY
trailblazer
UNDERGROUND RESERVOIR
FF
EE
TO BARBURY CASTLE
FYFIELD DOWN NNR
PATH LEVELS OUT THEN RISES BRIEFLY AFTER JUNCTION
B
STANDING STONE
GG
KEEP ON GRAVEL TRACK
0
1/4 mile
0
APPROX SCALE
500m
D
PATH ACROSS FIELD
STEEP ON GRAVEL TRACK
TO START OF RIDGEWAY
1
Marlborough to Avebury
MAP C
GREEN STREET/RIDGEWAY JUNCTION
25–40 MINS
TRACK JUNCTION

Leaving the gallops behind, and having passed an underground **reservoir** to the right of the path which looks rather anomalous in this landscape, you soon enter the weird but wonderful world of **Fyfield Down National Nature Reserve (NNR)** (Map C). To most people it's just another attractive area for a stroll, but for geologists it's one of the most important sites in Britain. The sides and bottom of the valley in the reserve are littered with sarsen stones – the very same kind of stones that were used to build Avebury and many of the more recent buildings in the vicinity. Some of these sarsens are also home to rare mosses and lichens. There is something of a fantasy-world feel to this place, as if you might pass a wandering hobbit or see an elf resting on a sarsen.

This NNR takes you all the way to the Ridgeway trail itself; turn left to reach the beginning or right to start the trail just under two miles in. To reach Avebury, cross over the Ridgeway and drop down the track opposite, **Green Street** – also known as Herepath, an Anglo-Saxon road meaning 'army road'; this snakes its way into the centre of Avebury and **The Red Lion**, the perfect place to enjoy a well-earned drink!

❑ Crop circles

If you are in the Wiltshire area, particularly around Avebury, during the summer months you have a good chance of seeing a crop circle. It's usually free to go into the field to have a look inside the formation but as you'll be just one of many doing this they get damaged very quickly. It's not often easy to get good photographs of crop circles because although they are generally on hillsides, the gradient isn't steep enough to present a clear view of the pattern.

However, nearly every formation that appears in Wiltshire will have an aerial photograph taken of it and these are easily found on the internet. Websites such as 🖳 www.cropcircleconnector.com often have photos of crop circles within a day of them first being reported.

The appearance of crop circles in Wiltshire certainly dates back as far as the early 1980s and some farmers say they noticed them earlier than that. In the 1990s, when the more elaborate designs started to appear, the media became interested. However, within a few years much of the media interest faded, though the circles continue to appear, getting more elaborate every year. By the end of July 2016 there had been about 20 crop circles in the area.

Theories abound as to how the circles are created. There is no doubt that some are man-made and people have comprehensively demonstrated how to make complex designs in just a few hours. But that still leaves some designs which appear simply too intricate to be created in a few hours in the middle of the night. You can take your pick of the theories out there, some more 'out there' than others. Are they created by a 'plasma vortex', UFOs, the presence of ley lines, or something completely different that no one has even thought of yet?

If it all gets a bit confusing, you might like to unwind with a pint of Crop Circle, a beer produced by Hop Back Brewery (see box p22) and available in some local pubs. Alternatively, head to the Barge Inn (☎ 01672 851705, 🖳 www.the-barge-inn.com) at Honeystreet for a pint of Honeystreet Ales' Croppie.

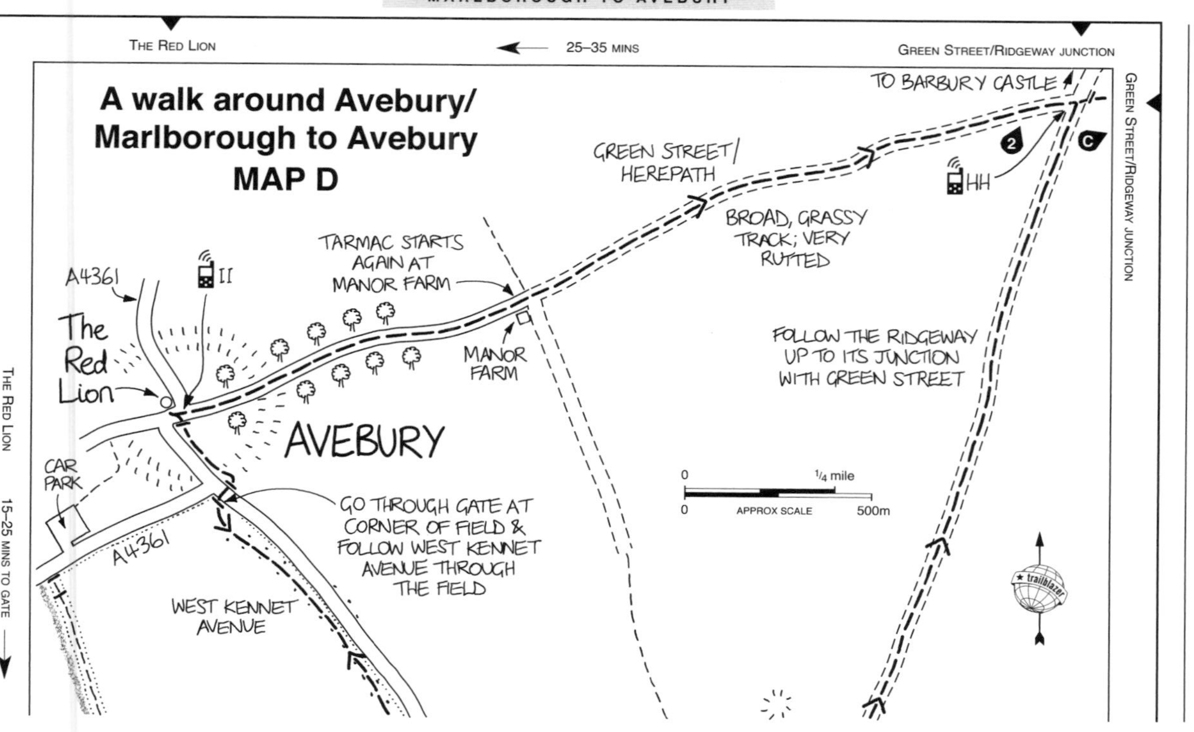
The Red Lion
25–35 mins
Green Street/Ridgeway junction
Green Street/Ridgeway junction
The Red Lion
15–25 mins to gate
The Red Lion
A walk around Avebury/
Marlborough to Avebury
MAP D
TO BARBURY CASTLE
GREEN STREET/
HEREPATH
HH
BROAD, GRASSY
TRACK; VERY
RUTTED
A4361
II
TARMAC STARTS
AGAIN AT
MANOR FARM
The
Red
Lion
MANOR
FARM
FOLLOW THE RIDGEWAY
UP TO ITS JUNCTION
WITH GREEN STREET
AVEBURY
CAR
PARK
0
1/4 mile
0
APPROX SCALE
500m
GO THROUGH GATE AT
CORNER OF FIELD &
FOLLOW WEST KENNET
AVENUE THROUGH
THE FIELD
A4361
WEST KENNET
AVENUE
trailblazer

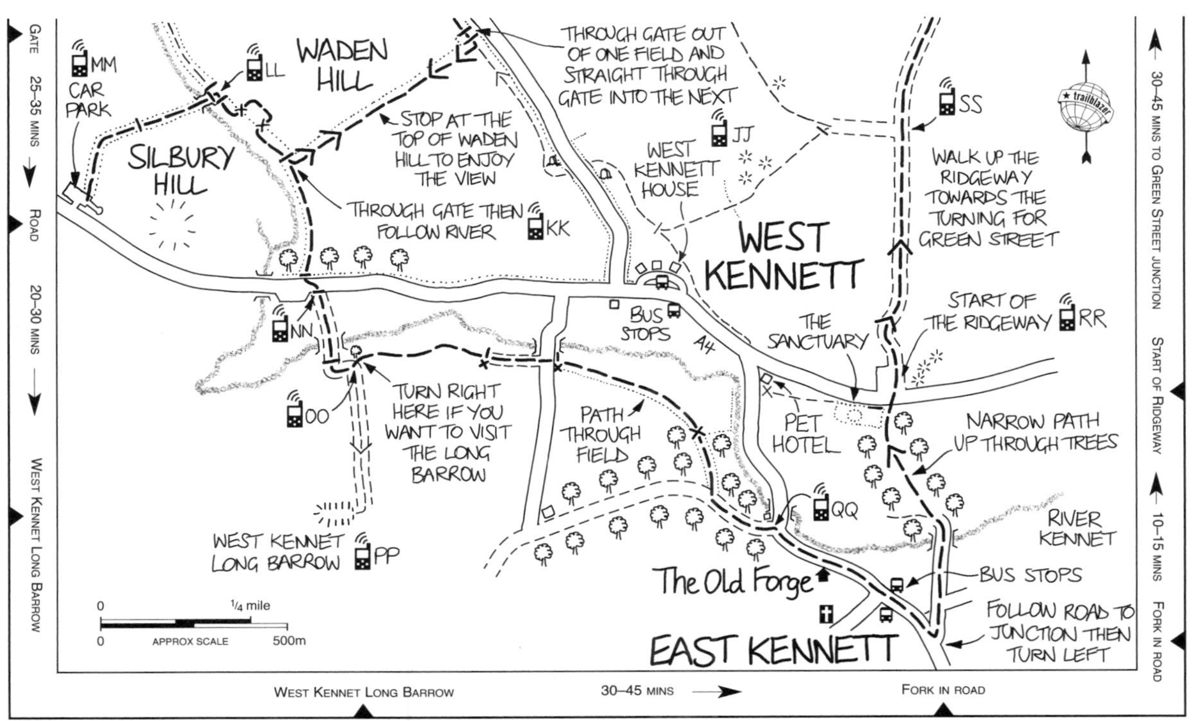
Gate
25–35 mins
Road
20–30 mins
West Kennet Long Barrow
30–45 mins to Green Street junction
Start of Ridgeway
10–15 mins
Fork in road
trailblazer
MM
Car park
LL
Waden Hill
Silbury Hill
Through gate out of one field and straight through gate into the next
Stop at the top of Waden Hill to enjoy the view
Through gate then follow river
KK
JJ
West Kennett House
West Kennett
SS
Walk up the Ridgeway towards the turning for Green Street
Start of the Ridgeway
RR
Bus stops
A4
The Sanctuary
NN
Turn right here if you want to visit the long barrow
OO
Path through field
Pet Hotel
Narrow path up through trees
QQ
River Kennet
West Kennet Long Barrow
PP
The Old Forge
Bus stops
Follow road to junction then turn left
East Kennett
0
1/4 mile
0
Approx scale
500m
West Kennet Long Barrow
30–45 mins
Fork in road

Avebury and around

AVEBURY

This small village, spread around one of the most important Neolithic sites (see box pp86-7) in Europe, attracts thousands of visitors every year, but for all that, it's still essentially a quiet and unassuming place. Most tourists are here for just a couple of hours on a whistle-stop coach tour and those day-trippers who arrive by car are usually gone by mid-afternoon, too. It's remarkable how you can walk just a few minutes away from the throngs of visitors around the stone circle and be on your own in the countryside. Another remarkable thing about this place, that's impossible to miss, is how the busy A4361 road from Beckhampton to Swindon zig-zags straight through the stone circle itself. It really couldn't be any less subtle.

It is well worth spending as much time as you can in and around Avebury. There is so much to see and the walking is easy – an ideal warm-up for the Ridgeway proper. Not only is there the stone circle, but the Great Barn and museums, West Kennet Avenue, Silbury Hill, West Kennet Long Barrow, the Sanctuary and Windmill Hill. And if you're really lucky you might even see a crop circle (see box p81)! A useful website for information about the sights is 💻 www.avebury-web.co.uk.

The **Alexander Keiller Museum** (💻 www.english-heritage.org.uk; daily Easter-Oct 10am-6pm, Nov-Easter 10am-4pm) is spread over two locations: the **Barn Gallery**, in the magnificent late 17th-century **Great Barn** and the **Stables Gallery**, a few minutes' walk away. This museum was started in 1935 to gather together archaeological finds from Avebury and the surrounding area dating back 6000 years. A visit is recommended as it really helps to put the surviving monuments in and around the village in context. Entry is £4.40/2.20 for adults/children (£4.90/2.50 inc Gift Aid; free for members of English Heritage); one ticket admits you to both galleries.

Close to the Stables Gallery is **Avebury Manor and Gardens** (☎ 01672 539250, 💻 www.nationaltrust.org.uk/avebury; Easter-Oct daily 11am-5pm; £9.50/4.50 adults/children, £10.50/5 inc Gift Aid; free for NT members). There was originally a Benedictine Priory on this site dating back to the 13th century, but the current buildings date from the 16th century with renovations made by a Colonel Jenner in the early 20th century.

The immaculate gardens, with their box hedges and medieval walls, are open to the public, as is most of the Manor House including the Tudor and Georgian dining rooms. Unusually, you are allowed to sit on many of the chairs, lie on many of the beds and touch many of the exhibits in the Manor. There is also a tea room here but the opening times vary.

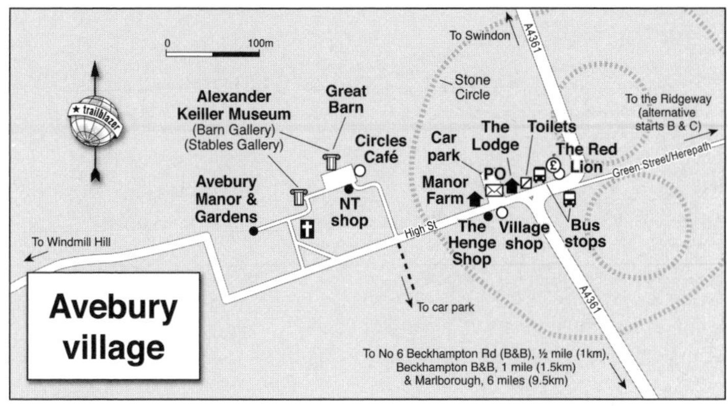

Services

The **post office** in the small car park on the High St, opposite the shop, operates limited hours (Mon 9am-noon, Wed-Fri 2-5pm). The **village shop** (Mon-Sat 9am-5pm, Sun 10.30am-4.30pm) itself stocks a selection of groceries and a range of sandwiches. There is no longer a tourist information centre, though the **National Trust Shop** (☎ 01672 539384; daily Apr-Oct 10am-5.30pm, Nov-Mar 11am-4pm) close to the Great Barn has some tourist information leaflets. They also have a good range of postcards and souvenirs.

If you need cash you should head to The Red Lion pub (see p88) where there is an **ATM** (£1.85 charge per withdrawal). **The Henge Shop** (☎ 01672 539229; daily late Mar to late Oct 9.30am-5.30pm but to 6pm in summer holidays, late Oct to late Mar to 5pm) is a large souvenir shop that sells some interesting Avebury paraphernalia as well as shelf upon shelf of generic tourist tat.

There are frequent **bus** services to Marlborough (Thamesdown's No 42 service) and to Swindon (Stagecoach's No 49); see pp47-51 for further details. For a **taxi**, call one of the firms in Marlborough, see p74.

Where to stay

B&B options in Avebury village are expensive and even if you can afford to stay here you should book well ahead to secure a room.

There is, however, a cheaper option just outside the village, at ***No 6 Beckhampton Road*** (☎ 01672 539588; 1D en suite/1T shared bathroom; WI-FI; Ⓛ). It's run by the friendly Mrs Dixon who charges £30-37.50pp (sgl occ from £50). You could walk here from the village as it's only about half a mile (1km) along the A4361 towards Beckhampton though there isn't a pavement all the way. The B&B is in the line of cottages on the main road at the top of the hill. A quieter and safer but less straightforward route would be to follow the High St to its western end then take the series of paths to Trusloe village and cut through to the B&B. *(continued on p88)*

❑ Avebury Stone Circle

A visit to the Neolithic stone circle complex at Avebury is undoubtedly one of the highlights of the Ridgeway. This is one of the largest stone circles in the world though it's often overshadowed by the more famous Stonehenge, about 24 miles away. Although most tourists are here for just a couple of hours, it would be easy to spend a day or two investigating Avebury and the surrounding monuments.

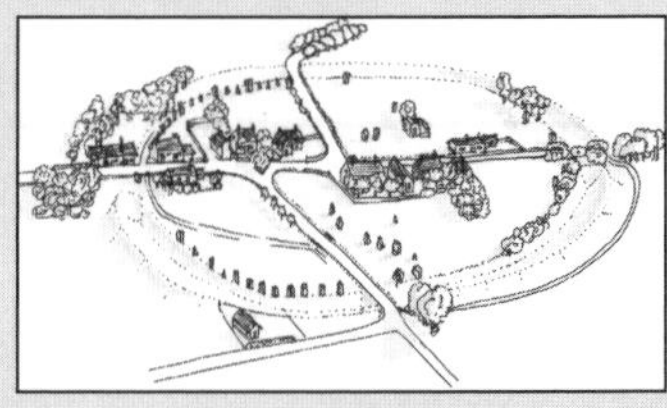

The immense task of constructing this site spanned about 500 years, starting around 2500BC. The irregularly shaped stones come from the Marlborough Downs, a few miles from where they were set up in the henge, and were transported here with great effort though it's still unclear why. There are several clear solar alignments within the formation but an overall theory about the purpose and usage of the stone circle remains elusive. If you are in need of an answer, you'll find plenty of ideas out there, with many entering the realms of fantasy, but none of which can comprehensively explain this huge site.

Starting from the outside and working in there is a roughly circular earth bank about 400 metres in diameter immediately dropping down into a deep ditch. Lining the other side of this ditch is the main stone circle. It is highly significant that the earth bank is on the outside of the ditch as this means that the site cannot have been defensive in nature, unlike all the later hill forts which have the ditch outside the bank and therefore are defensive. The alignment of outer bank and inner ditch is what defines a '**henge**', though there is one exception to this of course – Stonehenge itself!

The **Outer Circle**, the main stone circle, once consisted of nearly 100 stones, but today just 30 are standing. There are two main reasons for the disappearance of the stones: some were pulled over and buried in pits during the 14th century and others were broken up and used as building materials for houses in the village in the late 17th and 18th centuries. Most of the stones standing today were unearthed during excavations and re-erected. The two smaller **inner circles** (Northern and Southern) are both about 100 metres in diameter. Like the outer circle, many of the stones that once formed these circles are now missing and have been replaced by concrete markers.

Two of the best-known stones in the outer circle are the 'Swindon Stone' and the 'Barber Surgeon Stone'. The '**Swindon Stone**', roughly square in shape, is one of the largest and marks the northern entrance to the circle. It weighs in at an estimated 60 tonnes and is one of the only stones never to have fallen.

The '**Barber Surgeon Stone**', towards the south of the outer circle, is so named because a skeleton was found under it during excavations in the 1930s. The story goes that, during the 14th century when many of the stones were pulled over and buried one unfortunate man happened to be in the wrong place and was squashed. When Alexander Keiller excavated this stone the man's skeleton was found underneath it, along with a pouch containing scissors and some coins. Research indicated this unfortunate individual was probably an itinerant craftsman who performed many roles including that of a barber and a surgeon.

What you can see today is the result of immense excavation work and restoration projects, mainly led by Alexander Keiller during the 1920s and 1930s; up till then, the site had suffered centuries of deliberate damage and neglect. Keiller relied heavily on the previous work of two antiquarians, John Aubrey and William Stukeley,

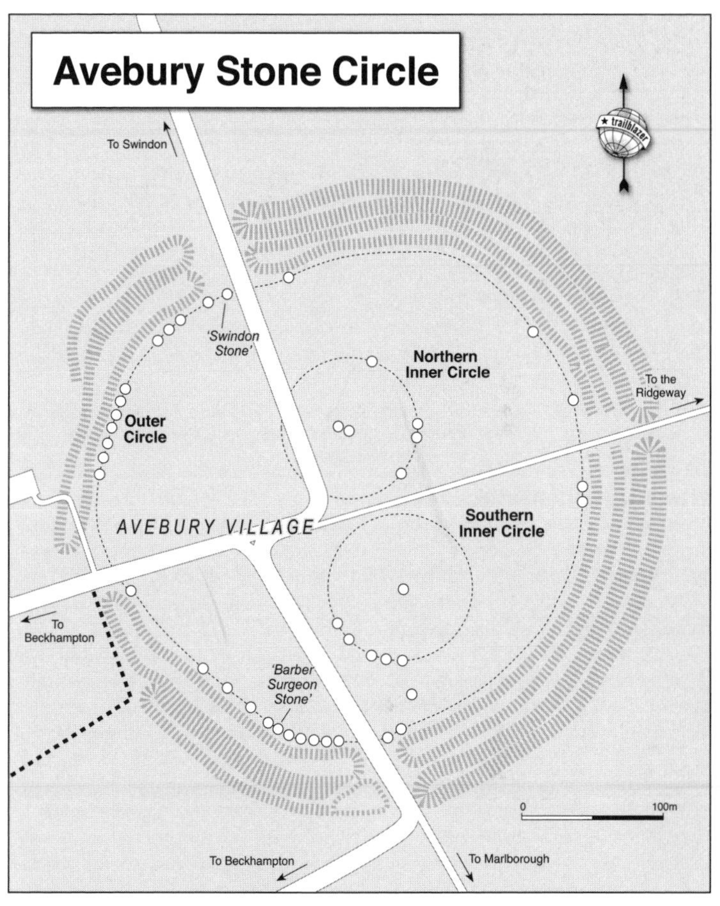

to interpret the remains of the stone circle. Aubrey was the first person to study Avebury in detail and record what he found. His main findings were written up in 1690 and proved an invaluable resource for William Stukeley who in the 18th century drew maps of the entire complex of stones and also wrote extensively about his findings. As the period following Aubrey's and Stukeley's work was one of the most destructive in Avebury's history, had it not been for their surviving records much of Keiller's work, and indeed even modern archaeology in the Avebury area, would have proved an impossible task.

There is no entrance fee to the circle, mainly because it would be impractical to enforce such a scheme; hence it is open for visitors all day, every day.

(continued from p85) Alternatively, you could get a bus (Stagecoach's No 49, see pp47-51): the first bus stop out of Avebury village is more or less opposite the B&B. ***Beckhampton B&B*** (☎ 01672 539534, 🖳 www.aveburyworld.co.uk; 1D en suite, 1S/1D share facilities; WI-FI; Ⓛ £6.95; Mar-Oct) is on the A4 but is a quiet place. B&B costs £37.50-42.50pp (sgl £50, sgl occ £65-75); guests receive a 15% discount for meals at the pub opposite and 10% at The Red Lion (see below). ***Manor Farm*** (☎ 01672 539294, 🖳 www.manorfarmavebury.com; 1D/1T, private bathroom ▼; intermittent WI-FI; Ⓛ) is a large red-brick farmhouse offering B&B for £50pp (sgl occ £80). Since only one room is let out at a time, unless a group book, effectively the bathroom is private; a group would have to share the bathroom. Note: this is a different Manor Farm from the one on Green Street (see Map D, p82). ***The Lodge*** (☎ 01672 539023, 🖳 www.avebur ylodge.co.uk; 1D private bathroom ▼/1Tr en suite; WI-FI; Ⓛ), just up the High St, charges £87.50pp (sgl occ £140, three sharing is £225). The food is vegetarian and, where possible, organic.

In addition there is the accommodation listed on **Airbnb** (see p20), including one at the end of West Kennet Avenue and one pretty close to the centre of the village.

Where to eat and drink

Most people head to ***Circles Café*** (☎ 01672 539514; daily Apr-Oct 10am-5.30pm, Nov-Mar 10am-4pm) which is in a good location next to the Great Barn. They have various sandwiches and rolls from £3.95, jacket potatoes from £4.95 and, of course, cakes, tea and coffee. Note dogs are not allowed inside though there are a few tables outside.

The Red Lion (☎ 01672 539266, 🖳 www.oldenglishinns.co.uk/our-locations/the-red-lion-avebury; food generally Mon-Sat noon-3pm & 5-9pm, Sun noon-3.30pm & 5.30-8pm) is right in the centre of the stone circle and is also the only pub in the village. The building dates back to the early 17th century but it was only in the early 18th century that it became a pub. Since then the original building has been enlarged. Naturally, the place has its own ghost – a murdered lady – who might or might not put in an appearance depending on how long you've spent at the bar. The pub is always busy and lunchtimes can be particularly crowded with long waiting times for food. Food-wise it's fairly standard pub grub, though with a good line in steaks (£11.79 for an 8oz rump up to £15.99 for a 10oz rib-eye). Note that the pub's car park is free to customers; it's the most central parking in the village.

WEST OVERTON [see map p93]

This village is about a mile/1.6km from the start of the Ridgeway. On the A4 at the main turning for the village is ***The Bell*** (☎ 01672 861099, 🖳 www.thebell westoverton.co.uk; Tue-Sat food noon-2.30pm & 6-9pm, Sun noon-3pm, bar to 6pm), which has a very good reputation for its food. Main courses (£12-24) include a range of fresh fish from Cornwall. They also serve around three locally brewed real ales. Thamesdown's No 42 **bus** stops here en route between Calne and Marlborough; see pp47-51 for further details.

WEST KENNETT & EAST KENNETT [see map p93]

The hamlet of **West Kennett** consists of a pet hotel and a few houses spread out along the main A4 road. Apart from the **bus** stops (Thamesdown's No 42 stops here, see pp47-51), there is nothing of practical use to the traveller (though there may still be an **Airbnb** property, see p20). **East Kennett**, a very picturesque village, provides the closest B&B to the Ridgeway, though very little else.

The Old Forge (☎ 01672 861686, 💻 www.theoldforge-avebury.co.uk; 1T/2D, all en suite, 1D private bathroom; ●; WI-FI; Ⓛ; 🐕 £5-10) really is a lovely B&B. They charge £37.50-45pp (£65-80 for single occupancy). This place is often busy so book as far in advance as possible. For an evening meal they offer a tray supper (from £7) if arranged in advance but The Bell (see opposite) at West Overton is about 10 minutes' walk down the road.

From East Kennett the start of the path is only about half a mile/1km away. Should you need a shop, it's a straightforward half-hour stroll along West Kennet Avenue to Avebury.

A WALK AROUND AVEBURY [MAP C p80; MAP D pp82-3]

If you have some spare time before starting the Ridgeway, you might like to explore the area around Avebury. Detailed below is a walk designed to take in the main attractions outside the village. As this walk is circular and starts from the centre of Avebury, you can do it in either direction. It will take between 2½ and 4 hours. The general theme of this walk is Avebury–West Kennet Avenue–Silbury Hill–West Kennet Long Barrow–East Kennett village–The Sanctuary–the Ridgeway–Green Street–Avebury. It's about 6 miles/9.5km and the walking is generally easy going with just a couple of mildly tiring uphill stints.

Starting from **The Red Lion** follow the main road south through the stone circle then enter the field and follow **West Kennet Avenue** (see box below). When you reach the **gates** at the end of the field follow the fence line up **Waden Hill** from the top of which you get very good views of Silbury Hill. At the bottom of the hill you have a choice, the route you take depending on how close

❑ West Kennet Avenue [see map p93]

West Kennet Avenue dates from about 2400BC and runs south from the henge at Avebury to The Sanctuary, a distance of about 1½ miles/2.5km. The course of the avenue was originally marked by two parallel rows of around one hundred sarsen stones, though today only the first 750 metres of the avenue is lined with them.

These stones were excavated and re-erected by Maud Cunnington in 1912 and by Alexander Keiller in the 1930s. As with the henge at Avebury, concrete markers replace stones that have disappeared or been destroyed. Despite various sources of evidence – the 18th-century records of William Stukeley and excavations in both the 20th century and in 2002 – the exact course of the avenue is still a subject of debate. There is a second avenue of stones at Avebury, leading away from the henge to the west. This was first noticed by William Stukeley in the 18th century, but no longer shows above ground and was only rediscovered following excavations in 1999. It is called Beckhampton Avenue because it heads out towards the long stones at Beckhampton.

❑ West Kennet Long Barrow

Even if you don't plan to do the whole walk around Avebury (see p89) you should make the effort to go up to West Kennet Long Barrow, located on a ridge about a mile from Silbury Hill. At 100 metres long it's one of the largest Neolithic burial mounds in the country and dates back to 3600BC, nearly a thousand years before Wayland's Smithy (see box p114). It's thought that this long barrow was used for around a thousand years before it was filled in with earth and sealed with the huge sarsen stones that currently stand across the entrance. During several excavations, the last in 1955-6, the remains of 45 people of all ages were discovered in the various chambers.

The main advantage this site has over Wayland's Smithy is that you can actually enter this long barrow and walk into all five of the burial chambers, but don't expect the underground passage to take you along the entire length of the long barrow – it only extends about ten metres into the mound. There is no entrance fee for the long barrow and it is open all the time. Take a torch though.

you want to get to Silbury Hill. For most, the distant view of Silbury Hill from here is enough, and they should turn left to cross the A4 and head towards the West Kennet Long Barrow. However, if you want a closer look, you should turn right and follow the stream to the junction where you need to take the left turn and go over the bridge – straight ahead leads back to Avebury, if you are already tired. After turning left you will skirt around **Silbury Hill** (see box opposite), eventually arriving at a car park. Here you can get a closer view of the Hill from a special viewing area. You are not allowed to walk any nearer. That said, the road does in fact pass much closer if you do want that closer look – though this does involve a rather unpleasant schlep along the A4. You must then look for a turning on the other side of the road which leads up to **West Kennet Long Barrow** (see box above). The climb up is a bit tiring but will get you in good shape for the Ridgeway.

After visiting the Long Barrow and admiring the views you should retrace your steps to the path junction where you need to take a right turn, heading for **East Kennett** village. This is an idyllic place; take a few minutes to look at the church and wander past the attractive village houses before you get to the fork in the road. At this point you should follow the other lane, almost doubling back

❑ The Sanctuary

Opposite the official start of the Ridgeway is The Sanctuary. It's not one of the more memorable relics in the Avebury area, but is worth a visit nonetheless. It consists of various concentric circles marked out with small concrete posts in the ground.

This was the site of a circular wooden building, possibly a temple, dating back as far as 2500BC. The smaller circle marks out the boundary of the original building while the larger ones suggest that the structure was considerably and repeatedly expanded over the course of the next thousand years. Eventually the wooden buildings were replaced by two stone circles, noted by John Aubrey in 1648, and these were connected to Avebury by a stone avenue (West Kennet Avenue), parts of which you can still follow. The views from here over to Silbury Hill and West Kennet Long Barrow are particularly good.

❑ **Silbury Hill**

Despite the enormity of this hill it's often neglected in favour of the stone circle up the road. But do make the effort to come here as it's only at this closer proximity that you can start to understand the almost super-human effort that must have been required to build this structure.

The history of the hill dates back to around 2600BC when construction started. The first phase created a stepped structure. The steps were then filled in with chalk and after that earth was shaped over the steps to create a smooth face. You can still see one of these steps near the top of the hill but it's only clear when viewed from the eastern side. The top of the mound was left flat, but not level, and is 39m high and 30m wide. The base is perfectly round with a diameter of 167m. Just to really impress you, the hill contains around a quarter of a million cubic metres of chalk.

Why was it built? No one really knows, but there have been some earnest efforts to find out. The first of these was in 1776 when a shaft was dug from the summit down to the base. Nothing was found apart from construction materials. In 1849 another approach was tried, this time digging a tunnel from the base to the centre. Again, nothing was found. Yet another investigation took place in the late 1960s but the new tunnel into the base, again, revealed no evidence to point to Silbury Hill's raison d'être.

The hill was previously open to the public but slippages of the top soil were detected and any more human trampling would have only accelerated this deterioration. In 2000 a large hole also opened up on the summit, owing to a collapse of the shaft dug in 1776. It was infilled with polystyrene blocks and then covered with chalk. Investigations by English Heritage around the base of Silbury Hill in 2007 discovered evidence of a Roman settlement and later in the same year a major task was undertaken to stabilise the hill. Tunnels which had previously been dug into the hillside were filled with hundreds of tonnes of chalk to prevent any more collapses. As this work was sealing up the tunnels for good, English Heritage also took the opportunity to undertake one final archaeological survey in a bid to finally understand why the hill was built. Although they ultimately didn't come any closer to finding an answer to the question, the stabilisation work on the hill was carried out successfully.

Naturally, various theories regarding Silbury Hill's purpose have been developed to fill the vacuum, among them that it was a solar observatory or was symbolic of a Mother Goddess, but none really explains why such a gargantuan effort was made to build something so seemingly purposeless.

on yourself. This lane turns into a path and you cross the River Kennet once more, heading up to **The Sanctuary** (see box opposite) by the side of the A4. When you feel you have soaked up the atmosphere of this place you should cross the road to the official start of the Ridgeway and make your way up the hill to the junction with **Green Street/Herepath**. Turn left onto this track and follow it down to the Red Lion at Avebury. It's a handy place to finish for obvious reasons.

GETTING TO THE START OF THE RIDGEWAY [See map p93]

Anyone who has walked the Ridgeway will agree that even though it is a national trail the official start, by the side of the A4 road, is rather lacking in atmosphere. It is a shame, especially when one considers how packed with character the surrounding area is. There have been many calls to change the starting point though at the time of writing the situation hasn't changed much from when the first edition of this book was published. Avebury is, of course, the obvious place to which it should be relocated. So, until it is changed, here are four routes (A-D) from Avebury to the start of the trail. Deciding which to take will depend to a large degree on whether you want to start the Ridgeway at the official beginning, or whether you are happy to join it a little way along. Each has its own advantage. **Route A** takes you along the stones down the West Kennet Avenue, but also leads to the beginning of the national trail, so you still get to experience the Ridgeway in its entirety. Thanks to a couple of permissive paths that have recently been introduced, you no longer have to walk along any pavement-less roads either. At the other end of the spectrum, **Route D** takes you from the centre of Avebury along Green Street, to where it joins the Ridgeway. By taking this route you actually miss out on the first 1.8 miles/2.7km of the Ridgeway.

Routes B and C, meanwhile, meet the Ridgeway at the same point, a little way along the trail, but not as far along as Route D, but get there in different ways. Route B starts the same way as Route A (the West Kennet Avenue), but instead heads past four intriguing tree-covered tumuli before joining the national trail just a few minutes from its start; so those who want to begin at the beginning don't have far to head down the hill (before heading back up again); this is my favourite route. Route C, like Route D, uses Green Street/Herepath but it then turns south towards the official start.

Alternative start – Routes A & B

Route A is the longest alternative start. It involves walking out of the village along West Kennet Avenue which runs parallel to the B4003. It's easy walking on the soft grass along here with the large sarsen stones flanking you on either side. Begin by taking the gate opposite The Red Lion to the stones, and head past them south towards the line of trees, ignoring the first gate on your right (just 100m from the start) but taking the second gate (after the line of trees).

Crossing the road, you come to a second gate and the continuation of the avenue. The path continues through the stones and down into the next field, where a permissive path leads on, hugging the busy B4003. A gate on your left (by a couple of minor stones either side of the road) shepherds you across the tarmac once more, the path now bending away east behind a house to the A4. Cross the road to the pet hotel – and head down the road opposite. Just after the pet hotel and shop there is a stile on your left leading into a field. Climb over this and walk up the field, parallel to the A4, to reach the top corner where you should climb over another stile and find yourself in The Sanctuary. From here you simply have to cross the A4 to arrive at the official start of the Ridgeway.

For **Route B**, having crossed over the B4003 and reached the kissing gate where the permissive path divides, take the steeper path heading due east up the hill, past a total of four tumuli, to reach the Ridgeway approximately 500m and minutes from the beginning of the National Trail itself.

Alternative start – Routes C & D

Both of these leave Avebury via Green Street/Herepath. The only part of Green Street that could be vaguely described as a conventional 'street' peters out very quickly before becoming a sealed track. Even on the busiest days in Avebury, you don't have to take many steps down Green Street before leaving the crowds behind. You'll pass several houses on your right as Green Street clears the village and then come to Manor Farm. This is the last building on the 'street' and is where the tarmac finishes. It can be muddy around here owing to the farm vehicles.

You will see Green Street stretching into the distance up the hillside; it's at this point that you need either to follow Green Street up the hill (D), or take the signposted track that turns off right, immediately after Manor Farm (C).

If you choose to follow Green Street straight up the hill (D) you'll find that the track broadens out and becomes grassy, making for easy walking despite the increasing gradient. Look behind on your way up here to see the view getting better all the time. As for Route C, soon after joining this track it becomes grassy but deeply rutted and can be really muddy after rain. The path is level for the first half-mile after which it bends left and begins to climb the side of Overton Hill and up to the Ridgeway. It does take you past a tumulus and it is a nice quiet trail, but Route B is more interesting.

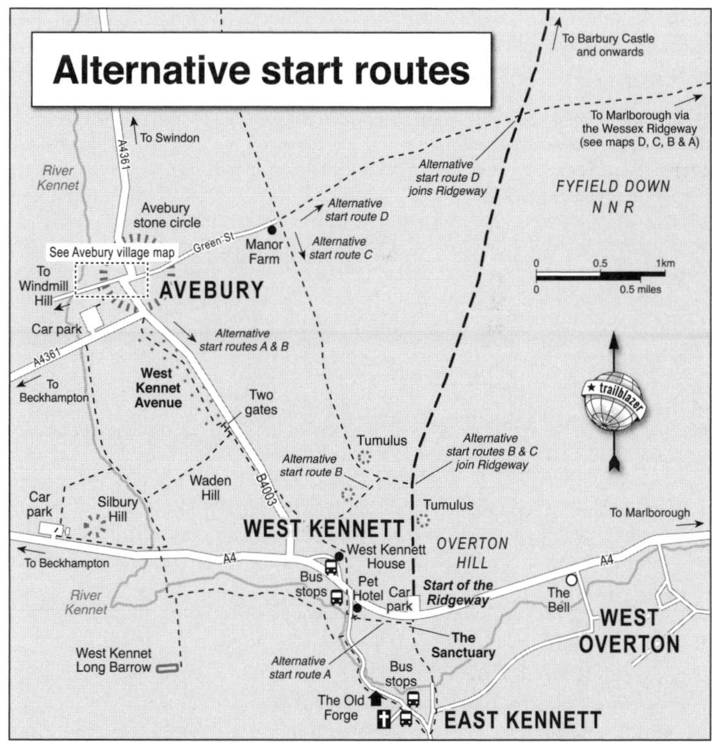

5 ROUTE GUIDE & MAPS

Using this guide

This route guide has been divided according to logical start and stop points. However, these are not intended to be strict daily stages since people walk at different speeds and have different interests. The maps can be used to plan how far to walk each day. The route summaries describe the trail between significant places and are written as if walking the path from west to east.

To enable you to plan your own itinerary practical information is presented clearly on the trail maps. This includes walking times for both directions, all places to stay, camp and eat, as well as shops where you can buy supplies. Further service details are given in the text under the entry for each place.

For a condensed overview of this information see **Itineraries** on pp30-6 and the **towns and villages facilities table** on pp32-3.

For **overview maps** and **profiles** see the colour pages at the end of the book.

TRAIL MAPS

Scale and walking times

The trail maps are to a scale of 1:20,000 (1cm = 200m; $3^{1}/_{8}$ inches = one mile). Walking times are given along the side of each map and the arrow shows the direction to which the time refers. Black triangles indicate the points between which the times have been taken. **See box below about walking times**.

The time-bars are a tool and are not there to judge your walking ability. There are so many variables that affect walking speed, from the weather conditions to how many beers you drank the previous evening. After the first hour or two of walking you will be able to see how your speed relates to the timings on the maps.

❑ **Important note – walking times**
Unless otherwise specified, **all times in this book refer only to the time spent walking**. You will need to add 20-30% to allow for rests, photography, checking the map, drinking water etc. When planning the day's hike count on 5-7 hours' actual walking.

Up or down?

Other than when on a track or bridleway the trail is shown as a dotted line. An arrow across the trail indicates the slope; two arrows show that it is steep. Note that the arrow points towards the higher part of the trail. If, for example, you are walking from A (at 80m) to B (at 200m) and the trail between the two is short and steep it would be shown thus: A— — — >> — — — B. Reversed arrow heads indicate downward gradient.

Accommodation

Apart from in large towns where some selection of places has been necessary, almost everywhere to stay that is within easy reach of the trail is marked. Details of each place are given in the accompanying text. The number and type of rooms is given after each entry: **S** = Single, **T** = Twin room, **D** = Double room, **Tr** = Triple room and **Qd** = Quad. Note that most of the triple/quad rooms have a double bed and one/two single beds (or bunk beds); thus for a group of three or four, two people would have to share the double bed, but it also means that the room can be used as a double or twin. See also pp18-20.

Rates quoted for B&B-style accommodation are **per person (pp) based on two people sharing a room** for a one-night stay; rates may well be discounted for longer stays. Where a **single room (sgl)** is available, the rate for that is quoted if different from the rate per person. The rate for **single occupancy (sgl occ)** of a double/twin may be higher and the per person rate for three/four sharing a triple/quad may be lower.

Unless specified, rates are for bed and breakfast. At some places the only option is a **room rate**; this will be the same whether one or two people (or more if permissible) use the room. In tourist towns, particularly, you can expect to pay extra at weekends (whereas in the few places on this route that cater to business people the rate is likely to be higher during the week). Note that a few places accept only a two-night stay, particularly at weekends and in the main season.

Rooms either have **en suite** (bath or shower) facilities, or a **private** or **shared** bathroom or shower room, often just outside the bedroom. The text notes if a bath (🛁) is available for those who prefer a relaxed soak at the end of the day.

The text also indicates whether the premises have: **wi-fi** (WI-FI); if a **packed lunch** (Ⓛ) can be prepared, subject to prior arrangement; and if **dogs** (🐕 – see also p29 and pp191-2) are welcome, again subject to prior arrangement, either in at least one room (many places have only one room suitable for dogs), or at campsites. The policy on charging for dogs varies; some places make an additional charge per day or per stay, while others may require a refundable deposit against any potential damage or mess.

Other features

Other features are marked on the map only when they are pertinent to navigation. To avoid clutter, not all features are marked all the time.

The Ridgeway route guide

OVERTON HILL TO FOXHILL [MAPS 1-10]

Overview

This first **16½-mile/26.5km (6¾-8½hrs)** stage of the Ridgeway includes many interesting sights but most of them are before Ogbourne St George. By comparison, thereafter, it can seem a bit of a slog in parts, especially the last section from Liddington Hill to Foxhill.

The full length of this stage will leave you tired after your first day but you'll have to push on to Bishopstone to find accommodation (a further 1.2 miles/2km). Alternatively you could stay at Ogbourne St George which is only 9 miles/14.5km from the start of the Ridgeway. It would make an easy first day's walking and would also allow time to investigate Fyfield Down National Nature Reserve and take a long break at Barbury Castle.

Route

There are several alternative starts to the Ridgeway (see pp91-3) that are all more interesting than the official one. It just depends how serious you are about following every step of the real path.

The official, but rather uninspiring, starting point is at the side of the Beckhampton to Marlborough road (the A4) and if you've taken Alternative start route A you will arrive here. However, you soon gain enough height on the broad track on **Overton Hill** to lose the sight and noise of the busy road.

In clear weather there are excellent views west to the obelisk monument on Cherhill Hill, 5 miles/8km away. It was built on an Iron Age hillfort in 1845/6 in memory of Sir William Petty, the 17th-century economist. **Windmill Hill** (see box opposite), 2½ miles/4km to the west, is another easily spotted landmark. After the track levels out, you'll arrive at the Green Street junction (Map 2).

If you have taken Alternative start route D from Avebury you will join the Ridgeway from the left, while to the right is a gate leading into **Fyfield Down**

ROUTE GUIDE AND MAPS

> ❏ **Tumuli**
>
> Especially on the western half of the Ridgeway, and in particular on the first 15 miles of it, you will see many tumuli – burial mounds dating from around 4500 to 4000 years ago which now just look like raised grassy humps. In fact there are three right next to the start of the Ridgeway (see Map 1, p98) and you'll see a couple more just 10 minutes up the path. Sometimes they are planted over with trees, so if you see an isolated bunch of trees in the middle of a field, this could suggest a tumulus underneath.
>
> They are generally marked on Ordnance Survey maps, though not all features marked as tumuli are necessarily burial mounds. They could be just, as yet, unidentified lumps on the landscape.

❑ Windmill Hill

This 20-acre site forms the largest of the 66 known Neolithic causewayed enclosures in Britain, with evidence of activity here dating from about 3700BC. A causewayed enclosure is a piece of land, usually oval in shape, bounded by one or more segmented banks or ditches. Windmill Hill has three such series of banks and ditches, with the outermost series being by far the most substantial. These sites represent the earliest examples of artificially enclosing an open area in Britain.

The findings of excavations by Rev H G O Kendall and Alexander Keiller, that took place here in the 1920s, not only established Neolithic causewayed enclosures as a distinct class, but also granted Windmill Hill its status as the most important one in Britain. The site even lent its name to 'Windmill Hill Ware', a distinctive type of pottery found at this and other similar sites in Britain.

From the 1920s onwards, the theory was that Neolithic people had lived in 'pit dwellings' – in the ditches of the enclosure – owing to the large quantity of animal bones and pottery found there. Keiller's findings from the 1920s were not properly written up at the time and it wasn't until 1965 that a summary of the excavations was published. This led to renewed excavations on the site and by the late 1960s the theory of 'pit dwellings' had totally lost favour. Although we now know that this was not a site of permanent settlement it is still unclear exactly what its purpose was. We can presume that ceremonies and feasts took place here, but the size of the enclosure would suggest a more substantial use. Several round burial mounds on Windmill Hill have also been excavated but these have been dated to the Bronze Age.

Despite the significance of Windmill Hill to archaeologists, a casual visit can prove disappointing. Apart from the views of the surrounding countryside there really isn't much to see on the hill itself as large sections of the banks and ditches have been ploughed into farmland. It's certainly far less visually dramatic than an Iron Age hill fort like Barbury Castle, only 5 miles/8km along the Ridgeway from Avebury.

If you want to visit Windmill Hill you should walk to the western end of Avebury High St and follow the signposts from there; it's about 2 miles (3km) from the village.

NNR (see p81). Up here it's exposed to the elements with few trees or bushes to shelter you and the walking is mainly level on a broad, grassy track with numerous byways and bridleways joining from both sides.

When you get to the junction (Map 3) where the Broad Hinton to Marlborough road crosses the Ridgeway you'll have the opportunity to see the **Hackpen White Horse** (see box p117) cut into the chalk of the hillside. You can't see it from the track as you are above it so you'll need to make a slight diversion. It is not an ancient White Horse – this one was cut into Hackpen Hill in 1838 – so don't feel the steep detour is obligatory, especially as you will be seeing the original white horse at White Horse Hill, further along the Ridgeway. This section of the Ridgeway path is also part of the White Horse Trail (see box p117).

At the foot of **Barbury Castle** (Map 4) the 'Ridgeway Route For Vehicles' continues straight ahead across the road but walkers, cyclists and horses can follow the steep grassy slopes up onto the top of Barbury Castle itself. Apart from this one there are two more Iron Age forts on the Ridgeway (Liddington Castle, p108, and Uffington Castle, p116), but this is the only one that the path cuts directly through. *(continued on p102)*

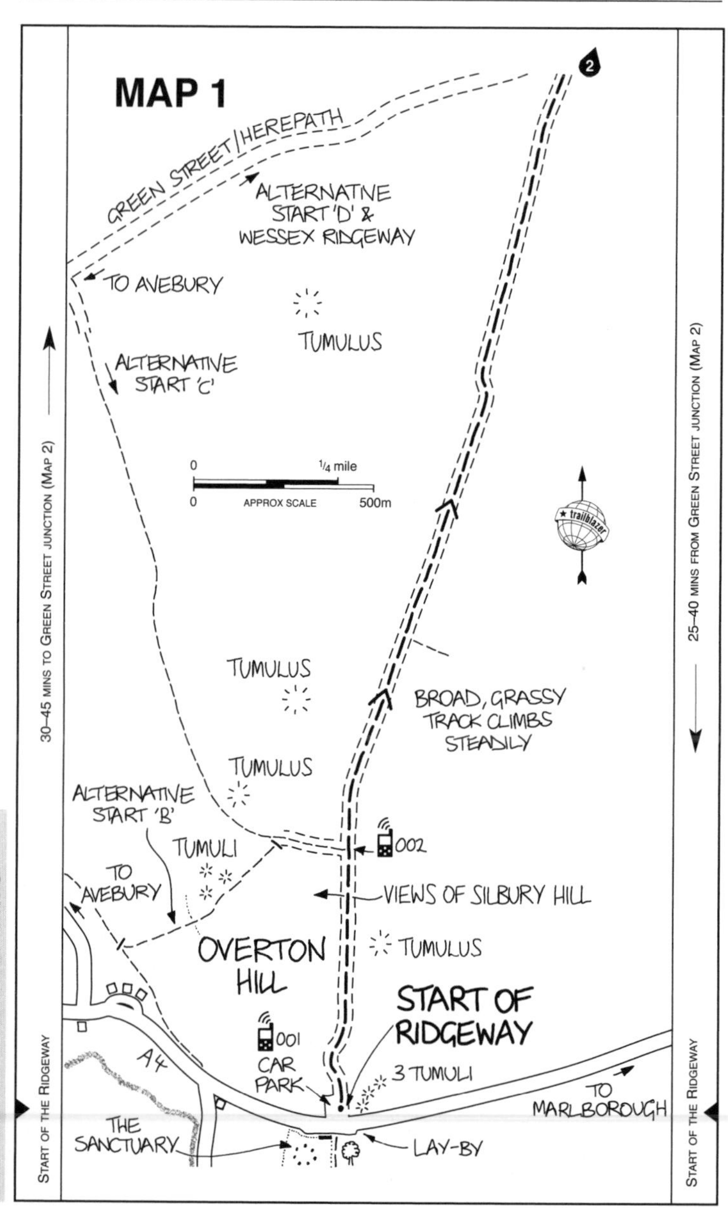
MAP 1
GREEN STREET/HEREPATH
ALTERNATNVE START 'D' & WESSEX RIDGEWAY
TO AVEBURY
TUMULUS
ALTERNATIVE START 'C'
0 1/4 mile
0 APPROX SCALE 500m
trailblazer
TUMULUS
BROAD, GRASSY TRACK CLIMBS STEADILY
TUMULUS
ALTERNATIVE START 'B'
TUMULI
002
TO AVEBURY
VIEWS OF SILBURY HILL
OVERTON HILL
TUMULUS
START OF RIDGEWAY
001
A4
CAR PARK
3 TUMULI
TO MARLBOROUGH
THE SANCTUARY
LAY-BY
30–45 MINS TO GREEN STREET JUNCTION (MAP 2)
25–40 MINS FROM GREEN STREET JUNCTION (MAP 2)
START OF THE RIDGEWAY
START OF THE RIDGEWAY

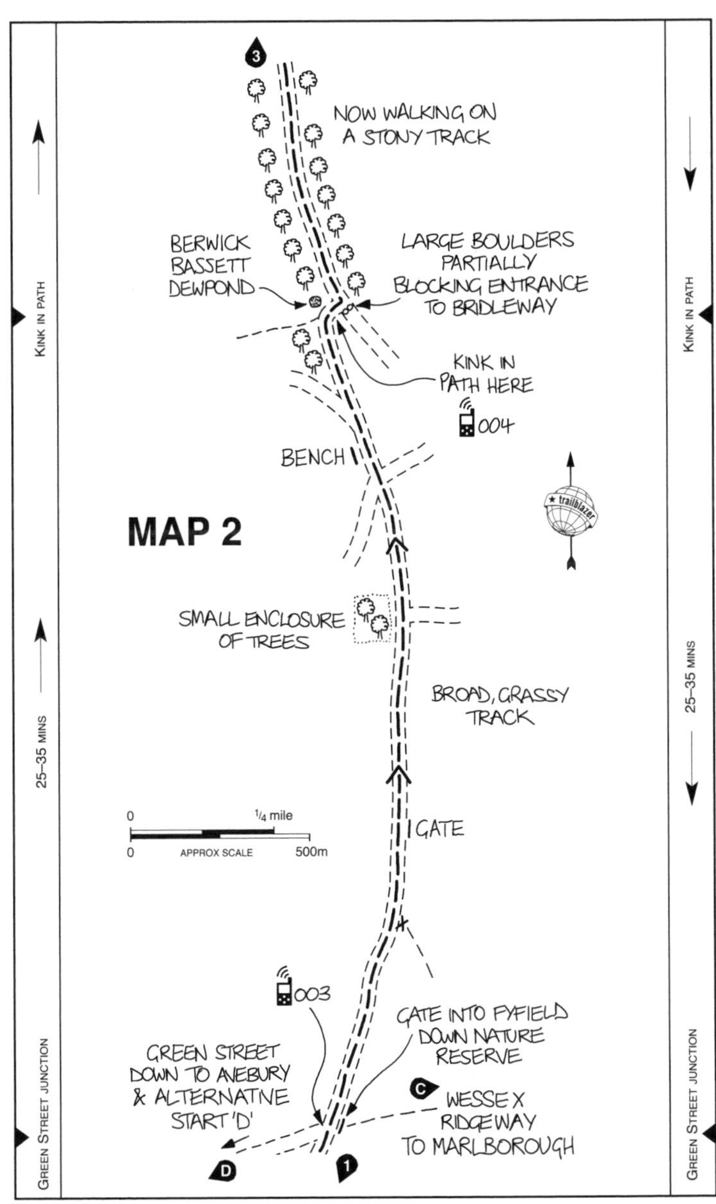

ROUTE GUIDE AND MAPS

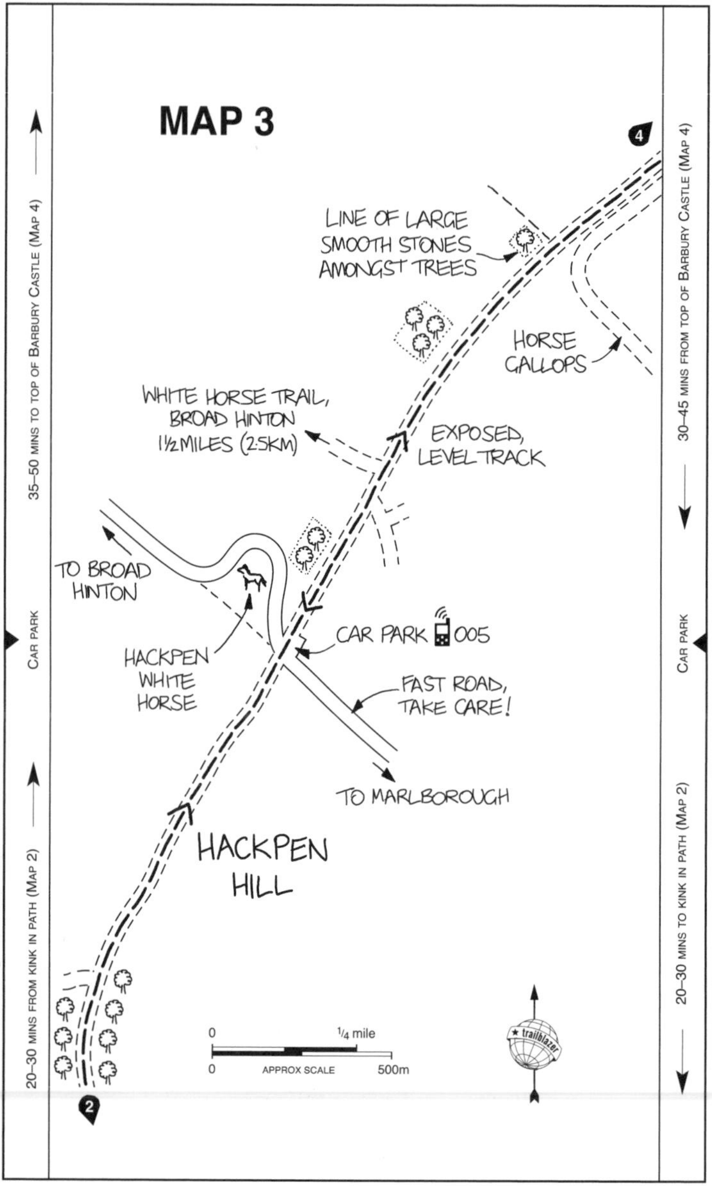

35–50 mins to top of Barbury Castle (Map 4)

Car park

20–30 mins from kink in path (Map 2)

MAP 3

LINE OF LARGE SMOOTH STONES AMONGST TREES

HORSE GALLOPS

WHITE HORSE TRAIL, BROAD HINTON 1½MILES (2.5KM)

EXPOSED, LEVEL TRACK

TO BROAD HINTON

CAR PARK 005

HACKPEN WHITE HORSE

FAST ROAD, TAKE CARE!

TO MARLBOROUGH

HACKPEN HILL

0 ¼ mile

0 APPROX SCALE 500m

trailblazer

30–45 mins from top of Barbury Castle (Map 4)

Car park

20–30 mins to kink in path (Map 2)

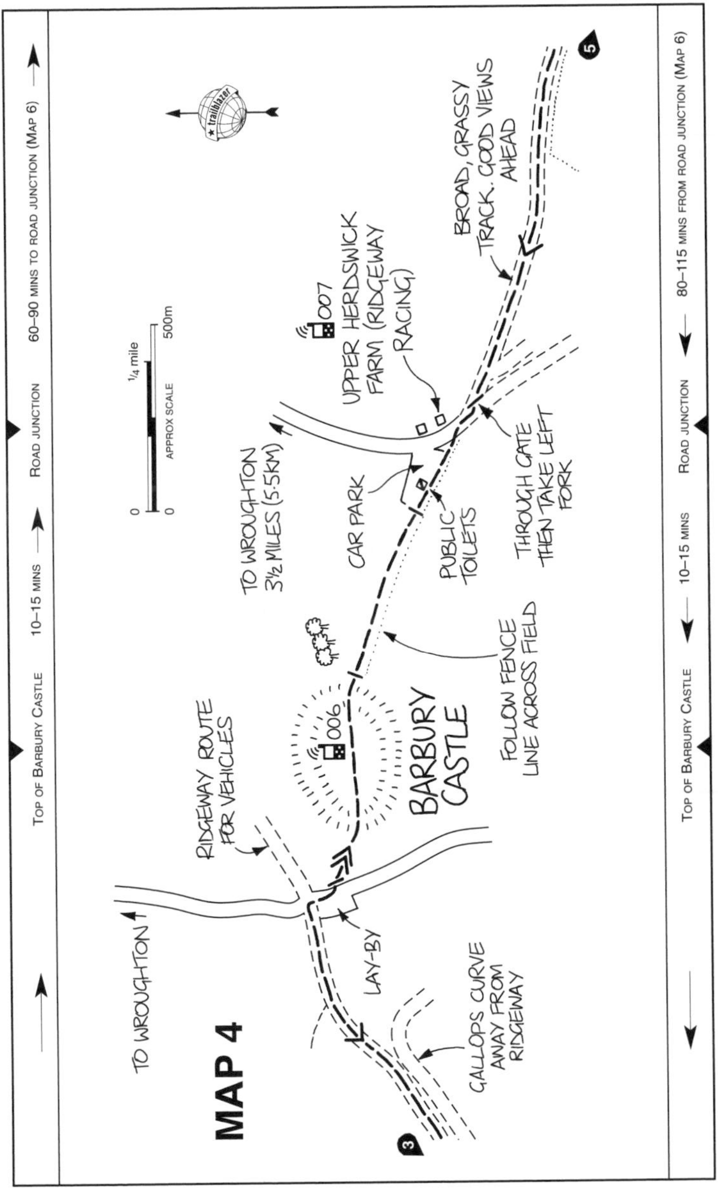

Top of Barbury Castle — 10–15 mins → Road junction — 60–90 mins to road junction (Map 6) →

MAP 4

TO WROUGHTON

RIDGEWAY ROUTE FOR VEHICLES

LAY-BY

GALLOPS CURVE AWAY FROM RIDGEWAY

006

BARBURY CASTLE

FOLLOW FENCE LINE ACROSS FIELD

TO WROUGHTON 3½ MILES (5.5KM)

CAR PARK

PUBLIC TOILETS

THROUGH GATE THEN TAKE LEFT FORK

007

UPPER HERDSWICK FARM (RIDGEWAY RACING)

BROAD, GRASSY TRACK. GOOD VIEWS AHEAD

0 — 1/4 mile

0 — APPROX SCALE — 500m

★ trailblazer

← Top of Barbury Castle ← 10–15 mins — Road junction ← 80–115 mins from road junction (Map 6)

(continued from p97) The 11-acre fort is ringed by double ramparts and deep ditches with entrances at both ends through which the Ridgeway passes. Some Iron Age finds from the castle are on display at Wiltshire Museum (💻 www.wiltshiremuseum.org.uk), in Devizes. The castle's defensive position is indisputable and this guaranteed its importance long after the Iron Age finished. In fact the name 'Barbury' is thought to come from the Old English name, 'Bera', after the Saxon chief who controlled the castle around AD550. Even as late as World War II it was being used as a potentially defensive position by allied troops.

The views from up here on a clear day are fantastic and it's a popular place at weekends with walkers, cyclists and horseriders. On some weekends it's also home to the White Horse Kite Fliers. You might wonder how all the people managed to get up here but when you get to the other side of the castle you'll understand. There you'll find a large car park, picnic tables, public toilets and the road north to Wroughton, 3½ miles/5.5km away.

When the weather is good the walking on **Smeathe's Ridge** (Map 5) makes for some of the most enjoyable parts of this stage; the soft grass underfoot means walking is easy. Although the official path doesn't go into **Ogbourne St George** you can follow the signposted footpath (see Map 6), about half a mile/1km, into this attractive village if you want to stop here.

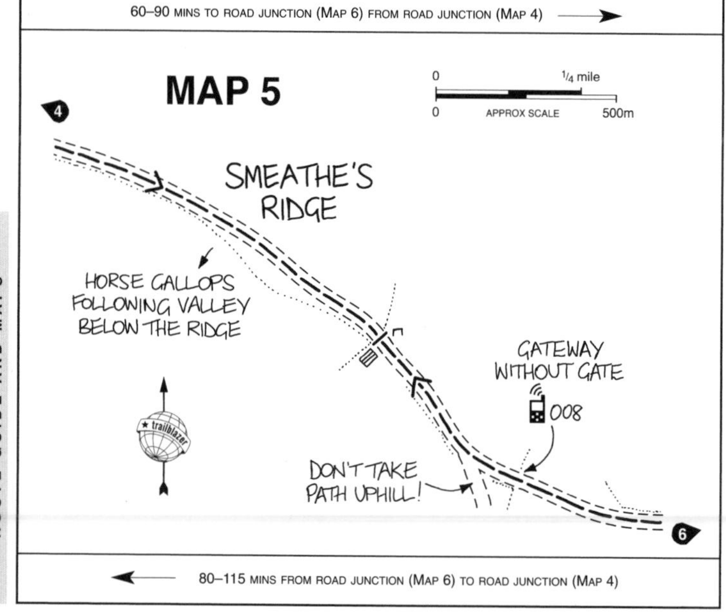

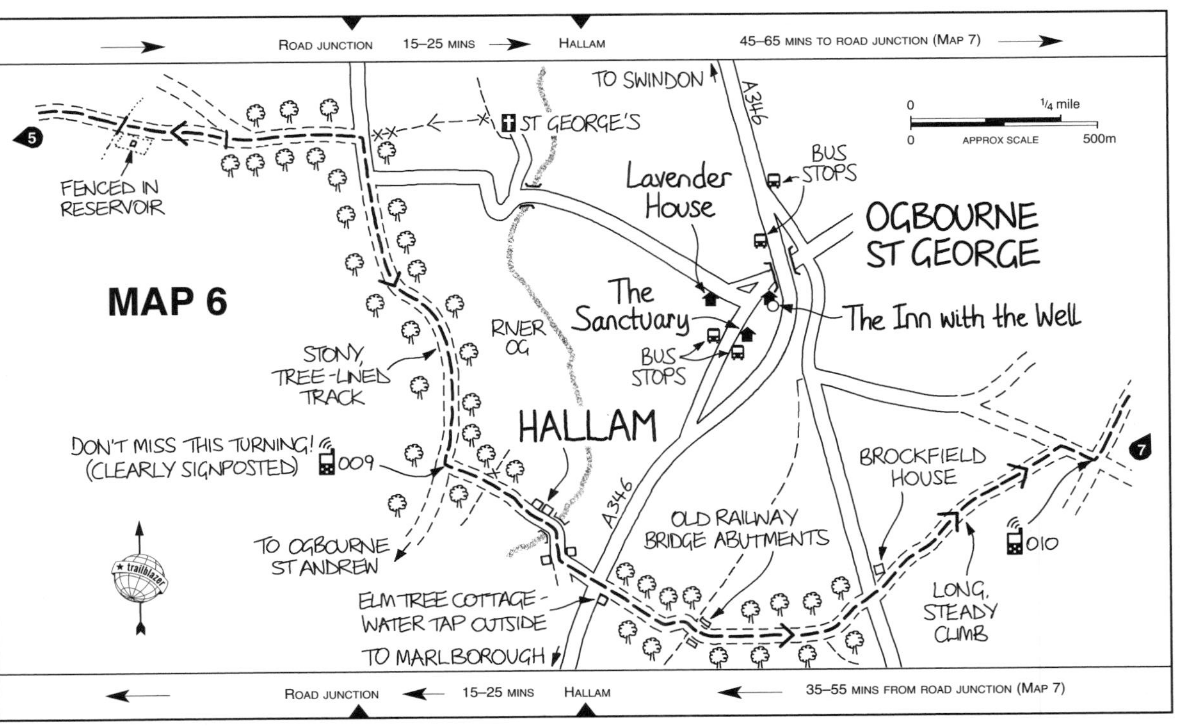
ROAD JUNCTION
15–25 MINS
HALLAM
45–65 MINS TO ROAD JUNCTION (MAP 7)
TO SWINDON
A346
ST GEORGE'S
0
1/4 mile
0
APPROX SCALE
500m
FENCED IN RESERVOIR
BUS STOPS
Lavender House
OGBOURNE ST GEORGE
MAP 6
The Sanctuary
The Inn with the Well
RIVER OG
BUS STOPS
STONY, TREE-LINED TRACK
HALLAM
DON'T MISS THIS TURNING! (CLEARLY SIGNPOSTED)
009
BROCKFIELD HOUSE
A346
OLD RAILWAY BRIDGE ABUTMENTS
TO OGBOURNE ST ANDREW
010
trailblazer
LONG, STEADY CLIMB
ELM TREE COTTAGE - WATER TAP OUTSIDE
TO MARLBOROUGH
ROAD JUNCTION
15–25 MINS
HALLAM
35–55 MINS FROM ROAD JUNCTION (MAP 7)
5
7

OGBOURNE ST GEORGE

[MAP 6, p103]

The name of this village refers to the river Og (Map 6) and the name of its church, St George's. A mile/1.5km or so south of here is the village of Ogbourne St Andrew, named in the same way. Ogbourne St George is a pretty-enough village but unless you are planning to stay the night, there really isn't much point making the detour, especially as there aren't any shops.

Ogbourne is a stop on Thamesdown's/ Stagecoach's No 70A/72A, and Stagecoach's No 80, **bus** services which operate between Swindon and Marlborough; all stop in the village. See pp47-51 for further details.

If you need a **taxi**, call one of the firms in Marlborough, see p74.

Where to stay, eat and drink

Wherever you stay, arranging to have a packed lunch is useful, as there is no shop in the village.

The first B&B you come to from the trail is ***Lavender House*** (☎ 07725 324869, 🖳 lavenderhouse53@yahoo.com; 1D or T en suite; WI-FI; Ⓛ £5; 🐕 £5), on the High St, a simple B&B with a friendly host and good breakfasts. Rates are £32.50pp (£45 for single occupancy). They allow dogs if you bring their bedding.

A couple of minutes away is ***The Sanctuary*** (☎ 01672 841473, ☎ 07850 325344, 🖳 www.the-sanctuary.biz; 2D or 1T/1Tr, all en suite or private facilities; ☕; WI-FI; Ⓛ from £3.25; 🐕), a well-run, friendly B&B that's used to walkers. They serve large, tasty breakfasts to set you up for the day. B&B costs from £40pp (sgl occ from £65, three sharing from £120). They welcome dogs in return for a donation to their favourite canine charity (£5 to Black Retriever X Rescue), but be aware that they also have chickens running free in their garden. Luggage transfer by arrangement.

The only place for food in the evenings is ***The Inn with the Well*** (☎ 01672 841445, 🖳 www.theinnwiththewell.co.uk; 3D/2T/ 1Tr, all en suite, ☕; WI-FI; Ⓛ £5.95; 🐕); it is a deservedly popular place with both locals and people travelling from the surrounding area. Their varied menu (**food** served Sat & Sun noon-2.30pm, Mon-Sat 5-9pm, May-Aug Sun 5-8pm) has dishes such as venison pie with veg and mash (£10.95). **B&B** costs from £40pp (sgl occ from £70, from £100 for three sharing).

Do remember to check on **airbnb** (see p20); at the time of writing there was one in a modern annex of an old farmhouse but there may be more by the time you are here.

❑ Racehorses

From virtually the start of the Ridgeway up until past East Ilsley you are likely to see racehorses. They won't be on the path itself, but will be training along the gallops that often run parallel to the path, sometimes with brushwood hurdles set up on them. As you may have noticed, the ground here is soft and springy and very open which makes it ideal for racehorse training. The early morning is the best time to see the small groups of horses being put through their paces with their trainers. When the Ridgeway is right next to the gallops you can feel the power of the horses as they thunder by.

When you are at Barbury Castle you can look down onto the Marlborough Downs and see Barbury Castle racecourse, but it's the Lambourn Downs area, further east, that is really famous as a centre for racehorse training. There are around 50 racing yards around Lambourn which train up to 2000 horses at any one time.

If you visit the Crown & Horns pub in East Ilsley (see pp133-4), you'll notice that the walls in the bar are covered with horse-racing memorabilia, connected to the landlord's involvement in the business.

❑ Signposts on the Ridgeway

The Ridgeway is one of the most comprehensively signposted long-distance trails in the country. At nearly every junction on the path there is a dedicated and distinctive black 'Ridgeway' signpost (see photo p6), not only to keep you going in the right direction, but also to inform you of other options.

At a glance these waymarkers look to be made in the traditional manner from wood that has been treated with creosote, but in fact the material used is Plaswood. This is an environmentally friendly plastic material made from 30% consumer waste and 70% from other waste sources. It is strong, durable and impervious to water so it will not rot or splinter as wood does. This also means that it is maintenance free.

You will see many traditional wooden signs along the Ridgeway in various states of decay but the Plaswood signs will remain looking the same as the day they were set into the ground for years to come. Some have been there for more than 10 years already.

Plaswood is now used for many other products, often as a substitute for wood in outdoor areas. Items such as benches, planters, walkways and street furniture are all being constructed from the material.

The official path skirts around the south of the village on shady farm tracks. You get occasional glimpses of Ogbourne St George through the trees on your left and you soon arrive in the hamlet of **Hallam** (Map 6). This must rate as one of the most picturesque collections of cottages anywhere and is so perfect it's almost twee. Apart from the few buildings at Barbury Castle, this is the most heavily built-up area you have passed through since setting off. There is a water tap at Elm Tree Cottage.

After the hamlet you start a steady climb up a stony track closed in by trees and bushes and come to pass between the hefty stone abutments of an old railway bridge which was once the route of the Midland and South Western Junction Railway. This section opened in the 1880s but has long since disappeared. It linked Swindon and Chiseldon, to the north, with Marlborough, to the south. It's now been developed into the Chiseldon & Marlborough Railway Path and is popular but muddy.

Much later on when you arrive at the crossroads with the **reservoir** (Map 7) on the left corner that looks like a fortified concrete bunker, there is the opportunity to visit the former village of **Snap**. A small farming community existed on this site for hundreds of years until the late 19th century when farming became less economically viable owing to cheap imports and spare land was bought up by wealthy local landowners for use as sheep-grazing. Most of the population left the village to find work elsewhere and by the early 20th century the village was empty. To get there turn right and follow the track straight on for about half a mile/1km. Since being abandoned, the village has all but disappeared into the landscape, so unless you have plenty of time…

The 'Snap crossroads' is worth noting because just a short way down the track to the left is the **radio mast** that you'll probably have seen by now. If you haven't it will certainly be a prominent landmark every time you do look back, all the way to Liddington Castle. *(continued on p108)*

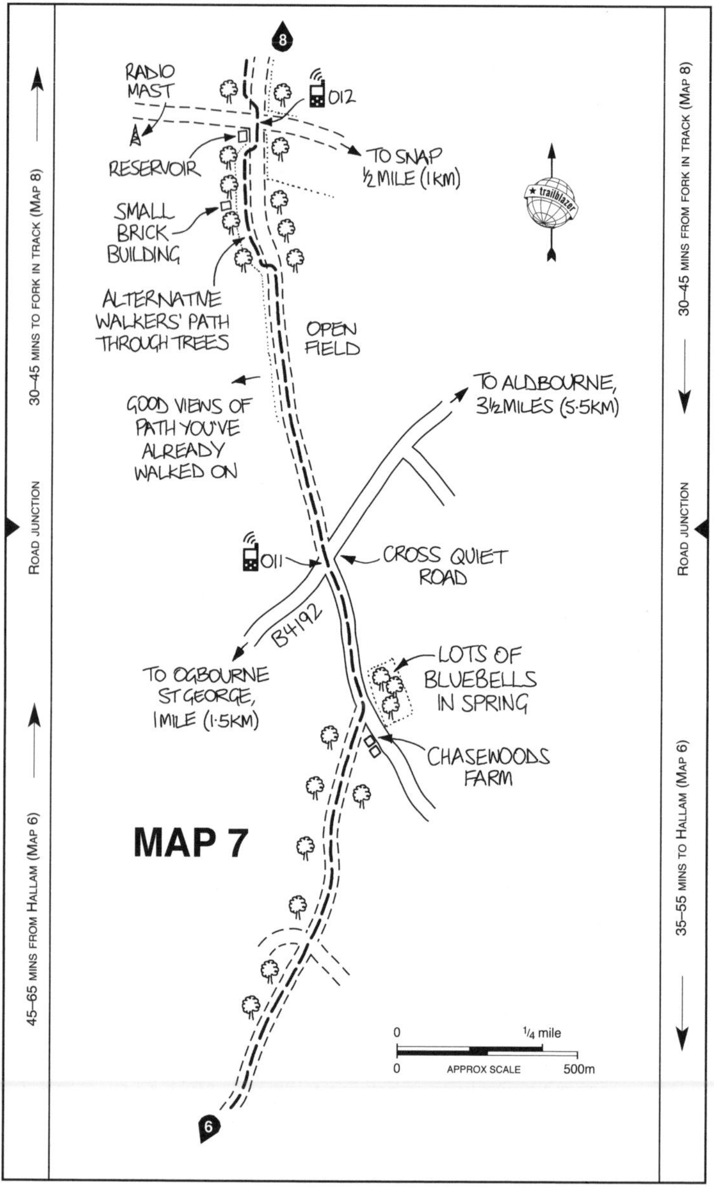

30–45 MINS TO FORK IN TRACK (MAP 8)

ROAD JUNCTION

45–65 MINS FROM HALLAM (MAP 6)

8

RADIO MAST

012

TO SNAP ½ MILE (1KM)

RESERVOIR

SMALL BRICK BUILDING

ALTERNATIVE WALKERS' PATH THROUGH TREES

OPEN FIELD

GOOD VIEWS OF PATH YOU'VE ALREADY WALKED ON

TO ALDBOURNE, 3½ MILES (5.5KM)

011

CROSS QUIET ROAD

B4192

TO OGBOURNE ST GEORGE, 1 MILE (1.5KM)

LOTS OF BLUEBELLS IN SPRING

CHASEWOODS FARM

trailblazer

MAP 7

0 ¼ mile

0 APPROX SCALE 500m

6

30–45 MINS FROM FORK IN TRACK (MAP 8)

ROAD JUNCTION

35–55 MINS TO HALLAM (MAP 6)

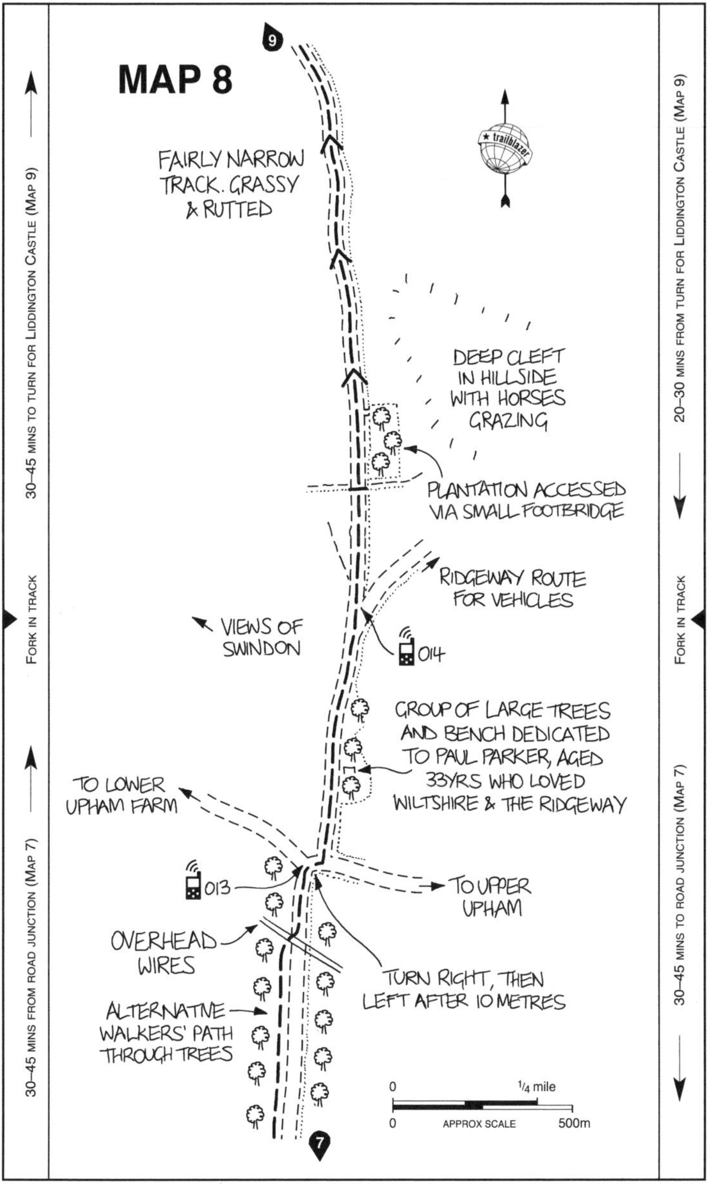

MAP 8

30–45 MINS TO TURN FOR LIDDINGTON CASTLE (MAP 9)

FORK IN TRACK

30–45 MINS FROM ROAD JUNCTION (MAP 7)

20–30 MINS FROM TURN FOR LIDDINGTON CASTLE (MAP 9)

FORK IN TRACK

30–45 MINS TO ROAD JUNCTION (MAP 7)

9

trailblazer

FAIRLY NARROW TRACK. GRASSY & RUTTED

DEEP CLEFT IN HILLSIDE WITH HORSES GRAZING

PLANTATION ACCESSED VIA SMALL FOOTBRIDGE

RIDGEWAY ROUTE FOR VEHICLES

VIEWS OF SWINDON

014

GROUP OF LARGE TREES AND BENCH DEDICATED TO PAUL PARKER, AGED 33YRS WHO LOVED WILTSHIRE & THE RIDGEWAY

TO LOWER UPHAM FARM

013

TO UPPER UPHAM

OVERHEAD WIRES

TURN RIGHT, THEN LEFT AFTER 10 METRES

ALTERNATIVE WALKERS' PATH THROUGH TREES

0 1/4 mile

0 APPROX SCALE 500m

7

(continued from p105) When you eventually reach **Liddington Castle** (Map 9), you'll get views of the M4 over to the north-east and if you turn around you'll see the aforementioned radio mast, now on the horizon behind you. The Ridgeway does not actually go through Liddington Castle so if you'd like to visit follow the signpost that directs you along the fence line rather than going directly to the castle; it's about 500m. The trig point on top of the castle displays a height of 277m and the hill is a popular launch site for paragliders. After descending Liddington Hill and joining the fast B4192 you'll have the possibility of walking to Liddington; though it is only worth going if you want to eat, drink, stay, or to get a bus. To get there simply continue down the B4192 for about half a mile (1km), crossing the M4 en route; or, even better, take a bus.

LIDDINGTON

The Village Inn (☎ 01793 790314, 💻 www.villageinn-liddington.co.uk; 1S/1D/1T, shared bathroom, ♥; WI-FI; Ⓛ) provides a friendly focus for the village and is usually busy. This creeper-clad inn, originally called The Bell, was built in the late 19th century. **B&B** costs from £35pp (£55 for single occupancy). Their excellent **food**

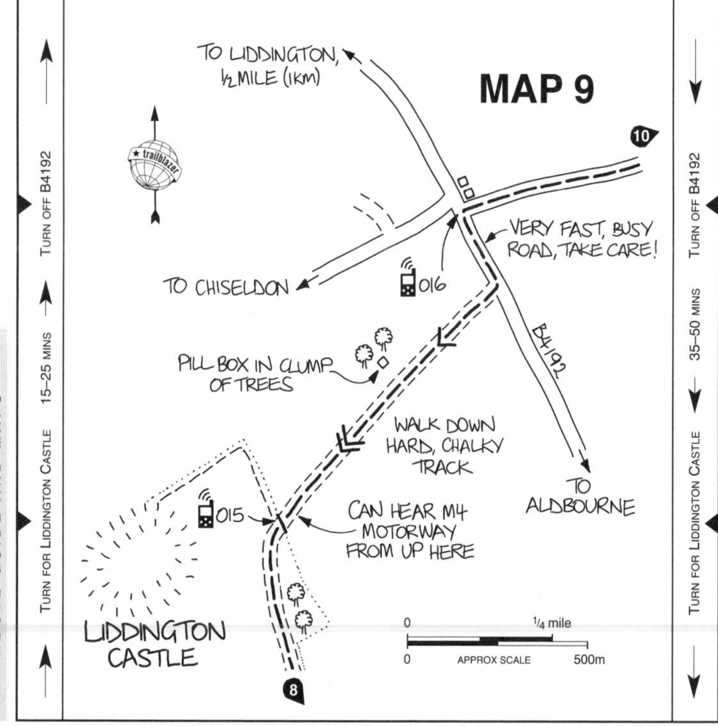

(Mon-Sat noon-2pm & 6-9pm, Sun noon-9pm) keeps the place full, particularly at weekends. Apart from Sunday the pub is closed between 3pm and 6pm.

The other B&B option in the village is ***Meadowbank*** (☎ 01793 791401, 🖳 meadowbankhouse.com; 1D en suite/2D share bathroom, ▾; WI-FI; Ⓛ); it is a supremely comfy place with B&B for £35-45pp (sgl occ £60-75); guests have access to a sitting room and a drying room. The house lies less than a mile from the path on Medbourne Lane, near the B4192. They are very happy to pick up from the B4192 (and drop off the next day) if arranged in advance; if a two-night stay is booked they will take you to where you want to start walking.

There are three **bus** stops. Thamesdown's No 46/46A (Swindon to Hungerford) service stops by The Village Inn and their No 48 (Swindon to Marlborough) calls at Spinney Close. Their X47 service (Wantage to Swindon) stops at the turning off the B4192 into the village; see pp47-51 for further details.

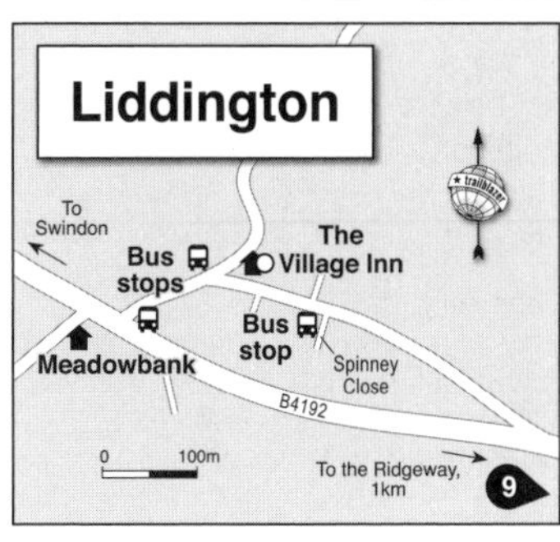

After enduring a stretch of road walking you must cross the **bridge over the M4** (Map 10). You'll be surprised just how noisy and smelly it is; although the fumes disappear quickly when you reach the other side, the noise will stay with you all the way to Foxhill at the end of this stage. There is still about 700m of walking to go after the bridge but it's all on a neat grassy verge.

The crossroads at **Foxhill** are dominated by ***The Burj*** (☎ 01793 791888, 🖳 www.theburj.co.uk; daily noon-2.30pm & 5.30-11.30pm), an Indian restaurant. This place used to be Shepherds Rest pub, a most welcoming stop during a Ridgeway walk. Since the closure of this pub, there is now no pub directly on the western half of the Ridgeway. Anyway, The Burj does cook some very tasty food from an extensive menu and has plenty of interesting vegetarian options, too. Main courses cost £9-18 but they also have set menus (from £21.50pp).

Thamesdown's Nos 46/46A, 48/48A and X47 **buses** call here; see pp47-51 for further details.

FOXHILL TO COURT HILL (& WANTAGE) [MAPS 10-16]

Overview

This second stage of the Ridgeway totals **11½ miles/18.5km (3¾-5½hrs)**; plus 2 miles/3km to reach Wantage); on the whole the walking is easy along very broad grassy tracks. Although there are a few ascents, they're not too draining. There are some great views plus several interesting archaeological sites and natural phenomena worth investigating. This is also the most remote section of the Ridgeway and is completely exposed to the elements with little shelter available. If it rains there is little you can do but continue walking and get very wet. But on a sunny day in spring it's quite delightful, and colourful too: the bright white of the chalk path contrasting nicely with the green of the vegetation, picked out here and there with the vivid sunshine of the dandelion and the

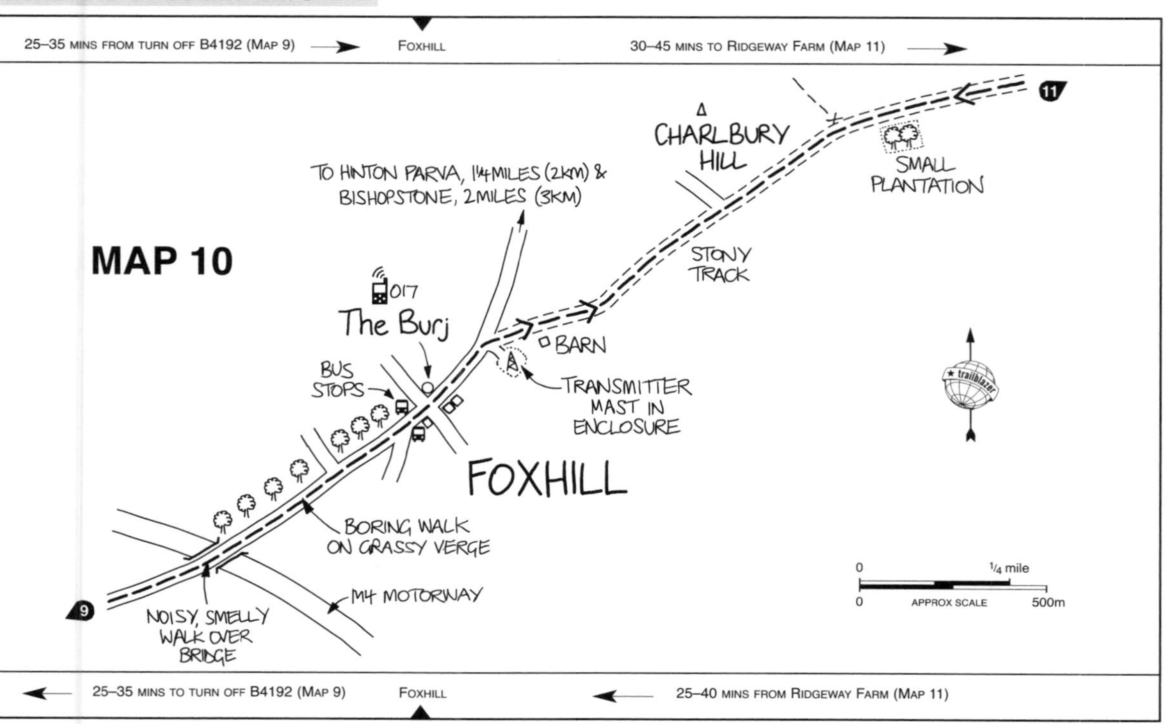
25–35 MINS FROM TURN OFF B4192 (MAP 9)
FOXHILL
30–45 MINS TO RIDGEWAY FARM (MAP 11)
MAP 10
11
CHARLBURY HILL
SMALL PLANTATION
TO HINTON PARVA, 1¼ MILES (2KM) & BISHOPSTONE, 2 MILES (3KM)
STONY TRACK
017
The Burj
BARN
BUS STOPS
TRANSMITTER MAST IN ENCLOSURE
trailblazer
FOXHILL
BORING WALK ON GRASSY VERGE
0
¼ mile
0
APPROX SCALE
500m
9
M4 MOTORWAY
NOISY, SMELLY WALK OVER BRIDGE
25–35 MINS TO TURN OFF B4192 (MAP 9)
FOXHILL
25–40 MINS FROM RIDGEWAY FARM (MAP 11)

creamy white of the hawthorns – all against a backdrop of the screaming yellow rape fields and (hopefully) the blue of the sky.

Route

About 200m past the Foxhill crossroads you leave the road that goes to the villages of Hinton Parva and Bishopstone and take the track on the right. If you are heading to Bishopstone it is best to wait and take the first turning on Map 11. A large **transmitter mast** is in the field on your right protected by a gate with a dozen padlocks on it. The path levels out after a short climb and you can see the trig point on **Charlbury Hill** ahead and to the left of the path.

The ever-spreading town of Swindon is clearly visible to the west and you can also see villages down in the valley, parallel to the Ridgeway. These include Hinton Parva, Bishopstone, Idstone and Ashbury. Paths run down off the Ridgeway to these villages and many people from the surrounding area bring their dogs up here for exercise.

The first turning off (on Map 11) left to Bishopstone is a bridleway down a very steep-sided cleft, followed just a few hundred metres later by a narrow surfaced road headed to the same place from the crossroads at **Ridgeway Farm**. From this latter turning it's about half a mile/1km to the village.

BISHOPSTONE

Although this is a fairly large village, facilities for the walker are a little thin on the ground. There is no shop or post office but there are some great places to stay and the pub serves delicious food. It's an attractive place for a wander, especially by the village pond and on the shady short-cut paths around the village. However, like some of the other settlements on this stretch, it's only worth coming all the way down off the Ridgeway if you plan to stay or eat here.

Connect's No 47 **bus** passes through on its way between Swindon, Ashbury and Lambourn. You can also take Thamesdown's Sat X47 (Wantage to Swindon); see pp47-51 for further details.

Where to stay and eat

The Royal Oak (☎ 01793 790481, 💻 www.helenbrowningsorganic.co.uk; WI-FI), in a grand building set on a quiet lane, has been here for about two hundred years and is well worth stopping off at. They serve Arkell's ales, amongst others, and have an excellent restaurant (booking is recommended) serving a regularly changing selection of organic **food** (Mon-Sat noon-2.30pm & 6-9.30pm, Sun noon-5pm) and much of the meat comes from their own farm. They are opening a 12-bed **hotel** in a building behind their car park in 2017; at the time of research the details were not available but it is likely there will be a range of en suite rooms.

Cheney Thatch (☎ 01793 790508; 2D, both with private facilities; ☕; Ⓛ £7.50; 🐕) is a 400-year-old cottage hidden away

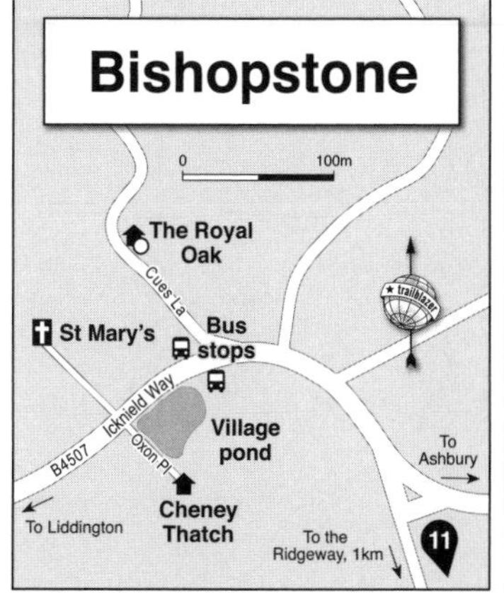

ROUTE GUIDE AND MAPS

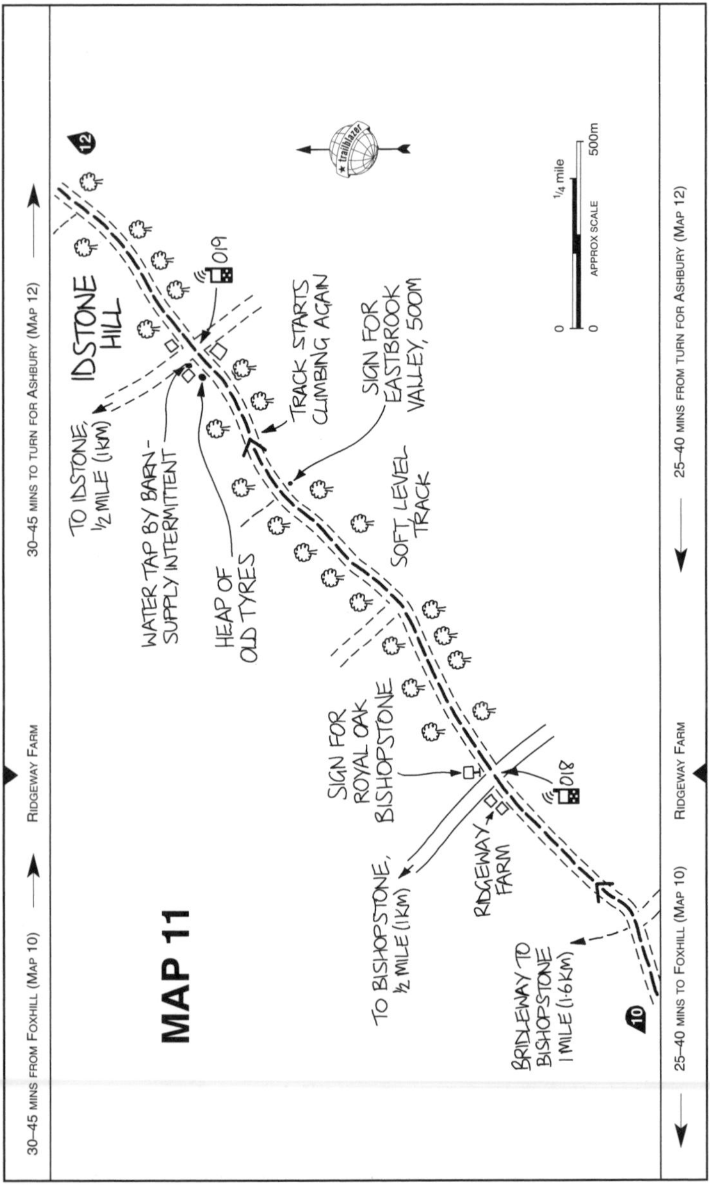

30–45 MINS FROM FOXHILL (MAP 10) → RIDGEWAY FARM 30–45 MINS TO TURN FOR ASHBURY (MAP 12) →

MAP 11

TO IDSTONE, ½ MILE (1KM)

IDSTONE HILL

WATER TAP BY BARN – SUPPLY INTERMITTENT

HEAP OF OLD TYRES

019

TRACK STARTS CLIMBING AGAIN

SIGN FOR EASTBROOK VALLEY, 500M

SOFT, LEVEL TRACK

SIGN FOR ROYAL OAK BISHOPSTONE

TO BISHOPSTONE, ½ MILE (1KM)

RIDGEWAY FARM

018

BRIDLEWAY TO BISHOPSTONE 1 MILE (1·6KM)

10

12

trailblazer

0 ¼ mile

0 APPROX SCALE 500m

← 25–40 MINS TO FOXHILL (MAP 10) RIDGEWAY FARM ← 25–40 MINS FROM TURN FOR ASHBURY (MAP 12)

at the end of the lane by the village pond (look for a sign 'Oxon Place leading to The City') and is a very popular place for B&B. The lady has been running the show for years and provides first-rate accommodation and also a swimming pool, though be wary of two things: firstly, there's no internet; and secondly, you'll need to book well ahead as this place has many admirers and is beloved by some of the walking companies. B&B costs from £30pp (sgl occ £55).

Airbnb (see p20) options may include a room in an 18th-century cottage and one in a manor house.

After the junction at Ridgeway Farm the track becomes lined with trees on both sides and the walking is easy along here owing to the track being surfaced with stone chippings and the banning of motor vehicles.

At the next barn there is a track left, down Idstone Hill, to the hamlet of Idstone (half a mile/1km); Connect's 47 and Thamesdown's Sat X47 **bus** services stop here; see pp47-51 for further details. From this junction to Bishopstone, via Idstone, it's a little over 1¼ miles/2km. There is also a **water tap** by the barn a few metres down the Idstone Hill turning.

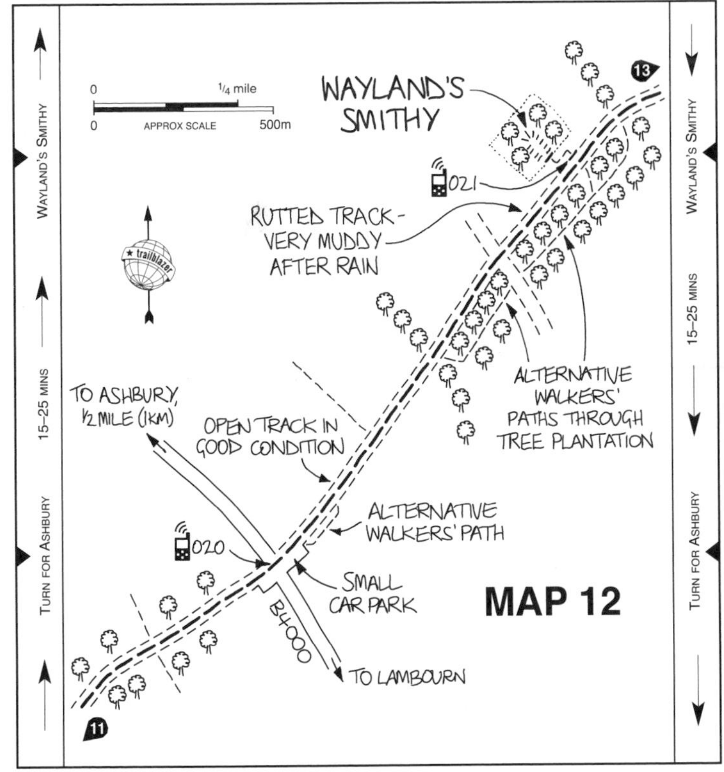

You're likely to hear the noise of the upcoming B4000 road crossing a good few minutes before you reach it. It comes up Ashbury Hill from Shrivenham and Ashbury, in the north, to cross the Ridgeway and continue south to the Lambourn villages. From this crossing (Map 12) it is about half a mile/1km down to the village of Ashbury.

ASHBURY

This is another delightful village in the string of settlements running parallel to the Ridgeway. The centre of Ashbury – spiritually, if not geographically – is the **Village Shop** (☎ 01793 710068, 🖳 www.ashburyshop.co.uk; Mon-Sat 8am-5.30pm) and its ***Jam Jar Tea Room*** (same hours), serving good coffee and cakes as well as home-made sandwiches from its fridge (from £1.50) but not lunches as such.

There is also a **post office**, though it has limited opening hours (Wed & Fri 9.30-11.30am), in the ***Rose & Crown Inn*** (☎ 01793 710222, 🖳 www.roseandcrowninn.co.uk; 2S/2T/4D, most en suite others share bathroom, ☕; WI-FI; Ⓛ; 🐕), occupies a commanding position in the centre of the village. Rates start from £40pp (sgl/sgl occ £65). Bar snacks are available and the menu (**food** Mon-Sat noon-2pm & 6-9pm, Sun noon-3pm) has a wide range of main courses including Wiltshire ham, hand-cut chips & fried eggs (£9.95). This is a popular place for Ridgeway walkers to stay and they are always made to feel welcome.

Connect's 47 and Thamesdown's X47 **bus** services stop here; see pp47-51 for further details.

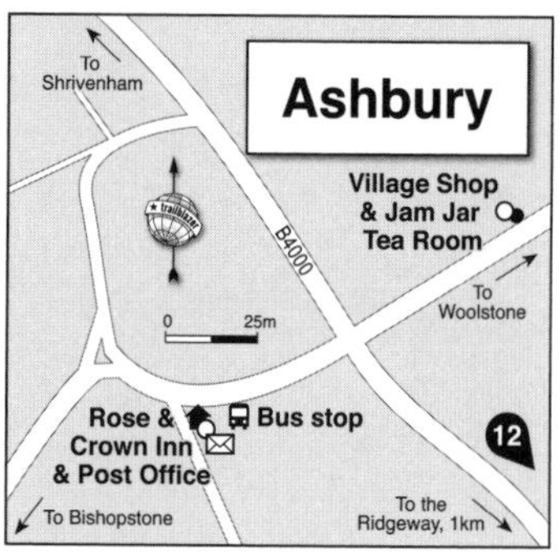

Around 15 minutes further along the closed-in track you will come to a short path on your left for Wayland's Smithy and by this time tall stands of trees will also be lining the track to your right. There is something a little eerie about this place, especially on a misty morning. **Wayland's Smithy** (see box below) isn't, and never really was, a smithy (blacksmith's/forge).

❑ Wayland's Smithy

This is a Neolithic long barrow. It was built in stages but was started around 3590BC as a burial place for members of the important ruling families in this area. The barrow itself is set in a small fenced wood and the entrance passageway that leads to the burial chamber is flanked by four huge sarsen stones. It's not possible to go far into the underground chambers, but nevertheless it's still an impressive construction when viewed just from the outside.

The name of this long barrow dates from a couple of thousand years after it was built and comes from 'Wayland', the Saxon god of smiths. Apparently he made the shoes for the Uffington White Horse and will even shoe your horse for you if you leave it here, overnight, with some payment – cash only.

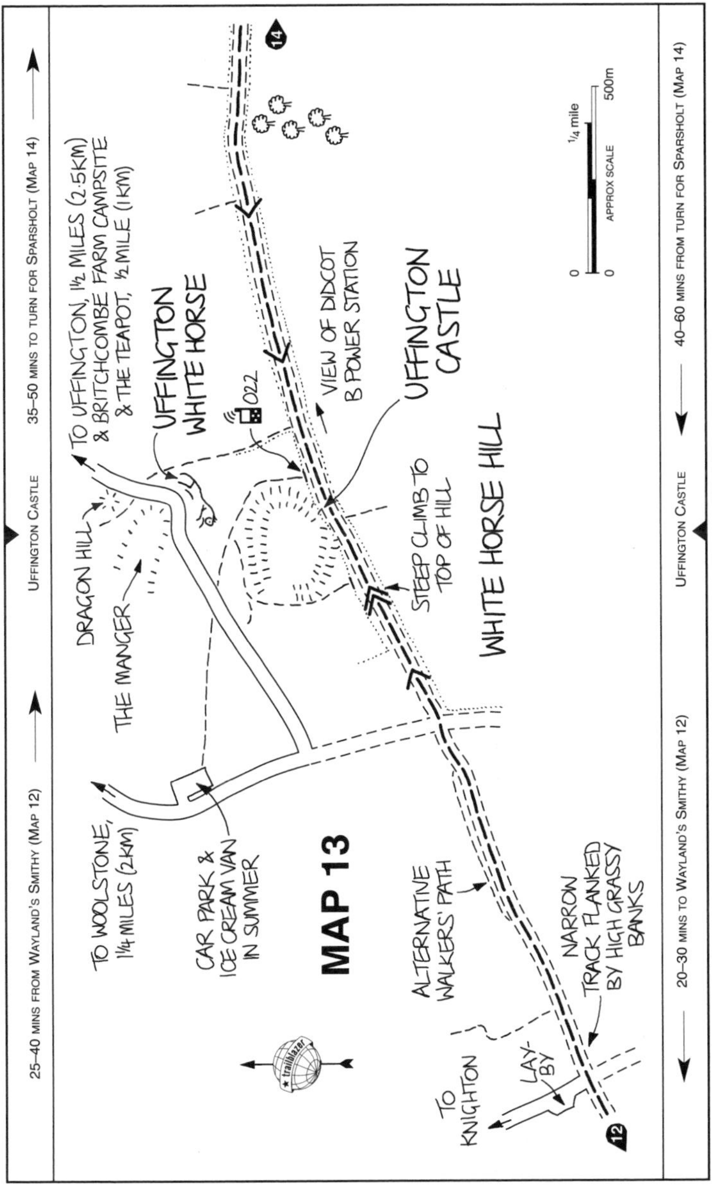

25–40 mins from Wayland's Smithy (Map 12) →
Uffington Castle
35–50 mins to turn for Sparsholt (Map 14) →

MAP 13

TO WOOLSTONE, 1¼ MILES (2KM)
THE MANGER
DRAGON HILL
TO UFFINGTON, 1½ MILES (2.5KM) & BRITCHCOMBE FARM CAMPSITE & THE TEAPOT, ½ MILE (1KM)
UFFINGTON WHITE HORSE
CAR PARK & ICE CREAM VAN IN SUMMER
022
VIEW OF DIDCOT B POWER STATION
ALTERNATIVE WALKERS' PATH
STEEP CLIMB TO TOP OF HILL
UFFINGTON CASTLE
TO KNIGHTON
LAY-BY
WHITE HORSE HILL
NARROW TRACK FLANKED BY HIGH GRASSY BANKS
12
14
trailblazer
0 ¼ mile
0 APPROX SCALE 500m

← 20–30 mins to Wayland's Smithy (Map 12)
Uffington Castle
← 40–60 mins from turn for Sparsholt (Map 14)

The village of Woolstone can be reached by taking a left turn down the hill at the next crossroads (Map 13). It's about 1¼ miles/2km to the village.

WOOLSTONE

This is a very small, picturesque village at the foot of the steep Uffington Hill. There are many attractive buildings and the only place offering food and accommodation is one of the most enchanting buildings of all, ***The White Horse*** (☎ 01367 820726, 🖳 www.whitehorsewoolstone.co.uk; 4D/2T, all en suite; ▾; WI-FI; Ⓛ; 🐕 £15 per night). It is an attractive 16th-century coaching inn situated in the 'centre' of the village that's open every day 11am-11pm. The comfortable **accommodation** is in the more modern building next to the pub and costs from £42.50pp (sgl occ £70). They serve **food** (daily noon-2.30pm & 6-9pm, in the summer pizzas only 3-9pm) in the bar and the restaurant; delicious open sandwiches cost from £6.50 and in the evening main courses such as lamb three ways (roast rump, pan-fried crispy belly and slow-cooked shoulder wrapped in pancetta) with roasted beetroot, sweet potato and mint jus (£18.95) are on the menu; there are also specials every day.

Thamesdown's Sat X47 **bus** service stops here; see pp47-51 for further details.

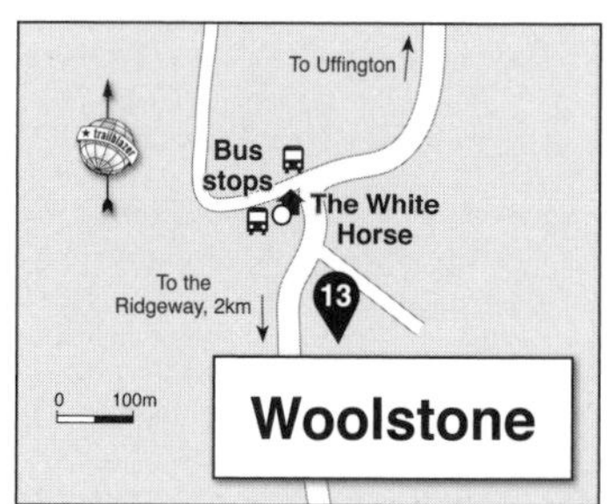

The climb up White Horse Hill to Uffington Castle is on a good track but it certainly gets steep towards the top; this is the toughest climb of this section but it doesn't last for long so count yourself lucky.

The National Trust area around this hill contains not only the aforementioned Uffington Castle and Uffington White Horse but also The Manger, a stunning coombe, lined with terraces, best viewed from the White Horse itself, and the perfectly formed, flat-topped Dragon Hill, just north of the White Horse, where St George battled with and slew the dragon.

Uffington Castle is the third of the big Iron Age hill forts you will have passed – the previous two being Barbury Castle (see p97) and Liddington Castle (see p108). The setting is certainly no less dramatic than Barbury's, though it's seven metres lower and only two-thirds its size. The double banks and ditches are still steep and well defined and the views from up here are magnificent.

Uffington White Horse lies on the side of the hill to the north of the castle and although it really is spectacular this is certainly not the best place from which to view it. In fact it's very difficult to get a good view of the horse from the ground. Short of hiring a helicopter, the better views are from down in the valley: a steep descent and a very disappointing walk back up. If you don't think you can manage it, don't worry – even from down there the views are frustratingly incomplete. Perhaps remember to drive along the B4507 (the road running parallel to the Ridgeway along here) another time for views of the horse.

❏ White horses

The **Uffington White Horse** (see Map 13) is the one that inspired them all. Scientists now think, after much debate, that it was first cut into the hillside around 800BC. It's over 100 metres long and superbly suggests the form of a horse rather than simply defining its outline. It's a mystery how the creators of the horse could cut it so well, given that the whole horse is only properly viewable from around a mile/1.5km away in the valley.

Without a shadow of a doubt, Uffington White Horse is the best of the lot, but there are various other white horses scattered around the countryside near here. None of them is nearly as ancient and they don't even get close to the fluid beauty of the Uffington horse. By the time you reach this horse you'll have already passed another example at Hackpen Hill (Map 3) that was cut into the hillside in 1838.

The oldest and one of the most visible of all the modern horses is the **Westbury White Horse**. This was cut in 1778 but at some point in the 1950s it was concreted over. The concrete was then painted white. Owing to some unsightly deterioration and discolouration in the concrete, the horse was given another coating of concrete and paint in 1995. The logic was that concrete is easier to maintain. Using that logic maybe there should be concrete over the Ridgeway, too?

Cherhill White Horse is on a hill of the same name that is south of the A4 near Cherhill village, 3¾ miles/6km west of Avebury. This horse is one of the older ones in the area having been cut into the hillside in 1780. It was fully restored in 2002 and is easily visible from the A4.

There are other **white horses**: between Milk Hill and Walkers Hill, close to the village of Alton Barnes, about 3¾ miles/6km due south of Avebury is a good specimen, cut in 1812 and cleaned up in 2002. There is a further example of a well cared for horse near Broad Town on a north-west-facing slope. This horse is about 3 miles/5km north-west of the Hackpen Hill horse, though it's unclear when it was cut – probably in the 1860s. On Pewsey Hill, just south of the village of Pewsey, about 4¼ miles/7km south of Marlborough, is a well-groomed 1937 white horse.

The youngest white horse in the area is on Roundway Hill in Devizes, about 7½ miles/12km south-west of Avebury. It was created for the millennium and is unusual in that it faces to the right. There was a much older white horse close to here but it has long since disappeared.

There is now a recognised **White Horse Trail** that follows a roughly circular route and visits all the white horses in Wiltshire. The trail is around 90 miles/145km long and illustrated guides can be bought from tourist information centres in the area.

For further information visit 💻 www.wiltshirewhitehorses.org.uk.

The **White Horse Hill area** really is one of the highlights of the Ridgeway trail so do take some time out to relax here and enjoy it. You've also got a fairly long stretch of plodding ahead, so you'll need the energy.

If you have decided to finish your day's walking at this point, you can walk down to the **campsite** at ***Britchcombe Farm*** (☎ 01367 821022, 💻 www.britchcombefarm.co.uk; over 70 pitches; 🐕 on a lead; all year); the location is hard to beat. Pitches are £7pp including use of the shower/toilet facilities. You are also allowed to have an open fire as long as it is on a site where there has previously been a fire and also is not near the tents – bags of firewood are sold by the campsite owner. There is also a tearoom called ***The Teapot*** (Mar-Dec, weekends & Bank Holidays 2-6pm) that serves cream teas.

To book one of the three **tipis and yurt** here call ☎ 07340 256631 (between 10am and 5pm); these cost from £70 per night and sleep up to four people. You need to bring your own bedding but can use the campsite's toilet/shower facilities; there is no electricity. The Shepherds Hut (from £50 for two people) does have electricity.

This is also the place to leave the trail and head down to the village of Uffington, if you so desire.

UFFINGTON

It's a bit of a trek to get to Uffington from the Ridgeway, and certainly a strenuous start to the day if walking back up to the trail, but there a couple of very good places to stay here, along with a decent pub, a shop with a post office, and even a museum.

Tom Brown's School Museum (💻 www.museum.uffington.net; Easter-end Oct, weekends & Bank Hols only 2-5pm; free) is logically located in the classroom featured in the 1857 novel *Tom Brown's School Days* by Thomas Hughes. Exhibits centre on local history and archaeology.

The **Post Office and Stores** (☎ 01367 820977; Mon-Sat 7am-6pm, Sun 8am-6pm; post office daily but opens one hour later than the shop) is well stocked with groceries and general supplies.

In the centre of the village is the cream-coloured ***Norton House*** (☎ 01367 820230, 💻 www.smoothhound.co.uk/hotels/nortonfaringdon; 1S/1D/1Qd, with two bathrooms, ☕; WI-FI; 🐕 £5 per visit) which offers B&B in a large 18th-century family home. Rates start at £32.50pp (sgl £40-45, three/four sharing costs £95/120). The owners can pick you up from, or drop you off at, the Ridgeway which could be a godsend if you're finding the going a bit tough; they just ask for a donation to their favourite charity.

The other permanent option for eating in the village is at ***The Fox & Hounds*** (☎ 01367 820680, 💻 www.uffingtonpub.co.uk; bar Mon-Sat 11am-11pm, Sun noon-10.30pm; **food** Mon-Fri noon-2pm & 6-9pm, Sat noon-3pm & 6-9pm, Sun noon-3pm), near the cottage where John Betjeman lived. It's not often that you find a village pub with such accommodating opening hours and as such there is little excuse to pass it by. Being a freehouse, there is a good selection of real ales; there may be some that you might not have tried before. The menu is fully of hearty pub grub which should satisfy the hungry walker. Mains start at £10.95 rising to £19.95 for the 28-day matured rib-eye steak. Their new conservatory means you can eat and have views of the White Horse. They also have four **rooms** (2T/1Tr/1Qd, all en suite; WI-FI; Ⓛ; 🐕 £15); rates are £34.50-37pp (sgl occ full room rate, £94-104 for three/four sharing); breakfast is £10 extra. The Icknield Way Morris Men (see box opposite) perform here several times a year.

Finally, a mobile van serving fish and chips stops by the village hall on a Tuesday evening (5-9pm).

Thamesdown's X47 **bus** (Swindon to Wantage Sat only) stops in the village; see pp47-51 for further details.

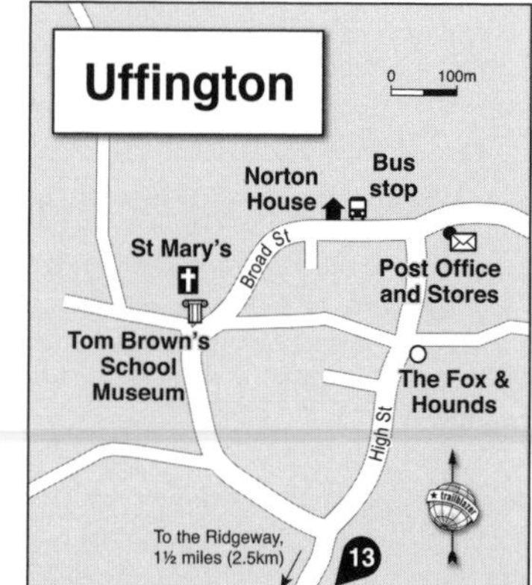

ROUTE GUIDE AND MAPS

❑ Morris dancing

If you hang around the pubs along the Ridgeway for long enough during the summer, you are likely to see some Morris dancing. Essentially the Morris teams (or sides) are performing traditional country dances and will often be accompanied by musicians. Each group of Morris men has its own particular outfit: embroidered smocks, waistcoats, decorated hats, neckerchiefs and clusters of bells abound. Depending on the dance they might also be waving handkerchiefs or hitting sticks together, sometimes with great force.

It is thought that these dances, often named after the villages where they were originally performed (such as Adderbury, Bampton, Ducklington or Stanton Harcourt), have also been influenced by traditional European dances. It's fairly safe to say that they were performed as long as 500 years ago, though many traditions died out in the 18th and 19th centuries.

The beginning of the 20th century saw a concerted effort to record the dances and music before they disappeared forever and the last 30 years in particular have seen an increased interest in performing the traditions.

Morris groups based in the Ridgeway area include the White Horse Morris Men (💻 www.whitehorsemorris.org.uk), Liddington Hall and Icknield Way Morris Men (💻 www.icknieldwaymorrismen.org.uk), the latter being one of the more active.

Many of the village pubs along the western half of the Ridgeway are popular venues for Morris dancers including the Fox & Hounds at Uffington, Royal Oak at Bishopstone, the Rose & Crown at Ashbury, and The Bell at Aldworth to name a few.

At the next crossroads (Map 14) a sealed road cuts across the Ridgeway. Turn right here for **Seven Barrows**, a group of, well, yes, seven barrows.

After you descend **Kingston Hill** you will reach a **track crossroads** that is an important junction: turn left here for Sparsholt (see p121); to stay on the route and for Hill Barn B&B (see below) go straight across; or turn right to reach Down Barn Farm (also see below), about half a mile/1km away. The turning is marked as a byway though there is no sign for Down Barn Farm; the farm itself is not visible from here as it's round a corner and in a dip.

SPARSHOLT FIRS [MAP 14, p120]

For a unique experience you might like to stay at ***Down Barn Farm*** (☎ 01367 820272, mob ☎ 0779 983 3115, 💻 pennydownbarnfarm@gmail.com; 1D/2T, ☛; limited WI-FI; Ⓛ £4.50; 🐕 £5). This place really is out on its own, set on a grassland farm that rears organic pigs and cattle. You might occasionally hear the cows mooing or the cock crowing but that's about it at this haven of peace and quiet. One twin is en suite and the other rooms share a bathroom if both are let. **B&B** costs £37.50-45pp (sgl occ £45). There are several pitches for **campers** (£5pp; available all year), but it is exposed up here. Campers can use the toilet and a sink; a shower costs £4 by arrangement. **Booking is essential**, even if you are camping. If arranged in advance the owner can prepare evening meals (£15-20pp for three courses) and breakfast for campers (£8), which is just as well as the next nearest place offering food is a good couple of miles (3km) away.

Booking is also recommended for ***Hill Barn B&B*** (☎ 01235 751236, ☎ 07885 368918, 💻 www.hillbarnbedandbreakfast.co.uk; 1S private bathroom, 1D/1T, both en suite, ☛; WI-FI; Ⓛ; 🐕 £5). B&B costs £40pp (sgl £40, sgl occ £50). The welcome is very friendly, there are drying facilities and evening meals are available by prior arrangement.

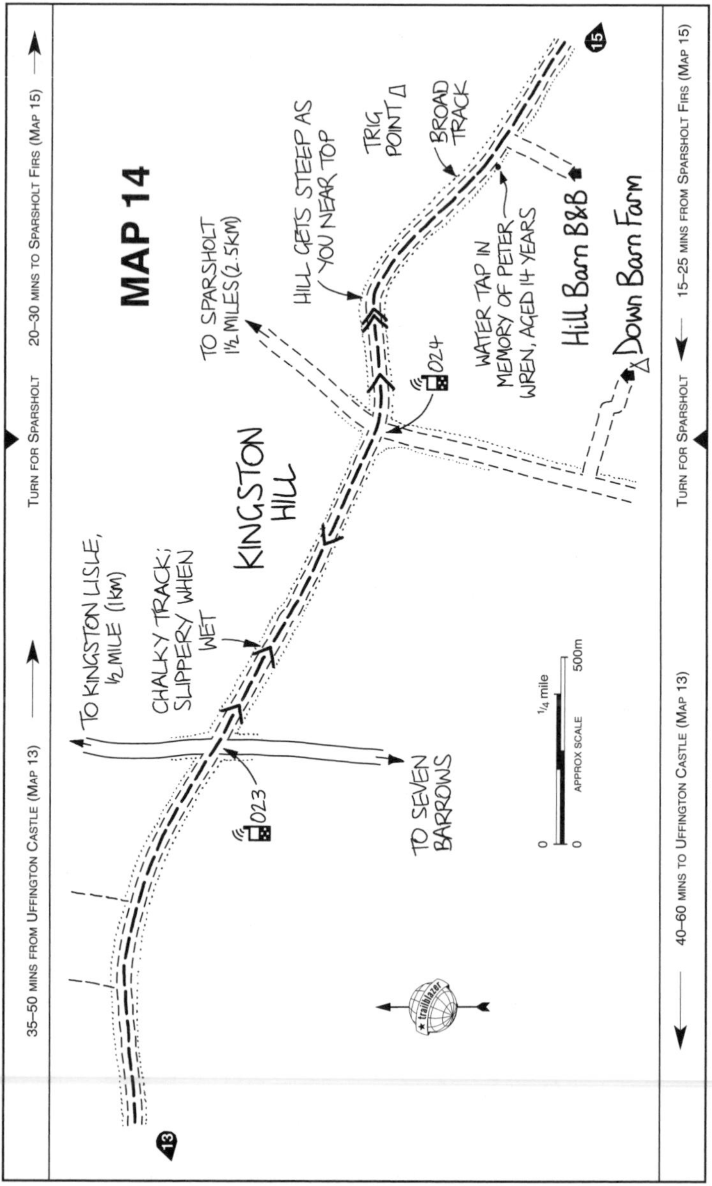

MAP 14

35–50 mins from Uffington Castle (Map 13) →

Turn for Sparsholt

20–30 mins to Sparsholt Firs (Map 15) →

TO KINGSTON LISLE, ½ MILE (1KM)

CHALKY TRACK; SLIPPERY WHEN WET

023

TO SEVEN BARROWS

KINGSTON HILL

TO SPARSHOLT 1½ MILES (2.5KM)

HILL GETS STEEP AS YOU NEAR TOP

TRIG POINT

024

BROAD TRACK

WATER TAP IN MEMORY OF PETER WREN, AGED 14 YEARS

Hill Barn B&B

Down Barn Farm

0 ¼ mile

0 APPROX SCALE 500m

← 40–60 mins to Uffington Castle (Map 13)

Turn for Sparsholt ←

15–25 mins from Sparsholt Firs (Map 15)

The furthest option for accommodation from the track crossroads is The Star Inn at Sparsholt; it is a 1½-mile/2.5km walk from the crossroads. Follow the track to the main road, turn right onto the road and follow it for 500m before turning left into the quiet village of Sparsholt. You can also reach Sparsholt via the turning off Map 15, but this route requires more road walking.

SPARSHOLT **[off MAP 14]**

The Star Inn (☎ 01235 751873, 🖳 www.thestarsparsholt.co.uk; 4D/2T/2Tr, all en suite, ▾; WI-FI; Ⓛ; 🐕 £10) is an inviting 17th-century country inn with well-kept accommodation; **B&B** costs from £52.50pp (sgl occ full room rate, three sharing room rate plus £10 extra) in a converted barn. Their menu (**food** Mon-Sat noon-2.30pm, Mon-Thur 6.30-9pm, Fri & Sat to 9.30pm, Sun noon-8pm) has plenty of filling dishes to satisfy the hungry walker.

There is no shop or post office in the village, but Thamesdown's X47 (Sat only) **bus** stops here; see pp47-51 for further details.

On your way up **Hackpen Hill** the valley drops away very steeply to the north giving excellent views of the **Devil's Punchbowl** (Map 15). You can get closer to the punchbowl by taking the path that branches left from the track where there is a stile structure marking the path junction. Although this should be a path, it seems to run straight through a planted field with no visible trail.

You'll soon cross the road junction (Map 16) that has a left turn down to Letcombe Bassett and further on there is a track on the left that joins up with the road; using either of these turnings **Letcombe Bassett** is about half a mile/1km away. You could also use these to walk to Wantage but it'd probably be better to wait for the next road junction for that. Shortly ahead there is a path on the left – yet another opportunity to head down to Letcombe Bassett. If you have no pressing matters to attend to in the village, it's probably not worth a detour. However, Thamesdown's X47 **bus** (Sat only) stops here; see pp47-51.

It was just a little further on from here that I once passed a nun on the track. She had walked from St Mary's Convent in Wantage, around three miles/5km away. You might have some unlikely encounters on the Ridgeway – owls or deer, for instance, but meeting a nun up here must now be added to the list.

On reaching **Segsbury Farm** (on your right), there is a 100-metre track (to the left) up to **Segsbury Camp**: this is also called Letcombe Castle. It's more than double the size of Barbury Castle but far less popular; you'll usually have the place to yourself. Like Barbury Castle (see p97), this was an Iron Age hill fort and evidence of roundhouses were found during excavations in the 1990s.

It's also this track that you should take if you want to visit Letcombe Regis. This isn't the only way to the village – you could follow the road past the Court Hill Centre – but it's the most convenient. *(continued on p124)*

❑ Important note – walking times

All times in this book refer only to the time spent walking. You will need to add 20-30% to allow for rests, photography, checking the map, drinking water etc.

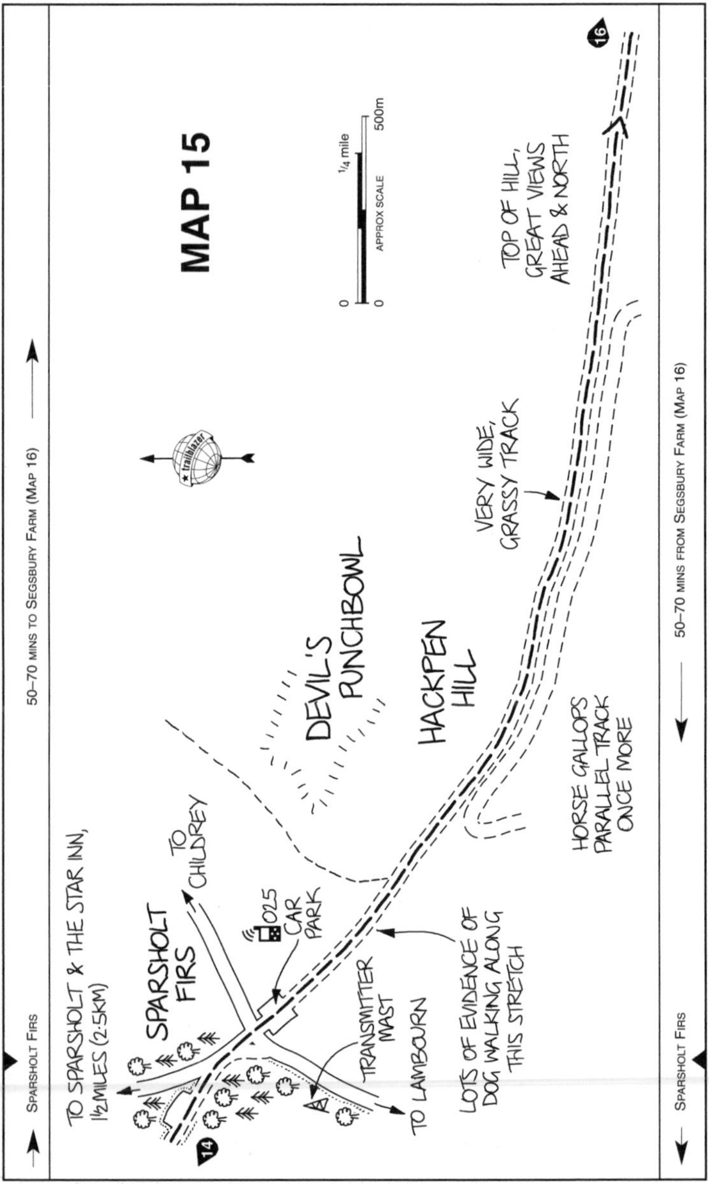

MAP 15

0 ¼ mile
0 500m
APPROX SCALE

→ SPARSHOLT FIRS — 50–70 MINS TO SEGSBURY FARM (MAP 16) →

← SPARSHOLT FIRS — 50–70 MINS FROM SEGSBURY FARM (MAP 16) ←

14

TO SPARSHOLT & THE STAR INN, 1½MILES (2·5KM)

SPARSHOLT FIRS

TO CHILDREY

025 CAR PARK

TRANSMITTER MAST

TO LAMBOURN

LOTS OF EVIDENCE OF DOG WALKING ALONG THIS STRETCH

DEVIL'S PUNCHBOWL

HACKPEN HILL

VERY WIDE, GRASSY TRACK

HORSE GALLOPS PARALLEL TRACK ONCE MORE

TOP OF HILL, GREAT VIEWS AHEAD & NORTH

16

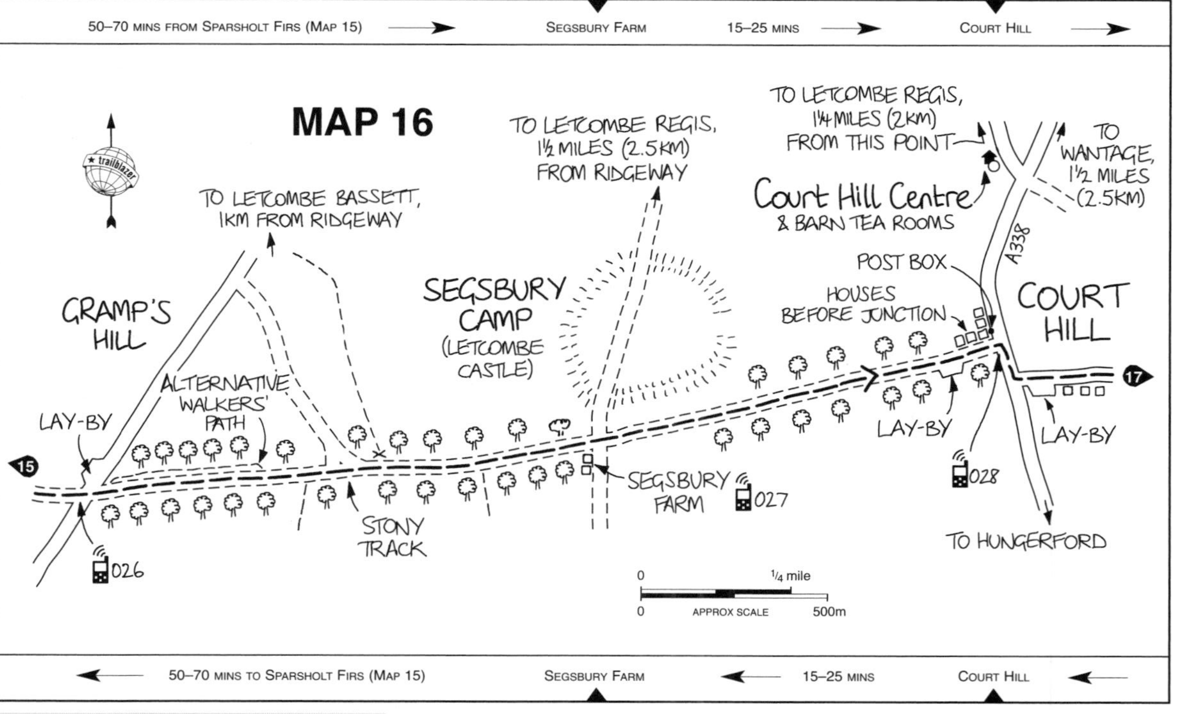
50–70 MINS FROM SPARSHOLT FIRS (MAP 15)
SEGSBURY FARM
15–25 MINS
COURT HILL
MAP 16
TO LETCOMBE BASSETT, 1KM FROM RIDGEWAY
TO LETCOMBE REGIS, 1½ MILES (2.5KM) FROM RIDGEWAY
TO LETCOMBE REGIS, 1¼ MILES (2KM) FROM THIS POINT
TO WANTAGE, 1½ MILES (2.5KM)
Court Hill Centre
& BARN TEA ROOMS
A338
POST BOX
HOUSES BEFORE JUNCTION
COURT HILL
GRAMP'S HILL
SEGSBURY CAMP
(LETCOMBE CASTLE)
ALTERNATIVE WALKERS' PATH
LAY-BY
15
17
LAY-BY
LAY-BY
SEGSBURY FARM
027
028
026
STONY TRACK
TO HUNGERFORD
0
¼ mile
0
APPROX SCALE
500m
50–70 MINS TO SPARSHOLT FIRS (MAP 15)
SEGSBURY FARM
15–25 MINS
COURT HILL

(continued from p121) You'll also have the bonus of passing through Segsbury Camp on your way. From Court Hill Centre, it's about 1¼ miles/2km to the centre of the village.

LETCOMBE REGIS

This village, another in the chain of 'spring line' settlements below the Wessex Downs, dates back well over a thousand years although the 'Regis' part of the name was only added during the reign of Richard II (1377-99). However, the regal connections date from well before then as it was the property of King Stephen in the 12th century and there was a royal hunting lodge here in the 13th and 14th centuries.

The oldest remaining building in the village is the church, St Andrew's, parts of which date back to the 12th century though some of the houses don't look as if they are a great deal younger.

Letcombe Regis and its neighbour, Letcombe Bassett, are known for the watercress beds that covered the land between them though 'Regis' is also home to four racing stables, which generate considerably more income.

There aren't any shops or services but nevertheless it would make a convenient and enjoyable overnight stop. Thamesdown's X47 **bus** stops here (Sat only); see pp47-51 for further details.

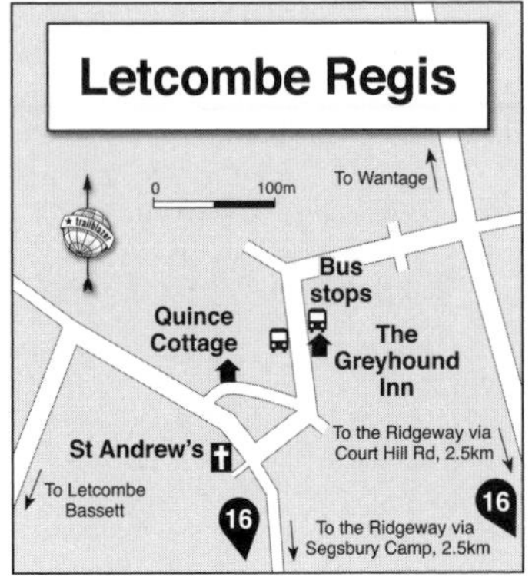

Where to stay, eat and drink

The Greyhound Inn (☎ 01235 771969, 🖳 www.thegreyhoundletcombe.co.uk; 6D/2D or T, all en suite, ▼; WI-FI; Ⓛ; 🐕 £15) is a Georgian-style, traditional country inn with some lovely rooms (£42.50-65pp, sgl occ from £65) some of which can sleep additional children, but not more than two adults. Breakfast is served Mon-Sat 7.30-9.30am, Sat & Sun 8-10am. They also serve superior **food** (Mon-Thur noon-2.30pm & 6-9pm, Fri & Sat noon-2.30pm & 6-9.30pm, Sun noon-3.30pm & 6-8.30pm) and booking is recommended; the menu may include such delights as salt-marsh pan-roast lamb rump and slow-cooked shoulder, with smoked garlic dumpling, turnips, hispi cabbage and cider sauce (£17), or sweet potato and goats cheese hash brown, pickled wild mushroom, kale pesto, mushroom and thyme velouté (£11.50).

Nearby is ***Quince Cottage*** (☎ 01235 763652, 🖳 www.quincebandb.com; 1S/1D/1Tr, shared facilities, ▼; WI-FI; Ⓛ £6), a charming 18th-century thatched cottage that charges £40pp (sgl/sgl occ from £40, three sharing £35pp). This is a great place to stay and you are assured a friendly welcome. An excellent cooked breakfast is also served. Book well ahead as this place is deservedly popular with walkers!

Soon after here, at the foot of **Court Hill**, the Ridgeway crosses the main A338 road coming from Wantage in the north and Hungerford in the south. Turn left for Wantage (see opposite), a town with plenty of shops, banks and other services just over 1½ miles/2.5km away, and also for Court Hill Centre, about 500 metres along the road. ***Court Hill Centre*** (☎ 01235 760253, 🖳 www.courthill.org.uk; 45 beds; Ⓛ; open all year) has accommodation in a **bunkhouse**:

there are family (4-bed bunk rooms) and dormitory rooms at £19.50pp (£16.50pp for under 18s). A limited number of **camping pitches** (£8.50pp, £7.50 for under 18s; all year) is also available. Breakfast and packed lunches, both from £6.50, and an evening meal, from £8.50, are available but all must be ordered in advance. There is a decent self-catering kitchen. Campers have access to a toilet during the night and use of the other facilities during opening hours. Advance booking for both the bunkhouse and the campsite is recommended, as the bunkhouse in particular is often booked by groups on a sole occupancy basis.

If you're just passing by and not staying the night, you could always stop off at ***Barn Tea Rooms*** (daily 10.30am-4pm) where you'll find teas, coffees and cold drinks along with cakes, light lunches and ice-creams; they also do a very tasty fishfinger sandwich for £3.50.

WANTAGE [see map p127]

Despite the lengthy walk from the Ridgeway, Wantage is a good place to stop and recharge your batteries. The town is famous as the birthplace of King Alfred the Great (849-99), the only Anglo-Saxon ruler who was not defeated by the Vikings. You can see his statue in the centre of Market Place.

Wantage has a compact centre with most of the shops, restaurants and pubs within a minute's walk of Market Place.

Vale & Downland Museum (☎ 01235 771447, 🖳 www.wantage-museum.com; Mon-Sat 9.30am-4pm; free but donations appreciated) is well worth a visit if you have some free time. There is a permanent historical exhibition and art gallery; the exhibition concentrates on the history of the town and features plenty of artefacts from King Alfred's time to the present. Part of the museum is housed in an 18th-century barn that was moved from a nearby village and rebuilt here, a gift shop, visitor information point (see below) and a **café** (see Where to eat and drink).

Services

There is a **visitor information point** (☎ 01235 760176; Mon-Sat 9.30am-4pm) at the museum (see above), with lots of free information about local attractions. For online information about Wantage visit 🖳 www.wantage.com.

There are branches of plenty of **banks** (such as HSBC, Barclays, NatWest & Nationwide), all with **ATMs**, around Market Place. You'll also find a Boots **chemist** (Mon-Sat 9am-5.30pm, Sun 10am-4pm) on Market Place and a large Waitrose **supermarket** (Mon-Thur & Sat 8am-8pm, Fri 8am-9pm, Sun 10am-4pm) just a few steps away. There's also a **farmers' market** (see box p21).

The **post office** (Mon-Fri 9am-5.30pm, Sat 9am-12.30pm) is in the Costcutter shop (daily 5am-11pm).

If you need **bike repairs** you should head to Ridgeway Cycles (☎ 01235 764445, 🖳 www.ridgewaycycles.com; Mon-Sat 9am-5.30pm), on Newbury St. There are free **public toilets** at the entrance to the pay and display car park.

Buses stop on Market Place and include services to: Oxford (Stagecoach's Nos 31 & X30, Thames Travel's X32); Letcombe Regis, Sparsholt, Kingston Lisle, Uffington and Swindon (Thamesdown's Nos X47, Sat only); Didcot Parkway and Abingdon (Thames Travel No 32A); see pp47-51 for further details.

Where to stay

If you are walking from the Ridgeway to Wantage, the chances are you'll be intending to stay overnight here, too.

Alfred's Lodge (☎ 01235 762409, ☎ 07884 002203; 🖳 www.alfredslodge.co.uk; 1S/2T/3D/1Qd, all en suite; WI-FI; Ⓛ £6.50; 🐕), 23 Ormond Rd, is at the junction of Ormond Rd and Trinder Rd. B&B costs £45pp (sgl/sgl occ costs from £65, three/four sharing room rate plus £15pp).

Right on Market Place is ***The Bear Hotel*** (☎ 01235 766366, 💻 www.thebearwantage.co.uk; 9S/16D/6T/4Tr/1Qd, all en suite, 🐕; WI-FI). B&B costs from £40pp (sgl/sgl occ £60-70, £90/100 for three/four sharing).

Just down the way, ***The Bell Inn*** (☎ 01235 763718, 💻 www.thebellinnwantage.co.uk; 3S/5D or T/3Tr/1Qd, most en suite; 🐕; WI-FI) is the cheap option in town, with singles for £25-35, while for two people sharing a room it's £30-40pp.

Apart from the above you're pretty much confined to the options listed on **Airbnb** (see p20).

Where to eat and drink

There are two very good upmarket eateries open during the day for lunch. ***Umami Deli*** (☎ 01235 766245, 💻 www.umami-deli.co.uk; Mon-Sat 8am-5pm), on Newbury St, does some lovely 'gourmet sandwiches' from £3.20 (for sweet chilli humous, roasted vegetables and herbs), and ***Wildwood Kitchen*** (☎ 01235 424327, 💻 www.wildwoodkitchen.co.uk/wantage.html; Tue-Sat 10am-11pm, Sun & Mon 10am-10pm), on Market Place, which also does some great sandwiches including lemon and thyme chicken, tomato and avocado (£8.35). They also open in the evenings, mainly pizzas (from £7.75) and pastas (from £9.45 for the wild mushroom tagliatelle).

Less fancy lunchtime snacks and sandwiches can be had at the branches of ***Subway*** (Sun-Thur 7am-8pm, Fri & Sat to 9pm), on Newbury St, and ***Greggs*** (Mon-Fri 7am-5pm, Sat 7.30am-5pm), by The Bear on Market Place. There is also a branch of ***Costa*** (Mon-Sat 6.30am-7.30pm, Sun 8am-6.30pm) coffee shop on Market Place if you fancy a hot drink and a snack.

For something different you can enjoy home-made soup of the day for £4.20, or a range of salads with jacket potatoes for £5.25-6.30, in the light and airy *café* area (9.30am-3.45pm) at the **Vale & Downland Museum** (see p125).

There are plenty of places in Wantage offering food in the evenings. This includes two good pubs in close proximity to each other on the western side of Market Square. ***King Alfred's Head*** (☎ 01235 771595, 💻 kingalfs.com; food daily noon-3pm, Tue-Sat 6.30-9pm) is one of the best. Their lunchtime snack menu includes sandwiches such as smoked salmon on brown country bread with chive cream cheese (£4.90). Prices on the bistro-style dinner menu range from £8.90; dishes vary but may include steak and fries (£14.90). **Dogs** are allowed and they serve a good and regularly changing selection of real ales.

The Bear Hotel (see Where to stay; food Mon-Sat 11.30am-2.30pm & 6-9.30pm, Sun noon-3pm) is also a good place for food. They serve breakfast (Mon-Fri 7-9am, Sat & Sun 8-10am) for non residents; their full English (£10) might be just the thing to prepare you for a day of walking. In the evening, main courses start at around £12 but a beef wellington with dauphinoise potatoes, carrot purée and broccoli and Madeira jus costs £22. Booking is recommended.

Away from the pubs, ***Bistro 14*** (☎ 01235 771200, 💻 bistro-14.co.uk; Tue-Sat 11.45am-2.30pm & 6-9.30pm, Sun noon-2.30pm), on Wallingford St, the A417, has a fairly standard menu of classic favourites (eg slow roast belly of pork, thyme jus, dauphinoise potatoes, braised red cabbage; £14.95), but it often has a good atmosphere and the food is heart and tasty.

Tasty Thai food can be found at ***Yummy Thai*** (☎ 01235 768222; Thur-Sun noon-2.30pm & daily 6-11pm) who also provide a takeaway service. The menu is guaranteed to make your mouth water and the prices are very reasonable – main dishes cost from £6.25, though most are around £9-11. The *masaman* chicken curry for £10.50 is recommended.

There are two 'Indian' restaurants in town vying for your custom – ***House of Spice*** (☎ 01235 760707, 💻 www.houseofspice-wantage.co.uk; daily noon-2pm, Sun-Thur 5.30-11.30pm, Fri & Sat 5.30pm-midnight), which is part of a chain (see also p160) and ***Sylheti Spice*** (☎ 01235 764164/762651, 💻 sylhetispice.webs.com; Sun-Thur 6-11.30pm, Fri & Sat 6pm-midnight). They are just what you would expect and there really isn't much to choose

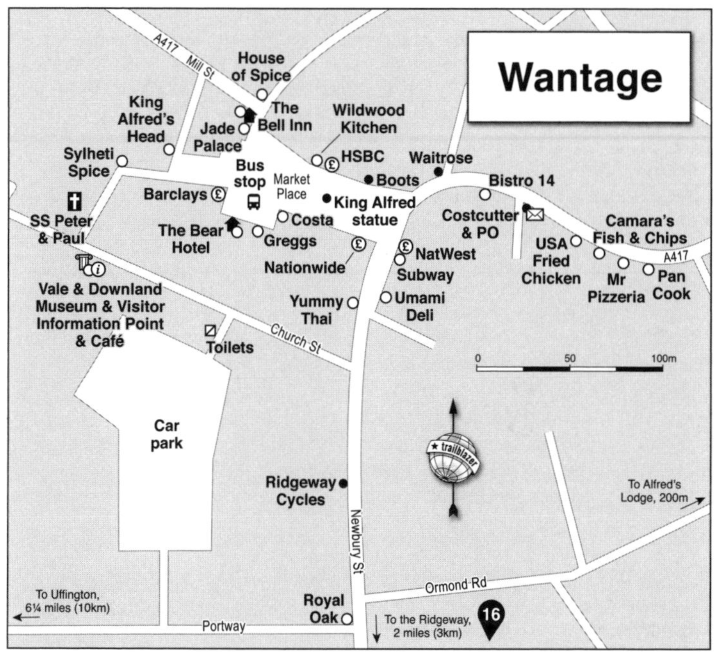

between them though you can take your own alcohol to Sylheti.

Fast food and takeaway outlets abound and include ***Camara's Fish & Chips*** (Mon-Thur 11am-2pm & 4-10.30pm, Fri-Sat 11am-10.30pm, Sun noon-10pm), ***Mr Pizzeria*** (daily 4pm-late) and ***USA Fried Chicken*** (Sun-Thur 3-11pm, Fri & Sat to 2.30am). ***Pan Cook*** (☎ 01235 766287; daily 5-11.30pm) and ***Jade Palace*** (☎ 01235 762832; Wed-Mon 5-11pm) are standard Chinese takeaways.

If you are after an excellent selection of real ales in a friendly atmosphere, you couldn't do better than head to the ***Royal Oak*** (☎ 01235 763129, 🖳 www.royaloakwantage.co.uk; bar Mon-Fri 5.30-11pm, Sat noon-2.30pm & 7-11pm, Sun noon-2pm & 7-10.30pm). With up to a dozen local ales on at any one time, not to mention a similar number of ciders, you'll be spoiled for choice – well worth a post-walk visit!

(WANTAGE &) COURT HILL TO GORING [MAPS 16-25]

Overview

This is an easy **14-mile/22.5km (4¼-6hrs)** section; add 2 miles/3km if you have stayed in Wantage. From Court Hill up to the crossing of the A34 road, the path is level, broad, grassy and exposed, similar to what you've become used to from the previous stages. After the A34 there is more tree cover and the path starts to undulate, though it hardly ever gets steep. The Ridgeway then gradually descends into the small town of Streatley, on the west bank of the river Thames, before crossing into Goring on the opposite bank. At the time of writing there is no source of drinking water on the trail between Court Hill and Streatley, so do make sure you set off with plenty.

This is actually something of a red-letter day on the trail. Once completed, you'll be virtually halfway on your Ridgeway odyssey. You'll notice that the path changes character after today, too, as you cross to the northern side of the Thames, leave the Wessex Downs behind and enter, in time, the more wooded upland scenery of the Chilterns. To appropriate that old footballing cliché, the Ridgeway is a trek of two halves – and after the end of this stage you'll have reached half-time.

Route

Where the Ridgeway arrives at the A338 (Map 16) to Wantage you need to make a right turn and follow it for all of a minute before turning left, back onto the track. The track is sealed for a while now and you'll pass several houses on your right before reaching Whitehouse Farm (Map 17) on the left; the tarmac fades to soft grass or mud, depending on the weather conditions. When you arrive at the T-junction, you'll have another chance to visit Court Hill Centre by turning left.

After you have crossed the B4494 and rejoined the broad grassy track, you will come to a **large monument**, on your right. It consists of a marble column set on a large square base with steps on all sides. At the top of the column is a cross; it is in memory of Baron Wantage (1832-1901) who, amongst other things, expanded the nearby Lockinge estate.

A further mile (1.5km) down the track, but this time on the left, you will see a **reservoir** (Map 18). It's a low, square red-brick structure, surrounded by trees and fenced in. The walking along here is on the same broad grassy track you have been on for some time and it will be with you for a while yet.

Around 20 minutes after passing the reservoir you will come to a sealed road (Map 19) crossing the Ridgeway. This is the road to East Hendred, 2½ miles/4km to the north. After this junction the Ridgeway is joined by gallops on the right that stick with the track until the next road junction at the **Bury Down** car parks – the road here goes north to Chilton and south to West Ilsley, about one mile (1.5km) away; Kennections' bus No 6a operates from West Ilsley to Newbury via Chievely.

Just before the car parks you'll begin to hear the noise of the A34 up ahead. Harwell International Business Centre is clearly visible just over a mile to the north from here.

When you arrive at the **A34 junction** (Map 20) you can either use the tunnel underneath or try to cross it. There are paths catering to both these options but it is far safer to use the tunnel. The track down to it drops steeply and bends to the right then the left. Inside the tunnel, on the right side, are some murals depicting traditional historical scenes from the area.

Just a few minutes after the tunnel, on the left of the track, almost enclosed by the shrubbery, is a **stone memorial** inscribed with the name of Hugh Frederick Grosvenor, a 2nd Lieutenant in the Lifeguards who, aged just 19, was killed here in an armoured car accident on 9 April 1947. *(continued on p132)*

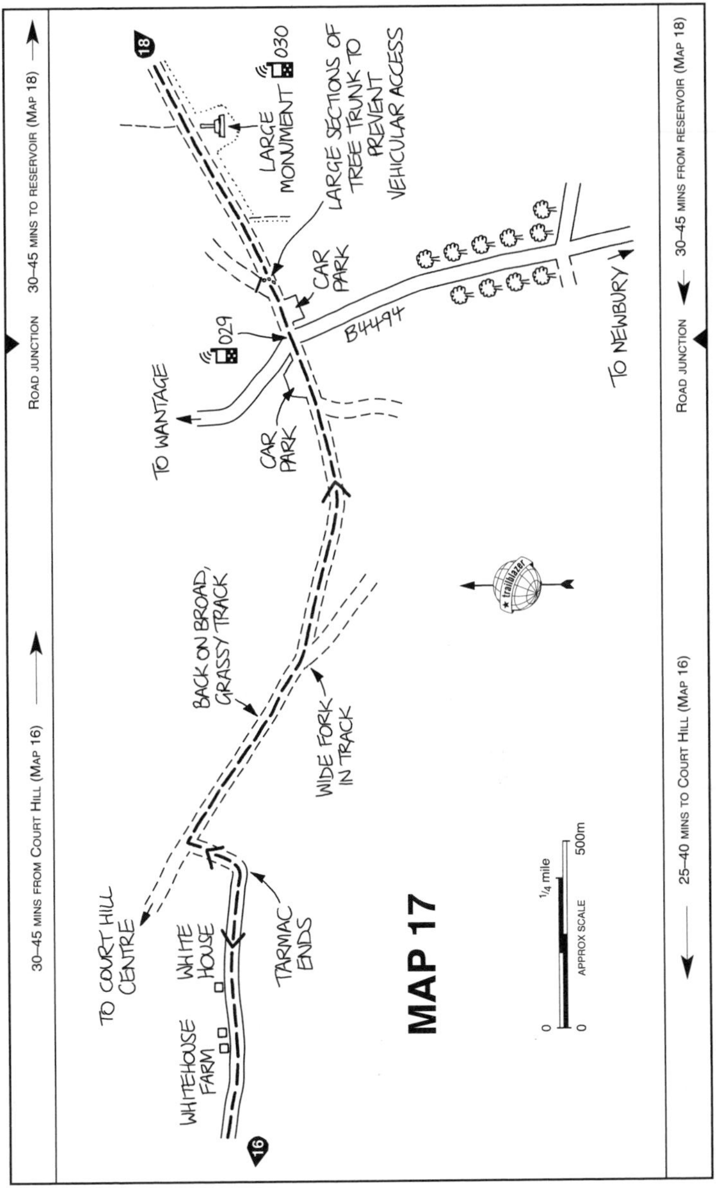

30–45 MINS FROM COURT HILL (MAP 16) →

ROAD JUNCTION

30–45 MINS TO RESERVOIR (MAP 18) →

← 25–40 MINS TO COURT HILL (MAP 16)

ROAD JUNCTION

← 30–45 MINS FROM RESERVOIR (MAP 18)

MAP 17

APPROX SCALE

0 ¼ mile

0 500m

16

WHITEHOUSE FARM

WHITE HOUSE

TARMAC ENDS

TO COURT HILL CENTRE

BACK ON BROAD, GRASSY TRACK

WIDE FORK IN TRACK

CAR PARK

TO WANTAGE

029

B4494

TO NEWBURY

CAR PARK

LARGE SECTIONS OF TREE TRUNK TO PREVENT VEHICULAR ACCESS

LARGE MONUMENT

030

18

trailblazer

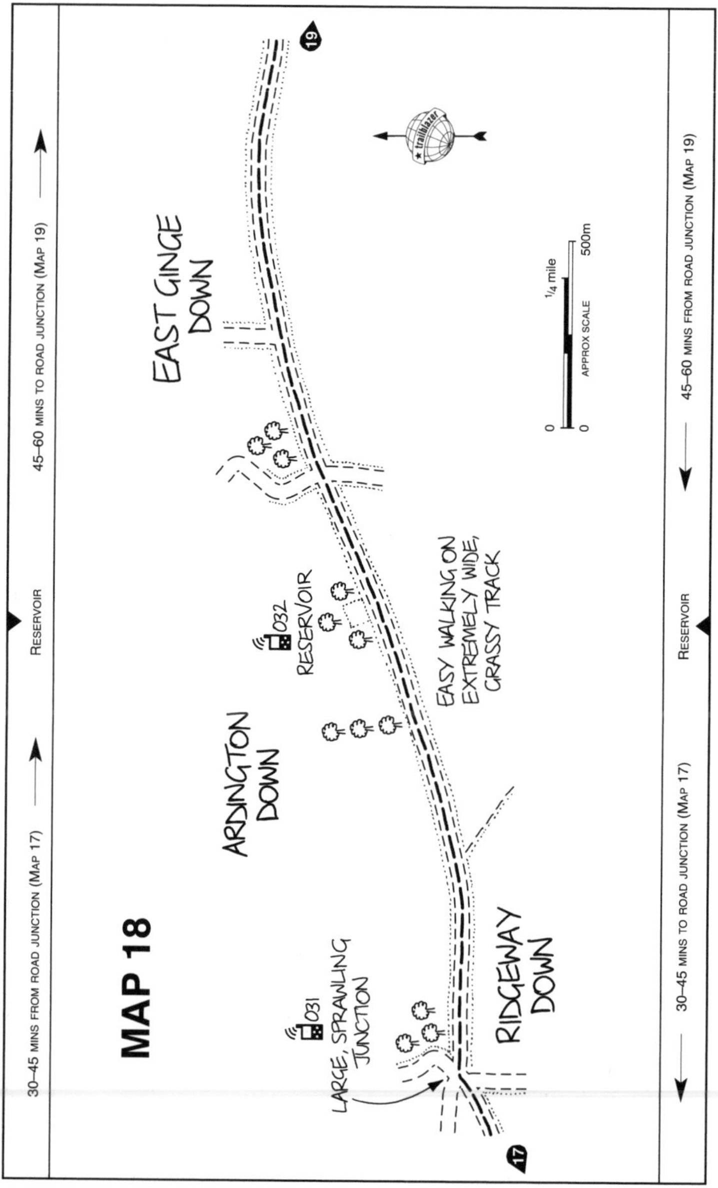

MAP 18

30–45 MINS FROM ROAD JUNCTION (MAP 17) →
RESERVOIR
45–60 MINS TO ROAD JUNCTION (MAP 19) →

LARGE, SPRAWLING JUNCTION
031
RIDGEWAY DOWN
ARDINGTON DOWN
032
RESERVOIR
EASY WALKING ON EXTREMELY WIDE, GRASSY TRACK
EAST GINGE DOWN
trailblazer
APPROX SCALE
0
0
1/4 mile
500m
17
19

← 30–45 MINS TO ROAD JUNCTION (MAP 17)
RESERVOIR
← 45–60 MINS FROM ROAD JUNCTION (MAP 19)

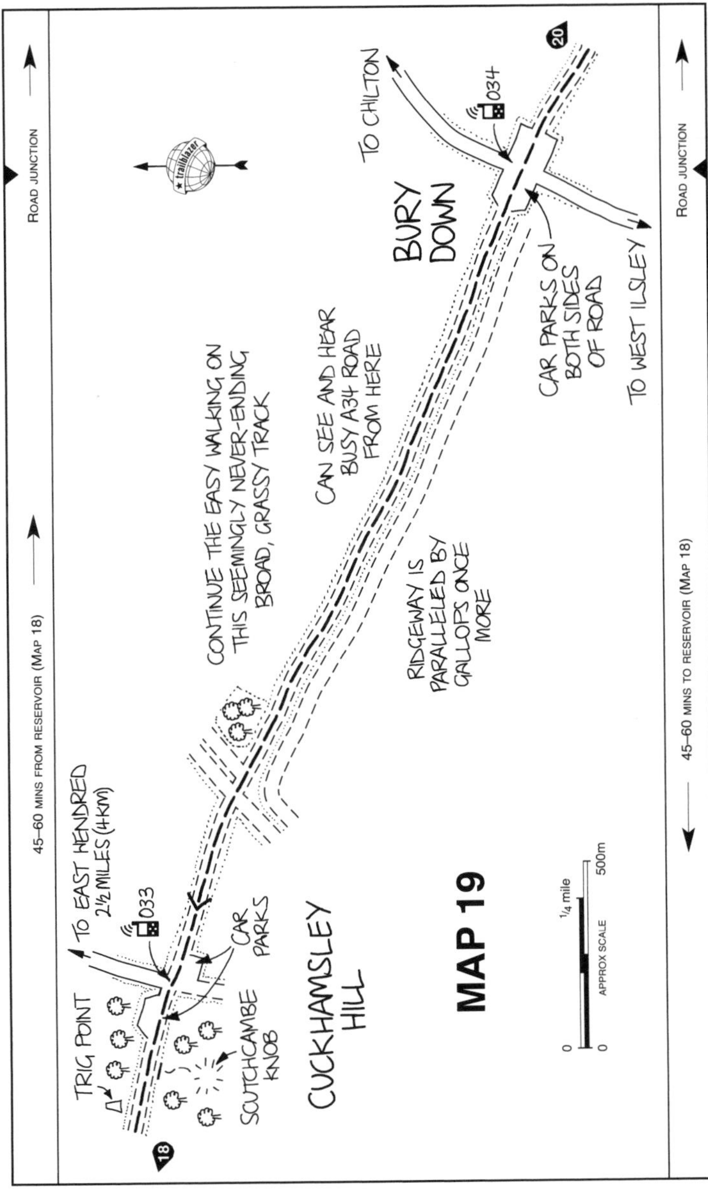

45–60 MINS FROM RESERVOIR (MAP 18) →
ROAD JUNCTION →

TRIG POINT
TO EAST HENDRED 2½ MILES (4KM)
033
18
SCUTCHCAMBE KNOB
CAR PARKS
CUCKHAMSLEY HILL
CONTINUE THE EASY WALKING ON THIS SEEMINGLY NEVER-ENDING BROAD, GRASSY TRACK
trailblazer
CAN SEE AND HEAR BUSY A34 ROAD FROM HERE
TO CHILTON
BURY DOWN
RIDGEWAY IS PARALLELED BY GALLOPS ONCE MORE
034
CAR PARKS ON BOTH SIDES OF ROAD
20
TO WEST ILSLEY

MAP 19

0 ¼ mile
0 APPROX SCALE 500m

← 45–60 MINS TO RESERVOIR (MAP 18)
ROAD JUNCTION →

(continued from p128) Look to the south occasionally and soon you'll get a glimpse of East Ilsley – a very welcome sight if you started at Foxhill earlier in the day. There is still the best part of two miles/3km to go, however, but the path follows the same broad grassy track that has by now become very familiar.

There are four possible ways down (Map 21) into **East Ilsley** from the Ridgeway and they are all less than a mile apart. The second way is probably the best choice – it's the most direct with easy walking. However, as the last two leave the Ridgeway that bit later, they give you slightly more of a head-start when you pick it up again. It doesn't really matter though – leaving by any of the tracks you'll have to walk about a mile into the village.

EAST ILSLEY [see map p134]

From the 17th century to 1934 East Ilsley was known as a venue for huge sheep markets. At their peak, drovers would descend on the village filling it with up to 70,000 sheep; it has been a lot quieter here since the market stopped. Today it's an attractive-enough place with two pubs, both of which provide food and accommodation, and this

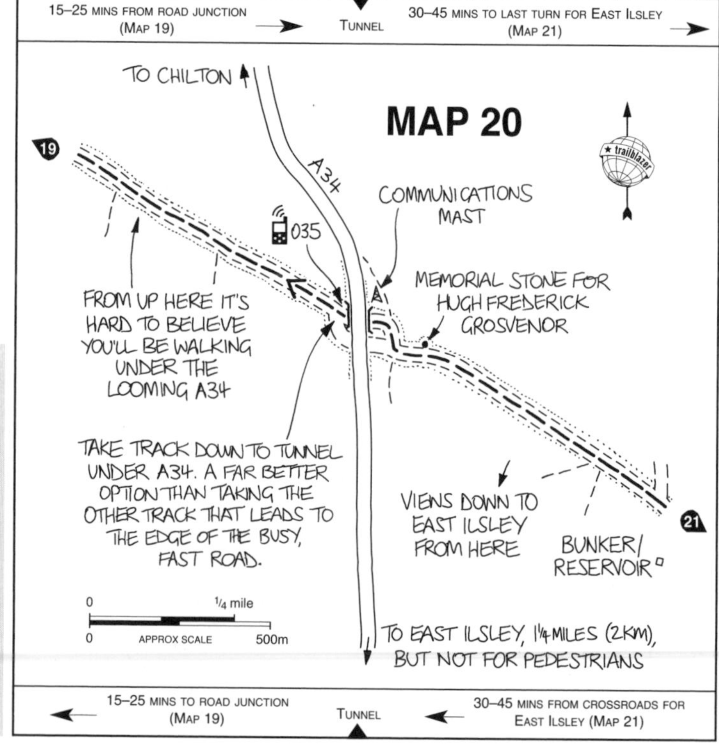

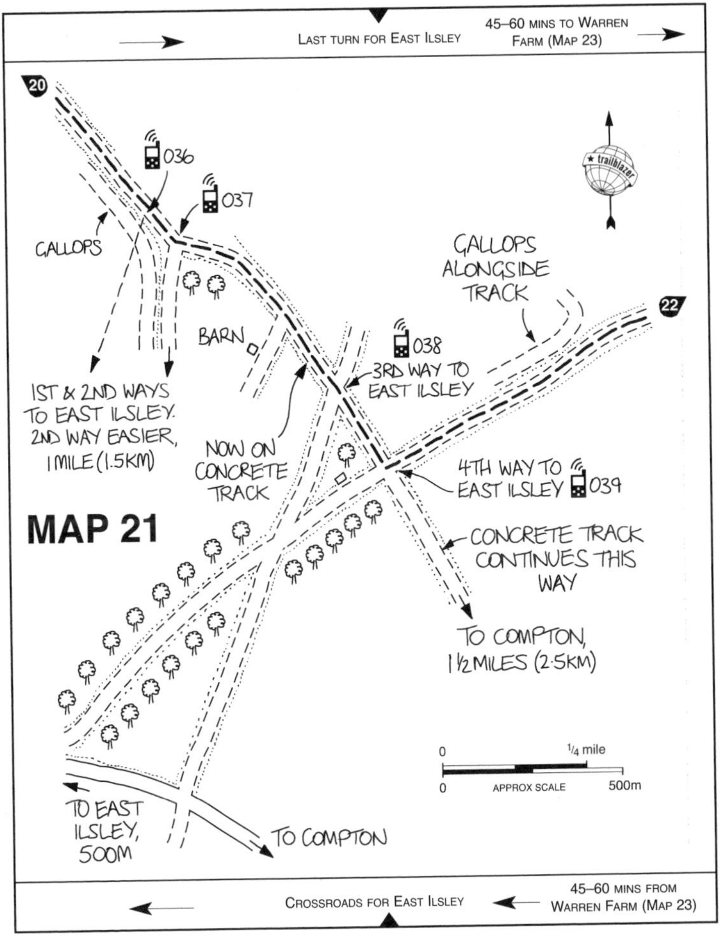

Last turn for East Ilsley
45–60 mins to Warren Farm (Map 23)

GALLOPS
036
037
BARN
038
GALLOPS ALONGSIDE TRACK
3RD WAY TO EAST ILSLEY
1ST & 2ND WAYS TO EAST ILSLEY. 2ND WAY EASIER, 1 MILE (1.5KM)
NOW ON CONCRETE TRACK
4TH WAY TO EAST ILSLEY 039
MAP 21
CONCRETE TRACK CONTINUES THIS WAY
TO COMPTON, 1½ MILES (2.5KM)
0 ¼ mile
0 APPROX SCALE 500m
TO EAST ILSLEY, 500M
TO COMPTON

Crossroads for East Ilsley
45–60 mins from Warren Farm (Map 23)

makes it a convenient place to break your journey.

There is no shop or post office but Kennections' **bus** No 6 calls here; see pp47-51.

Where to stay and eat

The ***Crown & Horns*** (☎ 01635 281545, 💻 crownandhorns.com; 8D/1T/2Tr, all en suite, ▼; WI-FI) has a cosy interior – in the colder months there is a welcoming open fire to sit beside – and a shady garden. It's always popular with walkers. The **accommodation** is in well-kept rooms and costs from £40pp (sgl occ full room rate, three sharing £120). Breakfast is extra and starts at £2.95 up to the full English for £7.95. The pub has separate dining areas and the walls in the bar are covered with horse-racing memorabilia (see box p104). The

menu (**food** Mon-Fri noon-3pm & 6-9pm, Sat noon-6pm & limited menu 6-9pm, Sun noon-6pm & limited menu 6-8pm) includes sausages with mash and onion gravy (£11.50); beer-battered cod (£12.95), and rump steak (£19.95), all of which can be washed down with one, two or several of their real ales.

Opposite is ***The Swan*** (☎ 01635 281238, 🖳 www.theswaneastilsley.co.uk; 2D/3T, all en suite, ▼; WI-FI; Ⓛ), a 16th-century coaching inn in the centre of the village with a pleasant garden that is open all day. **B&B** here costs £32.50-37pp (sgl occ from £65). **Food** is served (Mon-Sat noon-3pm & 6-8.45pm, Sun noon-2pm); the menu changes monthly but the food is standard pub food. On Sundays there is a two-course carvery for £13.45 (one course £9.95), but booking is required.

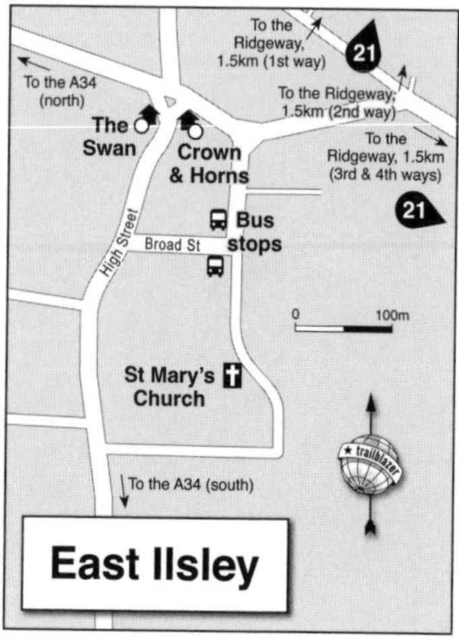

You start the Ridgeway again at the crossroads where the last of the four paths to East Ilsley turns off. If you want to go to Compton, 1½ miles/2.5km, it's best to leave the Ridgeway at this point.

COMPTON

The Saxon name given to this village means 'Coombe Town', or, 'town in the valley', but there is evidence of Bronze and Iron Age settlement in the area even before the Saxons were here. Plenty of Roman artefacts, coins in particular, have been found near Compton.

The **village shop** (☎ 01635 578682; Mon-Fri 7.30am-6.30pm, Sat 7.30am-6.30pm, Sun 8am-1pm) stocks a surprisingly large range of groceries; it also contains the local **post office** (Mon-Fri 9.30am-5.30pm, Sat 9.30am-12.30pm).

The ***Compton Swan*** (☎ 01635 579400, 🖳 thecomptonswan.com; 5D/1D or T, all en suite, ▼; WI-FI; Ⓛ; 🐕 in bar only) is a large, white building on the main road through the village. It is often busy with a mixture of locals and visitors and is deservedly a very popular place to eat. If you are here for lunch (**food** Mon-Sat noon-2.30pm, Sun noon-3pm, daily 5.30-9pm), try their rump of lamb baguette, mint Greek yoghurt and fries (£7.95). The smartly furnished **accommodation** is £45-50pp (sgl occ £90-100). Be sure to book ahead if you want to stay here.

From here you can take a **bus** (Kennections' bus No 6) to Newbury and East Ilsley; see pp47-51 for more details.

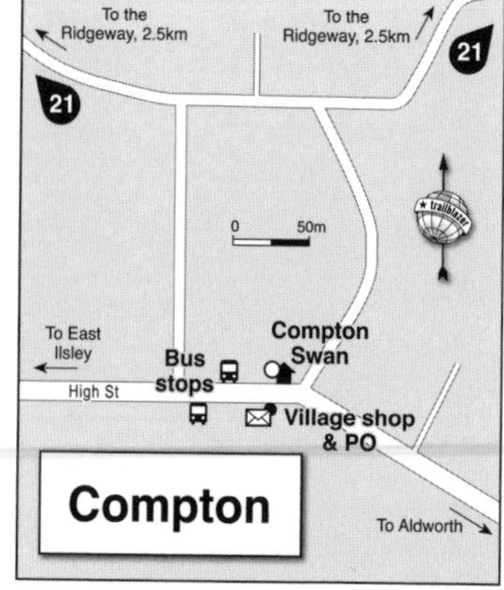

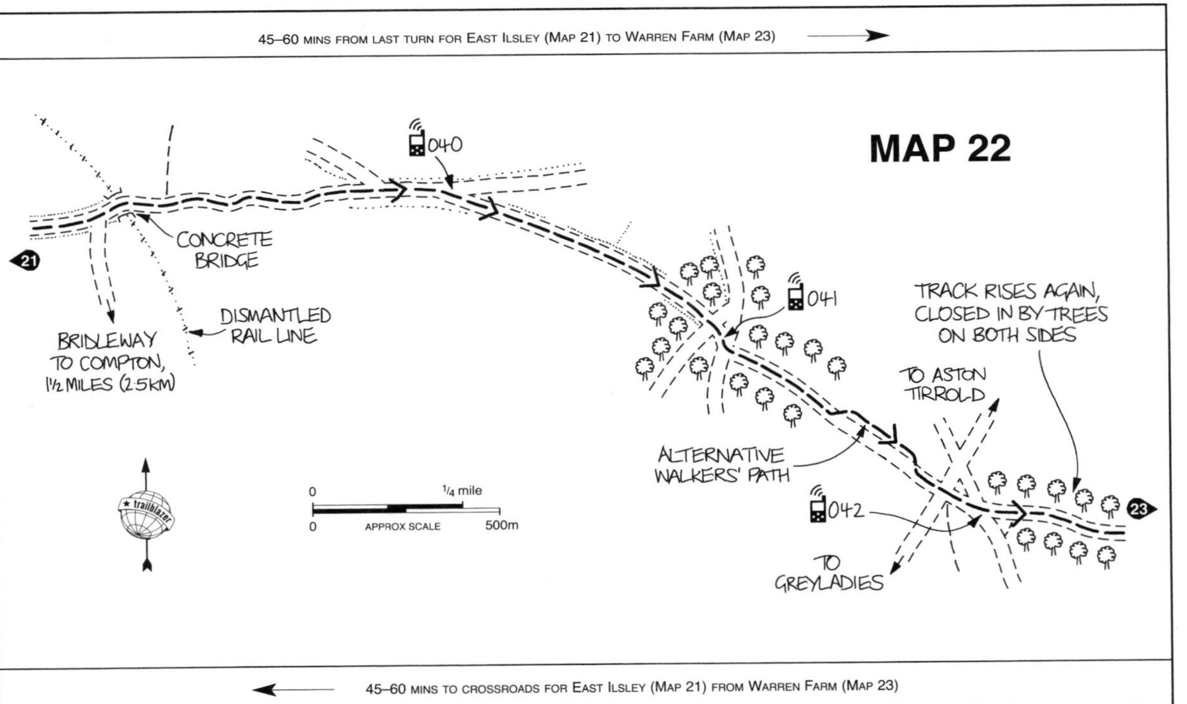

45–60 MINS FROM LAST TURN FOR EAST ILSLEY (MAP 21) TO WARREN FARM (MAP 23)
040
MAP 22
CONCRETE BRIDGE
21
DISMANTLED RAIL LINE
BRIDLEWAY TO COMPTON, 1½ MILES (2.5KM)
041
TRACK RISES AGAIN, CLOSED IN BY TREES ON BOTH SIDES
TO ASTON TIRROLD
ALTERNATIVE WALKERS' PATH
042
23
TO GREYLADIES
trailblazer
0
¼ mile
0
APPROX SCALE
500m
45–60 MINS TO CROSSROADS FOR EAST ILSLEY (MAP 21) FROM WARREN FARM (MAP 23)

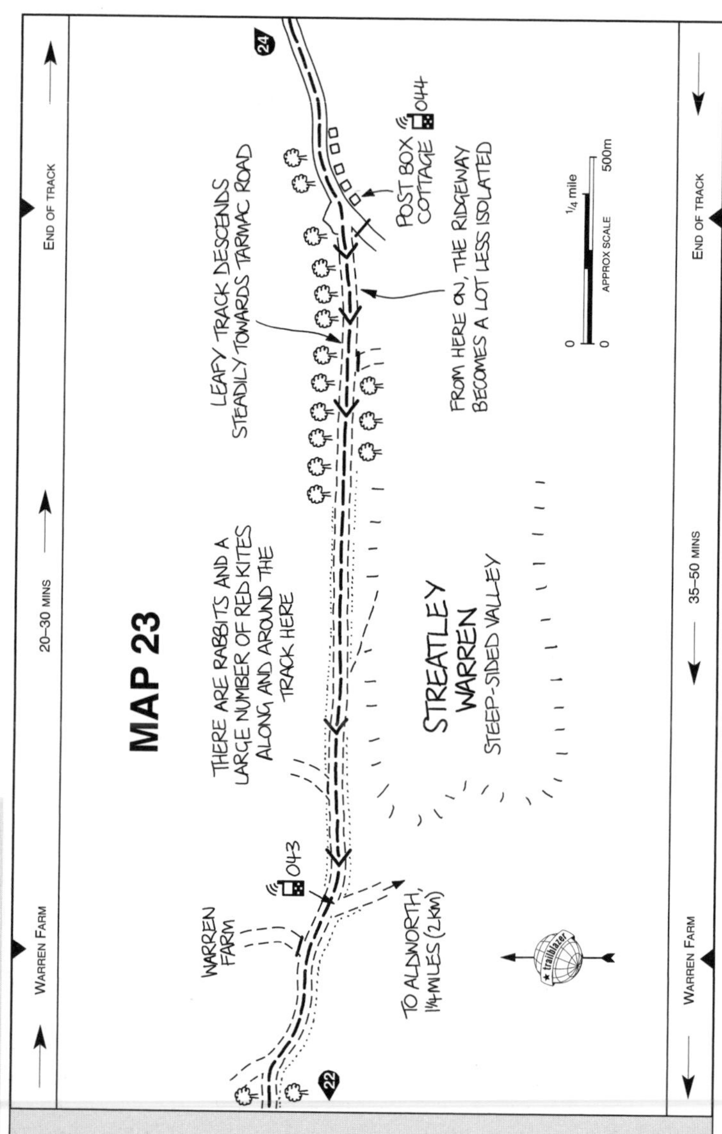

Symbols used in text (see also p95) Dogs allowed subject to prior arrangement
Bathtub in at least one room; Ⓛ packed lunch available if requested in advance.

Follow the broad grass track as it starts a slow descent, paralleled on the left by gallops. To a large extent, this is the last of the really exposed and lonely sections of the Ridgeway. The change isn't abrupt, but over the next few miles it will become obvious. After passing the bridleway from Compton that joins the track from the right, you will cross a **concrete bridge** (Map 22). This takes you over the old, and dismantled, railway that was once the Didcot, Newbury and Southampton Junction Railway. It's been closed since 1962 and the strip where the track once lay is now covered by bushes and trees. The section that you cross lies between the old stations of Churn and Compton. This part of the line was opened in 1882 and owing to its course through remote countryside was given the nickname of the 'Desert Line'.

When you arrive at the slightly **staggered crossroads**, at which the left turning heads north to the wonderfully named Aston Tirrold while the right turning heads for the less-enticing Greyladies, you should continue straight ahead for a short distance until the track forks. Make sure you are not daydreaming when you reach here as you need to take the less-obvious option, a turn to the left. It's an ascending flinty track, closed in by trees, which bends left after about 200m. It is signposted but if you're not paying attention the natural tendency is to carry straight on. Just after you pass the gate to **Warren Farm** (Map 23), on your left, there is a path leading off right, down a 1¼-mile/2km track to Aldworth.

ALDWORTH

The main reason why you might like to detour to this quiet village is to visit ***The Bell*** (☎ 01635 578272; food Tue-Sat 11am-2.30pm & 6-9pm, Sun noon-2.30pm & 7-9pm). No doubt about it, this is a real country pub. The building dates back to the 15th century and the pub has been in the same family for over 200 years. Take note that the pub is closed in the afternoons and on Mondays, except Bank Holidays lunchtime only. A wide selection of filled rolls and ploughman's is served to go with a choice of varied and interesting real ales and farmhouse cider. By the way, in case you need any more encouragement, it's been voted CAMRA (see box p22) 'National Pub of the Year' twice, won the regional award several times and even won an award for being 'the most unspoilt pub in England'. Its high regard amongst real ale drinkers means that it's often very busy despite its quiet location. Morris dancers (see box p119) can be seen here at certain times of the year.

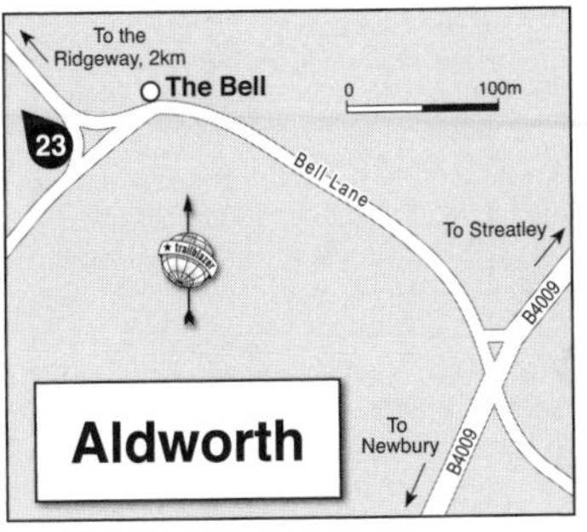

When you arrive at the sealed road by **Post Box Cottage** you have reached the beginning of a new type of Ridgeway. No more windswept wanderings up on grassy tracks 20 metres wide without a building in sight. For the next few miles at least, things are positively urban. You might welcome it after the previous stages, but it certainly lacks a lot of the wild feel. It's picturesque along this road, with each house having its own individuality; this helps to take your mind off the long walk on the tarmac. The final sure symbols that you are about to leave all the tranquillity behind are the 30mph speed limit signs and from here on there are houses on both sides of the road. Just 100m further on you'll come to a T-junction where you join the A417 into the centre of Streatley.

STREATLEY [MAP 24]

This West Berkshire village is now very much smaller than its neighbour, Goring (see pp140-4), across the river in Oxfordshire, but historically it was the larger of the two. Both places were mentioned in the *Domesday Book* with Streatley being valued higher than its neighbour. Even up until the early 19th century it was larger owing to its location on the road to Reading.

For shops, restaurants and other services you should head across the bridge to Goring, just a couple of minutes' walk away. Thames Travel's No 133 and Heyfordian's Nos 134/135 stop here; see pp47-51 for further details.

Where to stay, eat and drink

YHA Streatley (☎ 0845 371 9044, 🖳 www.yha.org.uk/hostel/streatley-thames; 48 beds – 2T, 2 quads, 2 x 5- & 4 x 6-beds; WI-FI; Ⓛ; Apr to end Oct) is the main reason to stay in Streatley, rather than in Goring. The hostel is in a large, white Victorian house, just off the road. There is a drying room, a bar and a self-catering kitchen; they also provide cooked meals. Beds in the dorm are £17-27.50pp; private rooms cost £29-129 depending on the number of people and time of year. Credit cards are accepted.

B&B options include ***The Bull*** (☎ 01491 872392, 🖳 bullinnpub.co.uk; 4D/2T, all en suite; ☕; WI-FI; Ⓛ; 🐕), a 15th-century former coaching inn where the spacious bar has a relaxed atmosphere. The restaurant (food Mon-Sat noon-8.45pm, Sun noon-8pm) here serves a wide variety of **food**; the steak and Marston's ale pie (£9.95) is recommended. The **accommodation** is in a separate building; B&B costs £35-45pp (sgl occ full room rate).

B&B at ***3 Icknield Cottages*** (☎ 01491 875152, 🖳 sueandmikebrodie@btinternet.com; 1S, private bathroom; ☕; WI-FI; Ⓛ) is very good value (£35) if you are walking on your own; it has a good location too.

Just before crossing the river to Goring is a large upmarket hotel known as ***The Swan*** (Map 25; ☎ 01491 878800, 🖳 www.theswanatstreatley.com; 5S/34D or T, all en suite; ☕; WI-FI; Ⓛ; 🐕 £20). It is right on the bank of the Thames and boasts a spa, gym, various options for eating as well as a spacious riverside terrace – an ideal spot for a break during a long day of walking. When you get here the refurbishment work should be finished so the details may have changed but at the time of research **B&B** here costs £50-95pp based on two sharing (sgl/sgl occ £120; at times this can be as low as £75). Food is available all day in The Swan itself (where they serve a good selection of afternoon teas, including a champagne version for £21.95pp), or in the ***Boathouse Deli & Café*** (details as above; Mon-Sat 8am-5.30pm, Sun 9.30am-5.30pm), which is part of the same building, but which feels more welcoming towards walkers. Sandwiches here start at £3.95.

Just a short walk across the double-span bridge from the village of Streatley is the town of Goring where you'll find pretty much everything you could need.

> ❑ **Important note – walking times**
> All times in this book refer only to the time spent walking. You will need to add 20-30% to allow for rests, photography, checking the map, drinking water etc.

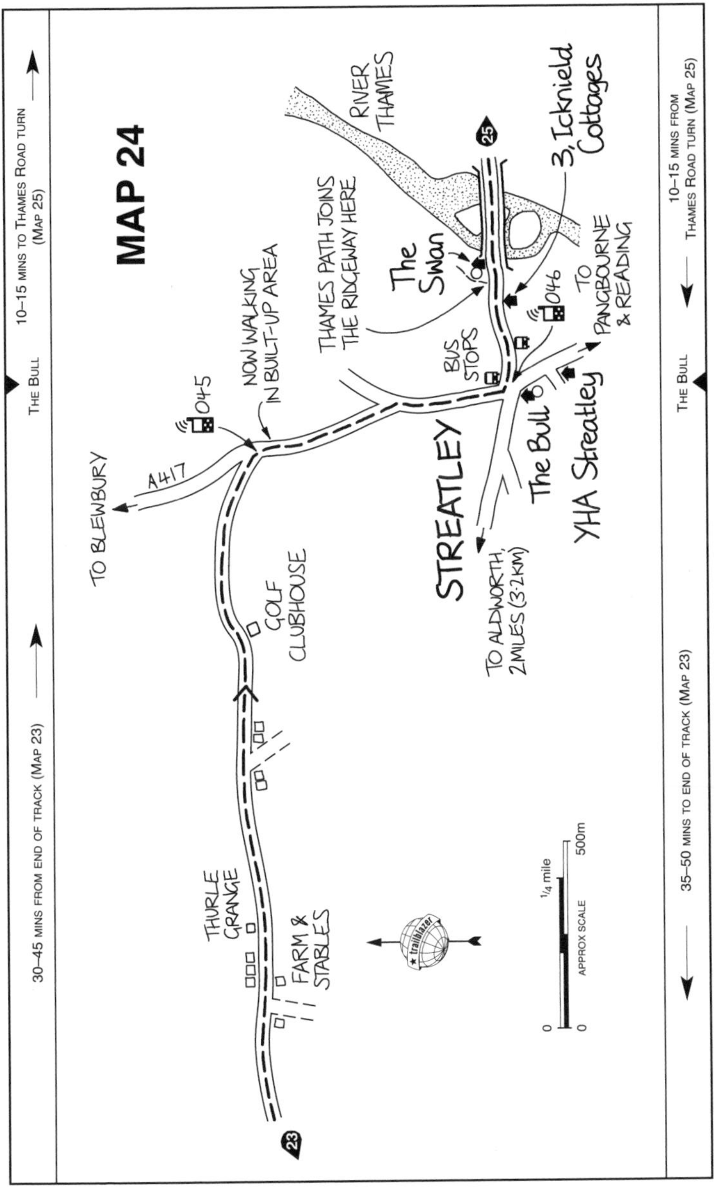

30–45 MINS FROM END OF TRACK (MAP 23) →

THE BULL

10–15 MINS TO THAMES ROAD TURN (MAP 25) →

TO BLEWBURY

MAP 24

A417

045

THURLE GRANGE

NOW WALKING IN BUILT-UP AREA

23

FARM & STABLES

GOLF CLUBHOUSE

THAMES PATH JOINS THE RIDGEWAY HERE

RIVER THAMES

trailblazer

The Swan

STREATLEY

BUS STOPS

25

TO ALDWORTH, 2MILES (3·2KM)

The Bull

0 — 1/4 mile

0 — 500m

APPROX SCALE

046

3, Icknield Cottages

YHA Streatley

TO PANGBOURNE & READING

← 35–50 MINS TO END OF TRACK (MAP 23)

THE BULL

← 10–15 MINS FROM THAMES ROAD TURN (MAP 25)

GORING [MAP 25]

After the Great Western Railway came through here in 1840, the town started to grow larger than its neighbour, Streatley. This growth has continued and as a result nearly all the shops, restaurants and services are located on this side of the river. The place seems to be at least 90% inhabited by young mums pushing their babies around – we don't know why.

Services

Tourist information (☎ 01491 873565; Mon-Fri 10am-noon, plus Sat 10am-noon in July & Aug) is available in the Community Centre on Station Rd. The office has a lot of leaflets about the area but staff are not able to do accommodation-booking, nor do they sell maps or books. Another source of information is 💻 www.visitgoringandstreatley.co.uk.

The **ATM** on the wall of the estate agents Davis Tate is the only one in town, but there is a branch of TSB (Mon-Fri 9am-2pm). On the High St you'll also find a **chemist** (Mon-Fri 9am-6pm, Sat 9am-5pm), **newsagent** (Mon-Sat 6am-10pm, Sun 7am-10pm) which sells most groceries and also houses the **post office** (Mon-Fri 6am-1pm & 2-5.30pm, Sat 9am-12.30pm). **The Goring Grocer** (Mon-Sat 9am-5pm) has a great selection of locally produced food including sandwiches and savouries, filos and tartlets (£3.25-3.50). There are some public **toilets** in the car park. A branch of the **bike store** Mountain Mania Cycles (☎ 01491 871721, 💻 www.mountainmaniacycles.co.uk; Mon-Sat 9am-6pm) is at 10 High St.

Go Ride's No 134 **bus** operates from the railway station to Wallingford via South Stoke and North Stoke; see pp47-51 for further details of **rail** services to Goring & Streatley.

If you need a **taxi** you could try Pangbourne Taxis (☎ 01491 671979); they are very helpful, but try to book well in advance.

Where to stay

There are several good accommodation options here: the first is ***Melrose Cottage*** (☎ 01491 873040, 💻 howarthr523@gmail.com; 1S/2T, share two bathrooms, ▼; WI-FI; Ⓛ £5), a 10-minute walk from the town centre. The rooms (£32.50pp, sgl/sgl occ from £40) are fairly self contained with their own fridges and microwaves. Walk straight up Wallingford Rd, looking out for Milldown Rd on your right, but be careful not to confuse this with Milldown Avenue, also on your right. The B&B is at No 36, pretty much at the far end of the road, again on your right.

You can also stay at one of the inns in town such as ***The Miller of Mansfield*** (☎ 01491 872829, 💻 www.millerofmansfield.com; 11D/2Tr, all en suite, ▼; WI-FI; Ⓛ; 🐕 £10). This lovely 18th-century building, situated right in the town centre, has a collection of striking, individually styled rooms with B&B for £45-97.50pp (sgl occ from £80, three sharing £160-180).

The John Barleycorn (☎ 01491 872509, 💻 www.thejohnbarleycornpub.co.uk; 3D, all en suite, ▼; WI-FI; Ⓛ) is a welcoming place to stay just two minutes' walk from the centre. B&B in the comfortable rooms costs £32.50-42.50pp (sgl occ from £65).

Don't forget **Airbnb** (see p20); save perhaps for the YHA hostel, it's your best chance of finding cheap-ish accommodation in either Goring or Streatley.

Where to eat and drink

If you're in one of the inns enjoying a drink anyway, you could try eating there. ***The Miller of Mansfield*** (see Where to stay; food Mon-Sat noon-2.30pm & 6-9pm, Sun noon-3.30pm & 6-8pm) serves some very interesting dishes; their prices aren't the cheapest but may include such treats as wild halibut fillet (£20.50), or oak-smoked Cornish cod (£18). They also do a set lunch during the week for £16/20 for two/three courses, on Sunday this costs £26/31.

The John Barleycorn (see Where to stay; food Mon-Sat noon-2pm & 6.30-9pm, Sun noon-2pm) has a more traditional-style menu with soup and bread (£4.95), pie of the day (£13.95), and ham, egg & chips (£10.25). A minute further along the road is

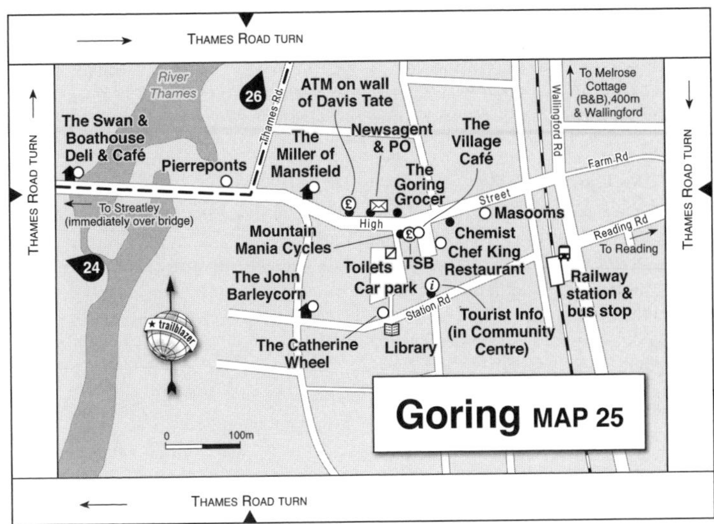

The Catherine Wheel (☎ 01491 872379, 🖳 www.tcwgoring.co.uk; food Mon-Sat noon-3pm & 6-9pm, Sun noon-4pm). This welcoming place is open all day and is probably the most traditional of the pubs in town, serving Brakspear's ales and generous portions of home-cooked food. Booking for an evening meal is recommended.

For lunch or snacks you could try ***The Village Café*** (☎ 01491 874264; Mon-Fri 8am-5pm, Sat 9am-5pm, Sun 10am-5pm; 🐕), a small, jolly, café in the centre of town serving cakes, sandwiches and drinks. The soup and sandwich (£6.50, takeaway £5) is ideal for lunch on a cold day.

Alternatively, just before the bridge, ***Pierreponts*** (☎ 01491 874464, 🖳 pierreponts.co.uk; Tue-Sat 8am-5pm, Fri 6-11pm) serves breakfast, lunch and afternoon tea – and an evening meal on Fridays. Their home-made cakes are delicious.

Chef King Restaurant (☎ 01491 872485, 🖳 www.chef-king.com; daily noon-2pm & 5.30-11pm), in the arcade by The Village Café, is a Chinese restaurant/takeaway; the menu has all the dishes you'd expect, most for around £5.50-8.50.

Masooms (☎ 01491 875078, 🖳 www.masooms.co.uk; Sat-Thur noon-2.30pm & daily 5.30-11pm), an Indian restaurant on the High St, has a mouth-watering and varied menu; most main courses cost between £8 and £15. The selection of fish curries is worth a look: the red mullet *biraan* is especially good.

GORING TO WATLINGTON [MAPS 25-33]

Overview

This stretch of the Ridgeway totals **14½ miles/23km (6½-9hrs)** and is very enjoyable, especially after the previous sections. From the twin towns of Streatley and Goring the path is easy and follows the Thames for around 5½ miles/9km, sometimes right on its bank, passing through the charming villages of South and North Stoke. Where the path turns east you can head into

Wallingford or keep on the Ridgeway, heading along Grim's Ditch (see box p152) for several miles before emerging at Nuffield.

One of the most bizarre sections of the Ridgeway is here – a walk across a golf course – after which you head into woodlands and across open fields for the section to Watlington, passing through Ewelme Park Estate.

Route

Soon after you've crossed the bridge into Goring you need to take a left turn on to Thames Rd. There is a 'Ridgeway' sign on the fence here but it's still possible to miss this turning if you're not looking for it.

You will now be walking parallel to the Thames but won't be able to see it just yet. The Ridgeway follows a succession of roads and paths behind gardens as it gradually gets closer to and level with the Thames. Along here you'll pass a turning down to ***Rossini at The Leatherne Bottel*** (Map 26; ☎ 01491 872667, 💻 www.leathernebottel.co.uk; food Tue-Sun 12.30-3pm, Tue-Sat 6.30-10.30pm) a riverside restaurant. It's a deservedly popular place serving high-quality food either on the terrace by the river bank or inside the restaurant itself. Main dishes on their à la carte menu are all around the £13 mark, and while the dishes themselves are the same that you'd see on any Italian menu anywhere in the world (carbonara, bolognese etc), the quality is undoubtedly finer than most. They also have a decent selection of fish dishes starting at £18 and including *tonno in crosta di sesamo* (grilled tuna on sesame seeds, cooked with soya sauce with wasabi on the side). Booking is recommended. The dress code is smart casual.

Further along the path you veer away from the busy rail line and head diagonally across an open field, towards the village of South Stoke.

SOUTH STOKE [MAP 26]

This is yet another attractive village on the route. The Ridgeway path follows 'The Street' through the village, lined with a real variety of old, new and renovated houses. You'll pass a primary school and a church, **St Andrew's**, but there are no shops.

The Goring to Wallingford **bus** (Go Ride's No 134) service stops on the main B4009 road just outside the village; see pp47-51 for further details.

The main place of interest to walkers will be ***The Perch & Pike*** (☎ 01491 872415, 💻 www.perchandpike.co.uk; 2D/1T, all en suite, ☕; WI-FI; 🐕 £10; bar Mon-Fri 11.30am-3pm & 5.30-11pm, Sat 11.30am-11pm, Sun noon-6pm), which is an excellent example of a rare phenomenon – a pub actually on the Ridgeway! For this reason it's a popular stop for many walkers and they are made more than welcome by the owners. The pub itself is a 17th-century coaching inn that has been tastefully refurbished and has open log fires in the colder months. They serve Brakspear ales, stock a select wine list and have both a lunchtime and a dinner menu (**food** daily noon-2.30pm, Mon-Sat 6-8.45pm) but the pub was changing ownership at the time of research so this may change. The **rooms** cost from £47.50pp (sgl occ full room rate). One of the rooms even has a Jacuzzi – just the thing after a long day's walk!

The other accommodation option is ***The Old Post Office*** (☎ 01491 871872, 💻 www.greenoakbarn.uk; 1Qd, en suite shower; WI-FI; Ⓛ); the accommodation is in a wonderful, self-contained apartment in a converted oak barn with a sitting area, internet and tea-/coffee-making facilities). B&B costs from £45pp (sgl occ £60, up to £135/180 for three/four sharing); additional £5 heating charge November to March.

Another option is **Airbnb** (see p20).

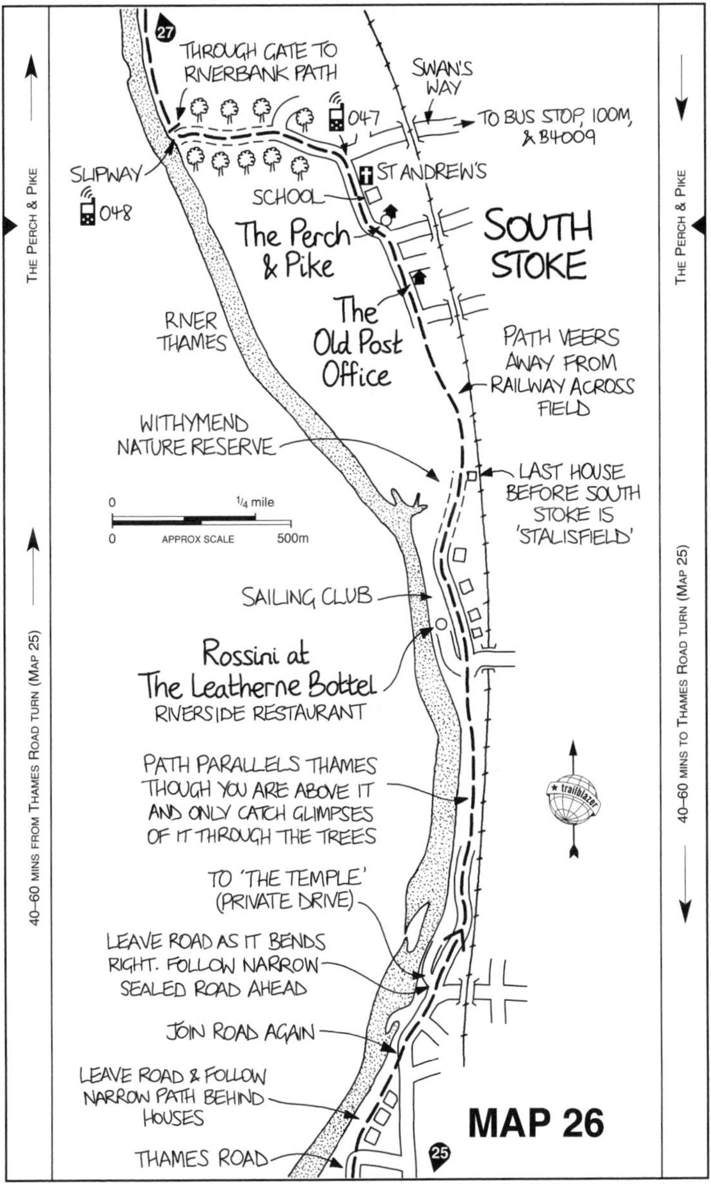

THE PERCH & PIKE

40–60 MINS FROM THAMES ROAD TURN (MAP 25)

27

THROUGH GATE TO RIVERBANK PATH

SWAN'S WAY

047

TO BUS STOP, 100M, & B4009

SLIPWAY

048

ST ANDREW'S

SCHOOL

The Perch & Pike

SOUTH STOKE

The Old Post Office

RIVER THAMES

PATH VEERS AWAY FROM RAILWAY ACROSS FIELD

WITHYMEND NATURE RESERVE

LAST HOUSE BEFORE SOUTH STOKE IS 'STALISFIELD'

0 1/4 mile

0 APPROX SCALE 500m

SAILING CLUB

Rossini at The Leatherne Bottel
RIVERSIDE RESTAURANT

PATH PARALLELS THAMES THOUGH YOU ARE ABOVE IT AND ONLY CATCH GLIMPSES OF IT THROUGH THE TREES

trailblazer

TO 'THE TEMPLE' (PRIVATE DRIVE)

LEAVE ROAD AS IT BENDS RIGHT. FOLLOW NARROW SEALED ROAD AHEAD

JOIN ROAD AGAIN

LEAVE ROAD & FOLLOW NARROW PATH BEHIND HOUSES

THAMES ROAD

25

MAP 26

THE PERCH & PIKE

40–60 MINS TO THAMES ROAD TURN (MAP 25)

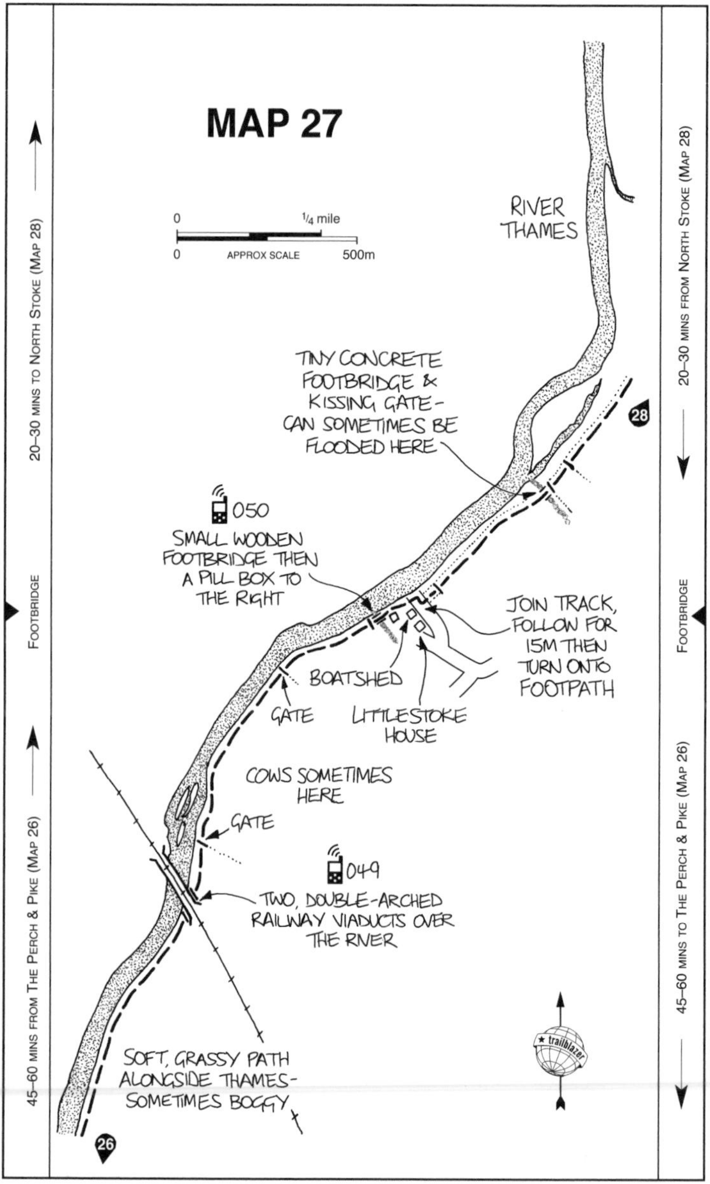

MAP 27

0 ¼ mile
0 APPROX SCALE 500m

20–30 mins to North Stoke (Map 28)
Footbridge
45–60 mins from The Perch & Pike (Map 26)

20–30 mins from North Stoke (Map 28)
Footbridge
45–60 mins to The Perch & Pike (Map 26)

RIVER THAMES

TINY CONCRETE FOOTBRIDGE & KISSING GATE - CAN SOMETIMES BE FLOODED HERE

050
SMALL WOODEN FOOTBRIDGE THEN A PILL BOX TO THE RIGHT

JOIN TRACK, FOLLOW FOR 15M THEN TURN ONTO FOOTPATH

BOATSHED

GATE

LITTLESTOKE HOUSE

COWS SOMETIMES HERE

GATE

049
TWO, DOUBLE-ARCHED RAILWAY VIADUCTS OVER THE RIVER

SOFT, GRASSY PATH ALONGSIDE THAMES - SOMETIMES BOGGY

28
26

trailblazer

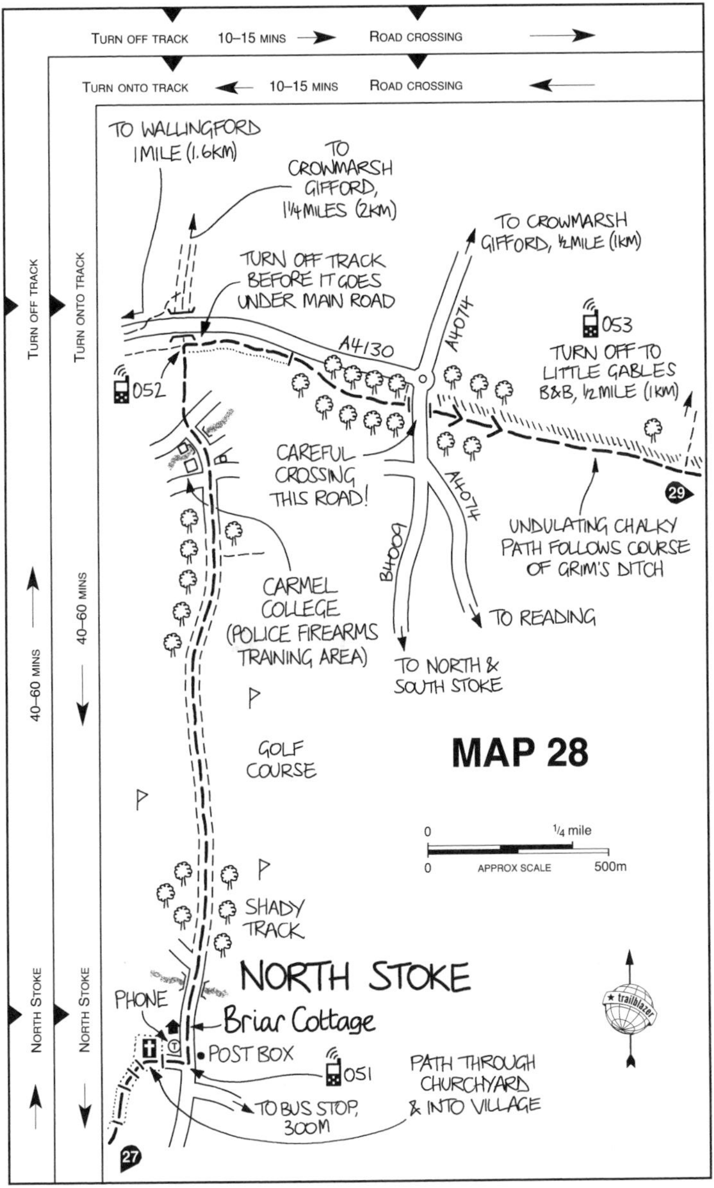

TURN OFF TRACK 10–15 MINS → ROAD CROSSING →
TURN ONTO TRACK ← 10–15 MINS ROAD CROSSING ←

TURN OFF TRACK
TURN ONTO TRACK
40–60 MINS
40–60 MINS
NORTH STOKE
NORTH STOKE

TO WALLINGFORD 1 MILE (1.6KM)
TO CROWMARSH GIFFORD, 1¼ MILES (2KM)
TURN OFF TRACK BEFORE IT GOES UNDER MAIN ROAD
TO CROWMARSH GIFFORD, ½ MILE (1KM)
A4074
A4130
052
053
TURN OFF TO LITTLE GABLES B&B, ½ MILE (1KM)
CAREFUL CROSSING THIS ROAD!
A4074
29
B4009
UNDULATING CHALKY PATH FOLLOWS COURSE OF GRIM'S DITCH
CARMEL COLLEGE (POLICE FIREARMS TRAINING AREA)
TO READING
TO NORTH & SOUTH STOKE
GOLF COURSE

MAP 28

0 ¼ mile
0 APPROX SCALE 500m

SHADY TRACK

NORTH STOKE

PHONE
Briar Cottage
POST BOX
051
PATH THROUGH CHURCHYARD & INTO VILLAGE
TO BUS STOP, 300M
27

trailblazer

ROUTE GUIDE AND MAPS

At the end of 'The Street' the Ridgeway branches left and Swan's Way turns right. Swan's Way is a 65-mile (105km), long-distance bridlepath starting in Salcey Forest, on the border with Northamptonshire and finishing at Goring. The Ridgeway crosses it on numerous occasions up ahead.

After leaving South Stoke and following the Thames you'll come to the low, wide **viaduct** (Map 27) that carries the railway over the Thames. From a distance it looks like a standard four-arched viaduct with flattened elliptical arches, as opposed to the semi-circular ones more favoured at the time of its construction. It's only when you get fairly close, and even right under the viaduct, that you see it is really something special. It's not a single viaduct, but two viaducts, built alongside each other with a narrow gap between them. You'll also see that the viaducts are heavily skewed as they cross the Thames on an angle. The red Berkshire brickwork is another interesting feature as the bricks are laid diagonally as opposed to horizontally. The visual effect of this, combined with the skewing of the viaduct, creates a sort of optical illusion as you stand under the arches following the lines of bricks with your eyes.

The path keeps alongside the Thames until it reaches **North Stoke** village, after which it starts to turn away from the river.

NORTH STOKE [MAP 28, p145]

You arrive in this village via the grounds of the 14th-century **church**, the main building of which remains largely unaltered since its construction. Even some of the original stained glass remains in the windows. Once you've had a look at it there isn't much else to do here; the village is smaller even than South Stoke and there are no facilities for the walker.

Go Ride's No 134 **bus** service stops on the main B4009 road just outside the village; see pp47-51 for further details.

When you reach the busy A4130 the Ridgeway branches off right, but if you want to visit either Wallingford or Crowmarsh Gifford you should continue on the bridleway that goes under the A4130. If heading for Wallingford, soon after you walk under the A4130 take the path on your left to lead you back up onto the road itself. Then follow the road bridge across the River Thames and descend from the bridge to the riverside path which leads straight to Wallingford (1 mile/1.6km).

To reach Crowmarsh Gifford (see pp150-2) from Wallingford you'll have to walk across the **19-arch stone bridge** crossing the Thames. Believe it or not this was the main road crossing of the Thames in this area until the A4130 bypass and new bridge were opened in 1993.

If heading directly for Crowmarsh Gifford (1¼ miles/2km) stay on the bridleway after going under the A4130. The bridleway turns into a road and you pass a farm on your left. On a curve in the road there is a footpath turning off to your left. Take this and stay on it to Crowmarsh Gifford. Alternatively, stay on the Ridgeway for another 500m and then walk to Crowmarsh Gifford on the A4074, though this is a less pleasant route.

WALLINGFORD [see map p149]

This is the largest town you will have come across 'on' the Ridgeway so far which might merit a visit, especially if you need to stock up, or just take some time out.

This historically important town was established by King Alfred in the 10th century and later a fortified castle was built here by William the Conqueror who arrived after the Battle of Hastings in 1066. The fortifications were added to over the years until it became one of the most important castles in England and remained so for several centuries. It was, however, completely destroyed on the orders of Oliver Cromwell in 1652. You can still visit the **Castle Gardens**, the site of the castle, to the north of town, but there is virtually no evidence of the castle itself.

Although the railway was closed to passengers in 1959, it has since reopened as the **Cholsey and Wallingford Railway**, linking Wallingford, via the old GWR branch line to Cholsey, and the national rail network. Trains run on various weekends and bank holidays during the year and are sometimes pulled by a steam engine. For more information call ☎ 01491 835067 (24-hour recorded message), or go to the railway's website: 💻 www.cholsey-wallingford-railway.com.

Wallingford Museum (☎ 01491 835065, 💻 www.wallingfordmuseum.org.uk; Mar-Nov Tue-Fri 2-5pm, Sat 10.30am-5pm, Sun (June-Aug only) and bank hols 2-5pm; £5 adults, children free if with an adult) traces the history of the town from its Saxon roots to the present day. Agatha Christie lived in the Wallingford area for over 40 years and a new exhibition includes details about her life and her books as well as some of her original letters.

Services

There is a **tourist information centre** (TIC; ☎ 01491 826972, 💻 www.wallingford.co.uk; Apr-Oct Mon-Fri 10am-1pm & 1.30-4pm, Sat 10am-2pm; Nov-Mar Mon-Sat 10am-2pm) in the Town Hall, built in 1670. The staff here are helpful and there is a huge amount of information for walkers in the form of free leaflets. They also have some information about accommodation but cannot do bookings. The **post office** (Mon-Sat 9am-5.30pm, Sat 9am-12.30pm) is just off Market Place near Waitrose's car park. On St Mary's St the branches of Nationwide, Lloyds and Barclays have **ATMs** as does the NatWest on the High St. There is a **Lloyds Pharmacy** (Mon-Fri 9am-6pm, Sat 9am-5.30pm) and a branch of **Boots** (Mon-Sat 8.30am-6pm, Sun 10am-4pm), the chemist, on Market Place and a **laundrette** (daily 9am-4pm) on the High St.

There is a large Waitrose **supermarket** (Mon-Fri 8am-9pm, Sat 8am-8pm, Sun 10am-4pm) on the corner of St Martin's St and the High St; you'll also find **public toilets** here; there are more public toilets in the car park on Wood St. There are also various **markets** here (see box p21).

If you need bicycle repairs try **Rides on Air** (☎ 01491 836289, 💻 www.ridesonair.com; Mar-Nov Mon-Fri 9am-5.30pm, Sat 8am-5pm, Sun 8am-2pm; Dec-Feb open from 9am) on St Martin's St.

Go Ride's No 134 **bus** service goes to Goring via North Stoke & South Stoke; Several Thames Travel services call here: No 136 (Cholsey to Benson via Crowmarsh Gifford): the No 139/139B (to Nuffield, Crowmarsh Gifford & Henley-on-Thames); the X2 (to Didcot & Abingdon); and the X39 & X40 (to Oxford & Reading via Crowmarsh). See pp47-51 for details. Check you are at the correct bus stop.

There is a **taxi** rank next to the Town Hall. Wally Cabs (☎ 01491 260029, 💻 www.wallycabs.co.uk) provides services in and around the area.

Where to stay

Right in the centre of the town you could try ***The Dolphin*** (☎ 01491 837377, 💻 www.thedollyinwally.co.uk; 2T, shared bathroom, 🐕; WI-FI) which has accommodation above the pub: it's handy for a drink, but isn't the most peaceful place to stay. B&B costs from £35pp (sgl occ from £50) and a hearty breakfast is served downstairs (see p150).

George Hotel (☎ 01491 836665, 💻 www.george-hotel-wallingford.com; 9S/

19D/8D or T/1Qd, one room sleeping up to six people, all en suite, ▼; WI-FI; Ⓛ) is a large, upmarket place with a central location. The hotel is in a 16th-century building also incorporating a 'tavern' and a separate restaurant and bar called Wealh's (see Where to eat). If you can afford the prices, you'll certainly be very comfortable: room rates start from £65pp based on two sharing (sgl from £110, rates on request for more than two sharing). Breakfast costs an extra £10pp.

The Partridge (☎ 01491 839305, 🖳 www.partridgeinnwallingford.co.uk; 1D en suite ▼, 3D share shower facilities; WI-FI; Ⓛ) is a new place at the southern end of St Mary's St. Rates are fair value, given that only one of the rooms has en suite facilities, with prices starting at £27.50pp, rising to £55pp for the en suite (sgl occ full room rate); breakfast is continental.

Opposite, the ***Coachmakers Arms*** (☎ 01491 838229, 🖳 www.coachmakersarms wallingford.co.uk; 2D/1Tr, ▼; WI-FI; Ⓛ; 🐕 £10) is the only place we found that allows **dogs**. B&B from £45pp (sgl occ full room rate, three sharing from £110).

Once again, apart from the pubs your best chance of securing accommodation might be **Airbnb** (see p20); there are several places advertised for both Wallingford and Crowmarsh Gifford.

Where to eat and drink

There are plenty of places to eat in Wallingford and lots of variety, too. All the places listed here are in or around the town centre.

Early risers just have a choice of the two ubiquitous chains, ***Greggs*** (Mon-Sat 7am-5.30pm, Sun 10am-4pm) and ***Costa*** (Mon-Sat 6.30am-7pm, Sun 8am-6pm), close to each other on Market Square.

For a quick pizza you could try ***The Pizza Café*** (☎ 01491 826222, 🖳 thepizza cafewallingford.co.uk; Mon-Sat 10am-2.30pm, Mon-Thur & Sun 5.30-10.30pm, Fri & Sat 5.30-11pm), on St Mary's St, which has a large range of pizzas (£5-12) for such a small place.

Also on St Mary's St is a branch of the chain restaurant, ***Pizza Express*** (☎ 01491 833431, 🖳 www.pizzaexpress.com/walling ford; Mon-Fri 11.30am-11pm, Sat 11am-11pm, Sun 11.30am-10.30pm) which dishes up various pizzas and pastas for slightly higher prices.

Avanti (☎ 01491 835500, 🖳 www .avantiitalian.com; Mon & Tue 6.15-10pm, Wed-Sat noon-2.30pm, Wed & Thur 6.15-10pm, Fri & Sat 5.45-10.30pm) serves a range of pasta dishes (£6.95-9.80), plus all the usual pizzas and fresh seafood too.

Just south of Market Place ***The Old Post Office*** (☎ 01491 836068, 🖳 www.opo wallingford.co.uk; Sun-Thur 8am-11pm, Fri & Sat to 1am) is described as 'a modern interpretation of an original public house'. Food is served all day, starting with cooked breakfasts (9am-noon; £4-8.50) and finishing with evening meals such as fillet of smoked haddock with fresh gnocchi, charred leek and onion cream sauce (£14).

Just along the street, ***Salvador's Deli*** (☎ 01491 825708, 🖳 www.salvadorsdeli .co.uk; Mon-Sat 8.30am-5pm) is another popular place with sandwiches from £2.95 and with a choice of over 25 fillings too, including Jamaican jerk chicken (£3.75).

The best Indian restaurant in town, ***Anokhi*** (☎ 01491 838077, 🖳 anokhicui sine.co.uk; daily noon-2.30pm & 5.30-11.30pm, Sun noon-3pm) is on the High St. They have an extensive choice of house specialities (£7.50-10.95).

Just past Anokhi is ***Delhi Brasserie*** (☎ 01491 826666, 🖳 www.delhibrasserie.co .uk; Mon-Sat noon-2pm & 5.30-11.30pm, Sun noon-11.30pm).

Alternatively try ***Wallingford Tandoori*** (Mon-Fri 5.30-11.30pm, Sat noon-2pm & 5.30-11.30pm, Sun noon-11.30pm) which has a standard menu and prices to match.

The only Thai restaurant in Wallingford is ***Thai Corner*** (Mon-Sat 5.30-11pm); it has an extensive and tasty menu and most main courses cost £6-11.

Both ***Hong Kong House*** (Sun-Thur 5.30-11pm, Fri & Sat 11.30am-1.30pm & 5-11.45pm) and ***Welcome Chinese Food*** (Sun-Thur 4.30-11.30pm, Fri & Sat noon-1.15pm & 4.30-11.30pm) are standard Chinese takeaways, but you can eat in at

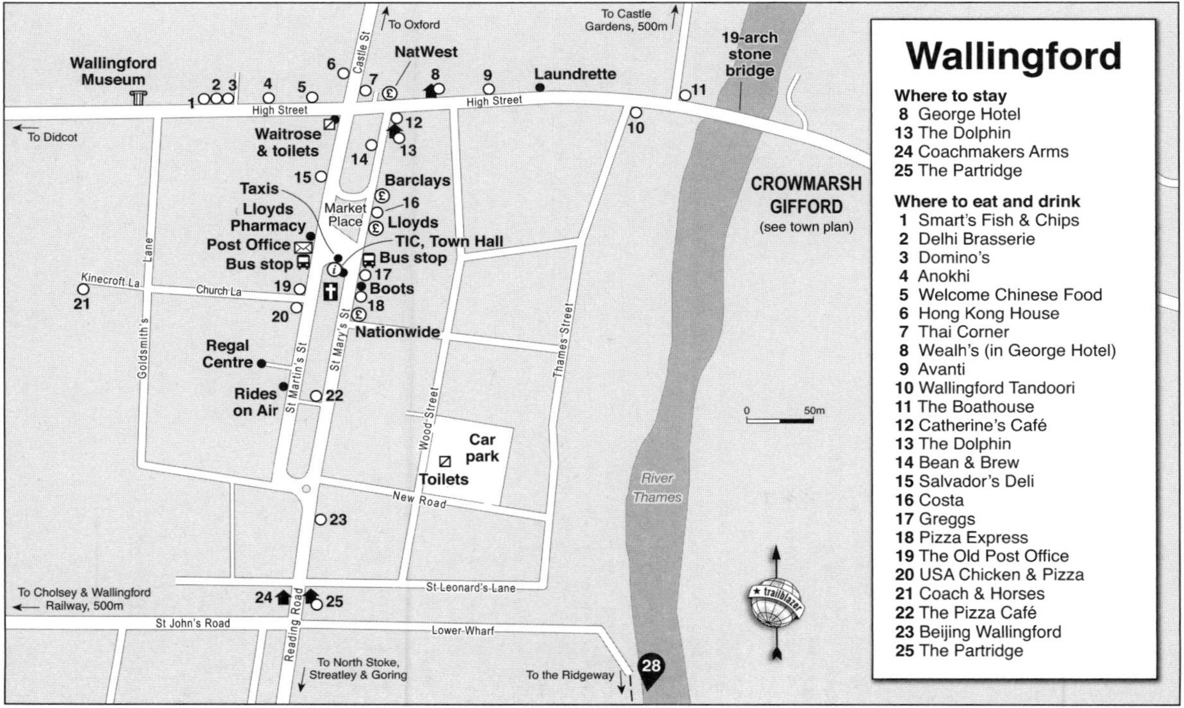
Wallingford
Where to stay
8 George Hotel
13 The Dolphin
24 Coachmakers Arms
25 The Partridge
Where to eat and drink
1 Smart's Fish & Chips
2 Delhi Brasserie
3 Domino's
4 Anokhi
5 Welcome Chinese Food
6 Hong Kong House
7 Thai Corner
8 Wealh's (in George Hotel)
9 Avanti
10 Wallingford Tandoori
11 The Boathouse
12 Catherine's Café
13 The Dolphin
14 Bean & Brew
15 Salvador's Deli
16 Costa
17 Greggs
18 Pizza Express
19 The Old Post Office
20 USA Chicken & Pizza
21 Coach & Horses
22 The Pizza Café
23 Beijing Wallingford
25 The Partridge
Wallingford Museum
To Oxford
To Castle Gardens, 500m
19-arch stone bridge
NatWest
Laundrette
High Street
To Didcot
Castle St
Waitrose & toilets
Taxis
Lloyds Pharmacy
Post Office
Bus stop
Barclays
Market Place
Lloyds
TIC, Town Hall
Bus stop
Boots
Nationwide
CROWMARSH GIFFORD
(see town plan)
Kinecroft La
Church La
Goldsmith's Lane
Regal Centre
Rides on Air
St Martin's St
St Mary's St
Wood Street
Thames Street
Car park
Toilets
New Road
River Thames
0
50m
To Cholsey & Wallingford Railway, 500m
St Leonard's Lane
St John's Road
Reading Road
Lower Wharf
To North Stoke, Streatley & Goring
To the Ridgeway
28
trailblazer

[*Wallingford cont'd*] ... ***Beijing Wallingford*** (Mon-Thur 5-11pm, Fri-Sun noon-2.30pm & 5-11pm) at the southern end of St Mary's St. Although the menu is fairly standard (eg crispy chilli beef £6) they do have plenty of vegetarian options and even an indoor fish pond!

Fast-food options in Wallingford include ***Smart's Fish & Chips*** (Mon-Fri 11.30am-2pm & 4.30-10pm, Sat 4-10pm, Sun 4-9pm), on the High St, a branch of ***Domino's*** (☎ 01491 833000, 🖳 www.dominos.co.uk/Wallingford; daily 10am-11pm), the pizza chain, nearby, and ***USA Chicken & Pizza*** (Tue-Thur & Sun 3-11pm, Fri & Sat to 3pm-1.30am), on St Martin's St.

Plenty of **pubs** here serve food. If the weather is good you should visit the ***Coach & Horses*** (☎ 01491 598827, 🖳 www.coachandhorseswallingford.co.uk; food daily noon-2pm & 5-9pm) that faces out onto a large grassy park. The food here is good and includes an all-day brunch of sausage, bacon, egg, beans & chips (£6.95). They serve a range of cask ales.

The Dolphin (see Where to stay; food Tue-Sat 8am-9pm, Sun 9am-2pm), nearer the centre of town, has Greene King ales though only has a standard bar menu. From 8am to noon they serve 'full English' breakfasts for £6. ***The Boathouse*** (☎ 01491 834100, 🖳 boathouse-pub.co.uk; food daily noon-10pm) has a large patio area for dining, right on the bank of the Thames. Although the menu is standard pub food it is done well. It can get quite noisy at weekends but you can always sit outside if the weather is warm enough.

Wealh's (food daily noon-3pm & 6-9pm) in George Hotel (see Where to stay), has a lovely outdoor eating area in the hotel courtyard; main courses here are £8-15 and may include moules marinières with fries and bread (£13.95).

For a cup of tea and a fancy cake there is ***Catherine's Cafe*** (☎ 01491 838122, 🖳 www.catherinescafe.co.uk; Mon-Sat 9am-5pm, Sun 10am-4pm). Our favourite place for lunch, however, is just round the corner. ***Bean & Brew*** (☎ 01491 520685, 🖳 www.beanandbrew.co.uk; Mon-Sat 8.30am-5.30pm, Sun 9.30am-4pm) does some delicious ciabattas (from £4.30) including a chicken, halloumi and pesto ciabatta, as well as all-day breakfasts including porridge (£2.50).

The Partridge (see Where to stay; Tue-Sat 5.30-9pm, Sun noon-3pm) is a new place but one that's quickly garnered a strong reputation for good food, with adventurous dishes such as wild monkfish tail served with steamed new potatoes, steamed greens and a creamy white wine, wild prawn and onion sauce (£21) regularly appearing on the menu. They serve a pre theatre menu £14/17 for 2/3 courses daily 5.30-7.15pm.

CROWMARSH GIFFORD

This town has now become an extension of Wallingford. It's separated from its larger neighbour only by the bridge and, to be honest, most shops and services are located in Wallingford, on the other side of the bridge. There are, however, two campsites and a B&B here and it's easy to walk into Wallingford should you need to.

The main claim to fame for this place is that **Jethro Tull** lived here. No, not them, but him, the inventor of the seed drill. You can still see his house on The Street where he lived from 1700 to 1710. It's only a couple of minutes' walk from the bridge, but is not open to the public. It's the middle one of the three terraced Tudor houses.

The seed drill was essentially a device that enabled you to plant three rows of seeds at the same time. He also invented other machines in an effort to improve crop yields. At the time his ideas weren't implemented fully but, looking back, he is now recognised as one of the most important figures in the modernisation of farming methods.

Services

There is a well-stocked **village shop** (☎ 01491 837176; Mon-Sat 6.30am-7.30pm, Sun 8am-2pm) on The Street.

Go Ride's No 134 and Thames Travel's **bus** Nos 136, 139/139B, X39 and

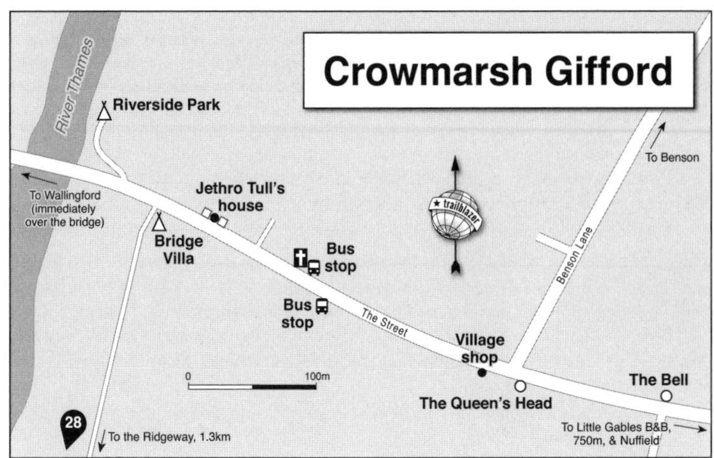

X40 stop here; see pp47-51 for further details.

Where to stay

There are two very good **campsites** here.

On the right as you walk in from the Ridgeway is ***Bridge Villa*** (☎ 01491 836860, 🖳 www.bridgevilla.co.uk; Feb-Dec; WI-FI; 🐕 allowed if kept on a lead). They charge £10-12 per night for a tent and one person, £15-21 for two people. The rate includes use of the shower and toilet facilities. They also offer a **room** (1T en suite) for £25pp (sgl occ £45), but do not serve breakfast. They recommend you book ahead, especially in the summer months and at weekends, for both forms of accommodation.

On the banks of the Thames, ***Riverside Park*** (☎ 01491 835232, 🖳 www.better.org.uk/venues/riverside-park-and-pools; late May to early Sep) is a very well-run campsite, with a heated open-air swimming pool (£4.45; daily 7am-6pm). There are 18 pitches (£14.50 per night per tent) and shower/toilet facilities. It can get busy so you are advised to book ahead.

You could try the excellent B&B at ***Little Gables*** (☎ 01491 837834, 🖳 www.littlegables.co.uk; 1T/1D/2Tr; private facilities; WI-FI; Ⓛ £7; small and medium 🐕 £15 per stay), at 166 Crowmarsh Hill. The rooms are en suite apart from the toilet for one of the twin rooms which is separate but next door to the room. Rates are £35-42.50pp (sgl occ from £70, £150 for three sharing). If arranged in advance they can provide an evening meal (£18); they will also transport your luggage to your next B&B – rates on request. Little Gables is in a cul-de-sac running parallel to the main road, a couple of hundred metres east of the large roundabout. Although you can walk here from Crowmarsh Gifford, the Ridgeway passes within about half a mile of this place (see Map 28, p145). To get there follow the Grim's ditch and look for a path leading off through a field to your left. Take this path and when it joins a minor road continue on that, in the same direction. You will soon arrive at the cul-de-sac.

Where to eat and drink

There are basically two options. ***The Bell*** (☎ 01491 835324; food Mon-Fri 11am-9pm, Sat & Sun 10am-9pm), on The Street, is a Greene King pub with a Hungry Horse restaurant and lots of facilities – the aim being that it will appeal to anyone who might walk through its doors. The menu is the same in all their branches: burgers with chips, steaks, or vegetable lasagne, but they pride themselves on the large servings and low prices. They also hold special evenings such as their Wednesday night curry feast, where a curry and a pint will only set you back £5. The other place, the 13th-century ***Queen's Head*** (☎ 01491 839857, 🖳 www .queensheadcrowmarsh.co.uk; food Mon-Fri noon-3pm & 5-9.30pm, Sat noon-9.30pm, Sun to 8pm), is more upmarket, and includes such delicious dishes as roast chicken supreme with oven-roasted sweet potato, curried corn and ranch cream cheese (£13.50).

From the junction at the A4130 the section of the Ridgeway almost all the way to Nuffield comprises narrow, undulating paths following the **Grim's ditch** (see box below). Sometimes the path is on top of the ditch and sometimes to one side. Most of the way is shaded by trees and you also pass through some attractive woodland. You are much more likely to meet other people, most of whom will be accompanied by a dog or two, on this stretch than on previous ones.

Several areas of woodland along this section (for example '**Oaken Copse**', Map 29) are carpeted with bluebells in the late spring and make for a much-visited and very colourful sight.

Before you can finish this stage you must do something quite unexpected: walk across several fairways (watch out for the bunkers!) of a golf course rather than skirting discreetly around it. It's called Huntercombe Golf Course (Map 30) and to cross it you'll need to follow the strategically placed wooden posts. On the other side you enter a small wooded area on a muddy path; this quickly turns into a gravelled track that leads you through a narrow gap between the two houses here, right past their front doors and down their drive. You may feel like a trespasser but this is the correct route. The path then disappears into the trees before taking you on a path cutting straight through the middle of a field. In the summer, when the crops are at their highest, the bare trail cutting straight between them can look quite dramatic.

NUFFIELD [MAP 30, p154]

Nuffield is basically a small, quiet village with a church, a pub and a golf course: there is no post office, shop, accommodation or food. Actually, that's not strictly true. **Holy Trinity** church, built in 1189, is the final resting place of Viscount William Morris (1877-1963), founder of Morris Motors. He was the Henry Ford of England, starting a mass-production car factory to build the Morris Oxford car. Inside the church they offer help-yourself tea and biscuits for a donation; if they are shut when you drop by, you can at least use the **water tap** by the bench next to William Morris's grave.

Thames Travel's No 139/139B **bus** services (Wallingford to Henley via Crowmarsh Gifford) stops at The Crown (now closed); see pp47-51 for further details.

❑ Grim's ditches

There are many Grim's ditches in England. The reason is that Grim is the Anglo-Saxon word for the devil and his name was often attributed to unnatural features in the landscape. This particular Grim's ditch (see Map 28, p145, but also Map 29, opposite) & Map 30, p154) was probably built during the Iron Age, probably to mark a boundary as it's not big enough to be a defensive earthwork. 'Probably' being the operative word, as even now little is known about this stretch.

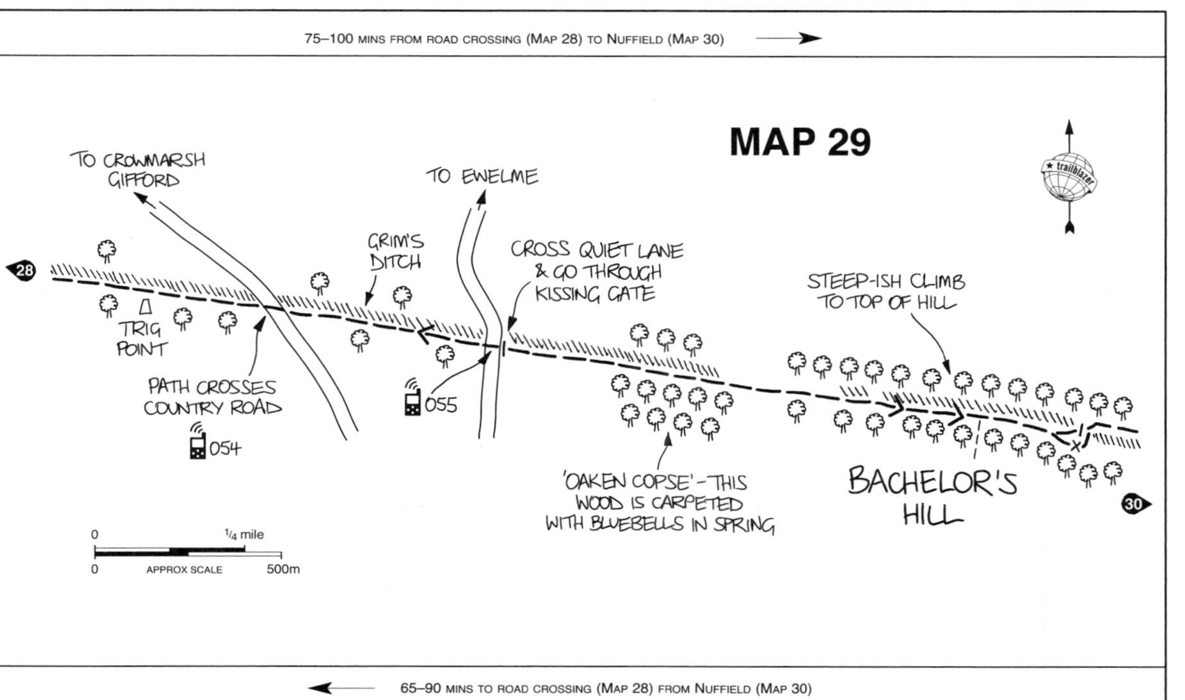
75–100 MINS FROM ROAD CROSSING (MAP 28) TO NUFFIELD (MAP 30)
MAP 29
trailblazer
TO CROWMARSH GIFFORD
TO EWELME
28
GRIM'S DITCH
CROSS QUIET LANE & GO THROUGH KISSING GATE
STEEP-ISH CLIMB TO TOP OF HILL
TRIG POINT
PATH CROSSES COUNTRY ROAD
055
054
'OAKEN COPSE' - THIS WOOD IS CARPETED WITH BLUEBELLS IN SPRING
BACHELOR'S HILL
30
0
1/4 mile
0
APPROX SCALE
500m
65–90 MINS TO ROAD CROSSING (MAP 28) FROM NUFFIELD (MAP 30)

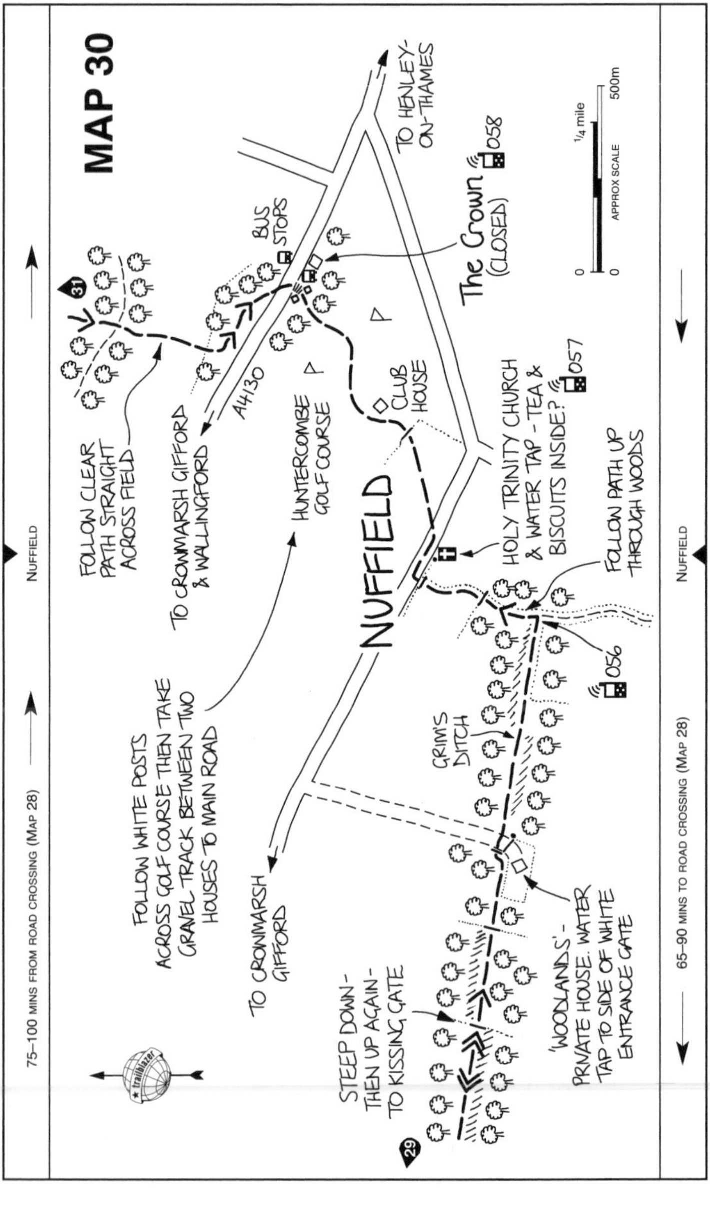

MAP 30

75–100 MINS FROM ROAD CROSSING (MAP 28)

NUFFIELD

65–90 MINS TO ROAD CROSSING (MAP 28)

NUFFIELD

FOLLOW CLEAR PATH STRAIGHT ACROSS FIELD

31

TO CROWMARSH GIFFORD & WALLINGFORD

A4130

BUS STOPS

TO HENLEY-ON-THAMES

The Crown (CLOSED)

058

HUNTERCOMBE GOLF COURSE

CLUB HOUSE

NUFFIELD

HOLY TRINITY CHURCH & WATER TAP - TEA & BISCUITS INSIDE?

057

FOLLOW PATH UP THROUGH WOODS

056

GRIM'S DITCH

FOLLOW WHITE POSTS ACROSS GOLF COURSE THEN TAKE GRAVEL TRACK BETWEEN TWO HOUSES TO MAIN ROAD

TO CROWMARSH GIFFORD

'WOODLANDS' - PRIVATE HOUSE. WATER TAP TO SIDE OF WHITE ENTRANCE GATE

STEEP DOWN - THEN UP AGAIN - TO KISSING GATE

29

trailblazer

APPROX SCALE

0 — 1/4 mile

0 — 500m

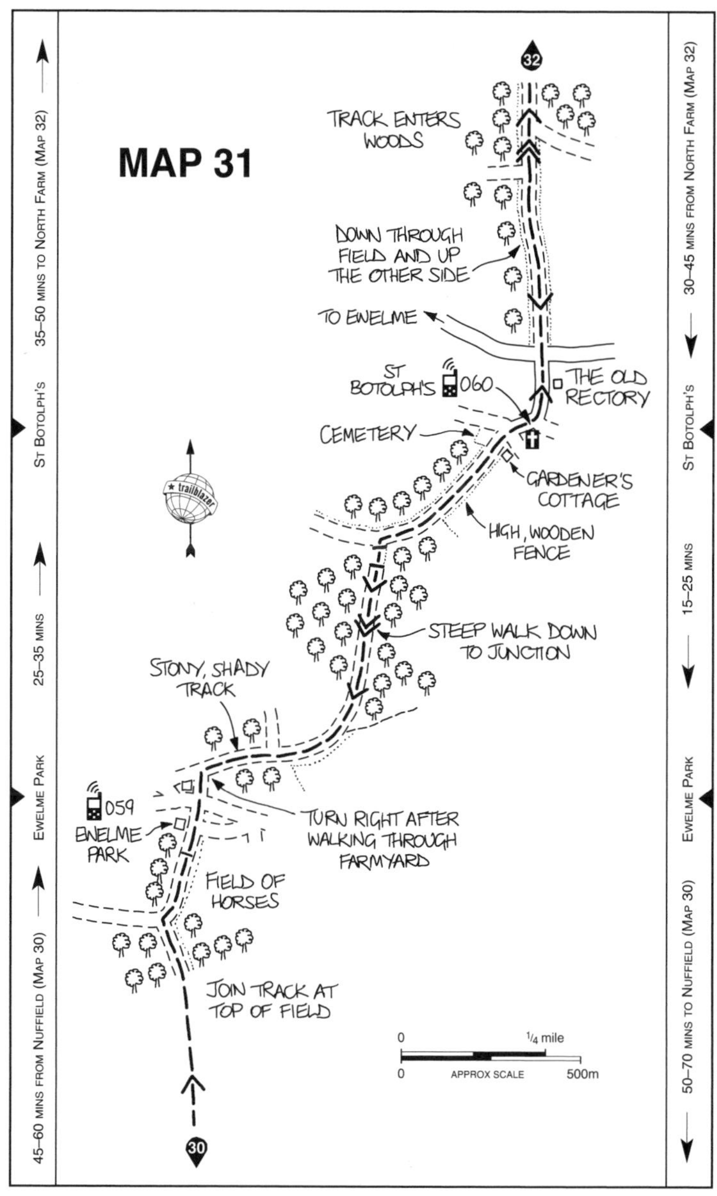
MAP 31
TRACK ENTERS WOODS
DOWN THROUGH FIELD AND UP THE OTHER SIDE
TO EWELME
ST BOTOLPH'S 060
THE OLD RECTORY
CEMETERY
GARDENER'S COTTAGE
HIGH, WOODEN FENCE
STEEP WALK DOWN TO JUNCTION
STONY, SHADY TRACK
059
EWELME PARK
TURN RIGHT AFTER WALKING THROUGH FARMYARD
FIELD OF HORSES
JOIN TRACK AT TOP OF FIELD
32
30
0
¼ mile
0
APPROX SCALE
500m
45–60 MINS FROM NUFFIELD (MAP 30)
EWELME PARK
25–35 MINS
ST BOTOLPH'S
35–50 MINS TO NORTH FARM (MAP 32)
30–45 MINS FROM NORTH FARM (MAP 32)
ST BOTOLPH'S
15–25 MINS
EWELME PARK
50–70 MINS TO NUFFIELD (MAP 30)

The first buildings you come to after leaving Nuffield are those of the picturesque **Ewelme Park Estate** (Map 31). This estate was formed around 450 years ago from several smaller estates and was an important royal deer park under Henry VIII, Elizabeth I, James I, and Charles I, before being broken up and sold. Nowadays the estate is better known for its pheasants rather than deer, though the finale for both animals is the same. A large cache of Roman coins was also found on the estate, among several other finds in the area. Local

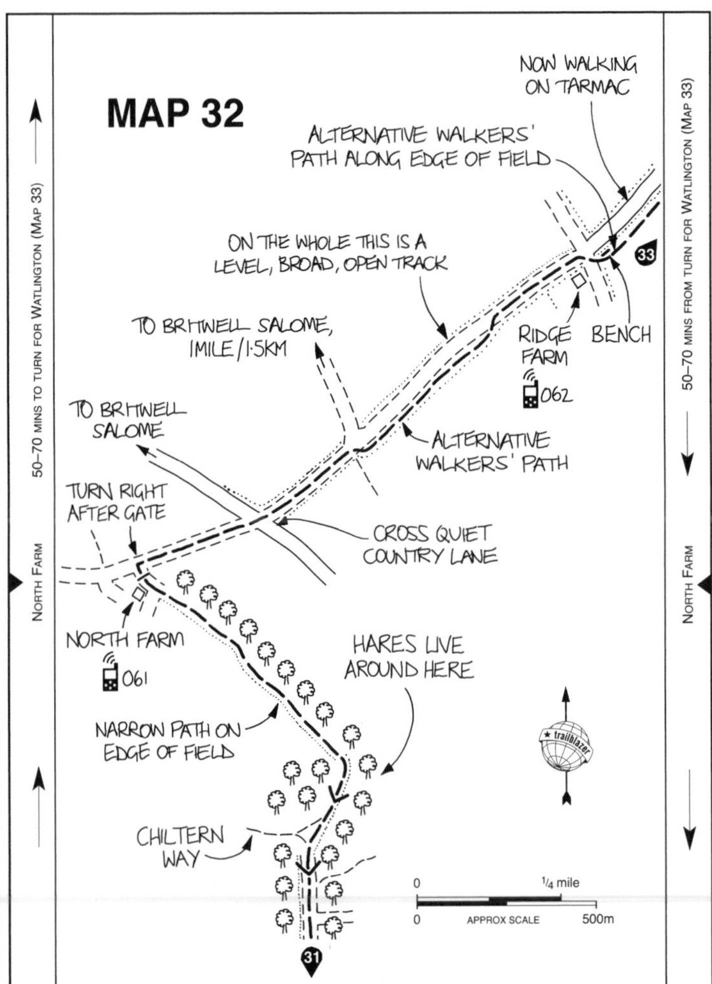

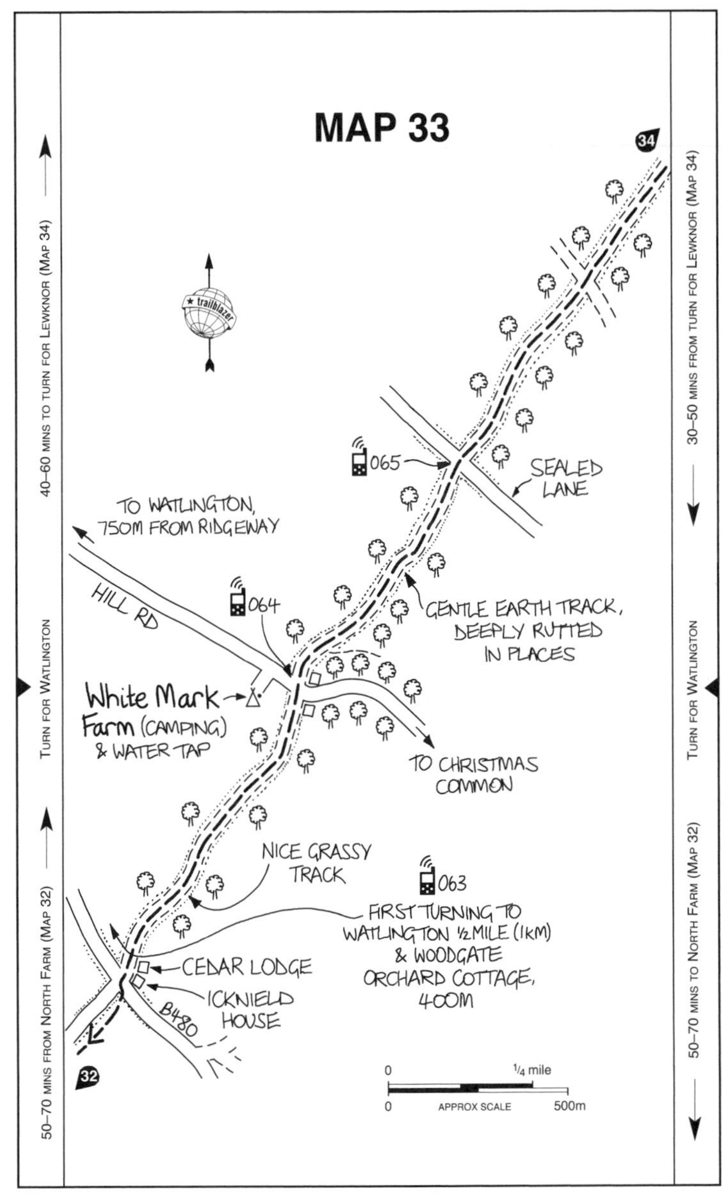
MAP 33
40–60 MINS TO TURN FOR LEWKNOR (MAP 34)
TURN FOR WATLINGTON
50–70 MINS FROM NORTH FARM (MAP 32)
30–50 MINS FROM TURN FOR LEWKNOR (MAP 34)
TURN FOR WATLINGTON
50–70 MINS TO NORTH FARM (MAP 32)
34
32
trailblazer
065
SEALED LANE
TO WATLINGTON, 750M FROM RIDGEWAY
HILL RD
064
GENTLE EARTH TRACK, DEEPLY RUTTED IN PLACES
White Mark Farm (CAMPING) & WATER TAP
TO CHRISTMAS COMMON
NICE GRASSY TRACK
063
FIRST TURNING TO WATLINGTON ½ MILE (1KM) & WOODGATE ORCHARD COTTAGE, 400M
CEDAR LODGE
ICKNIELD HOUSE
B480
0
¼ mile
0
APPROX SCALE
500m

schools make trips to the estate to learn about its history and see the archery corridor used by Henry VIII. When you walk through you'll see the beautiful gatehouse and views of the main house itself which, despite its appearance, is not very old. You may also see some peacocks and will definitely hear several dogs barking, announcing your arrival in the area.

Not much further on is the 11th-century **St Botolph's church**, Swyncombe. Considering the remote location it's a large place. The cemetery around the church is full and there is another diagonally across the crossroads. You may recognise the name of the church as it's famous for the carpet of snowdrops that grows around it in early February; so famous, in fact, that there have even been cases of snowdrop-bulb rustling in the churchyard.

A good couple of hours after leaving Nuffield you'll get to the two turnings (Map 33) for Watlington. If you're heading for the centre of town it matters little which you take, but if aiming for Woodgate Orchard Cottage B&B you'll need the first turning and if aiming for White Mark Farm campsite or Carriers Arms you'll need the second (see Where to stay below for details of all of these). Either way it's about half a mile into the town.

WATLINGTON

This is officially the smallest town in England. However, some people, the residents of Manningtree in Essex for instance, might like to take issue with this. For the record the royal charter giving town status to Watlington was issued in 1154.

If you are stopping here for the day most services and shops that you'll need are on one of two streets. The town is pleasant enough and has a few interesting old buildings to look at so it might be nice to relax here for an hour or two over lunch.

Services

There's a **post office** (Mon, Tue, Thur & Fri 9am-5.30pm, Wed 9am-1pm, Sat 9am-12.30pm) on the High St.

For an **ATM**, you'll have to go to the Co-op **supermarket** (daily 6am-10pm), on Couching St; the ATM is located just inside the door. Near the Co-op there is a **chemist** (Mon-Fri 9am-1pm & 2-6pm, Sat 9am-1pm) should you need it. There are **public toilets** on the High St; and the **library** (Mon 2-7pm, Tue 9.30am-12.30pm & 2-5pm, Thur 2-6pm, Fri 9.30am-12.30pm & 2-5.30pm, Sat 9.30am-1pm) has internet access and free WI-FI.

Thames Travel's No T1 **bus** goes to Lewknor and Chinnor (some of the services continue to Oxford) from the stops near the library; see pp47-51 for further details.

Where to stay

Campers should head for ***White Mark Farm*** (☎ 01491 612295, 🖳 www.whitemarkfarm.co.uk; 🐕 allowed if kept on a lead; Mar-Oct), just a few minutes' walk from the Ridgeway. There are around 40 pitches for tents on this friendly, well-run campsite and they charge from £7pp. The rate includes use of the toilet and shower facilities as well as a microwave oven, kettle and fridge and they can charge your phones/laptops etc for 50p-£1 per item. It's no more than 10 minutes to walk to the centre of town from here. Officially they are closed from the end of October to the beginning of March but if you are walking between November and February and would like to camp here, contact them.

Close to the Ridgeway is a B&B at ***Woodgate Orchard Cottage*** (☎ 01491 612675, 🖳 ronnie.m.roper@gmail.com; 1D/2T; shared bathroom, ☕; WI-FI; Ⓛ; 🐕). B&B starts at £40pp (sgl occ £55-65) including afternoon tea on arrival. The owner can provide luggage transfer if arranged in advance. Make sure to book well ahead if you want to stay here as it's

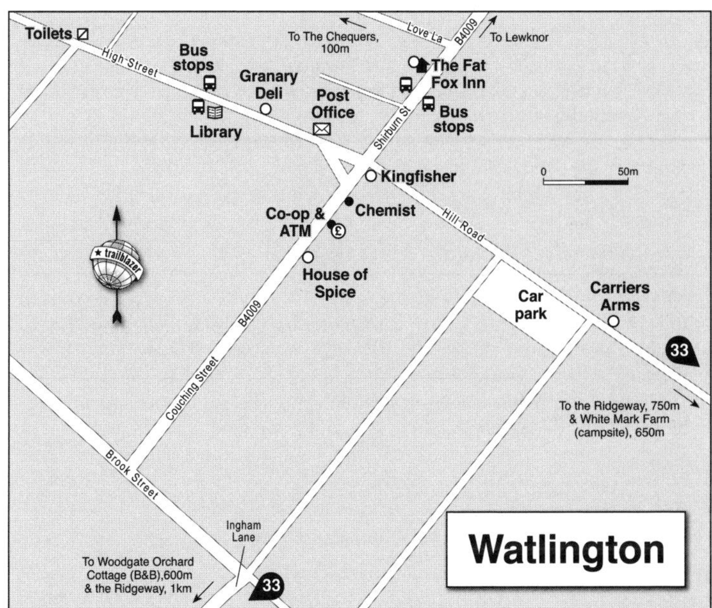

very popular, especially with walkers. This place is just 400m from the Ridgeway; the easiest way to get here is to leave the path where it crosses the B480. Icknield House is on this junction. Head down the B480 towards Watlington and the B&B is on your right near the restriction signs.

Another good choice would be ***The Fat Fox Inn*** (☎ 01491 613040, 💻 www.thefatfoxinn.co.uk; 5D/4T, all en suite, ☕; WI-FI; Ⓛ; 🐕 £10). This is a delightful old pub near the centre of town. The accommodation here is in a tastefully converted coach barn next to the pub and each room is different. B&B costs £42.50-62.50pp (sgl occ £75-115).

Airbnb (see p20) boasts several options in and around the town so that may be your best bet for accommodation.

Where to eat and drink

A relatively new place – and the best option for lunch – is ***Granary Deli*** (☎ 01491 613585, 💻 www.granarydeli.co.uk; Mon-Sat 9am-5pm, Sun 10am-2pm) with a fine array of wholesome sandwiches, cakes and lunches.

On the way into Watlington, from the second turning off the Ridgeway, is the ***Carriers Arms*** (☎ 01491 613470; food Mon-Sat 10am-2pm, Sun 10am-3pm, Thur, Fri & Sat 7-9pm). Breakfast is served daily till 11.30am and on Sunday they serve a roast from 11.30am-3pm. At other times you can get standard pub grub. This freehouse serves some decent real ales and the location is convenient if you're staying at White Mark Farm Campsite. However, they don't accept cards.

The Fat Fox Inn (see Where to stay; food Mon-Sat noon-2.30pm, Mon-Thur 6.30-9pm, Fri & Sat 7-9.30pm, Sun noon-3pm & 7-9pm) offers a more interesting menu which changes regularly and where possible includes locally sourced food; example: chorizo-stuffed rabbit loin, pancetta, confit leg, braised beans (£18), but there are also burgers from £14.

The Chequers (☎ 01491 612874, 🖳 www.thechequerswatlington.co.uk; food Mon-Sat noon-2pm, Sun to 2.30pm, Tue-Sat 7-9pm), a pub on Love Lane, is well known as one of the best places in town for food and it has friendly staff. The menu varies but in the evening it may include delicious pan-seared calves' liver and bacon, onion gravy, mashed potatoes and vegetables (£13.75). At ***House of Spice*** (☎ 01491 613865, 🖳 www.houseofspice.uk.com; daily 5.30-11pm), the menu contains all the usual Indian dishes; lamb dopiaza rice costs £7.95 (takeaway £6.50).

Alternatively ***Kingfisher*** (Mon-Sat 11am-2pm & 4-10pm) serves fish & chips and fried chicken.

WATLINGTON TO PRINCES RISBOROUGH [MAPS 33-39]

Overview

Although this **11.2 mile/18km (4-5¼hrs)** section of the Ridgeway is pleasant enough, it's fairly uneventful. The walking is easy with few steep sections so you can really slow down, relax and enjoy the scenery. Perhaps take a diversion into Lewknor, Kingston Blount or Chinnor for a drink, or press on and finish early in Princes Risborough.

Route

Continuing on the Ridgeway from the road turn-offs for Watlington it's a long, straight 2½ miles/4km along shady tracks and through open fields, until you get to the turning for Lewknor. It's about half a mile/1km along this minor road to the village.

LEWKNOR [MAP 34]

Lewknor is a small, picturesque village, much like many others around here. Easy access to the M40, and therefore London, has added to its value on the property market. It's a very quiet place as nearly all the traffic coming through is for the village itself.

The Oxford Tube and Oxford Bus 'airline' **coach** services (see box p46) stop on the B4009, just off junction 6 of the M40 near Lewknor. Carousel's link40 **bus** (High Wycombe to Thame) and Thames Travel's T1 (Watlington to Chinnor) services also call in Lewknor. See pp47-51 for details.

At the crossroads in the village, and a good reason to come here, is ***Ye Olde Leathern Bottel*** (aka ***The Leathern Bottle***; ☎ 01844 351482, 🖳 www.theleathernbottle.co.uk; food Mon-Thur noon-2pm & 7-9.30pm, Fri noon-2pm & 6-9.30pm, Sat noon-2.30pm & 6-9.30pm, Sun noon-2.30pm & 7-9.30pm). It closes in the afternoons, so don't make the trek out here between 2.30pm and 6pm on weekdays or 3.30pm and 6pm at weekends. However, when it is open it can get very busy, especially at weekends, as they don't have a booking policy other than for large groups. You can expect traditional pub food here – sandwiches at lunchtimes and steak with chips (from £16.95), or ham, egg & chips (£10.95) in the evenings. They also have vegetarian options.

Another good reason to visit is for the excellent **B&B** at ***Moorcourt Cottage*** (☎ 01844 351419, 🖳 moorcourt2002@yahoo.co.uk; 1D private bathroom/1T en suite; ▼; WI-FI; Ⓛ). Accommodation in this picture-perfect house is from £37.50pp, or £48 if you're on your own. The friendly owners will even pick you up from where the Ridgeway joins the road to Lewknor, saving you a fairly tedious stretch of road walking at the end of the day. This is another popular place for walkers to stay so be sure to book well in advance. If arranged in advance they will transport your luggage to your next destination on the Way; a charge is made. Credit cards are not accepted.

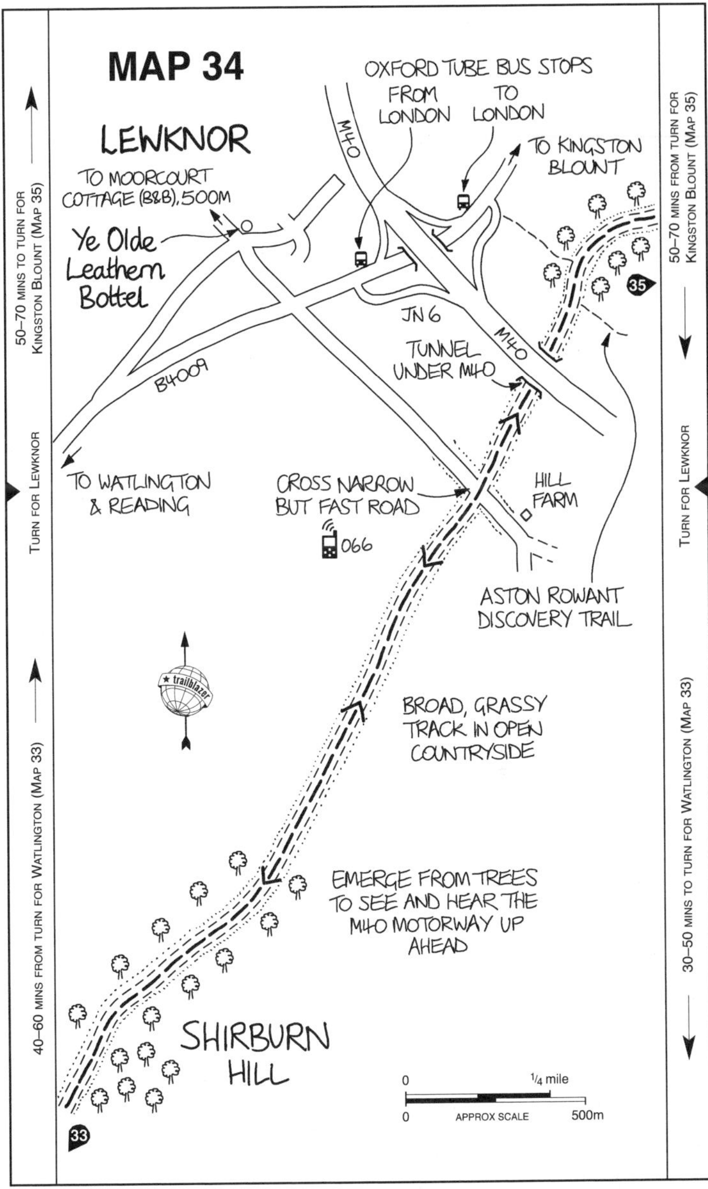
MAP 34
LEWKNOR
OXFORD TUBE BUS STOPS
FROM LONDON
TO LONDON
M40
TO KINGSTON BLOUNT
TO MOORCOURT COTTAGE (B&B), 500M
Ye Olde Leathern Bottel
JN 6
M40
TUNNEL UNDER M40
B4009
TO WATLINGTON & READING
CROSS NARROW BUT FAST ROAD
066
HILL FARM
ASTON ROWANT DISCOVERY TRAIL
trailblazer
BROAD, GRASSY TRACK IN OPEN COUNTRYSIDE
EMERGE FROM TREES TO SEE AND HEAR THE M40 MOTORWAY UP AHEAD
SHIRBURN HILL
35
33
0
1/4 mile
0
APPROX SCALE
500m
50–70 MINS TO TURN FOR KINGSTON BLOUNT (MAP 35)
TURN FOR LEWKNOR
40–60 MINS FROM TURN FOR WATLINGTON (MAP 33)
50–70 MINS FROM TURN FOR KINGSTON BLOUNT (MAP 35)
TURN FOR LEWKNOR
30–50 MINS TO TURN FOR WATLINGTON (MAP 33)

ROUTE GUIDE AND MAPS

You'll hear the M40 motorway up ahead long before you see it. There are no two ways about it: this motorway completely dominates the countryside it passes through. The physically elevated status of the M40 at this point only acts to reinforce its dominance over the landscape. Luckily for walkers there is a large tunnel underneath it, albeit without murals, unlike the tunnel under the A34 back near East Ilsley. See p36 for details of the Aston Rowant Discovery Trail.

Around 1½ miles/2.5km after you pass through the tunnel you'll come to a road crossing the path (Map 35). Turn left down this road to get to the village of Kingston Blount, about half a mile/1km away.

KINGSTON BLOUNT

This small village is sadly now only worth a visit if you're planning to stay for two nights and are happy to self cater (see opposite) as at the time of writing the last pub, The Cherry Tree, had closed. In times gone by this place had a number of shops and pubs, a post office, a school and even a telephone exchange. The local people pronounce the 'Blount' part of the village name as 'blunt' – a reference to the Le Blunt family who were lords of this area for several hundred years.

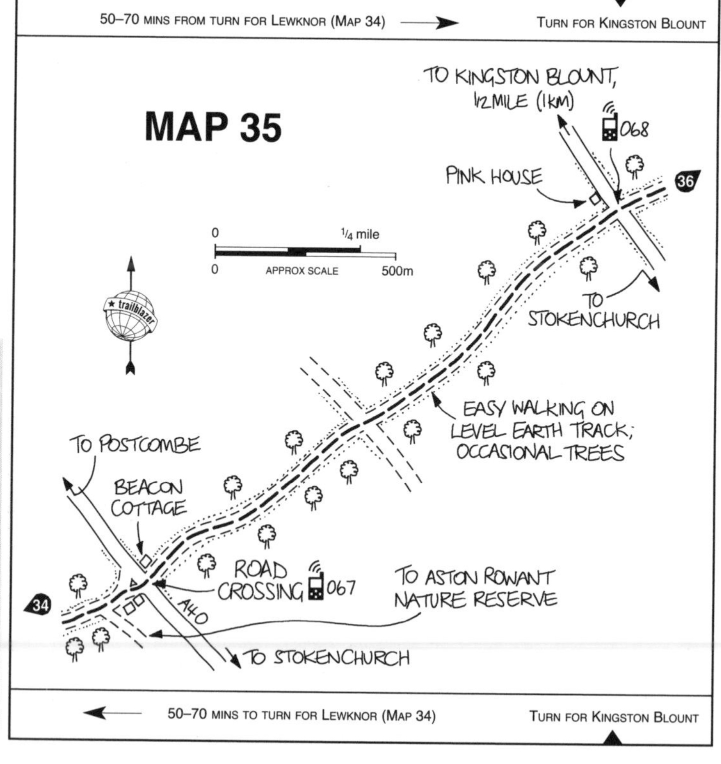

The only accommodation now is a self-catering cabin at ***Lakeside Town Farm*** (☎ 01844 352152, 0797 143 6504, 💻 townfarmcottage.co.uk; 1D, en suite; WI-FI; small kitchenette), a working farm with an old farmhouse that's full of character and has beautiful gardens. The rate is £110 per night (generally no sgl occ discount); a minimum stay of two nights is required. A welcome pack is provided for the first morning so you can make breakfast.

Carousel's Link40 and Red Rose's No 275 **bus** services stop here; see pp47-51 for further details. If you need a **taxi** you could call Chinnor Cabs (see p164).

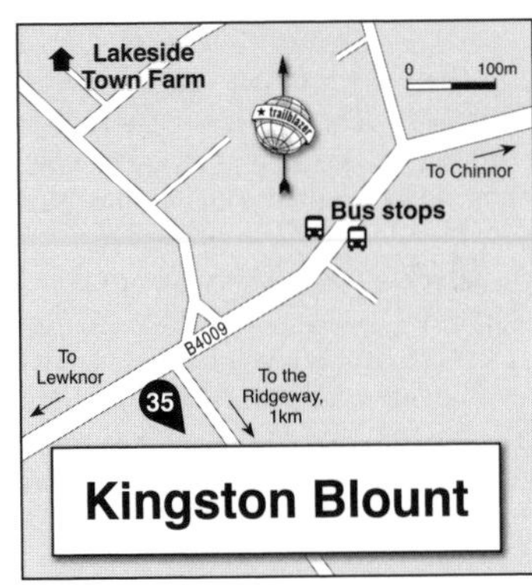

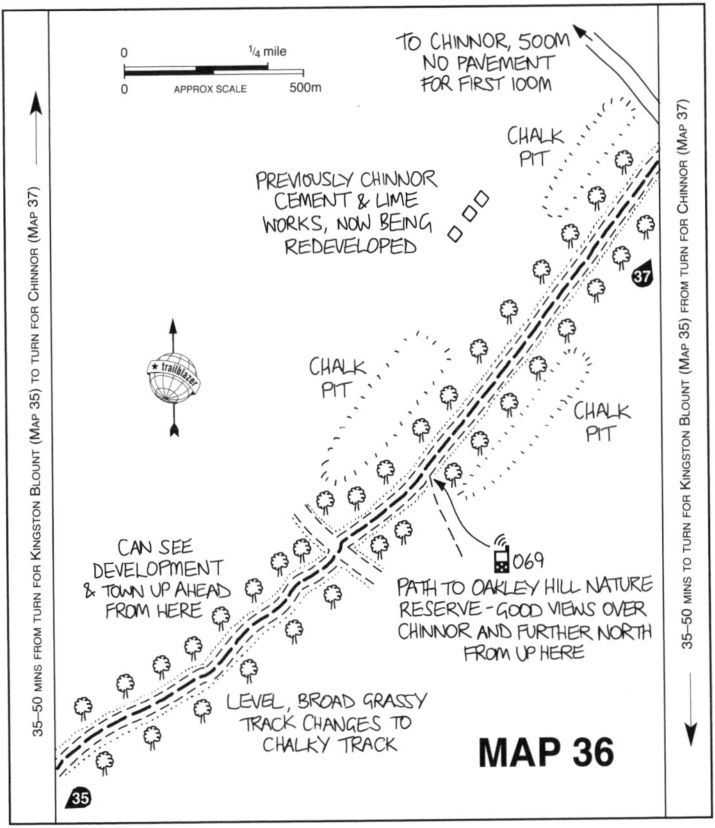

Lakeside Town Farm
0
100m
trailblazer
To Chinnor
Bus stops
B4009
To Lewknor
35
To the Ridgeway, 1km
Kingston Blount

0
1/4 mile
0
APPROX SCALE
500m
TO CHINNOR, 500M NO PAVEMENT FOR FIRST 100M
CHALK PIT
PREVIOUSLY CHINNOR CEMENT & LIME WORKS, NOW BEING REDEVELOPED
37
trailblazer
CHALK PIT
CHALK PIT
CAN SEE DEVELOPMENT & TOWN UP AHEAD FROM HERE
069
PATH TO OAKLEY HILL NATURE RESERVE - GOOD VIEWS OVER CHINNOR AND FURTHER NORTH FROM UP HERE
LEVEL, BROAD GRASSY TRACK CHANGES TO CHALKY TRACK
MAP 36
35
35–50 MINS FROM TURN FOR KINGSTON BLOUNT (MAP 35) TO TURN FOR CHINNOR (MAP 37)
35–50 MINS TO TURN FOR KINGSTON BLOUNT (MAP 35) FROM TURN FOR CHINNOR (MAP 37)

The developments (Map 36) at Chinnor stand out for a mile, or two, and not long after you have spotted them the path becomes flanked by the huge pits that are the result of previous activity at the works. Although it's not easy to get a proper view of these, most have water at the bottom. On a sunny day the water is bright turquoise which contrasts with the brilliant white chalk-pit sides – a bizarre sight in the middle of this countryside. On the opposite side is Oakley Hill (🖳 www.bbowt.org.uk/reserves/oakley-hill) nature reserve, run by Berks, Bucks & Oxon Wildlife Trust (see pp62-3).

When you reach the main road that crosses the Ridgeway (Maps 36 & 37), turn left and follow it into Chinnor, about a third of a mile/500m. Although Chinnor is a large village there isn't a great deal here, so if you don't want to go on the railway (see below) you might want to keep walking.

CHINNOR

This is the next village in the line of settlements along the Chilterns. In the 19th century this place was well known for producing lace and chair legs. The Chiltern beech forests were the source of wood for the legs. In the early 20th century a cement factory was opened and this steadily expanded as new technology allowed for ever-increasing production levels. The population in the village grew as the works expanded but they were eventually closed in 1999. Part of the land is now being redeveloped as housing.

One thing that has survived is the **Chinnor & Princes Risborough Railway** that runs steam trains along a section of track from here. By 1961 the line from Watlington to Chinnor had closed completely, though the section from Chinnor to Princes Risborough was used by the cement factory. In the early '70s Chinnor station and platform were demolished and by the late '80s all freight traffic had ceased. However, within five years the wholly volunteer-run Chinnor & Princes Risborough Railway Association had rebuilt the platform and station and started running their heritage steam services.

Since then the volunteers have extended the line three times and trains can now almost reach Princes Risborough providing a nearly 8-mile (12.6km) return trip. During spring 2017 a new platform is being built there to allow interchange with mainline trains. Steam and vintage diesel services run most Sundays and the tea room is open for walkers, but check their talking timetable (☎ 01844 353535), or their website (🖳 www.chinnorrailway.co.uk), before making your way down there.

Services

The village is centred on Church Rd where there is a line of shops. This comprises a Spar **supermarket** (daily 6.30am-9pm), **Lloyds Pharmacy** (Mon-Fri 9am-6pm, Sat 9am-1pm), and Godwins **Bakery** (Mon-Fri 6am-5pm, Sat 6am-4pm).

The **post office** (Mon-Fri 9am-5.30pm, Sat 9am-12.30pm) is just around the corner on the High St. There is an **ATM** outside the BP petrol station on Oakley Rd and also a Co-op supermarket (daily 6am-10pm) and a **public toilet** here.

Carousel's Link40 **bus** service stops at the Red Lion and at the other end of the High St. Redline's No 320 to Princes Risborough stops at the Red Lion. Red Rose's No 275 (High Wycombe to Oxford) and Thames Travel's T1 (Watlington to Lewknor) also call in Chinnor; see pp47-51 for further details.

If you want a **taxi** call Chinnor Cabs (☎ 01844 355252).

Where to stay, eat and drink

The only place to stay near Chinnor is ***Manor Farm Cottage*** (☎ 01844 353301, 🖳 www.manorfarmcottage.info; 1D en suite, 1D private bathroom ☕; WI-FI; Ⓛ; 🐕) a 400-year-old Grade II listed home about 1½ miles/2.5km east of the main village in the

ROUTE GUIDE AND MAPS

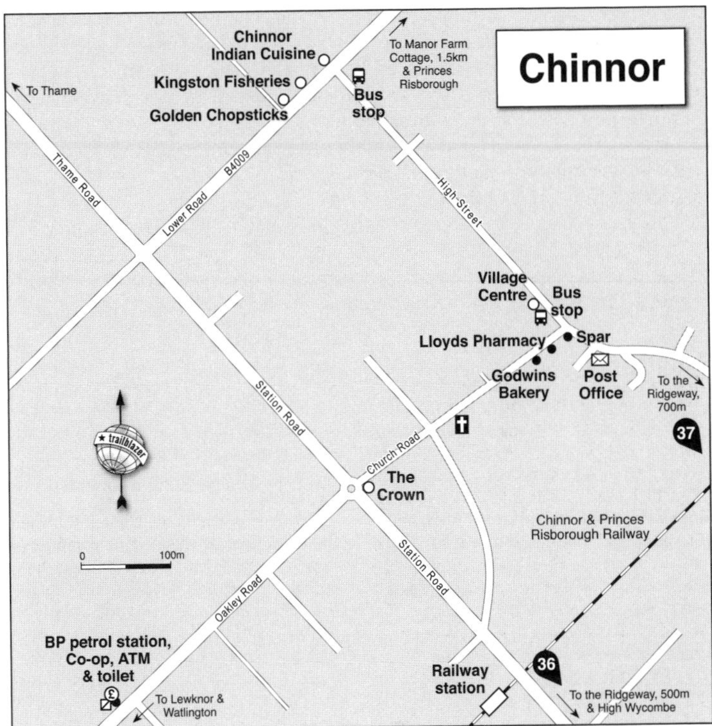

hamlet of **Henton**. Rates are from £32.50pp (sgl occ from £50).

For lunch or a cup of tea in Chinnor, pop into the ***Village Centre*** (☎ 01844 353733, 💻 www.chinnorvillagecentre.org; Mon-Fri 8.30am-4pm with lunch menu noon-2pm, Sat 8.30am-1.45pm) where the friendly staff serve tea, coffee, all-day breakfasts and toasted sandwiches.

There's also a good Indian: ***Chinnor Indian Cuisine*** (☎ 01844 354843, 💻 www.chinnorindiancuisine.co.uk; Tue-Sat noon-2pm & 5-11pm, Sun noon-3pm & 5.30-11pm) is a couple of minutes' walk from the 'centre', but worth it if you like Indian food as this place is good. Most main courses are £7.60 if you're opting for takeaway. If a Chinese takeaway is more your thing head to ***Golden Chopsticks*** (☎ 01844 354284; Mon & Wed-Sun 5.30-9.30pm). Alternatively, there is the rather grandly named ***Kingston Fisheries*** (☎ 01844 353874; Tue-Sat noon-1.45pm & 5-9pm, to 10pm on Fri). It's the only fish & chip shop in the village.

As for pubs, our favourite is ***The Crown*** (☎ 01844 351244, 💻 www.the-crownchinnor.co.uk; food Mon-Wed 9am-2.30pm & 6-8.30pm, Thur & Fri 9am-2.30pm & 6-7.30pm, Sat 10am-2pm, Sun 10am-3.30pm) on Station Rd; it does all-day breakfasts as well as lunches and evening meals (except at weekends). If breakfast is required at about 9am it must be prebooked. They have live music on Thursday and Friday evenings.

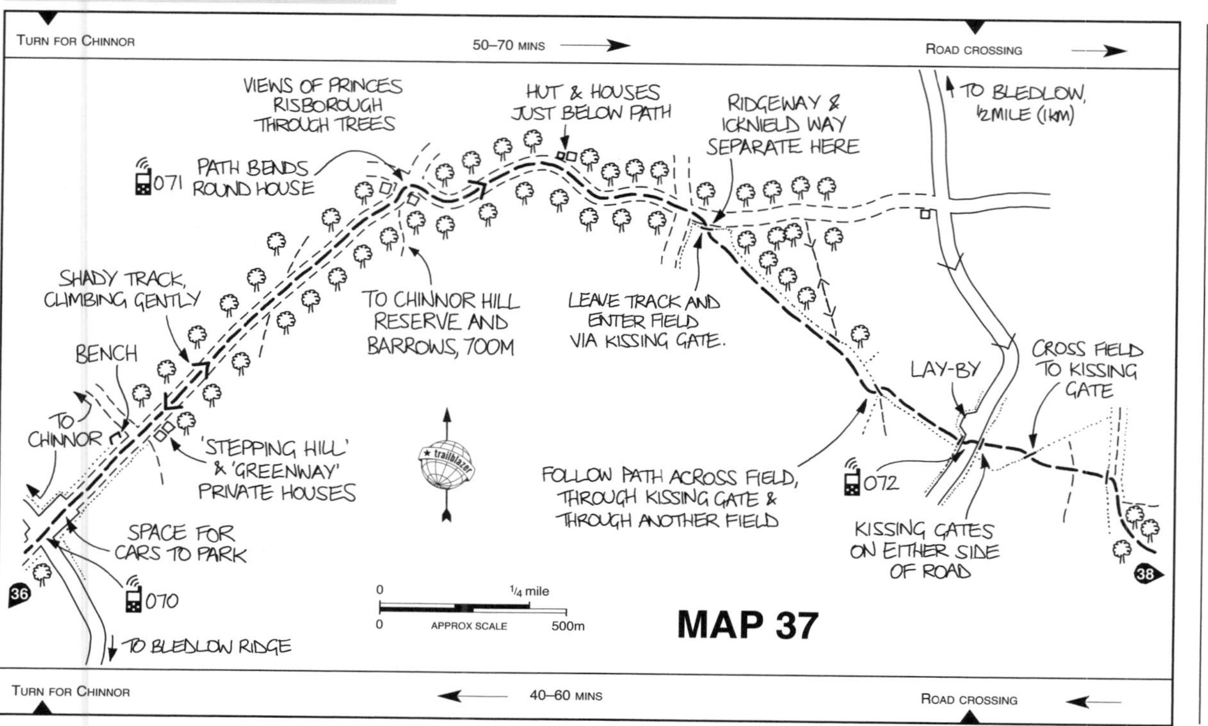
TURN FOR CHINNOR
50–70 MINS
ROAD CROSSING
VIEWS OF PRINCES RISBOROUGH THROUGH TREES
HUT & HOUSES JUST BELOW PATH
RIDGEWAY & ICKNIELD WAY SEPARATE HERE
TO BLEDLOW, ½MILE (1KM)
071
PATH BENDS ROUND HOUSE
SHADY TRACK, CLIMBING GENTLY
TO CHINNOR HILL RESERVE AND BARROWS, 700M
LEAVE TRACK AND ENTER FIELD VIA KISSING GATE.
BENCH
LAY-BY
CROSS FIELD TO KISSING GATE
TO CHINNOR
'STEPPING HILL' & 'GREENWAY' PRIVATE HOUSES
trailblazer
FOLLOW PATH ACROSS FIELD, THROUGH KISSING GATE & THROUGH ANOTHER FIELD
072
SPACE FOR CARS TO PARK
KISSING GATES ON EITHER SIDE OF ROAD
36
070
0
1/4 mile
0
APPROX SCALE
500m
MAP 37
38
TO BLEDLOW RIDGE
TURN FOR CHINNOR
40–60 MINS
ROAD CROSSING

Though the Ridgeway and Icknield Way have been sharing the same path since around Watlington, they eventually separate (Map 37) with the Icknield Way taking a straight course to Princes Risborough and the Ridgeway meandering along a much more roundabout route.

Depending on how you are feeling at this point in the day, you might decide to take the Icknield Way as it meets up again with the Ridgeway before going

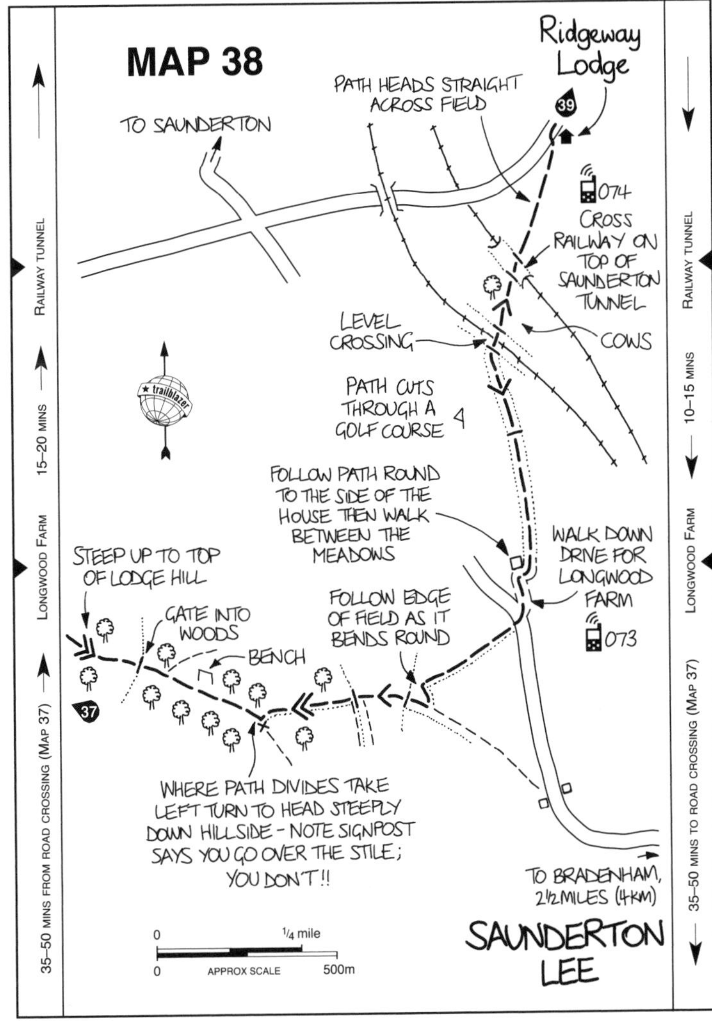

into Princes Risborough. From where the two paths divide to where they rejoin, the Icknield Way is 1½ miles/2.5km and the Ridgeway is 2¾ miles/4.5km.

Some time later the Ridgeway cuts through a golf course (Map 38), the second so far, and crosses a railway track. It hardly needs to be mentioned to take great care here. A couple of minutes further on there is another railway crossing but this time you are walking on the roof of **Saunderton Tunnel**. As you join the road, you pass Ridgeway Lodge (Map 38; see p167).

The final part of this section is along the busy A4010; it's as dull as most other walks along fast main roads. The Ridgeway only skirts the town so unless

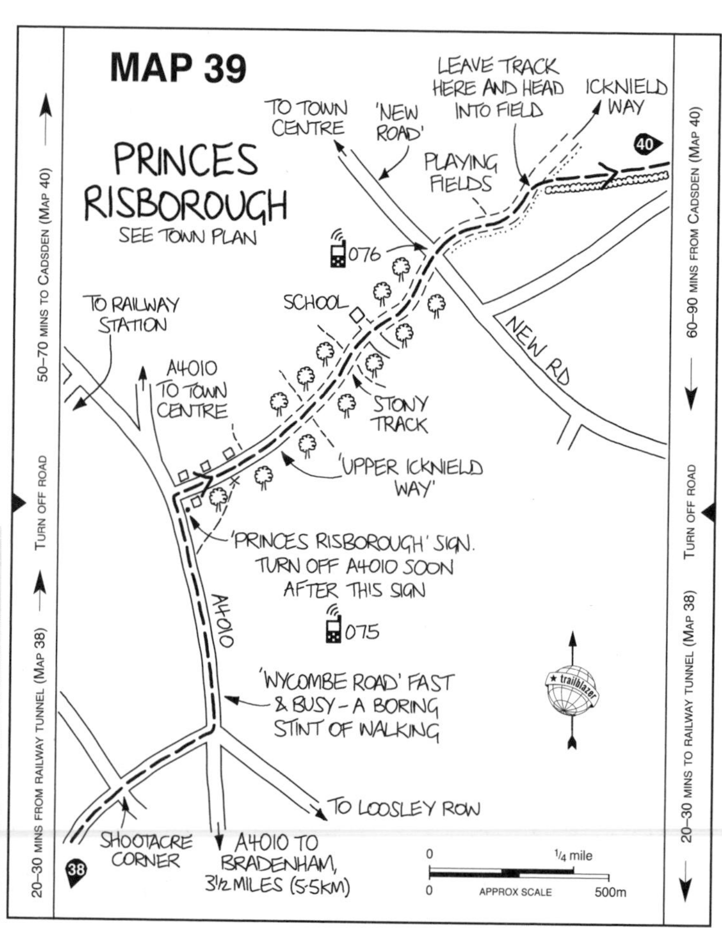

you're needing the railway station, the best way to get to the centre is to turn off the A4010 after the Princes Risborough sign (following the Ridgeway path) and then left when New Road crosses the path: it's then a quarter of a mile to the centre of town.

PRINCES RISBOROUGH

[see map p170]

This is the biggest town you'll have visited so far on the journey. Despite this, the centre is still compact with most of the shops and services occupying the old High St and large supermarkets at either end. As the Ridgeway passes more or less through the town it makes a convenient overnight or lunch stop.

Like many of the towns around here, this one dates back a very long way, possibly to Roman times. The Saxons were certainly here and a couple of hundred years after they arrived there is a mention of this town in the Domesday Book as 'Riseburg'.

Edward, 'The Black Prince', had his palace here in the 14th century, hence the town's name, though the site of the palace is now unfortunately a car park, so not really worth investigating.

The arrival of the railway in 1862 caused the town to grow considerably and by the 1930s the previously separate towns of Princes Risborough and Monks Risborough had merged.

Services

There is a **post office** (Mon-Fri 9am-5.30pm, Sat 9am-12.30pm) by the roundabout at the southern end of town. Across the High St, the library also now plays host to the **Information Centre** (☎ 01844 274795, 💻 risborough_office@wycombe.gov.uk; Tue 10am-1pm & 1.30-5.30pm, Wed 10am-1pm, Thur 10am-1pm & 1.30-4pm, Fri 10am-1pm & 1.30-5pm, Sat 10am-1pm); they have local information as well as an accommodation list and can make bookings.

On the High St itself you'll also find branches of NatWest, Barclays, Nationwide and TSB banks, all with **ATMs**.

There is a **supermarket** at either end of the High St: Tesco (Mon-Sat 6am to midnight, Sun 10am-4pm) at the top – which has **toilets** – and M&S Simply Food (Mon-Sat 8am-8pm, Sun 10am-4pm) at the bottom; there are also public **toilets** in the car park nearby. Next to M&S Simply Food there is a **newsagent** (Mon-Fri 6am-7pm, Sun 8am-2pm). You'll also find two branches of Lloyds Pharmacy, a **chemist**; one at 62-68 High St (Mon-Fri 8am-6pm, Sat 9am-5.30pm), the other (Mon-Fri 9am-6pm, Sat 9am-1.30pm) is at 52 High St.

There's also a shop for **cyclists**, Risboro' Car and Cycle Parts (☎ 01844 273092, 💻 www.risborocarcycleparts.co.uk; Mon-Sat 9am-5pm, Sun 9am-noon), on Church St; the staff offer a full service for your cycle for £44.99. There is a **farmers' market** once a month (see box p21).

If you need a **taxi** contact Risborough Cars (☎ 01844 274111, 💻 www.risboroughcars.co.uk.

Unlike in many of the surrounding towns the railway line is still open; there are regular **trains** to London Marylebone & Aylesbury via High Wycombe, see box p45. Arriva's No 300 **bus** from High Wycombe to Aylesbury passes through; Redline's Nos 320 and 321 also call here. See pp47-51 for further details.

Where to stay

There's not much choice in Princes Risborough, even **Airbnb** (see p20) was advertising only one option when we checked.

Slightly out of town, but directly on the Ridgeway, is ***Ridgeway Lodge*** (Map 38; ☎ 01844 345438, 💻 www.ridgewaylodge.co.uk; 1D/1T share facilities/1D or T, en suite; WI-FI; Ⓛ £6) which charges from £48pp (sgl occ £50-80). This is a very well-run B&B in a beautiful location. The owners can provide a packed lunch if given 24 hours' notice.

Right in the centre of town you could try ***The George & Dragon*** (☎ 01844

346785, 💻 georgeanddragonrisborough.co.uk; 2D/1T, all en suite, ☕; WI-FI; 🐕 £20 deposit). The rooms were refurbished in 2015 and are both smart and swish (and the bathrooms are huge!); rates are from £42.50pp (sgl occ £75).

Where to eat and drink

Crumbs Too (☎ 01844 344462; Mon-Sat 8am-5pm) is located at the top of the High St and continues to be a popular stop for coffee, cakes and lunchtime bites. There is a branch of ***Costa*** (Mon-Fri 6.30am-6.30pm, Sat & Sun 7.30am-6pm) serving the usual range of coffees, teas, cakes and savoury snacks.

At the other end of the street ***Fieldmouse Cheese Store & Deli*** (☎ 01844 344990; Mon-Fri 9am-5pm, Sat 9am-4pm) has a delicious selection of quiches, ploughman's and sandwiches to eat in or take away.

Also on the High St, ***La Crepe Escape*** (☎ 01844 275600, 💻 www.lacrepeescape.co.uk; Mon-Fri 10am-5pm, Sat 9.15am-5pm, Sun 10.30am-2pm) is proving very popular, with their Nutella crepe (£3.10/4.10 small/regular) an enduring favourite; gluten and dairy free options are available.

There's a good choice of curry houses for such a small town. ***Cinnamon Lounge*** (☎ 01844 347003, 💻 www.cinnamonloungerisborough.co.uk; Mon-Sat noon-2.30pm & 5.30-11.30pm, Sun noon-10.30pm), on the High St, is usually busy, but for a quieter Indian meal try ***Jaflong*** (☎ 01844 274443, 💻 www.jaflongbalti.co.uk; daily 5.30-11.30pm) further up the road; they don't serve alcohol here but you can bring

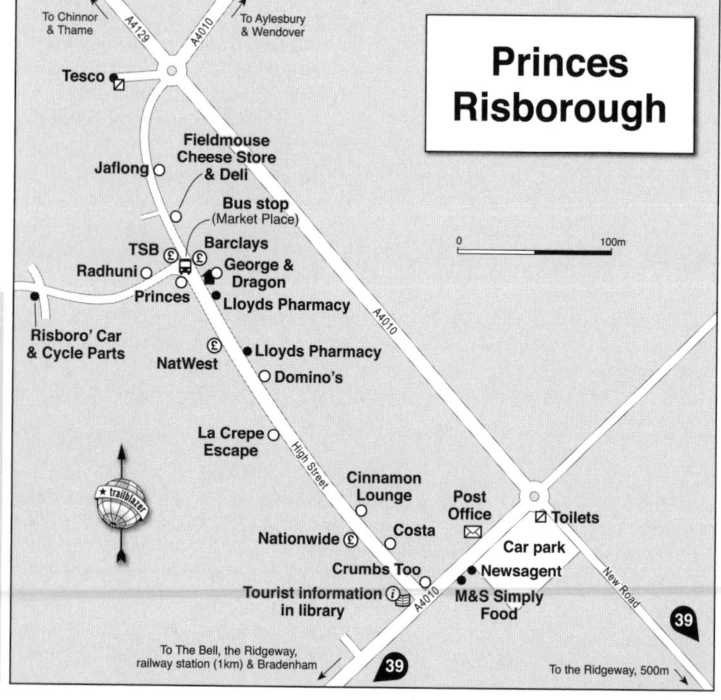

your own. There is also ***Radhuni*** (☎ 01844 273741, 🖳 www.radhunigroup.com/risborough; Mon-Sat 6-11pm, Sun to 10pm), on Church St, just off the High St.

Just down from the library, ***The Bell*** (☎ 01844 274702, 🖳 www.thebell-risborough.co.uk; bar Mon noon-11.30pm, Tue-Thur & Sun 11am-11.30pm, Fri & Sat 11am-1am), a lively bar with a decent line in cocktails; at the time of research they were not serving food but they were planning to.

There is also a very busy fish & chip shop on the High St called ***Princes*** (☎ 01844 343751; Mon-Thur & Sat 11.30am-2pm & 4.30-9.30pm, Fri to 10pm). Finally, for late-night fodder there's a branch of the pizza joint ***Domino's*** (☎ 01844 344244, 🖳 www.dominos.co.uk/princes-risborough; daily 11am-11pm), for take away or delivery.

PRINCES RISBOROUGH TO WIGGINTON (& TRING) [MAPS 39-46]

Overview

This section is **12½ miles/20km (6½-8hrs)**, but be aware that there are many steep ups and downs to tire you out before the end is in sight. A great deal of the walking is through mature woodlands on good paths and there is plenty of variety. You'll pass by Chequers, the Prime Minister's country house, visit a Boer War monument on top of a hill with stunning views, and pass through the attractive and useful town of Wendover, amongst other things.

If you decide you want to walk right through to Ivinghoe Beacon in one day, be prepared for a tough time. On paper the 17½ miles/28km doesn't sound unreasonable but the steep up and down sections will leave you weary well before you get your first sight of the Beacon. From there it's a strenuous last few miles to the end. Then there is the matter of walking from the Beacon to accommodation or to transport – a walk into Ivinghoe village is entirely possible but that would add another couple of miles. For this reason, starting the last day from somewhere closer, such as Wendover or Wigginton, can make a lot of sense. It'll also mean you'll have some energy left at the end of the day to celebrate finishing the Ridgeway.

Route

The section from Princes Risborough to Wendover is very popular with both day walkers and dog walkers. The Ridgeway and Icknield Way share the same path until they are out of Princes Risborough, then they separate. The Icknield Way continues on the main track and rejoins the Ridgeway later.

At the top of the first steep climb you'll enter **Whiteleaf Hill Nature Reserve** (Map 40; 🖳 www.buckscc.gov.uk/leisure-and-culture/whiteleaf-hill-nature-reserve); this nature reserve is known for its variety of butterflies and wild flowers. Even if you're not looking specifically, you're bound to notice a chalkhill blue butterfly (see opp p65) or two and you'll probably also see the common blue. Flowers that grow well on this chalky soil have wonderful names, such as squinancy wort and viper's bugloss.

On the west side of the hill, facing Monks Risborough, there is a chalk cross on a triangular base cut into the hill – the **Whiteleaf Cross**. The history of this monument is hazy to say the least, but it was recorded as far back as the mid 1750s. It's probably been enlarged since then and now a concerted effort has been made to restore and maintain it.

After descending this hill, you come to **Cadsden**, and more importantly a pub, ***The Plough*** (☎ 01844 343302, 💻 theplough.pub; 4D or T/1Tr, all en suite; ▼; WI-FI). It's a popular place and they charge £60-65pp (sgl occ from £75, three sharing from £150) for B&B. The menu (**food** Mon-Sat noon-2pm & 6.30-9.30pm, Sun noon-2.30pm & 6.30-8.30pm) features standard pub fare and main courses are served in small and large (£11.95/15.95) portions. For dogs

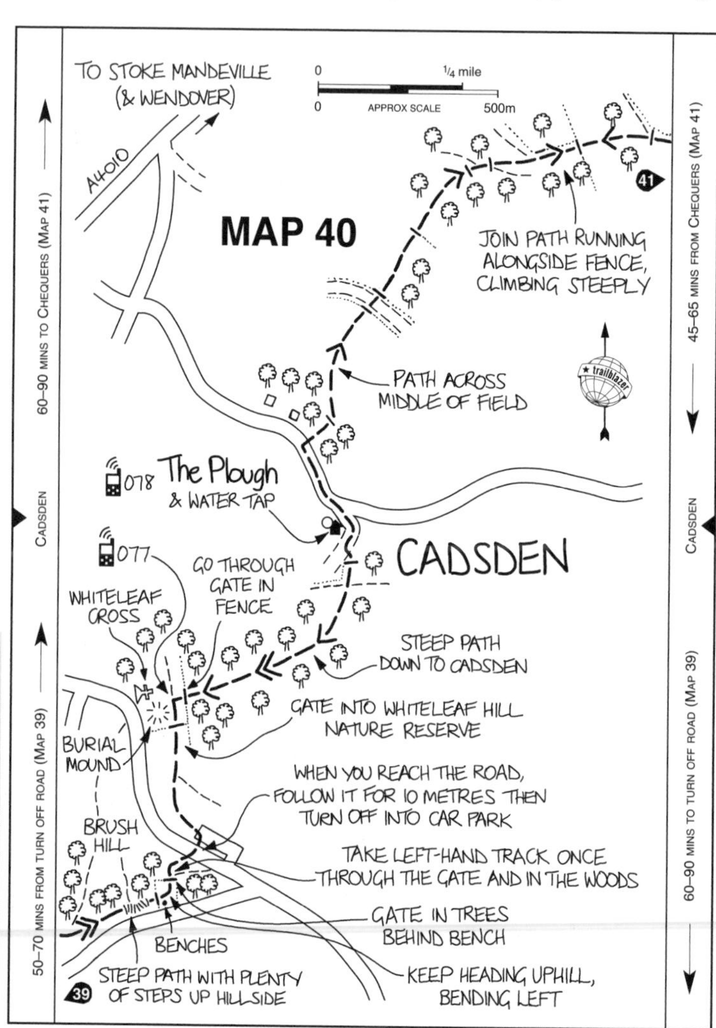

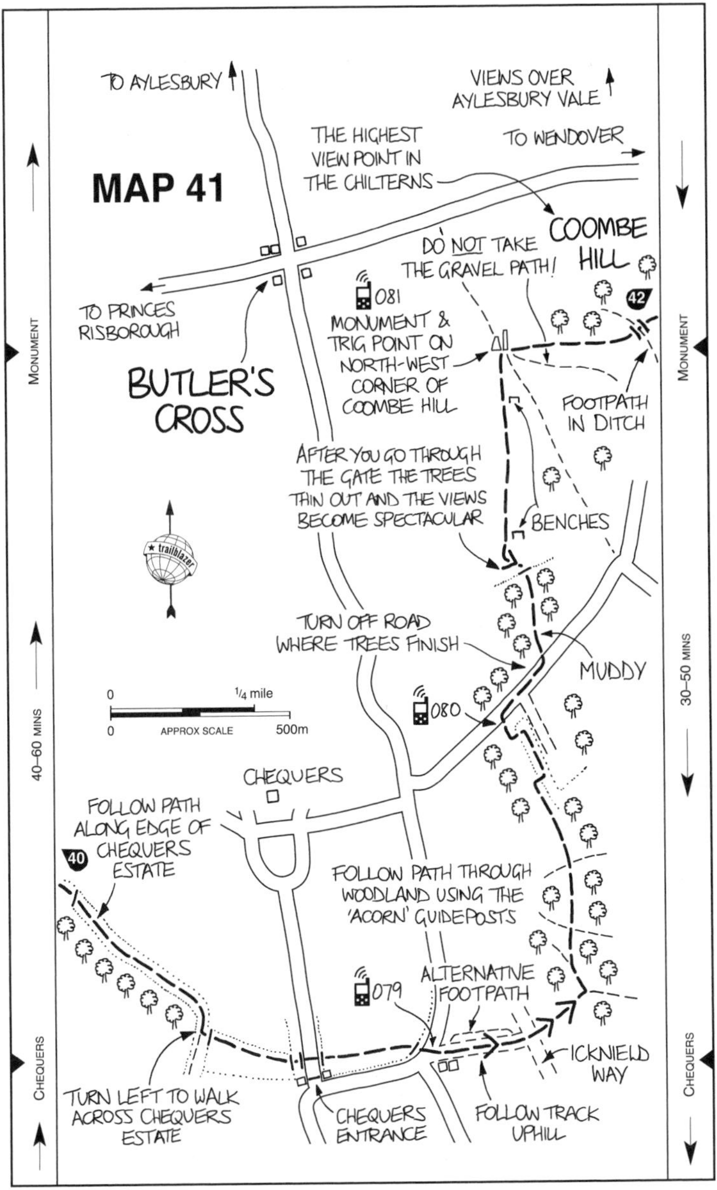

MAP 41

TO AYLESBURY

VIEWS OVER AYLESBURY VALE

THE HIGHEST VIEW POINT IN THE CHILTERNS

TO WENDOVER

COOMBE HILL

DO NOT TAKE THE GRAVEL PATH!

TO PRINCES RISBOROUGH

081

MONUMENT & TRIG POINT ON NORTH-WEST CORNER OF COOMBE HILL

42

BUTLER'S CROSS

FOOTPATH IN DITCH

AFTER YOU GO THROUGH THE GATE THE TREES THIN OUT AND THE VIEWS BECOME SPECTACULAR

BENCHES

trailblazer

TURN OFF ROAD WHERE TREES FINISH

MUDDY

0 ¼ mile

0 APPROX SCALE 500m

080

CHEQUERS

FOLLOW PATH ALONG EDGE OF CHEQUERS ESTATE

40

FOLLOW PATH THROUGH WOODLAND USING THE 'ACORN' GUIDEPOSTS

ALTERNATIVE FOOTPATH

079

ICKNIELD WAY

TURN LEFT TO WALK ACROSS CHEQUERS ESTATE

CHEQUERS ENTRANCE

FOLLOW TRACK UPHILL

MONUMENT

MONUMENT

40–60 MINS

30–50 MINS

CHEQUERS

CHEQUERS

and walkers (!) there is a **water tap** in the pub's garden on the other side of the road – though dogs are not allowed in the pub itself. The pub closes during the afternoon (3-5pm) Monday to Friday.

Another steep climb will take you through woodlands and you'll eventually catch sight of **Chequers** (Map 41). The dwelling you might be able to see today dates from the 16th century though there has been a house on this site since the 12th century. Over time, Chequers has been modified by its various inhabitants, but a Mr Arthur Lee and his wife Ruth restored the house to its original Tudor glory in the early part of the 20th century. During World War I Chequers was used as a hospital and convalescent home after which it was donated to the then prime minister, David Lloyd George, by the Lees. Since then it has been at the disposal of the current serving Prime Minister, though now it isn't used as much as it previously was. Its isolated position in the middle of the valley floor makes it impossible to miss.

Although the route cuts straight across the driveway to Chequers, no other part of the grounds or the house is open to the public. Naturally, security around here is tight: you'll certainly see surveillance cameras and perhaps police on patrol.

After Chequers you rejoin the Icknield Way and there is another steep climb back onto high ground followed by some good walking through mature woodland which stays fairly level for some time. There are many paths through here and you'll need to look out for the black 'acorn marker' posts and the occasional Ridgeway signpost, to keep on the right path.

As the path opens out you'll have amazing views to the west before reaching the monument and **trig point** on the north-west corner of Coombe Hill. This is a popular place for day-trippers and after the lonely effort of the last couple of miles it's quite surprising to see so many people up here. The **monument** commemorates those men from Buckinghamshire who were killed in the Boer War. It was completed in 1904 but had to be partially rebuilt in 1939 after being damaged when struck by lightning. In October 2010 major restoration work on the monument was completed.

From here you should be able to see Wendover, the next town on the Ridgeway, down below. It's all downhill (**Bacombe Hill**, Map 42) to the town but when leaving the monument do not take the obvious gravel path as this does not lead directly to Wendover. The correct path down the hill eventually joins a surfaced road to take you the last few hundred metres into the town itself.

WENDOVER [see map p177]

Even if the Ridgeway didn't go straight through the centre of Wendover it would still be a good idea to stop off here. It's an attractive town with a compact centre where all the shops and services you are likely to need are located.

This town was mentioned in the Domesday Book but probably dates from a good deal earlier than that. Its position on the road from London to Aylesbury has always ensured it plenty of passing trade and in days gone by it had a large number of inns to cater for weary travellers. There are still some very old pubs to stop off at for a few drinks. Its proximity to London by train also means this is a popular place for

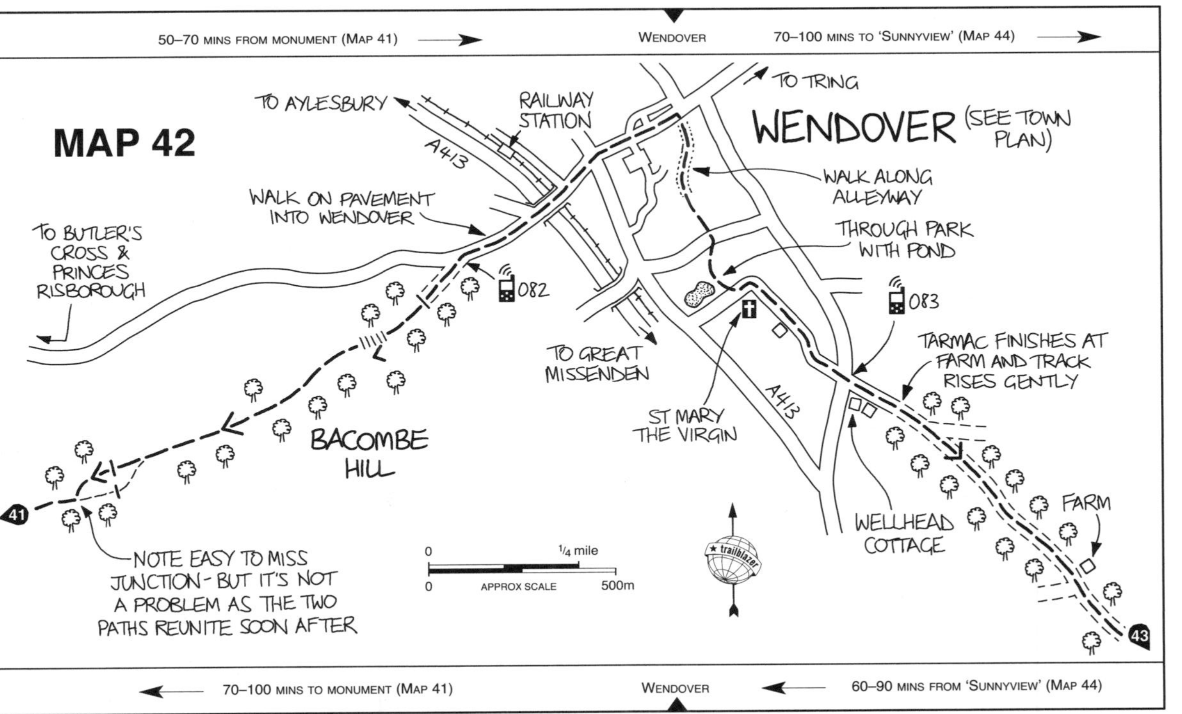
50–70 MINS FROM MONUMENT (MAP 41)
WENDOVER
70–100 MINS TO 'SUNNYVIEW' (MAP 44)
MAP 42
TO AYLESBURY
RAILWAY STATION
A413
TO TRING
WENDOVER (SEE TOWN PLAN)
WALK ALONG ALLEYWAY
WALK ON PAVEMENT INTO WENDOVER
TO BUTLER'S CROSS & PRINCES RISBOROUGH
THROUGH PARK WITH POND
082
083
TO GREAT MISSENDEN
TARMAC FINISHES AT FARM AND TRACK RISES GENTLY
A413
ST MARY THE VIRGIN
BACOMBE HILL
41
FARM
WELLHEAD COTTAGE
NOTE EASY TO MISS JUNCTION - BUT IT'S NOT A PROBLEM AS THE TWO PATHS REUNITE SOON AFTER
0
1/4 mile
0
APPROX SCALE
500m
trailblazer
43
70–100 MINS TO MONUMENT (MAP 41)
WENDOVER
60–90 MINS FROM 'SUNNYVIEW' (MAP 44)

city workers to commute from; as a result the town has an air of affluence.

Services

The **post office** (Mon-Fri 9am-5.30pm, Sat 9am-12.30pm) is on the High St along with a Lloyds **bank** and ATM. Other useful services on this street include a branch of **Lloyds Pharmacy** (Mon-Fri 8.30am-6.30pm, Sat 9am-5.30pm).

At the top end of town there's a Budgens **supermarket** (Mon-Sat 6.30am-10pm, Sun 9am-6pm). There are also some **markets** here (see box p21).

There is no tourist information centre as such but there are lots of leaflets in the **Wendover Community Library** (☎ 0845 230 3232; Tue & Thur 9.30am-5pm, Fri 9.30am-7pm, Sat 10am-4pm) and the librarians do their best to help. In the adjacent car park is a noticeboard with contact details for local accommodation and there are **public toilets** here too.

Arriva's and Redline's respective No 50 **bus** services call here; see pp47-51. There is a **taxi** firm called Alexander's (☎ 01296 620888) at the railway station.

Wendover **railway** station is on the Chiltern Line which runs from Aylesbury to London Marylebone; see box p45.

Where to stay

The most atmospheric place in which to stay is ***Red Lion Hotel*** (☎ 01296 622266, 🖳 www.redlionhotelwendover.co.uk; 2S/16D/3T, all en suite; ▼; WI-FI; Ⓛ). This is a 16th-century coaching inn that used to be the start/end point for coaches to/from London. The front of the hotel looks as if it has changed little since those days and it really is a place worth stopping off at even if you are not staying here – but if you are you can have a very comfortable room from £35pp rising to £45pp (based on two sharing) for the four-poster (sgl £59-69, sgl occ full room rate). They also have two rooms which sleep a couple and up to two children but these are not suitable for a group of adults. This is another popular place so book well in advance.

The **Airbnb** website (see p20) may mention a room just off the High St for £65. But given the paucity of other options in Wendover, it may be worth checking to see if any others have been added.

Where to eat and drink

If you just want something quick you have several good choices. A popular place is ***Whitewaters Deli Café*** (☎ 01296 623331, 🖳 www.whitewatersdeli.co.uk; Mon-Thur 9am-5pm, Fri & Sat to 6pm, Sun 10am-4pm); it serves delicious cakes, quiches and salads.

Close by, ***Rumsey's Chocolaterie*** (☎ 01296 625060, 🖳 www.rumseys.co.uk/our-shops/wendover; Mon-Sat 8.30am-6pm, Sun 10am-6pm) specialises in handmade chocolates, but also serves breakfast (8.30-11.30am) tea, coffee and light lunches.

There's a branch of ***Costa*** (Mon-Sat 8am-6pm, Sun 9am-5pm) on Aylesbury Rd. My favourite, however, is ***Lady Grey Tearoom*** (☎ 07519 834251, 🖳 ladygreytearoom.co.uk; daily 10am-5pm) in a lovely little spot in Barn Courtyard – and thus away from the noise of the traffic on the main drag – with some tasty fare including sandwiches from £4.30 and cream teas from £4.20.

For more substantial fare, on Pound St, ***Shoulder of Mutton*** (☎ 01296 623223, 🖳 www.chefandbrewer.com; food Mon-Fri noon-10pm, Sat 11.30am-10pm, Sun noon-9.30pm) is a large, old, Chef & Brewer establishment serving a decent range of pub grub such as slow-cooked pork belly (£12.49) in a toffee apple glaze, served with mashed potato, braised red cabbage, honey-roasted parsnips, a rich red wine sauce and sweet baked apple served all day, every day.

Further down Pound St, ***Tres Corazones*** (☎ 01296 622092, 🖳 www.trescorazones.co.uk; Tue 6-11pm, Wed-Sat noon-2.30pm & 5.30-11pm, Sun noon-4pm) is a spacious tapas restaurant with dishes from £3.95 (for the olives) to £12.95 (for oxtail cooked in red wine).

On High St, the bar at ***Red Lion Hotel*** (see Where to stay; restaurant Mon-Thur noon-9pm, Fri & Sat noon-9.30pm, Sun noon-8.30pm) serves hot and cold sandwiches (£5.75-7.25) throughout the day and has four real ales that change on a regular

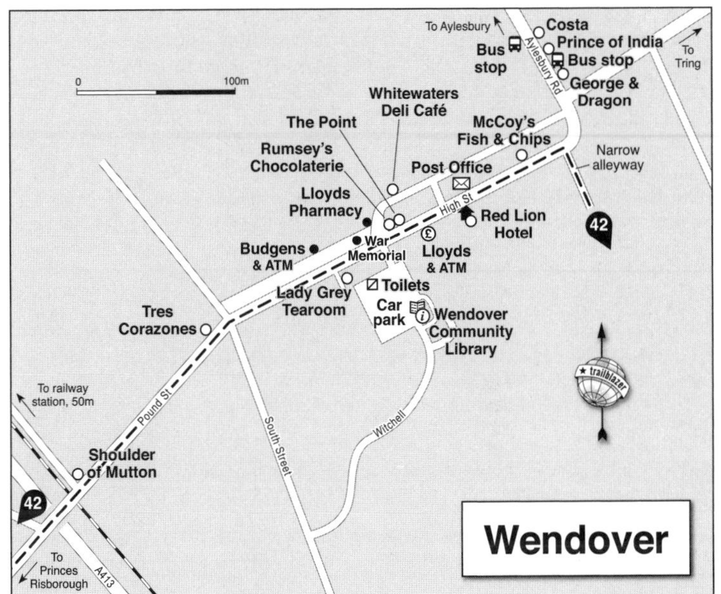

basis. The restaurant menu varies but usually includes a pie of the day (£12.95), burgers (£9.95) and a specials board.

Almost opposite, you'll find ***The Point*** (☎ 01296 696380, 💻 wendoverpoint.co.uk; Tue & Wed 10am-11pm, Thur-Sat 10am-1am, Sun 10am-5pm). It's a friendly place with a large array of tasty Italian dishes on offer, including lombatello steak (sliced steak of beef served with roast potatoes and a gorgonzola sauce) for £17.50.

Just down from the post office is a chippy, ***McCoy's Fish & Chips*** (☎ 01296 708243; Mon-Sat noon-2pm & 4.30-10pm). Inside the ***George & Dragon*** (☎ 01296 586152, 💻 www.georgeanddragonwendover.com; food Mon 6-8.30pm, Tue-Sat noon-2pm & 6-9.30pm, Sun noon-8.30pm) is a Thai restaurant and takeaway; mains are from £5.95 (takeaway), or £6.95 if you're eating in.

The ***Prince of India*** (☎ 01296 623233, 💻 www.prince-of-india.co.uk; daily noon-2.30pm & 6-11.30pm), almost next door to the George & Dragon, serves tasty Indian food.

The path out of Wendover follows a pleasant route between houses and parks before emerging at a T-junction in front of the church of **St Mary the Virgin**. This church was built in the 14th century and was used briefly as a camp by some of Oliver Cromwell's New Model Army troops during the English Civil War. Today it's still well used but for more sedate purposes such as afternoon tea (Apr-Sep Sun 2.30-5pm) and bellringing practice.

There's another long climb up into woodland that thankfully levels out for some time along the ridge through **Barn Wood** and the Forestry Commission's

Hale Wood (Map 43). This is a lovely walk along good paths surrounded by mature woodlands including many conifer trees. Although there are good views back to Wendover from here, the wood blocks them for most of the time.

For many miles now the Ridgeway and Icknield Way have often been following the same route and at times the Icknield Way can provide you with a shortcut if you are in a hurry. For instance, both paths leave Wendover at roughly the same place, but by the time they meet up again Ridgeway walkers have gone 2¾ miles/4.5km whereas Icknield Way walkers have only gone 1¾ miles/3km. However, if you're going to walk the Ridgeway, you might as well do it properly. Having said that, up ahead there is a part of the Ridgeway that it might be best not to do properly and I doubt many people do. You'll come to a **T-junction** (Map 44) in woodland (where the Icknield Way rejoins the path) and need to turn right. The official signpost for this is at the bottom of a steep ditch. So, you can either descend into the ditch and follow it up the hill, or simply continue walking on the woodland path parallel to the ditch. Having walked in the ditch I wouldn't recommend it unless you like muddy boots and swarms of flies for company.

After passing through the group of houses and farms collectively known as **Hastoe** (Map 45), you'll enter **Tring Park**, leased to the Woodland Trust (see

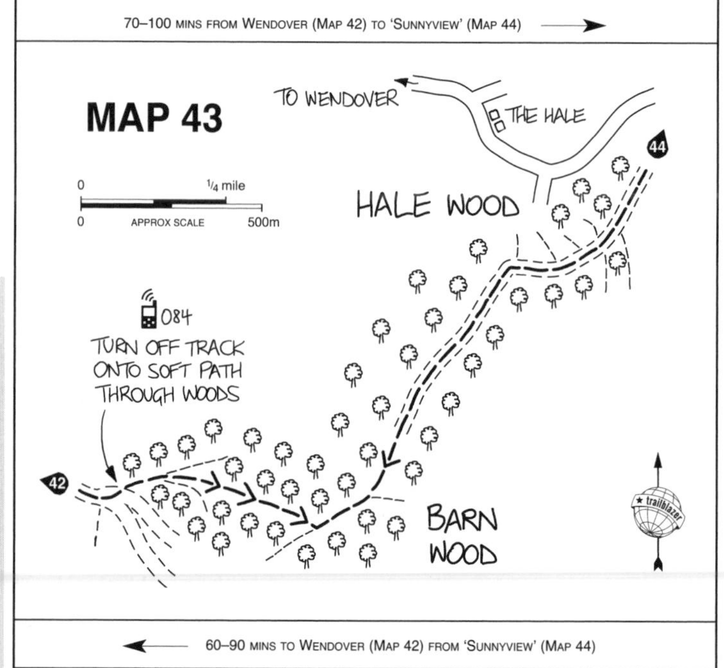

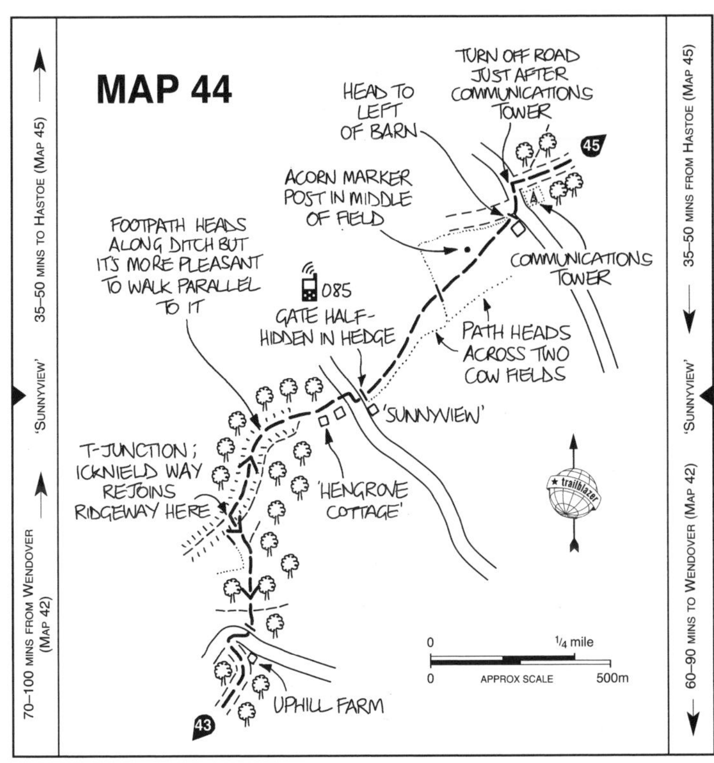

p63). This park used to be much bigger but in 1974 the A41 was cut straight through the centre of it in an east–west direction. The manor house is now located in the top half, while the Ridgeway passes through the bottom half. It's a really enjoyable section of the walk along decent paths with plenty of wildlife to look out for, including fallow deer.

The next village you come to is Wigginton (Map 46). The Ridgeway passes about 750m from the 'centre' and it's a good place to stay the night if you want a relaxed last day of walking up to Ivinghoe Beacon.

WIGGINTON [MAP 46, p181]

This small village has been here for centuries. It's probably now best known for the exclusive Champneys Health Spa just out of the village on the Chesham Road. It's a sleepy place with little to do, but there is good accommodation in the village pub – a perfect place to wind down after a long day on the Ridgeway. There are no shops, nor is there a post office.

A **taxi** can be ordered through Diamond Cars (☎ 01442 890303; Diamond also offer luggage transfer between Watlington and Ivinghoe Beacon) which is just as well because Red Rose's

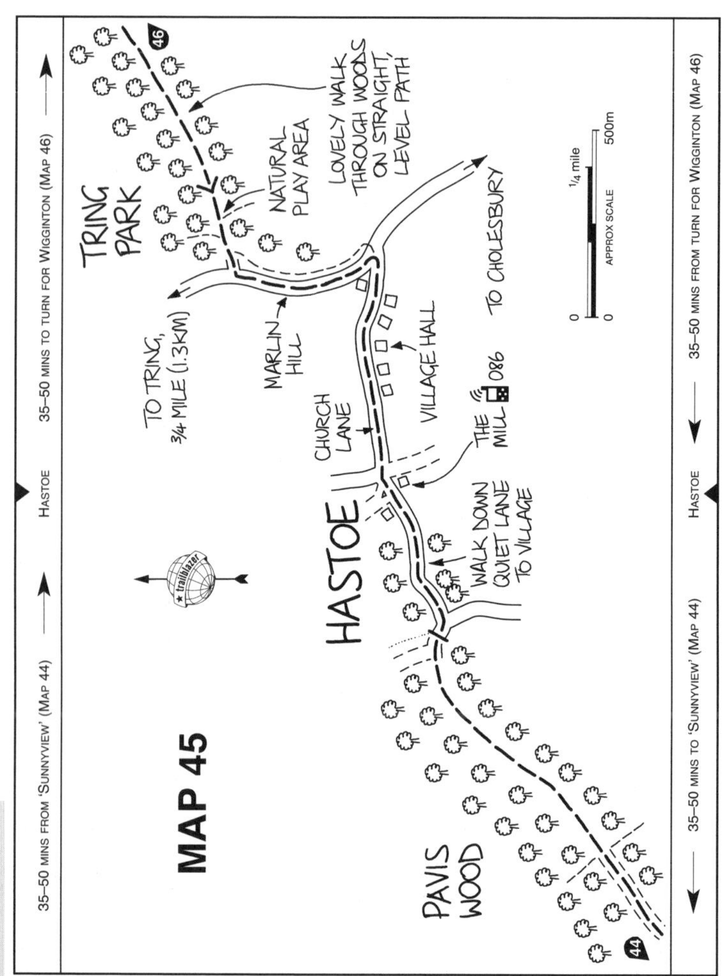

No 387 **bus** to Tring is the only service calling here; see pp47-51.

The Greyhound (☎ 01442 824631, 💻 www.greyhoundtring.co.uk; 2D/1T, all en suite; WI-FI bar only; Ⓛ; 🐕 £15) is the only pub in the village, hence its popularity with the locals – and also deservedly so with walkers, so book well ahead if you want to stay here. The rate (£32.50pp, £50 single occupancy) includes a continental breakfast only. This friendly place has a changing selection of real ales and their menu (**food** Mon-Sat noon-8.30pm, Sun noon-3.30pm) includes home-made pies and 10oz Aberdeen Angus steaks (£20.50).

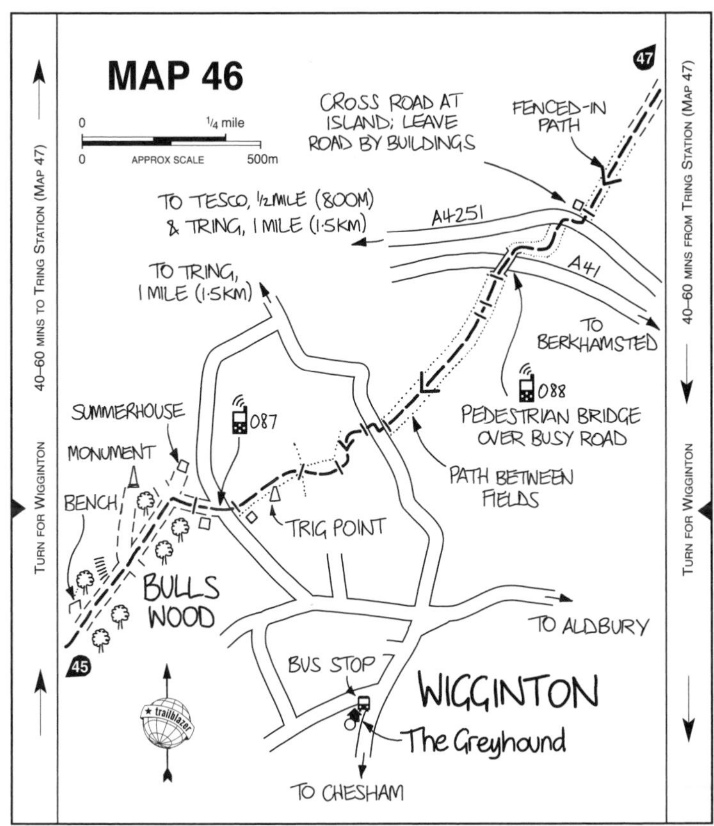

If you're heading for Tring you'll also need to leave the Ridgeway where the path crosses the roads at Wigginton; either road is fine. It's about a mile/1.5km to the centre of Tring from here. The advantage staying in Tring has over Wigginton is that there are far more facilities, but Wigginton is closer to the Ridgeway than Tring so you'll have to take into account the time and effort of walking there and back.

TRING

This is a large town near the end of the Ridgeway and it would be a good place at which to stop before you tackle the last stretch of walking up to Ivinghoe Beacon, but maybe it would be better to come here after you have finished the Ridgeway as, apart from all the shops and services you might need, there are good public transport links to get you back home. There aren't, however, many places to stay in Tring, so you might prefer to make your visit brief.

Like many of the towns in this chain of settlements along the edge of the Chilterns, there is evidence of Saxon settlement in Tring and it's also mentioned in the Domesday Book.

The town has always been on a natural pathway and when the Grand Junction Canal was cut through here in the late 18th century commerce in the town really started to expand. In the early 19th century a large silk mill was established in Tring and this gave employment to many of the town's women and children. In 1835 a railway was built along the course of the canal which runs to the east of Tring. Although this meant that the railway station was not built in the town it still further improved Tring's accessibility, especially to London.

You might well expect a museum in this town to include some of this history, but in fact its subject is something altogether different. The **Natural History Museum at Tring** (🖳 www.nhm.ac.uk/tring; Mon-Sat 10am-5pm, Sun 2-5pm; entry free) is at the corner of Akeman St and Park St, just a few minutes' walk from the High St. It comprises about 4000 stuffed animals from Walter Rothschild's personal collection. You'll be able to see anything from a coelacanth to a great auk to a platypus. It really is worth a visit!

Services

The **post office** (Mon-Fri 9am-5.30pm, Sat 9am-12.30pm) can be found on the High St. Nearby are branches of NatWest and HSBC **banks**, both with ATMs. There's also a Barclays with an ATM further along the High St.

If you need more local info, **Tring Information Centre** (☎ 01442 823347, 🖳 www.tring.gov.uk/information-centre.html; Mon-Fri 9.30am-3pm, Sat 10am-1pm) is conveniently located right in the middle of the High St but the entrance is on Akeman St. It has plenty of literature and advice about Tring and the surrounding area and also some information on accommodation but they can't do any bookings.

There is an M&S Simply Food **supermarket** (Mon-Sat 8am-8pm, Sun 10am-4pm) in a precinct just off the High St and a large branch of Tesco (Mon-Sat 6am-midnight, Sun 10am-4pm), to the east of town, on London Rd.

There's also a **cycle shop** here, Mountain Mania Cycles (☎ 01442 822458, 🖳 www.mountainmaniacycles.co.uk; Mon, Tue, Thur-Sat 9am-6pm, Wed to 7.30pm) at 10 Miswell Lane. The **farmers' market** (see box p21) is held on the Market Place. There are **public toilets** (Mon-Sat 8am-5pm) in the car park. The **library** (Mon & Fri 9.30am-6pm, Tue & Thur 1-6pm, Sat 9.30am-4pm) has free WI-FI and internet access (£1.25 for 30 mins). A branch of **Lloyds Pharmacy** (Mon-Fri 9am-6pm, Sat 9am-5.30pm) can be found on the High St.

Tring is a stop on London Midland's frequent **rail** service from London Euston to Milton Keynes/Cheddington, see box p45.

There is a reasonable number of **bus services** from Tring but the important thing is to make sure you go to the correct stop: Red Rose's No 387 stops at both the centre of Tring and the railway station, their 501 stops in the centre and also opposite Tesco (London Rd); Arriva's Nos 61 and 500 only stop at the Rose & Crown Hotel (now closed); Redline's No 50 and 164 stop opposite the Rose & Crown; see pp47-51 for further details.

If you need a **taxi** you should phone John's Taxis (☎ 01442 828828), based at Tring Station (Map 47).

Where to stay

In a great location, right in the town centre is ***97 High Street*** (☎ 01442 823678, 🖳 scharsachs@aol.com; 2D, both en suite, ♥; WI-FI) which charges £40pp, or £50 if you're on your own. Breakfast can either be a full English, continental, vegetarian or vegan. Booking is essential.

About 1¼ miles/2km west of the town centre there is a ***Premier Travel Inn*** (☎ 0871 527 9104, 🖳 www.premierinn.com/en/hotel/TRICRO; Tring Hill, HP23 4LD; 30D, en suite, ♥; free WI-FI) which has **rooms** from about £48.50 if you book online; there is also a Beefeater restaurant (daily Mon-Fri 6.30-10.30am & 5-10pm, Sat & Sun 8-10.30am & noon-10pm) on

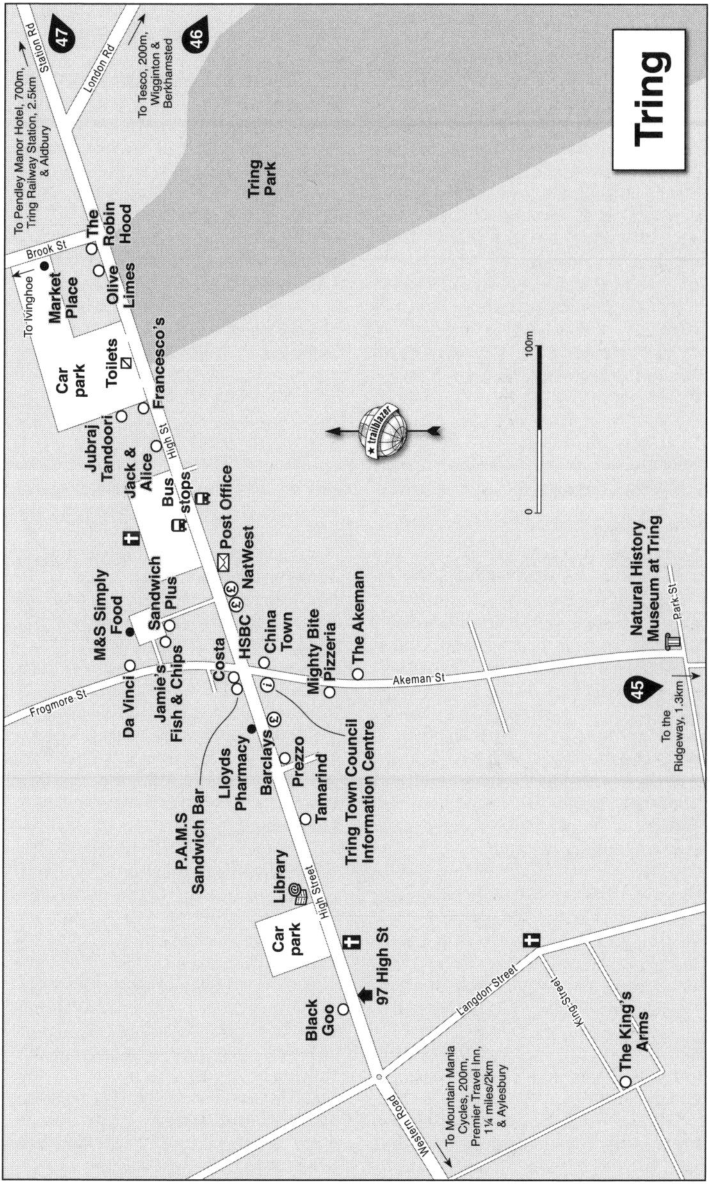

Tring
To Pendley Manor Hotel, 700m, Tring Railway Station, 2.5km & Aldbury
Station Rd
47
London Rd
To Tesco, 200m, Wigginton & Berkhamsted
46
To Ivinghoe
Brook St
Market Place
Car park
Toilets
The Robin Hood
Olive Limes
Francesco's
Jubraj Tandoori
Jack & Alice
High St
Bus stops
Post Office
NatWest
HSBC
M&S Simply Food
Da Vinci
Sandwich Plus
Jamie's Fish & Chips
Frogmore St
Costa
P.A.M.S Sandwich Bar
Lloyds Pharmacy
Barclays
China Town
Prezzo
Tamarind
Mighty Bite Pizzeria
The Akeman
Tring Town Council Information Centre
Library
Car park
High Street
Black Goo
97 High St
Western Road
To Mountain Mania Cycles, 200m, Premier Travel Inn, 1¼ miles/2km & Aylesbury
Langdon Street
King Street
The King's Arms
Akeman St
45
To the Ridgeway, 1.3km
Natural History Museum at Tring
Park St
Tring Park
trailblazer
0
100m

site; continental/full English breakfast costs £6.99/8.99.

Much nearer the path, ***Pendley Manor Hotel*** (off Map 47; ☎ 01442 891891, 🖳 www.pendley-manor.co.uk; 72 rooms, all en suite, ♥; WI-FI) is near Tring Railway Station. The rooms include doubles (some with four-poster beds), twins and some rooms which can sleep up to four people. As with most of these large, chain establishments the rates are complex and change according to the day and demand, but you're looking at upwards of £45pp and at peak times about £80pp (sgl occ from £79 and also rising depending on demand). The rate includes use of their indoor heated pool and other leisure facilities. **Food** is available throughout the day in their restaurant (smart casual appreciated).

If none of the above is suitable or available there is no shortage of options advertised on **Airbnb** (see p20).

Where to eat and drink

If you fancy a lunchtime sandwich you could head for ***P.A.M.S Sandwich Bar*** (☎ 01442 824262, 🖳 www.pamssandwichbar.co.uk; Mon-Fri 9am-3pm, Sat 9am-2pm, Sun 10.30am-1.30pm), on the High St. They do all the usual sandwiches, baguettes and rolls including tortilla wraps (£3.50). In the precinct near the M&S, ***Sandwich Plus*** (☎ 01442 826489, 🖳 www.sandwich-plus.com; Mon-Fri 8.30am-3pm) does much the same thing.

Coffee shops include the rather swish ***Black Goo*** (☎ 07786 434373, 🖳 www.blackgoocoffee.co.uk; Mon-Sat 9am-4pm, Sun 9am-1pm), at the top of town, and a branch of ***Costa*** (Mon-Sat 6.30am-6.30pm, Sun 7.30am-6pm) nearer the centre.

Perhaps the best option is ***Jack & Alice*** (☎ 01442 823993, 🖳 jackandalice.co.uk; food Mon-Sat 9am-10pm, Sun 10am-9pm), which is part café, part restaurant, part bar, and part holistic treatment centre – that last part being upstairs. The menu changes regularly but begins with a wide range of breakfasts (from £4.50) from bacon sandwiches and poached eggs to home-made Belgian waffles or American pancakes; this place serves up some wonderful dishes throughout the day and long into the night. It's a friendly place and, in our opinion, the best eatery in Tring.

There are several **Indian restaurants** and among them is the recommended ***Jubraj Tandoori*** (☎ 01442 825368; daily 6-10pm), just off the High St. The *balti zinga special* (chicken or lamb, hot or mild) is well worth £7.95. Other Indian restaurants include ***Tamarind*** (☎ 01442 822333; Sun-Thur 6-11.30pm, Fri & Sat 6pm to midnight) and ***Olive Limes*** (☎ 01442 828444; daily noon-2.30pm & 6-11pm) which has a more contemporary feel.

The **Italian** restaurant and café ***Francesco's*** (☎ 01442 827258, 🖳 www.amore-bella.co.uk; Tue-Sat noon-3pm & 5.30-11pm, Sun noon-11pm, Mon 5.30-11pm) is a really popular place, especially in the daytime when the café gets very busy, despite its location overlooking the car park. There's another Italian restaurant on Frogmore St called ***Da Vinci*** (☎ 01442 891300, 🖳 www.davincitring.co.uk; Mon-Thur noon-3pm & 6-10pm, Fri & Sat to 10.30pm, Sun noon-9pm); it has all the usual pizzas and pasta dishes and a selection of risottos for £8.95-9.95. On the High St is a branch of ***Prezzo*** (☎ 01442 822610, 🖳 www.prezzorestaurants.co.uk/restaurant/tring; Mon-Sat noon-11pm, Sun to 10.30pm), yet another Italian restaurant.

Several standard **takeaways** are dotted around Tring. They include: ***China Town*** (Wed & Thur noon-1.45pm & 5-11pm, Tue & Sun 5-11.30pm, Fri & Sat noon-1.45pm & 5pm-midnight) which serves exactly what you'd expect; ***Mighty Bite Pizzeria*** (Sun-Thur 5-11pm, Fri & Sat noon-11pm) serving pizzas, burgers and the like, and ***Jamie's Fish & Chips*** (Mon-Sat 11.30am-10pm).

There are plenty of **pubs** around town, most of them serving food. The most upmarket is ***The Akeman*** (☎ 01442 826027, 🖳 www.theakeman.co.uk; food Mon-Thur 8am-10pm, Fri & Sat to 10.30pm, Sun 9am-9pm), a café/pub/restaurant serving Mediterranean-style food. They serve an English-style breakfast (£8.50) and later on there's a wide choice of dishes ranging from £8 to £15, though the steaks are £19-26.

The Robin Hood (☎ 01442 824912, 🖳 www.therobinhoodtring.co.uk; food Mon-Fri noon-2.15pm & 6-9.15pm, Sat noon-9.15pm, Sun noon-2.15pm, Tip Khao menu Sun 6-10pm) serves Fullers beer and is far more sedate and really rather quiet.

The most interesting choice is just a short walk away from the western end of the High St; ***The King's Arms*** (☎ 01442 823318, 🖳 www.kingsarmstring.co.uk; food Mon-Thur noon-2.15pm, Fri & Sat to 2.30pm, Sun to 4pm, Mon-Sat 6-9.30pm) on King St. This is a friendly freehouse on a suburban street with five real ales and a relaxed atmosphere. It has won various CAMRA (see box p22) awards over the years and the food is good too. The menu varies but may include smoked haddock and crayfish chowder (£13), and 8oz ribeye steak (£17.50); they also have a specials board. Note that dogs are not welcome inside.

(TRING &) WIGGINTON TO IVINGHOE BEACON [MAPS 46-48]

Overview

This final **5-mile/8km (2¼-4hrs)** section of the Ridgeway may not seem much of a challenge but as most of this stage is uphill, with a steep climb to the finish itself, it'll probably be enough. From the finish you'll also have to walk at least to the nearest road, or probably to the nearest village, Ivinghoe. This will add around 1½ miles/2.5km to your walk and you don't want to be too tired to celebrate with a drink or two in one of the local pubs at the end.

Route

From Wigginton you'll soon come to the **pedestrian bridge** (Map 46) crossing the crowded A41 that runs from Bicester down to the M25. Next up it's the fast A4251 that you must cross without the aid of a bridge, so take care. Soon after these two road crossings, the Ridgeway crosses the **Grand Union Canal** (Map 47; see box below). After crossing two roads and a canal, next up is a railway line.

You pass by **Tring Railway Station**, now a stop for local services for trains to and from London Euston. There is a taxi company (see p182) in the station car park, but if you're not catching a train here there is little reason to stop. You follow the road for a few more minutes and when you leave it, you can consider yourself to be beginning the last stage of the Ridgeway. If you want to visit Aldbury, continue on the road for another half a mile/1km.

❑ The Grand Union Canal

This runs from the River Thames in Brentford, up through the Chilterns via many locks, then on to Birmingham where it finishes 137 miles/220km later. Initially this was the Grand Junction Canal, which opened in 1805 and ran only from Brentford, Middlesex, to Braunston, Northamptonshire, to link with the Oxford Canal. In 1929 it was linked to various other branches running up to Birmingham via Warwick and was renamed the Grand Union Canal. Nowadays the main traffic on the canal is boats rented by tourists. The towpath, from the Thames at Brentford to Birmingham, is now also recognised as an official walking path.

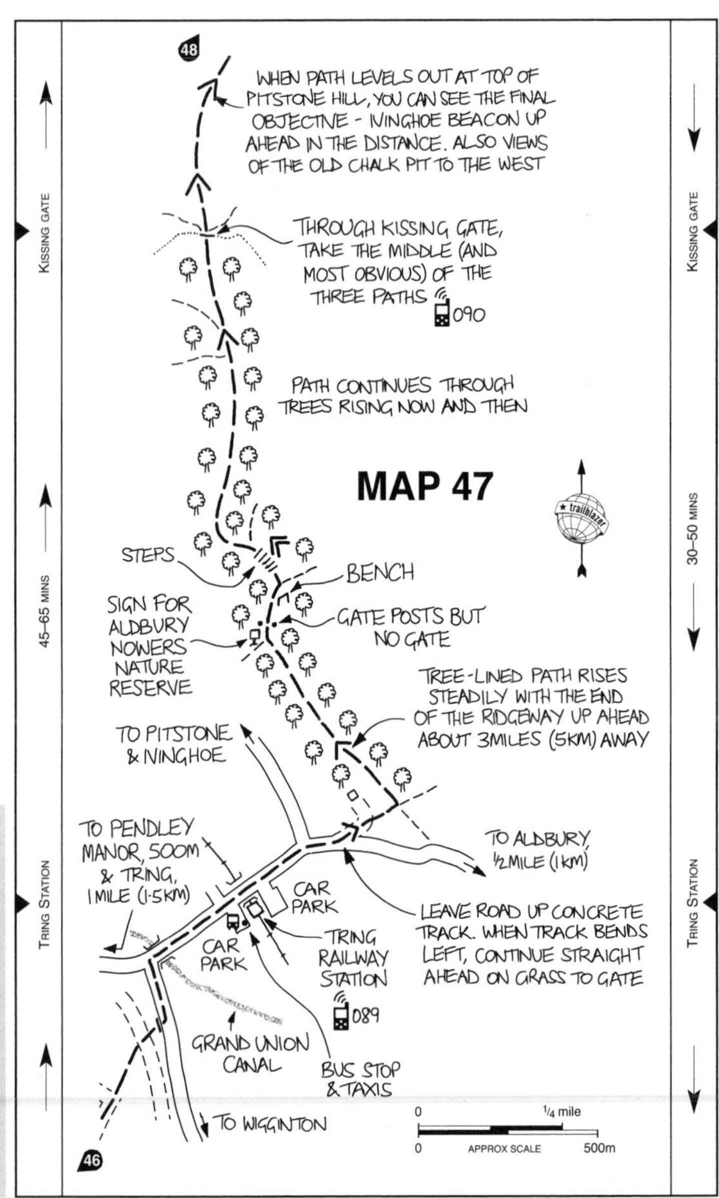

WHEN PATH LEVELS OUT AT TOP OF PITSTONE HILL, YOU CAN SEE THE FINAL OBJECTIVE - IVINGHOE BEACON UP AHEAD IN THE DISTANCE. ALSO VIEWS OF THE OLD CHALK PIT TO THE WEST
THROUGH KISSING GATE, TAKE THE MIDDLE (AND MOST OBVIOUS) OF THE THREE PATHS
090
PATH CONTINUES THROUGH TREES RISING NOW AND THEN
MAP 47
trailblazer
STEPS
BENCH
SIGN FOR ALDBURY NOWERS NATURE RESERVE
GATE POSTS BUT NO GATE
TREE-LINED PATH RISES STEADILY WITH THE END OF THE RIDGEWAY UP AHEAD ABOUT 3MILES (5KM) AWAY
TO PITSTONE & IVINGHOE
TO PENDLEY MANOR, 500M & TRING, 1MILE (1.5KM)
TO ALDBURY, ½MILE (1KM)
CAR PARK
CAR PARK
TRING RAILWAY STATION
089
LEAVE ROAD UP CONCRETE TRACK. WHEN TRACK BENDS LEFT, CONTINUE STRAIGHT AHEAD ON GRASS TO GATE
GRAND UNION CANAL
BUS STOP & TAXIS
TO WIGGINTON
0
¼ mile
0
APPROX SCALE
500m
Kissing gate
45–65 mins
Tring Station
Kissing gate
30–50 mins
Tring Station
48
46

ALDBURY

Aldbury is a picture-perfect English village, complete with duck pond, church and pub. It would be a good alternative to Wigginton if the accommodation there is full. This idyllic village has been captured on film many times: *The Avengers*, *The Dirty Dozen*, *Inspector Morse*, *Midsomer Murders* (inevitably) and, more recently, *Bridget Jones's Diary: The Edge of Reason*.

You'll be surprised when you look inside the **village shop** (☎ 01442 851233; Mon, Tue, Thur, Fri 6am-5.30pm, Wed & Sat 6am-7.30pm, Sun 7.30am-4pm; in the winter months they close for an hour 1-2pm). Not only is it very well stocked and much larger than it looks from the outside, but there is a **post office** (Mon, Tue, Thur, Fri 9am-1pm & 2-5.30pm, Wed & Sat 9am-1pm) in here as well as an **ATM** (the charge per withdrawal is £1.50).

Red Rose Travel's No 387 **bus** service operates to Tring; see pp47-51 for further details.

Where to stay and eat

Near the duck pond is ***The Greyhound Inn*** (☎ 01442 851228, 💻 greyhoundaldbury.co.uk; 5D/2D or T/1Qd, all en suite, ☕; WI-FI; Ⓛ), a much filmed and photographed place. **B&B** costs £40pp, £70 if you're on your own, £100/120 for three/four in a room. The **food** (food Mon-Fri noon-2.30pm & 6.30-9.30pm, Sat noon-9.30pm, Sun noon-7.30pm) is of a high standard and there is a varied menu: you could try a warm bacon, brie and red onion marmalade sandwich (£5.75) for lunch while the evening menu may include pan-fried fillets of sea bass on braised fennel, kale, yellow peppers and roti potato with a spicy tomato coulis (£14.95).

Another good option for **food** is ***The Valiant Trooper*** (☎ 01442 851203, 💻 www.valianttrooper.co.uk; food Mon noon-3pm, Tue-Fri noon-3pm & 6-9pm, Sat noon-9pm, Sun noon-4pm; they also serve breakfast Sat & Sun 10am-noon). This pub is less than five minutes' walk from the centre of the village. The menu changes weekly but includes daily specials as well as smart twists on standard pub fare such as smoked haddock fishcakes served with wilted spinach and sorrel sauce (£5.25) and free range pork sausages with bubble & squeak and homemade baked beans (£10.95).

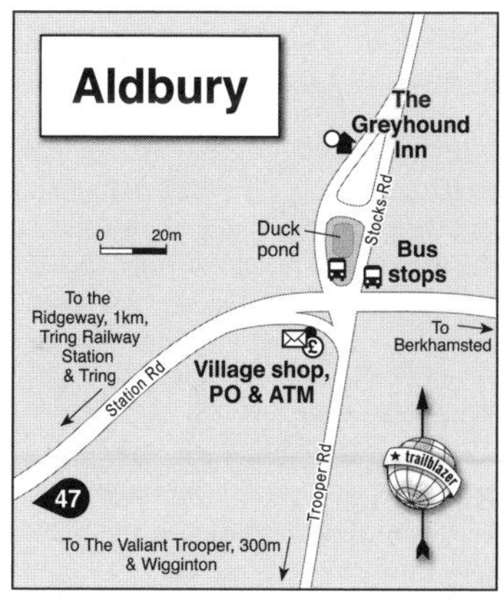

The path rises through woodland, sometimes level, but more often than not climbing. By now there are only a few miles left and you might think it will all be over soon. Then you'll get your first glimpse of Ivinghoe Beacon, up ahead in the far distance. The word 'far' is appropriate but at least the end is now always in sight. You can admire the increasingly stunning views from up here and plod on.

You can also see, down to your left a large, old **chalk pit**, now filled with water; this is a popular place for relaxing and swimming during the summer. The

❑ The butterflies of Aldbury Nowers

Probably tired and, with the end almost in sight, 99.99% of trekkers on the Ridgeway undoubtedly march through the woods after Tring with little thought as to what they're actually walking through. It's forgivable, of course, but it's also a bit of a shame, for this scrumptious little corner of Hertfordshire countryside is actually one of the main butterfly habitats in the UK.

Nobody is quite sure why **Aldbury Nowers Nature Reserve** (🖳 www.hertswildlifetrust.org.uk/reserves/aldbury-nowers; open all day all year but best Apr-Aug) is so popular with our colourfully winged friends but the truth is that the reserve plays host to over 30 species – out of the 59 species commonly accepted to live in the UK. Some of the Albury Nowers' residents, such as the meadow brown and the peacock, are commonplace enough. But several rarities also call the reserve home, including Essex skippers, marbled whites, green hairstreak, brown argus, and the scarce grizzled and dingy skippers.

Of course, you can't just turn up and expect to see all 30-plus species in one go; some butterflies (such as the orange tip) appear early in the season and are rarely seen after June, while others appear late in the summer. But if you have the time and inclination, there are few more enjoyable ways to spend a warm afternoon than to take a decent butterfly guide, a little magnifying glass or similar (to spot the sometimes subtle differences between the species) and to sit on the slopes of Albury Nowers, ticking off the different species.

water takes on a turquoise colour, adding something almost tropical to the atmosphere of the place. If you are plodding your way up to the Beacon on a hot day, just the sight of it can make you want to run down there and dive right in.

When you reach the **road and car park** (Map 48) the Icknield Way puts in an appearance once more and stays with you all the way to the end of the Ridgeway. Gradually the Beacon gets closer until you are left with just one last climb to the end. This will just about finish you off if you started the day at Princes Risborough.

There is a **Ridgeway information board** and **trig point** at the end of the walk to go with the panoramic views. There are often other people up on **Ivinghoe Beacon** but not many who have been on the Ridgeway for the last 87 miles, for sure. Take plenty of time to relax, enjoy the views and reflect on the previous stages. When you are ready to leave the Beacon you have several choices. If you are lucky, someone might be waiting to pick you up from the car park you passed on your way up here. If not, you'll need to walk down to Ivinghoe village. The best way to do this is to follow one of the many paths down the hillside to the main road. Be careful as it's very steep and there are plenty of hidden holes in the ground.

Most paths finish near to the B489 from where it's a boring walk into Ivinghoe (see p190). This road is not particularly wide yet people drive very fast along it so be careful. If you get on with it the 1¼-mile/2km walk from the top of Ivinghoe Beacon to Ivinghoe village shouldn't take more than about 20-30 minutes.

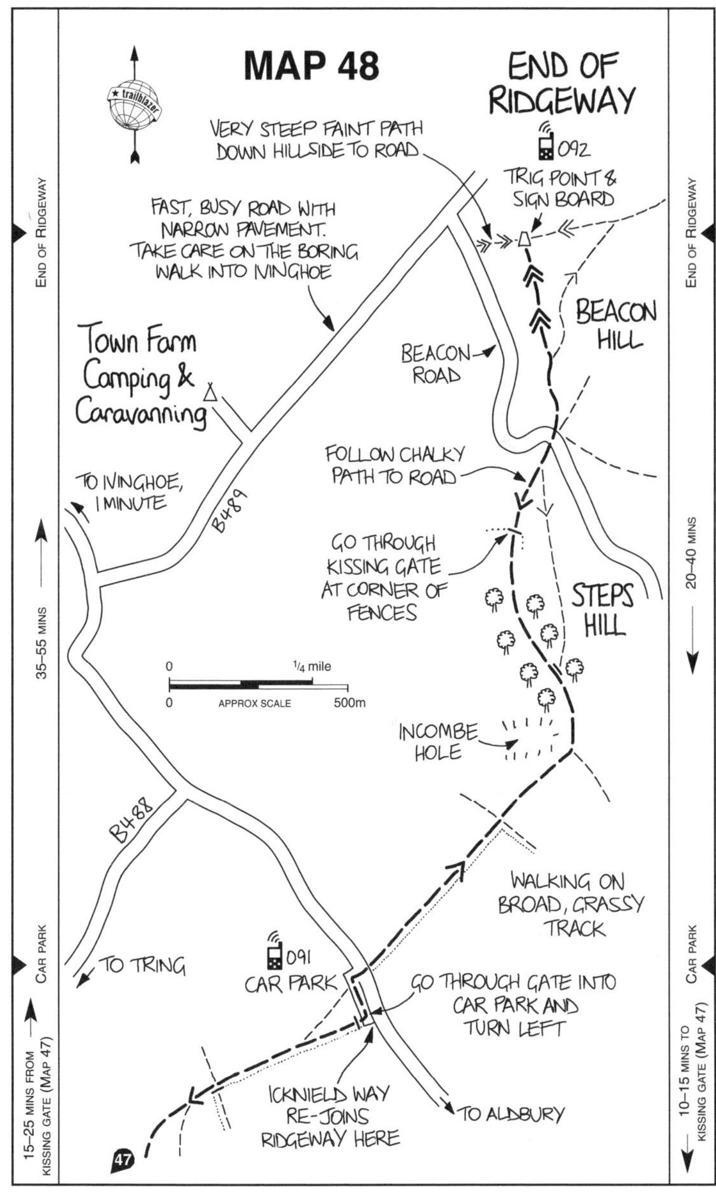
MAP 48
END OF RIDGEWAY
VERY STEEP FAINT PATH DOWN HILLSIDE TO ROAD
092
TRIG POINT & SIGN BOARD
FAST, BUSY ROAD WITH NARROW PAVEMENT. TAKE CARE ON THE BORING WALK INTO IVINGHOE
BEACON HILL
BEACON ROAD
Town Farm Camping & Caravanning
FOLLOW CHALKY PATH TO ROAD
TO IVINGHOE, 1 MINUTE
B489
GO THROUGH KISSING GATE AT CORNER OF FENCES
STEPS HILL
0 1/4 mile
0 APPROX SCALE 500m
INCOMBE HOLE
B488
WALKING ON BROAD, GRASSY TRACK
091
CAR PARK
TO TRING
GO THROUGH GATE INTO CAR PARK AND TURN LEFT
ICKNIELD WAY RE-JOINS RIDGEWAY HERE
TO ALDBURY
47
END OF RIDGEWAY
35–55 MINS
CAR PARK
15–25 MINS FROM KISSING GATE (MAP 47)
20–40 MINS
10–15 MINS TO KISSING GATE (MAP 47)

IVINGHOE

Given its name you'd be right in presuming that this village is the closest to the end of the Ridgeway at Ivinghoe Beacon. This means that most Ridgeway walkers will pass through, or stay here, at some point.

Services

The village **post office** and Best One **grocery shop** (☎ 01296 660325; opening times for both: Mon-Thur 8am-8.30pm, Fri & Sat 9am-9pm, Sun 9am-2pm) are in the Old Town Hall; also here is the Community Library with the library.

A larger shop with longer opening hours, **Mason's Stores** (☎ 01296 660052; Mon-Fri 6.30am-8pm, Sat 7.30am-8pm, Sun 8am-5.30pm) is on Marsworth Rd in **Pitstone village** about 10 minutes' walk away. It's also an **off-licence** and **newsagent**.

If you're in urgent need of plasters, there's a **chemist**, Windmill Pharmacy (Mon-Fri 8.30am-1pm & 2-6pm, Sat 9am-noon), 50m down from the post office.

Arriva's No 61 **bus** and Redline's No 50 (Sun & Bank hols only) stop here; see pp47-51 for further details.

Where to stay

If you want to **camp**, head for ***Town Farm Camping*** (Map 48; book online only at 🖳 www.townfarmcamping.co.uk; 50 pitches; 🐕 £2) which charges £10pp including use of toilet and shower facilities.

An excellent **B&B** near Ivinghoe is ***The Brownlow*** (☎ 01296 668787, 🖳 www.thebrownlow.com; 3D/1T/1Qd, all en suite, ☕; WI-FI; 🐕 £10 per stay), a former pub about a mile (1.5km) out of the village where the road crosses the Grand Union Canal. Light, spacious rooms are available for £40-60pp (sgl occ £70-110, four sharing £120). To reach here, head out of the village on Station Rd.

There may also be a couple of options on **Airbnb** (see p20).

Where to eat and drink

There's a great eatery, ***CuriosiTEA Rooms*** (☎ 01296 663853; Mon, Tue, Thur & Fri 9am-4.30pm, Wed to 2pm, Sat & Sun 10am-3pm), just below The Green in the centre of the village. Lots of outdoor seating, biscuits for the dog (not allowed in the tearooms themselves), friendly staff and a decent array of cakes, sandwiches, toasties, jacket potatoes and other lunchtime options. Reasonably priced (shepherds pie £3.99, for example), it's a pleasant place to relax those aching muscles while waiting for the bus.

For dinner, the 17th-century ***King's Head Restaurant*** (☎ 01296 668388, 🖳 www.kingsheadivinghoe.co.uk; Tue-Sun noon-2.15pm, Tue-Sat 7-9.15pm), right in the centre of the village, is known for its high-quality cuisine. It's not really the place for muddy walkers – the dress code is smart, particularly in the evening – and with *entrées* costing from £39.50 to £50 (though this includes an appetiser, dessert and coffee), you'll probably not find many walkers in there anyway. However, they do offer a Bon Appetit luncheon menu Tuesday to Saturday (three courses for £24.75, or à la carte) which might be worth considering for a celebratory meal.

The only other possible alternative, the cosy ***Rose & Crown*** (☎ 01296 668472, 🖳 www.roseandcrownivinghoe.com; bar Mon-Thur 5-11pm, Fri 4-11pm, Sat & Sun noon-11pm), down Vicarage Lane, is not doing food while they seek a new chef.

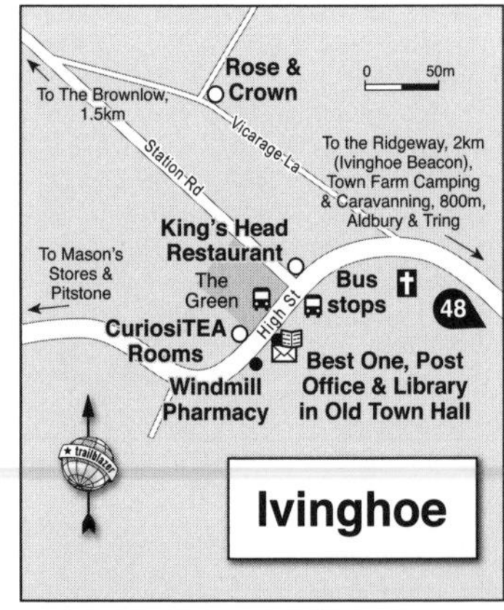

APPENDIX A: WALKING WITH A DOG

WALKING THE RIDGEWAY WITH A DOG

Many are the rewards that await those prepared to make the extra effort required to bring their best friend along the trail. You shouldn't underestimate the amount of work involved, though. Indeed, just about every decision you make will be influenced by the fact that you've got a dog: how you plan to travel to the start of the trail, where you're going to stay, how far you're going to walk each day, where you're going to rest and where you're going to eat in the evening etc.

If you're also sure your dog can cope with (and will enjoy) walking 10 miles or so a day for several days in a row, you need to start preparing accordingly. Extra thought also needs to go into your itinerary. The best starting point is to study the town and village facilities table on pp32-3 (and the advice below), and plan where to stop and where to buy food.

Looking after your dog

To begin with, you need to make sure that your dog is fully **inoculated** against the usual doggy illnesses, and also up to date with regard to **worm pills** (eg Drontal) and **flea preventatives** such as Frontline – they are, after all, following in the pawprints of many a dog before them, some of whom may well have left fleas or other parasites on the trail that now lie in wait for their next meal to arrive.

Pet insurance is also a very good idea; if you've already got insurance, do check that it will cover a trip such as this.

On the subject of looking after your dog's health, perhaps the most important implement you can take is the **plastic tick remover**, available from vets for a couple of quid. These removers, while fiddly, help you to remove the tick safely (ie without leaving its head behind buried under a dog's skin).

Being in unfamiliar territory also makes it more likely that you and your dog could become separated. For this reason, make sure your dog has a **tag with your contact details on it** (a mobile phone number would be best if you are carrying one with you); the fact that all dogs now have to be **microchipped** provides further security.

When to keep your dog on a lead

• **When crossing farmland**, particularly in the **lambing season** (around May) when your dog can scare the sheep, causing them to lose their young. Farmers are allowed by law to shoot at and kill any dogs that they consider are worrying their sheep. During lambing, most farmers would prefer it if you didn't bring your dog at all.

The exception to the dogs on leads rule is if your dog is being attacked by cows. A few years ago there were three deaths in the UK caused by walkers being trampled as they tried to rescue their dogs from the attentions of cattle. The advice in this instance is to let go of the lead, head speedily to a position of safety (usually the other side of the field gate or stile) and call your dog to you.

• **Around ground-nesting birds** It's important to keep your dog under control when crossing an area where certain species of birds nest on the ground. Most dogs love foraging around in the woods but make sure you have permission to do so; some woods are used as 'nurseries' for game birds and dogs are only allowed through them if they are on a lead.

What to pack

You've probably already got a good idea of what to bring to keep your dog alive and happy, but the following is a checklist:

• **Food/water bowl** Foldable cloth bowls are popular with walkers, being light and taking up little room in the rucksack. You can also get a water-bottle-and-bowl combination, where the bottle folds into a 'trough' from which the dog can drink. Where there are water taps along the Ridgeway, there is often a trough for your dog to drink from but this is not always the case.

- **Lead and collar** An extendable one is probably preferable for this sort of trip. Make sure both lead and collar are in good condition – you don't want either to snap on the trail, or you may end up carrying your dog through sheep fields until a replacement can be found.
- **Medication** You'll know if you need to bring any lotions or potions.
- **Bedding** A simple blanket may suffice, or you can opt for something more elaborate if you aren't carrying your own luggage.
- **Poo bags** Essential.
- **Hygiene wipes** For cleaning your dog after it's rolled in stuff.
- **A favourite toy** Helps prevent your dog from pining for the entire walk.
- **Food/water** Remember to bring treats as well as regular food to keep up the mutt's morale. That said, if your dog is anything like mine the chances are they'll spend most of the walk dining on rabbit droppings and sheep poo anyway.
- **Corkscrew stake** Available from camping or pet shops, this will help you to keep your dog secure in one place while you set up camp/doze.
- **Tick remover** See p191.
- **Raingear** It can rain!
- **Old towels** For drying your dog.

When it comes to packing, I always leave an exterior pocket of my rucksack empty so I can put used poo bags in there (for deposit at the first bin). I always like to keep all the dog's kit together and separate from the other luggage (usually inside a plastic bag inside my rucksack). I have also seen several dogs sporting their own 'doggy rucksack', so they can carry their own food, water, poo etc – which certainly reduces the burden on their owner!

Cleaning up after your dog

It is extremely important that dog owners behave in a responsible way when walking the path. Dog excrement should be cleaned up. In towns, villages and fields where animals graze or which will be cut for silage, hay etc, you need to pick up and bag the excrement.

Staying (and eating) with your dog

In this guide the symbol 🐕 denotes where a **hotel, pub, or B&B** welcomes dogs. However, this always needs to be arranged in advance – many places have only one or two rooms suitable for people with dogs. In some cases dogs need to sleep in a separate building. Some places make an additional charge (usually per night but occasionally per stay) while others may require a deposit which is refundable if the dog doesn't make a mess.

Hostels (both YHA and independent) do not permit them unless they are an assistance (guide) dog.

Smaller **campsites** tend to accept dogs, but some of the larger holiday parks do not; again look for the 🐕 symbol in the text.

When it comes to **eating**, most landlords allow dogs in at least a section of their pubs, though few cafés/restaurants do. Make sure you always ask first and ensure your dog doesn't run around the pub but is secured to your table or a radiator.

APPENDIX B: THE GREATER RIDGEWAY

LYME REGIS TO HUNSTANTON

After you've completed the Ridgeway you might like to consider a stroll along parts of the Greater Ridgeway that link Lyme Regis, in Dorset, with Hunstanton, in Norfolk. The Ridgeway covered in this book comprises just the middle section.

Starting from the popular seaside town of Lyme Regis, you can follow the **Wessex Ridgeway** 136 miles (219km) up to its finishing point at Marlborough in Wiltshire, crossing the Ridgeway near Avebury. From Lyme Regis the path goes through Beaminster before meandering through open country and numerous small villages and passing within a few miles of Shaftesbury.

You then skirt round the edge of Salisbury Plain taking in the towns of Heytesbury and Warminster. From here you head towards the Westbury White Horse and on to Devizes before arriving in Avebury and finally Marlborough.

From there the **Ridgeway** in this book takes you up to Ivinghoe Beacon from where you can follow the **Icknield Way** on to Knettishall Heath in Suffolk, 103 miles (166km) away. The long history of this trail equals that of the Ridgeway and is made evident by the wealth of archaeological remains found along here. The route continues on the high chalky ground visiting numerous towns along the way including Baldock, Royston and Linton. From here the Icknield Way continues to Cheveley and Icklingham before finishing at Knettishall Heath Country Park.

Picking up where the Icknield Way finishes, the **Peddars Way**, from Knettishall Heath to Hunstanton, clocks in at 46 miles (75km) and provides easy walking to the end of the

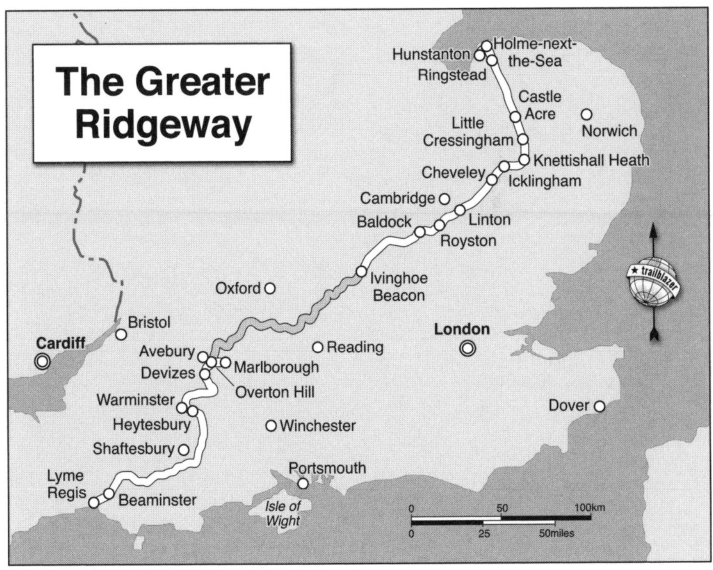

Greater Ridgeway. This largely straight inland route follows a Roman road in open countryside with few villages en route.

You will pass through Little Cressingham, Castle Acre and Ringstead before reaching the coast at Holme-next-the-Sea. From here you walk along the coast to reach Hunstanton, and the end of the Greater Ridgeway.

Further information

- *The Wessex Ridgeway*, Anthony Burton, Aurum
- *Ancient Trackways of Wessex*, HW Timperley & Edith Brill, Nonsuch
- *The Icknield Way Path: A Walkers' Guide*, by Sue Prigg and Nigel Balchi, Icknield Way Association
- *Peddars Way and Norfolk Coast Path*, Alexander Stewart, Trailblazer Publications

❏ Ridgeway National Trail Certificates

Now you have walked – cycled or ridden – along the Ridgeway what else can you do?

Firstly the Ridgeway National Trail team are very keen to encourage people to **give feedback** (🖳 www.nationaltrail.co.uk/ridgeway/contact-trail-team, or 🖳 ridgeway@oxfordshire.gov.uk) on their experiences because, not surprisingly, it's very useful for them. In return they will send you a free **certificate**!

Another way you can help is to upload **photos** of your walk so the NT team can build an online photo gallery (🖳 www.nationaltrail.co.uk/ridgeway/add-data).

Some of the work keeping the trail well maintained is done by volunteers but there are also lots of other costs in terms of making improvements to the trail and also providing free online information for everyone to benefit from so the NT team are grateful for any **donations** (🖳 www.nationaltrail.co.uk/ridgeway/donate).

APPENDIX C: MAP KEYS

Town plan key

Where to stay
Where to eat & drink
Campsite
Post office
Bank/ATM
Building
Tourist information
Library/bookstore
Internet
Museum/gallery
Church/cathedral
Public toilet
Bus stop/station
Rail line & station
Park
CP Car park
Other

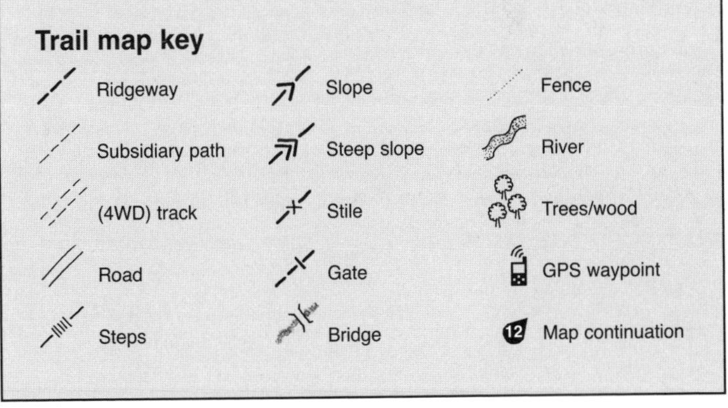

APPENDIX D: GPS WAYPOINTS

Each GPS waypoint below was taken on the route at the reference number marked on the map as below. This list of GPS waypoints is also available to download from the Trailblazer website – 🖳 www.trailblazer-guides.com.

MAP	REF	GPS WAYPOINT	DESCRIPTION
Marlborough to Avebury walk			
Map A	AA	N51° 25.113' W01° 44.031'	Southern end of Marlborough High Street
Map A	BB	N51° 25.565' W01° 44.213'	Gate into cemetery
Map A	CC	N51° 25.957' W01° 44.954'	Road crossing
Map B	DD	N51° 26.384' W01° 46.326'	Driveway to Manton House
Map C	EE	N51° 26.597' W01° 47.109'	Junction in path
Map C	FF	N51° 26.517' W01° 47.638'	Underground reservoir
Map C	GG	N51° 26.234' W01° 48.851'	Cross track
Map D	HH	N51° 26.191' W01° 51.236'	Junction with Green Street
Map D	II	N51° 25.712' W01° 51.236'	Red Lion, Avebury
A walk around Avebury			
Map D	II	N51° 25.712' W01° 51.236'	Red Lion, Avebury
Map D	JJ	N51° 25.246' W01° 50.749'	Gates to Waden Hill
Silbury Hill option			
Map D	KK	N51° 25.041' W01° 51.188'	Through gate and follow river
Map D	LL	N51° 25.130' W01° 51.336'	Left turn
Map D	MM	N51° 24.967' W01° 51.705'	Silbury Hill car park
Map D	NN	N51° 24.851' W01° 51.110'	Gate from A4 road up to the Long Barrow
Long Barrow option			
Map D	OO	N51° 24.732' W01° 51.045'	Turn right for the Long Barrow
Map D	PP	N51° 24.516' W01° 51.017'	West Kennet Long Barrow
Map D	QQ	N51° 24.496' W01° 50.096'	Join road into East Kennett
Map D	RR	N51° 24.711' W01° 49.834'	Start of the Ridgeway
Map D	SS	N51° 25.065' W01° 49.816'	Turn left for quickest route to Avebury
The Ridgeway			
Map 1	001	N51° 24.711' W01° 49.834'	Car park; start of the Ridgeway
Map 1	002	N51° 25.065' W01° 49.816'	Turn to Avebury
Map 2	003	N51° 26.191' W01° 51.236'	Junction with Green Street
Map 2	004	N51° 27.312' W01° 49.245'	Kink in path
Map 3	005	N51° 28.294' W01° 48.913'	Hackpen Hill car park
Map 4	006	N51° 29.115' W01° 47.178'	Barbury Castle
Map 4	007	N51° 29.004' W01° 46.469'	Upper Herdswick Farm
Map 5	008	N51° 28.325' W01° 44.461'	Gateway without gate
Map 6	009	N51° 27.752' W01° 43.303'	Turn to Hallam
Map 6	010	N51° 27.746' W01° 41.822'	Track crossroads
Map 7	011	N51° 28.618' W01° 41.520'	Cross B4192 road
Map 7	012	N51° 29.224' W01° 41.694'	Track crossroads by reservoir
Map 8	013	N51° 29.688' W01° 41.640'	Lower/Upper Upham junction

MAP	REF	GPS WAYPOINT	DESCRIPTION
Map 8	014	N51° 30.036' W01° 41.521'	Fork in path
Map 9	015	N51° 30.994' W01° 41.695'	Gate near Liddington Castle
Map 9	016	N51° 31.429' W01° 41.267'	Turn off B4192 to Foxhill
Map 10	017	N51° 31.803' W01° 40.100'	The Burj, Foxhill
Map 11	018	N51° 32.559' W01° 38.213'	Road junction to Bishopstone
Map 11	019	N51° 33.010' W01° 37.270'	Turn to Idstone
Map 12	020	N51° 33.432' W01° 36.427'	B4000 road crossing
Map 12	021	N51° 33.969' W01° 35.700'	Entrance to Wayland's Smithy
Map 13	022	N51° 34.459' W01° 34.013'	Second gate, Uffington Castle
Map 14	023	N51° 34.452' W01° 32.134'	Cross road Kingston Lisle to Seven Barrows
Map 14	024	N51° 34.217' W01° 31.436'	Tracks for Sparsholt/Down Barn Farm
Map 15	025	N51° 33.826' W01° 30.343'	Sparsholt Firs car park
Map 16	026	N51° 33.241' W01° 28.012'	Cross road to Letcombe Bassett
Map 16	027	N51° 33.317' W01° 26.871'	Segsbury Farm
Map 16	028	N51° 33.437' W01° 25.960'	A338 road crossing
Map 17	029	N51° 33.266' W01° 23.906'	B4494 road crossing
Map 17	030	N51° 33.411' W01° 23.408'	Large monument
Map 18	031	N51° 33.513' W01° 23.086'	Large, sprawling junction
Map 18	032	N51° 33.648' W01° 22.047'	Reservoir
Map 19	033	N51° 33.737' W01° 20.428'	Cross road for East Hendred
Map 19	034	N51° 33.194' W01° 18.598'	Bury Down car park
Map 20	035	N51° 32.880' W01° 17.679'	Tunnel under A34
Map 21	036	N51° 32.373' W01° 16.590'	First turn to East Ilsley
Map 21	037	N51° 32.362' W01° 16.544'	Second turn to East Ilsley
Map 21	038	N51° 32.125' W01° 16.175'	Third turn to East Ilsley
Map 21	039	N51° 32.016' W01° 16.059'	Fourth turn to East Ilsley
Map 22	040	N51° 32.262' W01° 14.490'	Fork in path
Map 22	041	N51° 32.021' W01° 13.844'	Tracks cross
Map 22	042	N51° 31.786' W01° 13.331'	Fork in path
Map 23	043	N51° 31.647' W01° 12.551'	Junction with tracks to Aldworth
Map 23	044	N51° 31.639' W01° 11.068'	Post Box Cottage
Map 24	045	N51° 31.726' W01° 09.064'	Path joins A417 road
Map 24	046	N51° 31.363' W01° 08.923'	Streatley crossroads
Map 26	047	N51° 32.929' W01° 08.335'	Turn towards River Thames
Map 26	048	N51° 32.951' W01° 08.701'	Slipway on bank of Thames
Map 27	049	N51° 33.454' W01° 08.544'	Railway viaduct
Map 27	050	N51° 33.862' W01° 08.072'	Small wooden footbridge
Map 28	051	N51° 34.306' W01° 07.271'	North Stoke
Map 28	052	N51° 35.304' W01° 07.232'	Turn before A4130 road
Map 28	053	N51° 35.121' W01° 05.983'	Turn to Little Gables B&B
Map 29	054	N51° 35.069' W01° 05.487'	Road to Crowmarsh Gifford
Map 29	055	N51° 35.012' W01° 05.012'	Cross road to Ewelme & Woodcote
Map 30	056	N51° 34.716' W01° 02.419'	T-junction in path; turn left
Map 30	057	N51° 34.862' W01° 02.281'	Holy Trinity Church, Nuffield
Map 30	058	N51° 35.048' W01° 01.607'	The Crown (closed), Nuffield
Map 31	059	N51° 35.833' W01° 01.732'	Ewelme Park
Map 31	060	N51° 36.393' W01° 00.979'	St Botolph's
Map 32	061	N51° 37.392' W01° 01.316'	North Farm
Map 32	062	N51° 37.831' W01° 00.254'	Ridge Farm
Map 33	063	N51° 38.022' W00° 59.954'	First turning to Watlington

MAP	REF	GPS WAYPOINT	DESCRIPTION
Map 33	064	N51° 38.413' W00° 59.528'	Turn to White Mark Farm
Map 33	065	N51° 38.714' W00° 59.110'	Cross road
Map 34	066	N51° 39.968' W00° 57.546'	Cross narrow but fast road to Lewknor
Map 35	067	N51° 40.404' W00° 56.903'	A40 road crossing
Map 35	068	N51° 40.908' W00° 55.741'	Cross road that goes to Kingston Blount
Map 36	069	N51° 41.309' W00° 54.704'	Turn to Oakley Hill Nature Reserve
Map 37	070	N51° 41.749' W00° 54.073'	Cross road to Chinnor
Map 37	071	N51° 42.264' W00° 53.218'	Path bends round house
Map 37	072	N51° 41.864' W00° 51.978'	Cross road that goes to Bledlow
Map 38	073	N51° 41.741' W00° 50.531'	Longwood Farm drive
Map 38	074	N51° 42.205' W00° 50.498'	Saunderton railway tunnel
Map 39	075	N51° 42.930' W00° 50.118'	Princes Risboro' sign; leave A4010 road
Map 39	076	N51° 43.251' W00° 49.502'	Cross road to Princes Risborough
Map 40	077	N51° 43.737' W00° 48.641'	Turn in road direction; go through gate in fence
Map 40	078	N51° 43.982' W00° 48.287'	The Plough, Cadsden
Map 41	079	N51° 44.221' W00° 46.578'	Leave road for track
Map 41	080	N51° 44.707' W00° 46.326'	Path joins road
Map 41	081	N51° 45.184' W00° 46.291'	Monument on Coombe Hill
Map 42	082	N51° 45.545' W00° 44.999'	Join road into Wendover
Map 42	083	N51° 45.366' W00° 44.098'	Cross road
Map 43	084	N51° 44.949' W00° 43.456'	Path leaves track
Map 44	085	N51° 45.825' W00° 41.816'	Gate half-hidden in hedge
Map 45	086	N51° 46.532' W00° 40.269'	The Mill, Hastoe
Map 46	087	N51° 47.138' W00° 38.777'	Road crossing
Map 46	088	N51° 47.460' W00° 38.133'	Pedestrian bridge over A41 road
Map 47	089	N51° 48.042' W00° 37.400'	Tring railway station
Map 47	090	N51° 48.956' W00° 37.379'	Take middle path after kissing gate
Map 48	091	N51° 49.496' W00° 36.931'	Car park
Map 48	092	N51° 50.531' W00° 36.502'	End of the Ridgeway

INDEX

Page references in **bold** type refer to maps

TRAILBLAZER TREKKING GUIDES

Europe
British Walking Guides – 15-title series
Scottish Highlands – The Hillwalking Guide
Tour du Mont Blanc
Walker's Haute Route: Mt Blanc – Matterhorn

South America
Inca Trail, Cusco & Machu Picchu
Peru's Cordilleras Blanca & Huayhuash

Africa
Kilimanjaro
Moroccan Atlas – The Trekking Guide

Asia
Nepal Trekking & The Great Himalaya Trail
Sinai – the trekking guide
Trekking in the Everest Region

Australasia
New Zealand – The Great Walks

Peru's Cordilleras Blanca & Huayhuash
The Hiking & Biking Guide
Neil & Harriet Pike, 1st edn, £15.99
ISBN 978-1-905864-63-8, 242pp, 50 maps, 40 colour photos
This region, in northern Peru, boasts some of the most spectacular scenery in the Andes, and most accessible high mountain trekking and biking in the world. This new practical guide contains 60 detailed route maps and descriptions covering 20 hiking trails and more than 30 days of paved and dirt road cycling.

Kilimanjaro – the trekking guide
Henry Stedman, 4th edn, £13.99
ISBN 978-1-905864-54-6, 376pp, 40 maps, 50 colour photos
At 5895m (19,340ft) Kilimanjaro is the world's tallest freestanding mountain and one of the most popular destinations for hikers visiting Africa. Route guides & maps – the 6 major routes. City guides – Nairobi, Dar-es-Salaam, Arusha, Moshi & Marangu.

Sinai – the trekking guide *Ben Hoffler,* 1st edn, £14.99
ISBN 978-1-905864-41-6, 288pp, 74 maps, 30 colour photos
Trek with the Bedouin and their camels and discover one of the most exciting new trekking destinations. The best routes in the High Mountain Region (St. Katherine), Wadi Feiran and the Muzeina deserts. Once you finish on trail there are the nearby coastal resorts of Sharm el Sheikh, Dahab and Nuweiba to enjoy.

Inca Trail, Cusco & Machu Picchu
Alexander Stewart, 5th edn, £13.99
ISBN 978-1-905864-55-3, 320pp, 65 maps, 35 photos
The Inca Trail from Cusco to Machu Picchu is South America's most popular trek. Practical guide with detailed trail maps, plans of Inca sites, guides to Lima, Cusco and Machu Picchu. Includes the Santa Teresa Trek, the Choquequirao Trail and the Vilcabamba Trail. With a history of the Incas by Hugh Thomson.

Trekking in the Everest Region
Jamie McGuinness 6th edn, £14.99 – **new edn Mar 2017**
ISBN 978-1-905864-81-2, 320pp, 95 maps, 30 colour photos
Sixth edition of this popular guide to the world's most famous trekking region. Covers not only the classic treks but also the wild routes. Written by a Nepal-based trek and mountaineering leader. Includes: 27 detailed route maps and 52 village plans. Plus: Kathmandu city guide

TRAILBLAZER'S LONG-DISTANCE PATH (LDP) WALKING GUIDES

We've applied to destinations which are closer to home Trailblazer's proven formula for publishing definitive practical route guides for adventurous travellers. Britain's network of long-distance trails enables the walker to explore some of the finest landscapes in the country's best walking areas. These are guides that are user-friendly, practical, informative and environmentally sensitive.

● **Unique mapping features** In many walking guidebooks the reader has to read a route description then try to relate it to the map. Our guides are much easier to use because walking directions, tricky junctions, places to stay and eat, points of interest and walking times are all written onto the maps themselves in the places to which they apply. With their uncluttered clarity, these are not general-purpose maps but fully edited maps drawn by walkers for walkers.

● **Largest-scale walking maps** At a scale of just under 1:20,000 (8cm or 3¹/₈ inches to one mile) the maps in these guides are bigger than even the most detailed British walking maps currently available in the shops.

● **Not just a trail guide – includes where to stay, where to eat and public transport** Our guidebooks cover the complete walking experience, not just the route. Accommodation options for all budgets are provided (pubs, hotels, B&Bs, campsites, bunkhouses, hostels) as well as places to eat. Detailed public transport information for all access points to each trail means that there are itineraries for all walkers, for hiking the entire route as well as for day or weekend walks.

Coast to Coast *Henry Stedman*, 7th edition, £11.99
ISBN 978-1-905864-74-4, 268pp, 110 maps, 40 colour photos

Cornwall Coast Path (SW Coast Path Pt 2) *Stedman & Newton*, 5th edition, £11.99
ISBN 978-1-905864-71-3, 3526pp, 142 maps, 40 colour photos

Cotswold Way *Tricia & Bob Hayne* 3rd edition, £11.99
ISBN 978-1-905864-70-6, 204pp, 53 maps, 40 colour photos

Dales Way *Henry Stedman* 1st edition, £11.99
ISBN 978-1-905864-78-2, 176pp, 45 maps, 40 colour photos

Dorset & South Devon (SW Coast Path Pt 3) *Stedman & Newton*, £11.99
ISBN 978-1-905864-45-4, 336pp, 88 maps, 40 colour photos

Exmoor & North Devon (SW Coast Path Pt I) *Stedman & Newton*, £11.99
ISBN 978-1-905864-43-0, 192pp, 68 maps, 40 colour photos

Great Glen Way *Jim Manthorpe*, 1st edition, £11.99 – due early 2017
ISBN 978-1-905864-80-5, 192pp, 55 maps, 40 colour photos

Hadrian's Wall Path *Henry Stedman*, 4th edition, £11.99
ISBN 978-1-905864-58-4, 224pp, 60 maps, 40 colour photos

Offa's Dyke Path *Keith Carter*, 4th edition, £11.99
ISBN 978-1-905864-65-2, 240pp, 98 maps, 40 colour photos

Peddars Way & Norfolk Coast Path *Alexander Stewart*, £11.99
ISBN 978-1-905864-28-7, 192pp, 54 maps, 40 colour photos

Pembrokeshire Coast Path *Jim Manthorpe*, 4th edition, £11.99
ISBN 978-1-905864-51-5, 224pp, 96 maps, 40 colour photos

Pennine Way *Stuart Greig*, 4th edition, £11.99
ISBN 978-1-905864-61-4, 272pp, 138 maps, 40 colour photos

The Ridgeway *Nick Hill*, 4th edition, £11.99
ISBN 978-1-905864-79-9, 208pp, 53 maps, 40 colour photos

South Downs Way *Jim Manthorpe*, 5th edition, £11.99
ISBN 978-1-905864-66-9, 192pp, 60 maps, 40 colour photos

Thames Path *Joel Newton*, 1st edition, £11.99
ISBN 978-1-905864-64-5, 256pp, 99 maps, 40 colour photos

West Highland Way *Charlie Loram*, 6th edition, £11.99
ISBN 978-1-905864-76-8, 208pp, 60 maps, 40 colour photos

'The same attention to detail that distinguishes its other guides has been brought to bear here'.
THE SUNDAY TIMES

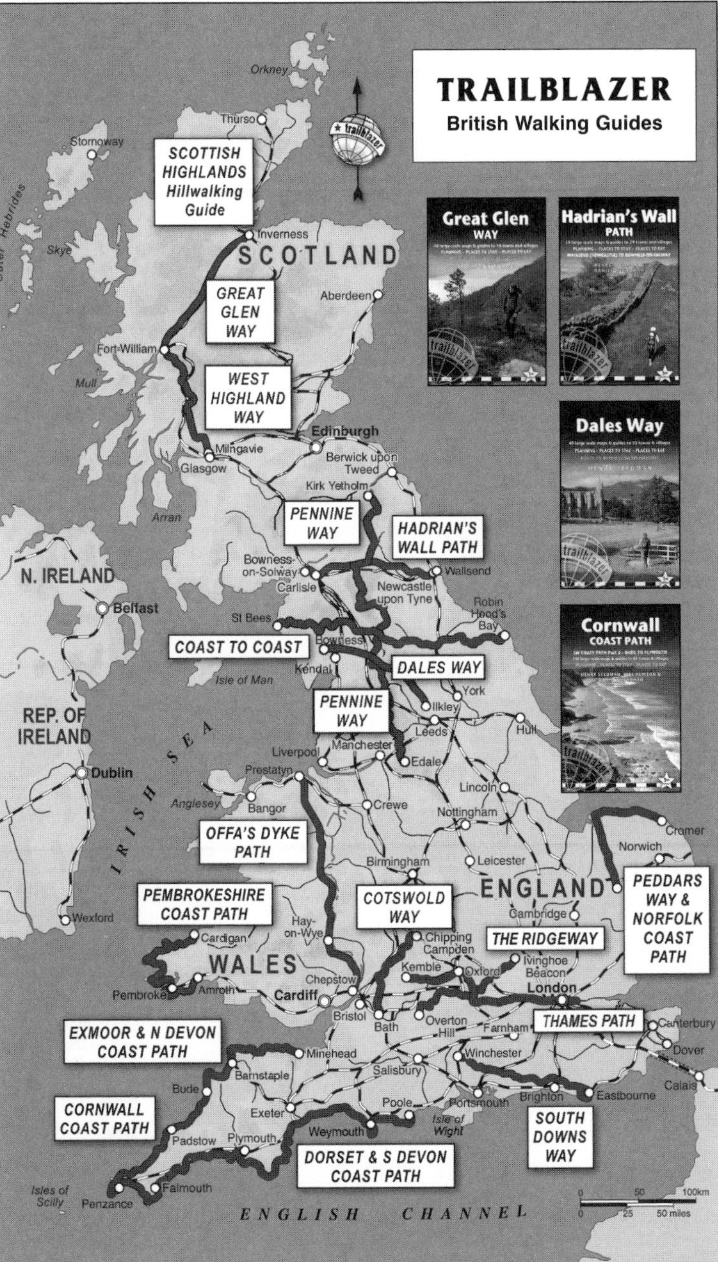
TRAILBLAZER
British Walking Guides
Great Glen
WAY
Hadrian's Wall
PATH
Dales Way
Cornwall
COAST PATH
trailblazer
SCOTTISH HIGHLANDS Hillwalking Guide
GREAT GLEN WAY
WEST HIGHLAND WAY
PENNINE WAY
HADRIAN'S WALL PATH
COAST TO COAST
DALES WAY
PENNINE WAY
OFFA'S DYKE PATH
PEMBROKESHIRE COAST PATH
COTSWOLD WAY
THE RIDGEWAY
PEDDARS WAY & NORFOLK COAST PATH
THAMES PATH
EXMOOR & N DEVON COAST PATH
CORNWALL COAST PATH
DORSET & S DEVON COAST PATH
SOUTH DOWNS WAY
SCOTLAND
N. IRELAND
REP. OF IRELAND
WALES
ENGLAND
IRISH SEA
ENGLISH CHANNEL
Orkney
Thurso
Stornoway
Outer Hebrides
Skye
Inverness
Aberdeen
Fort William
Mull
Edinburgh
Milngavie
Glasgow
Berwick upon Tweed
Kirk Yetholm
Arran
Bowness-on-Solway
Carlisle
Wallsend
Newcastle upon Tyne
Belfast
St Bees
Robin Hood's Bay
Bowness
Kendal
Isle of Man
York
Ilkley
Leeds
Hull
Liverpool
Manchester
Edale
Dublin
Prestatyn
Anglesey
Bangor
Crewe
Lincoln
Nottingham
Cromer
Norwich
Birmingham
Leicester
Cambridge
Wexford
Cardigan
Hay-on-Wye
Chipping Campden
Kemble
Oxford
Ivinghoe Beacon
London
Pembroke
Amroth
Chepstow
Cardiff
Bristol
Bath
Overton Hill
Farnham
Canterbury
Dover
Calais
Minehead
Barnstaple
Salisbury
Winchester
Bude
Exeter
Poole
Portsmouth
Brighton
Eastbourne
Isle of Wight
Padstow
Plymouth
Weymouth
Isles of Scilly
Penzance
Falmouth
0 50 100km
0 25 50 miles

TRAILBLAZER TITLE LIST

Adventure Cycle-Touring Handbook
Adventure Motorcycling Handbook
Australia by Rail
Azerbaijan
Coast to Coast (British Walking Guide)
Cornwall Coast Path (British Walking Guide)
Cotswold Way (British Walking Guide)
The Cyclist's Anthology
Dales Way (British Walking Guide)
Dorset & Sth Devon Coast Path (British Walking Gde)
Exmoor & Nth Devon Coast Path (British Walking Gde)
Great Glen Way (British Walking Guide)
Hadrian's Wall Path (British Walking Guide)
Himalaya by Bike – a route and planning guide
Inca Trail, Cusco & Machu Picchu
Japan by Rail
Kilimanjaro – the trekking guide (includes Mt Meru)
Moroccan Atlas – The Trekking Guide
Morocco Overland (4WD/motorcycle/mountainbike)
Nepal Trekking & The Great Himalaya Trail
New Zealand – The Great Walks
Offa's Dyke Path (British Walking Guide)
Overlanders' Handbook – worldwide driving guide
Peddars Way & Norfolk Coast Path (British Walking Gde)
Pembrokeshire Coast Path (British Walking Guide)
Pennine Way (British Walking Guide)
Peru's Cordilleras Blanca & Huayhuash – Hiking/Biking
The Railway Anthology
The Ridgeway (British Walking Guide)
Sahara Overland – a route and planning guide
Scottish Highlands – The Hillwalking Guide
Siberian BAM Guide – rail, rivers & road
The Silk Roads – a route and planning guide
Sinai – the trekking guide
South Downs Way (British Walking Guide)
Thames Path (British Walking Guide)
Tour du Mont Blanc
Trans-Canada Rail Guide
Trans-Siberian Handbook
Trekking in the Everest Region
The Walker's Anthology
The Walker's Anthology – further tales
The Walker's Haute Route – Mont Blanc to Matterhorn
West Highland Way (British Walking Guide)

For more information about Trailblazer and our expanding range of guides, for guidebook updates or for credit card mail order sales visit our website:

www.trailblazer-guides.com

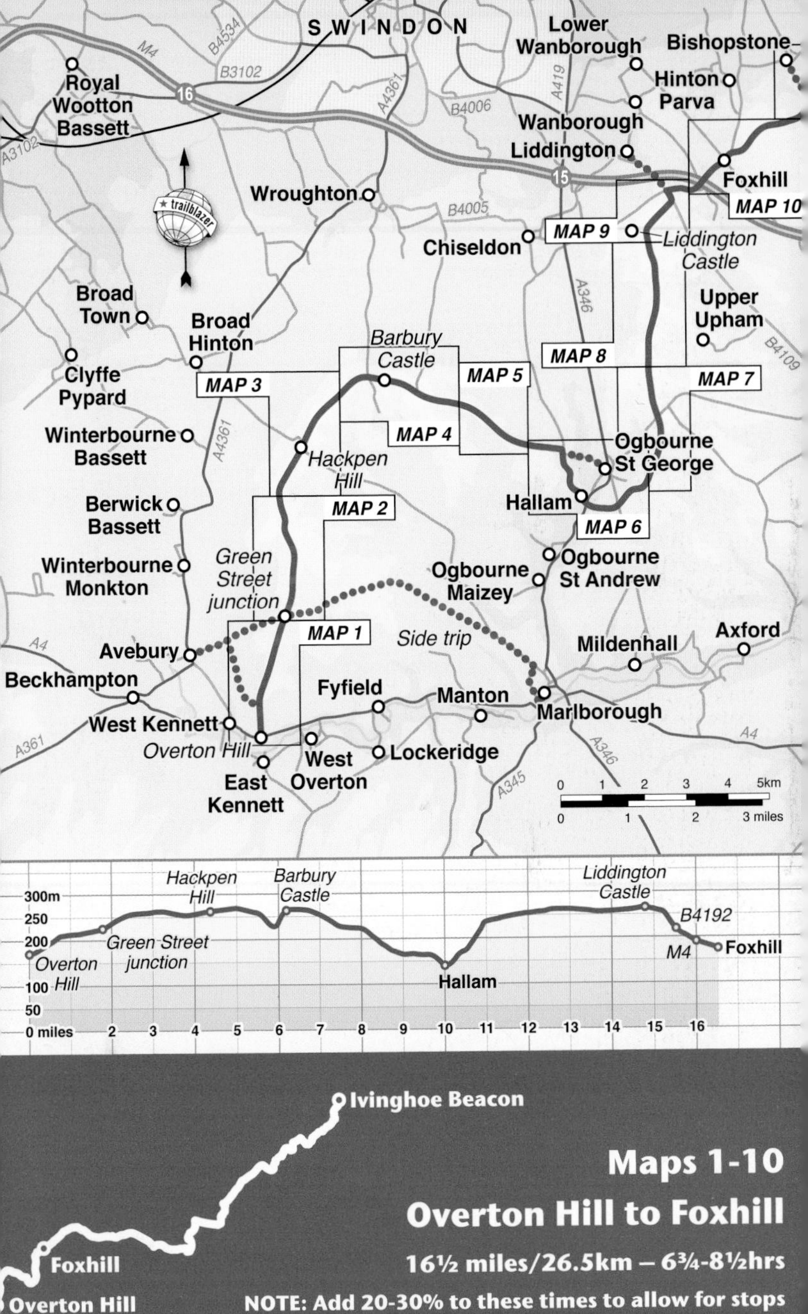
SWINDON
Lower Wanborough
Bishopstone
Royal Wootton Bassett
M4
B4534
B3102
16
A4361
B4006
A419
Hinton Parva
Wanborough
Liddington
A3102
trailblazer
Wroughton
15
Foxhill
MAP 10
B4005
Chiseldon
MAP 9
Liddington Castle
A346
Broad Town
Broad Hinton
Upper Upham
Barbury Castle
B4109
Clyffe Pypard
MAP 3
MAP 5
MAP 8
MAP 7
Winterbourne Bassett
A4361
MAP 4
Hackpen Hill
Ogbourne St George
Berwick Bassett
MAP 2
Hallam
MAP 6
Winterbourne Monkton
Green Street junction
Ogbourne Maizey
Ogbourne St Andrew
A4
Avebury
MAP 1
Side trip
Mildenhall
Axford
Beckhampton
Fyfield
Manton
Marlborough
West Kennett
A361
Overton Hill
West Overton
Lockeridge
A4
A346
East Kennett
A345
0 1 2 3 4 5km
0 1 2 3 miles
Hackpen Hill
Barbury Castle
Liddington Castle
300m
250
200
100
50
B4192
Green Street junction
Overton Hill
M4
Foxhill
Hallam
0 miles 2 3 4 5 6 7 8 9 10 11 12 13 14 15 16
Ivinghoe Beacon
Foxhill
Overton Hill
Maps 1-10
Overton Hill to Foxhill
16½ miles/26.5km – 6¾-8½hrs
NOTE: Add 20-30% to these times to allow for stops

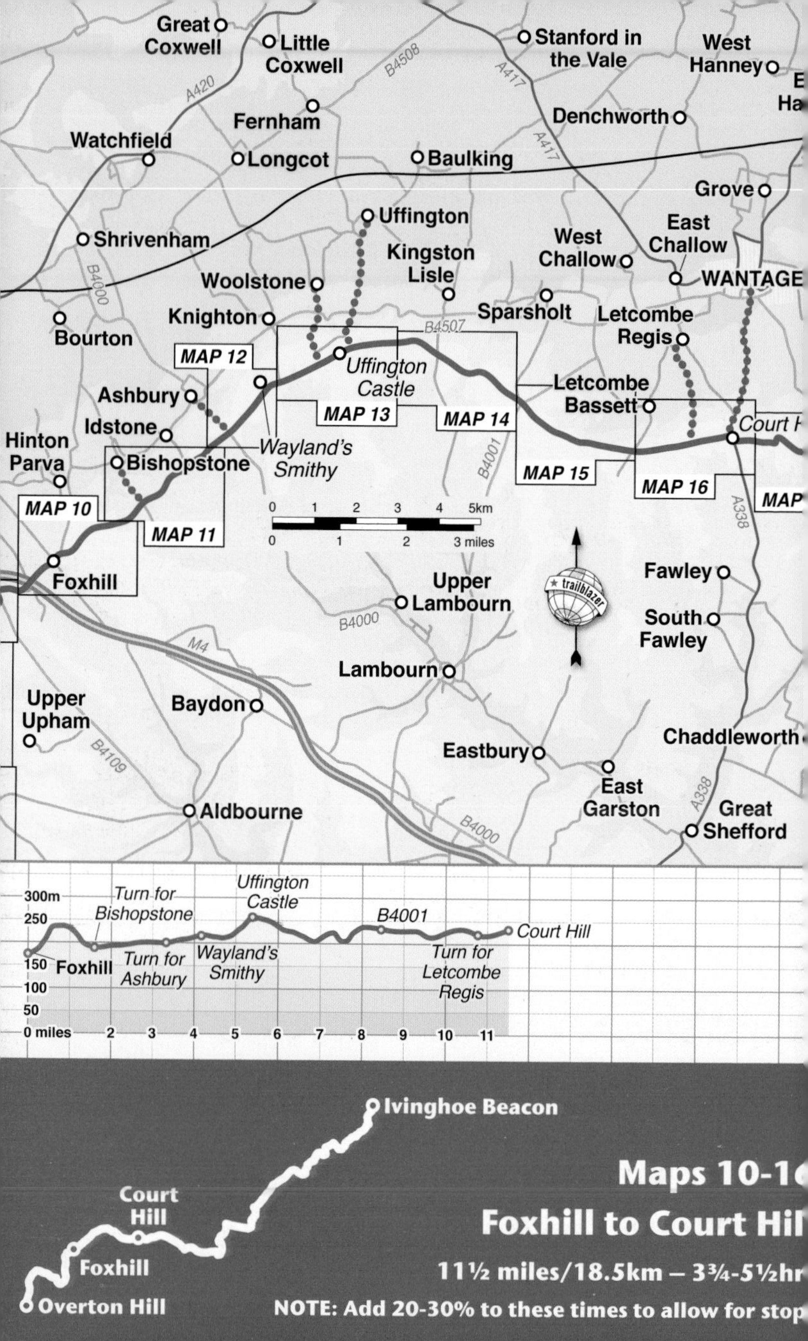

Great Coxwell
Little Coxwell
Stanford in the Vale
West Hanney
A420
B4508
A417
Fernham
Denchworth
Watchfield
Longcot
Baulking
Grove
Uffington
Shrivenham
East Challow
West Challow
Kingston Lisle
B4000
Woolstone
WANTAGE
Knighton
Sparsholt
Letcombe Regis
Bourton
B4507
MAP 12
Uffington Castle
Letcombe Bassett
Ashbury
MAP 13
MAP 14
Idstone
Hinton Parva
Wayland's Smithy
Bishopstone
B4001
MAP 15
MAP 16
A338
MAP 10
MAP 11
0 1 2 3 4 5km
0 1 2 3 miles
Foxhill
Upper Lambourn
trailblazer
Fawley
South Fawley
M4
Lambourn
Upper Upham
Baydon
Chaddleworth
B4109
Eastbury
East Garston
Great Shefford
Aldbourne
300m
250
150
100
50
0 miles 2 3 4 5 6 7 8 9 10 11
Turn for Bishopstone
Uffington Castle
B4001
Court Hill
Foxhill
Turn for Ashbury
Wayland's Smithy
Turn for Letcombe Regis
Ivinghoe Beacon
Court Hill
Foxhill
Overton Hill
Foxhill to Court Hil
11½ miles/18.5km – 3¾-5½hr
NOTE: Add 20-30% to these times to allow for stop

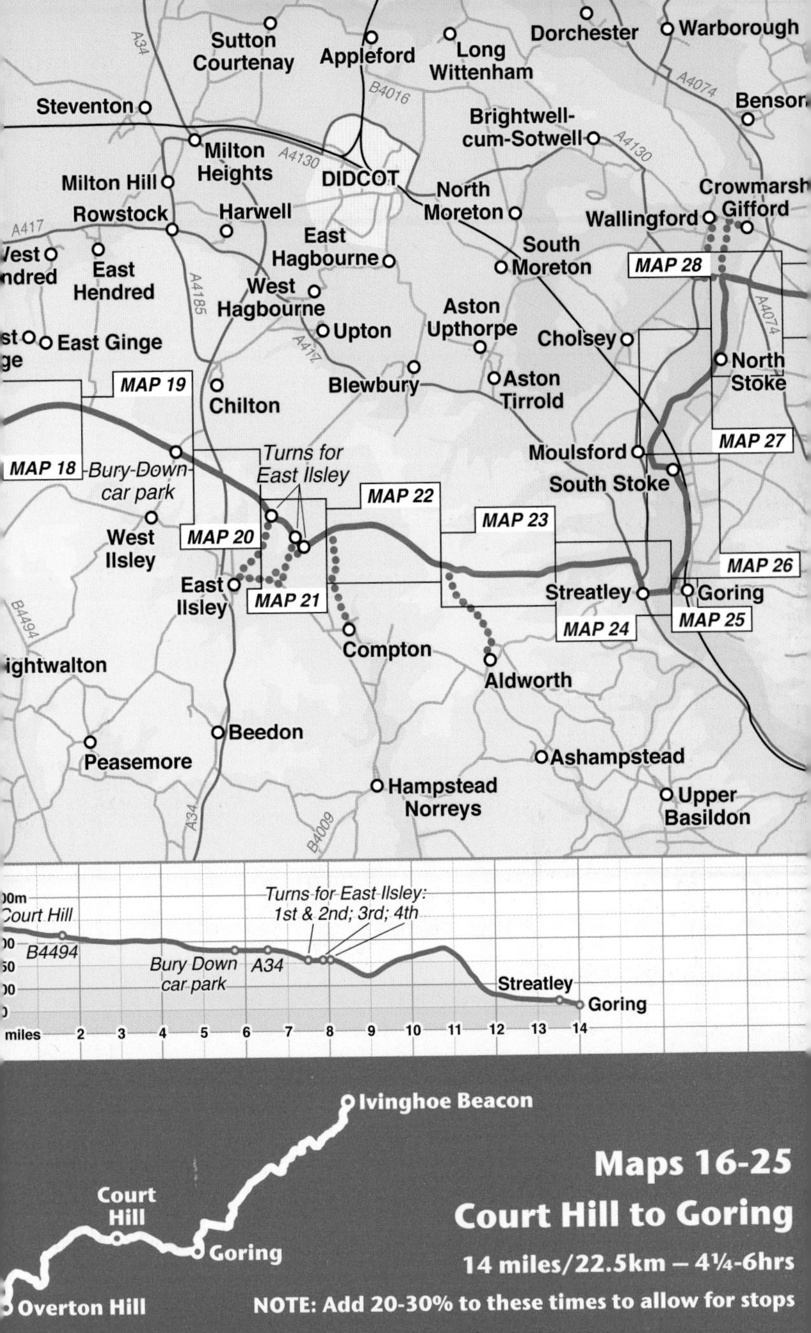

Maps 16-25

Court Hill to Goring

14 miles/22.5km – 4¼-6hrs

NOTE: Add 20-30% to these times to allow for stops

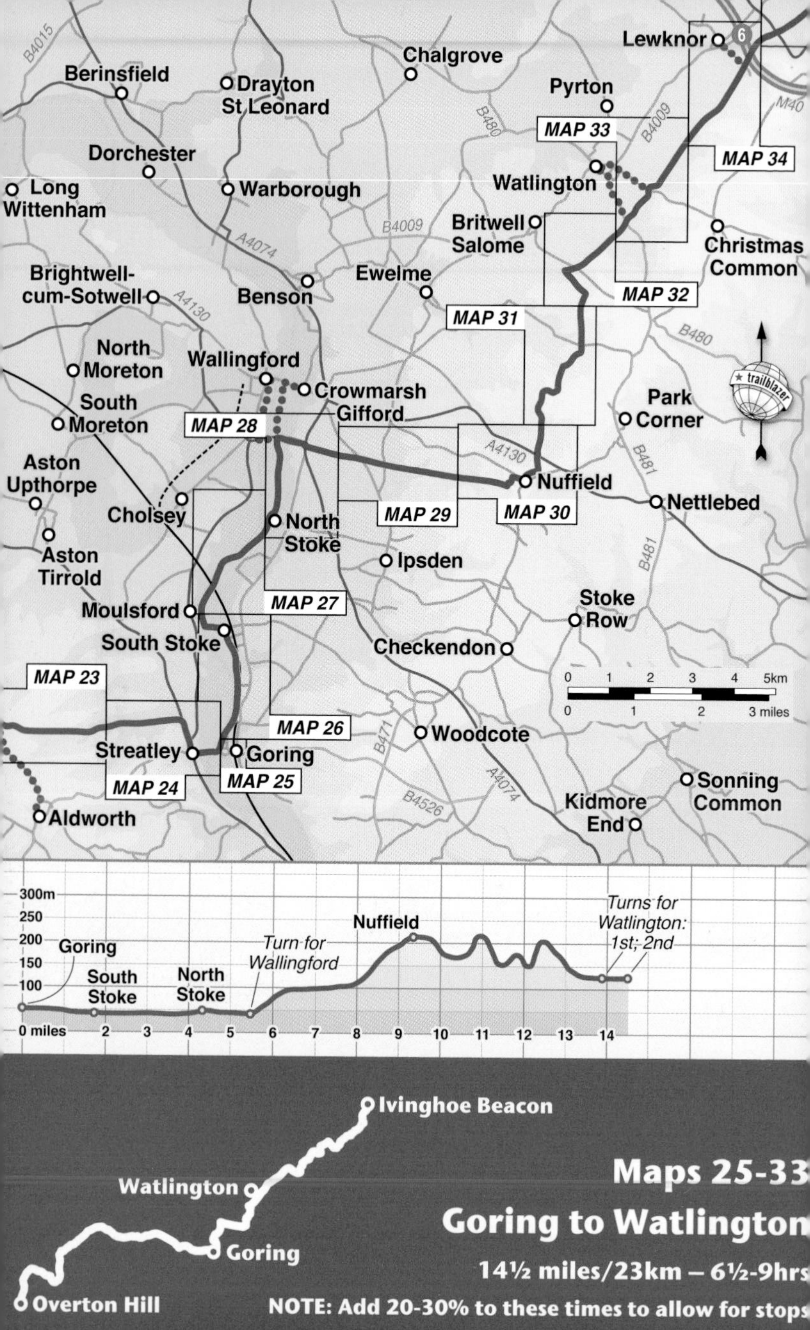

B4015
Berinsfield
Drayton
St Leonard
Chalgrove
Lewknor
6
Pyrton
M40
B480
B4009
MAP 33
MAP 34
Dorchester
Watlington
Long
Wittenham
Warborough
B4009
Britwell
Salome
Christmas
Common
A4074
Brightwell-
cum-Sotwell
Benson
Ewelme
MAP 32
A4130
MAP 31
B480
North
Moreton
Wallingford
Crowmarsh
Gifford
trailblazer
South
Moreton
Park
Corner
MAP 28
A4130
B481
Aston
Upthorpe
Nuffield
Cholsey
Nettlebed
MAP 29
MAP 30
North
Stoke
Aston
Tirrold
Ipsden
B481
Stoke
Row
MAP 27
Moulsford
South Stoke
Checkendon
MAP 23
0 1 2 3 4 5km
0 1 2 3 miles
MAP 26
B471
Woodcote
Streatley
Goring
MAP 24
MAP 25
A4074
Sonning
Common
Kidmore
End
B4526
Aldworth
300m
250
200
150
100
Goring
South
Stoke
North
Stoke
Turn for
Wallingford
Nuffield
Turns for
Watlington:
1st; 2nd
0 miles 2 3 4 5 6 7 8 9 10 11 12 13 14
Ivinghoe Beacon
Watlington
Goring
Overton Hill
Maps 25-33
Goring to Watlington
14½ miles/23km – 6½-9hrs
NOTE: Add 20-30% to these times to allow for stops

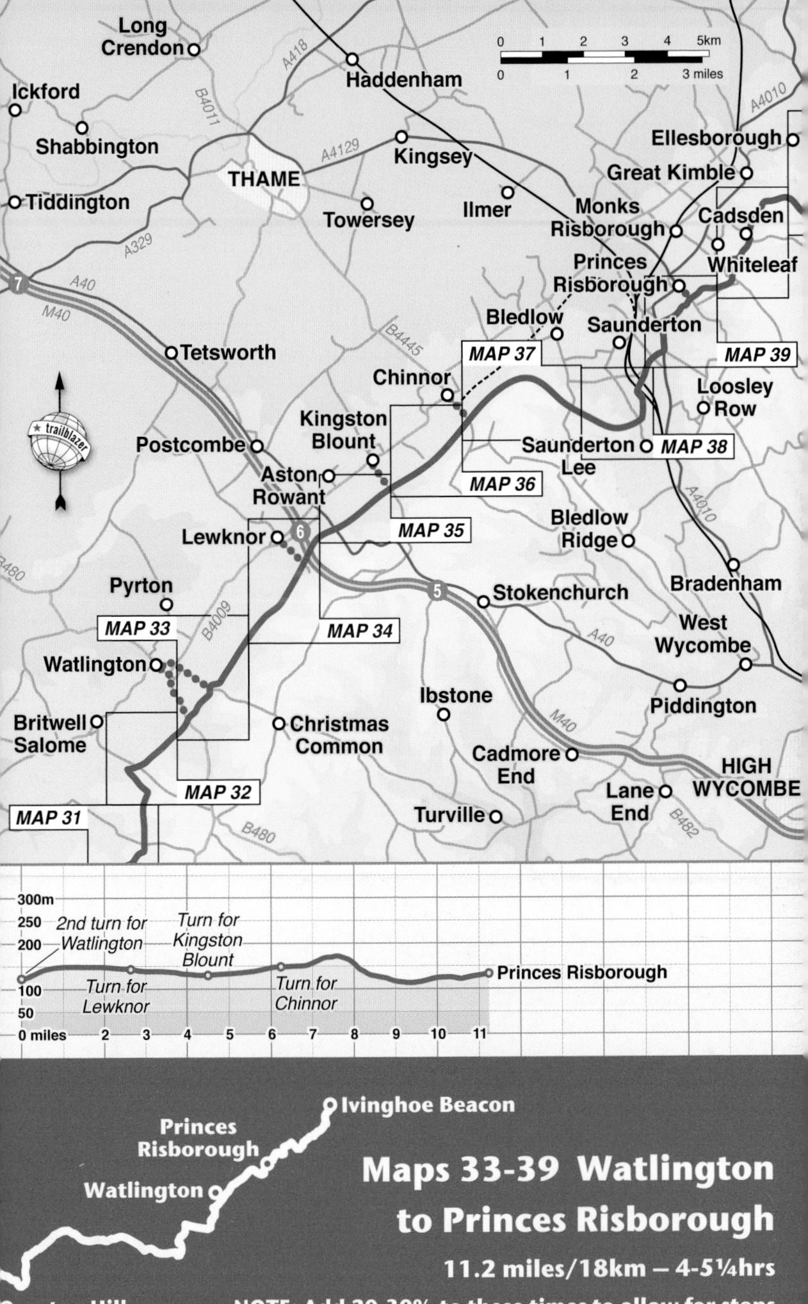
0 1 2 3 4 5km
0 1 2 3 miles
Long Crendon
Ickford
Shabbington
Tiddington
Haddenham
A418
B4011
THAME
A4129
Kingsey
Towersey
Ilmer
A329
A40
M40
7
Ellesborough
Great Kimble
Monks Risborough
Cadsden
Whiteleaf
Princes Risborough
A4010
Bledlow
Saunderton
MAP 37
MAP 39
Tetsworth
B4445
Chinnor
Loosley Row
trailblazer
Kingston Blount
Saunderton Lee
MAP 38
Postcombe
MAP 36
Aston Rowant
MAP 35
Lewknor
6
Bledlow Ridge
A4010
B480
Pyrton
5
Stokenchurch
Bradenham
MAP 33
B4009
MAP 34
West Wycombe
A40
Watlington
Ibstone
Piddington
Britwell Salome
Christmas Common
M40
Cadmore End
HIGH WYCOMBE
MAP 32
Lane End
MAP 31
Turville
B480
B482
300m
250
200
100
50
2nd turn for Watlington
Turn for Kingston Blount
Turn for Lewknor
Turn for Chinnor
Princes Risborough
0 miles 2 3 4 5 6 7 8 9 10 11
Ivinghoe Beacon
Princes Risborough
Watlington
Overton Hill
Maps 33-39 Watlington to Princes Risborough
11.2 miles/18km – 4-5¼hrs
NOTE: Add 20-30% to these times to allow for stops

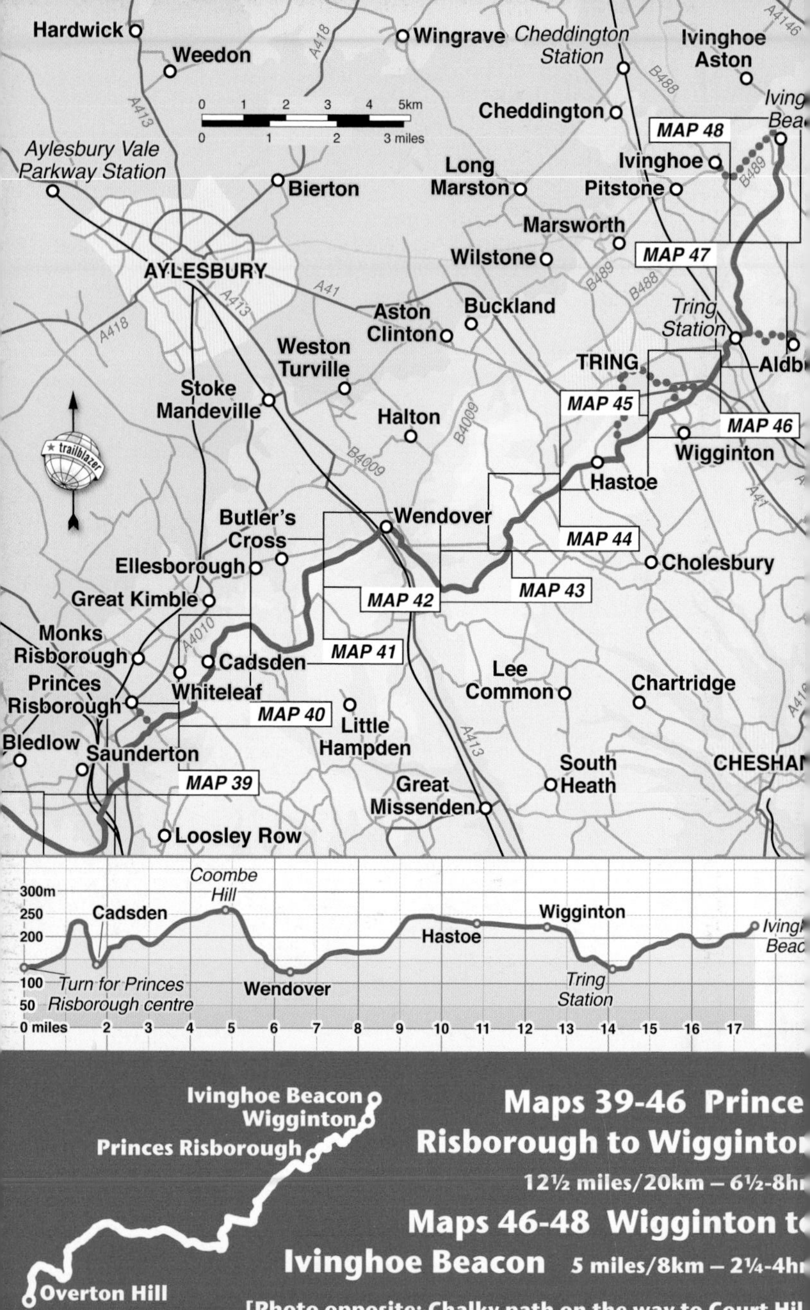

Hardwick
Weedon
Wingrave
Cheddington Station
Ivinghoe Aston
Cheddington
MAP 48
Ivinghoe
Pitstone
Long Marston
Aylesbury Vale Parkway Station
Bierton
Marsworth
Wilstone
MAP 47
AYLESBURY
A41
Aston Clinton
Buckland
Tring Station
TRING
Weston Turville
Stoke Mandeville
Halton
MAP 45
MAP 46
Wigginton
Hastoe
Butler's Cross
Wendover
MAP 44
Ellesborough
Cholesbury
Great Kimble
MAP 42
MAP 43
Monks Risborough
MAP 41
Cadsden
Whiteleaf
Princes Risborough
MAP 40
Lee Common
Chartridge
Little Hampden
Bledlow
Saunderton
MAP 39
South Heath
CHESHAM
Great Missenden
Loosley Row
A418
A413
A4010
B4009
B488
B489
A4146
0 1 2 3 4 5km
0 1 2 3 miles
Coombe Hill
Cadsden
Wigginton
Hastoe
Wendover
Turn for Princes Risborough centre
Tring Station
300m
250
200
100
50
0 miles
2 3 4 5 6 7 8 9 10 11 12 13 14 15 16 17
Ivinghoe Beacon
Wigginton
Princes Risborough
Overton Hill
Maps 39-46 Princes Risborough to Wigginton
12½ miles/20km – 6½-8hr
Maps 46-48 Wigginton to Ivinghoe Beacon
5 miles/8km – 2¼-4hr
[Photo opposite: Chalky path on the way to Court Hill